The Restorationist
Text One

a collaborative fiction by Jael B. Juba

Joyce Elbrecht
and
Lydia Fakundiny

STATE UNIVERSITY OF NEW YORK PRESS

This is a work of fiction. All names, characters, incidents, or places therein are either products of the authors' imaginations or are used fictitiously. Any resemblance to actual locales, events, or to any persons, living or dead, is entirely coincidental.

With gratitude to Phillis Molock.

Production by Ruth Fisher
Marketing by Lynne Lekakis

Published by
State University of New York Press, Albany

© 1993   State University of New York

For information, address State University of New York
Press, State University Plaza, Albany, NY 12246

Library of Congress Cataloging-in-Publication Data

Elbrecht, Joyce (Date)
      The restorationist text one : a collaborative fiction by Jael B.
   Juba / Joyce Elbrecht and Lydia Fakundiny.
         p.   cm. — (SUNY series, the margins of literature)
      ISBN 0–7914–1531–7 (alk. paper).   — ISBN 0–7914–1532–5 (pbk. :
   alk. paper)
      I. Fakundiny, Lydia (Date) II. Title. III. Series.
   PS3555.L24R47   1993
   813'.54—dc20
                                                            92–32586
                                                            CIP

10 9 8 7 6 5 4 3 2 1

SUNY Series,
THE MARGINS OF LITERATURE

Mihai I. Spariosu

...and the work stands as a ruin

—Walter Benjamin
*The Origin of
German Tragic Drama*

O mio dolor

—*La Traviata* (Act III)

I bear
my house inside me, everywhere

—Derek Walcott
Omeros

O mio dolor...the work...

I go to the things I love
with no thought of duty or pity

—H.D.
*The Flowering
of the Rod*

O mio dolor
...the things I love...

The Restorationist

Text One

Prologue

i

A trial run: May–August 1977, restoration of historic home on Florida
Gulf Coast. No more than a full line.

    Still early, says Harding, my last morning in Tarragona,
and Gulf breezes were offering themselves through the open
windows with all their old seductions. There I was, the house
spacious and empty around me, no place for myself in it, considering a rhetorical problem only because, clearing out the last
of my things a little after sunup, the typewriter in its film of
dust, the briefcase harboring one or two scripts of my profession—words pushing at me—I'd happened across my résumé
tucked away in a folder, ever ready. Out in the street, houses
stood idling in their unpeopled quiet. Sidewalks of rosy old brick
wound along in front of them greening over with moss, here
and there mounds of scrap, the viscera of demolition and construction as familiar to me by now as the summer heat, intellig-
ible, like entrails to augurers.

    I erased "home" and pencilled in "structure," put "total" in
front of "restoration," regretfully deleted it as excessive in context if not in fact, and, for "restoration," substituted the word in
The Bicentennial Guide To Old Tarragona, what all the more or
less official watchdogs of the town's historic district called it:
"rehabilitation." High time, this means, that certain building
projects are recognized for what they are, more than stripped
clapboard and cedar shingle roofs, nails and fresh paint, more
than just somebody doing up an old house: there's the moral
impact of it all on the community. And how could it be otherwise? Even houses fall into disrepute—run down—and need
uplifting now and then to their full potential for mirroring their
pristine origins. Houses above all, those molds of human intimacy. Hang the regulation attire on the old derelict, give her a

3

good bath and a shampoo and a few shrewd tips on successful communication, and *voila*! character regenerates.

That's about the way it went with me and the Boullet House, I must admit, but not as the gentlemen of the Committee for the Preservation of Historic Tarragona supposed. More brutally and before all else it had been a process of divestment, and self-divestment. Totalled: a self-world demolition. All the more reason to close off analytic peeps beyond the fashion code.

A résumé must always be available for viewing, and I was dallying, more or less guilelessly, with mine, the whole idea being—if I've got this right—to project an identity as carefully freed of narcissism as a realistic self-portrait, and as convincing on sight. Economy ought to be everything in this accounting of yourself, your time: no excesses allowed and, of course, no holes. Even when you're no longer seriously in the market, you tend to its standing as a public exhibit:

Elizabeth Harding Dumot
12 Quarry Way, Athena, New York
Birth: Colonus, Mississippi, December 5, 1935
Marital Status: Divorced (two daughters)

—and so on, down through all the tags of professional fitness honed just to a page in the dozen or so years of my career. If you are bent as I am on keeping to essentials for the record, updating your résumé may involve a sacrifice or two.

And there it was: the apparent irrelevancy of the divorce, and the daughters, taking up an entire line. Just the space I needed to gloss my late project.

My problem: how to write into the public record an episode so adulterated by privacy. Not how to find a language for rendering experience; that I already had. Who doesn't nowadays? Nor how to make the private public; that I know to be impossible in the strict sense. Having no private language, I understand that there is in language no private experience. (I too call a cat a cat, Alice by Gertrude being Alice being Gertrude notwithstanding.)

To see if it still worked, after three hot months in the back of a closet, I rolled the sheet with my revised trial run on it into my old Royal and toyed with the keyboard as I continued pondering how to encode my summer intrusion in Tarragona's dust, and no recourse to Faulkner. A machine is supposed to start where you leave off without anybody knowing the difference, which means in the case of a typewriter that you should be able to forget about it except at your fingertips. Keys sticking and bunching at every strike mire the thought in the mechanism, and, in one way or another, I'd been having far too much of that. All that back-breaking, joint-weakening summer, I'd come to expect trouble as sure as nightfall and time forever running out on me...now is the time...the quick brown fox.... Nudging up sticky keys I watched them strike, then hesitate and settle back into place like old women on stiff haunches...during this time...surely the quick brown fox as they used to say...the moving hand...during this time the reality of my possession marked mind and body as surely as the moving hand leaves its material traces...composing, but barely, till the keys were rebounding with only a hint of a drag...no remainder of myself with which to feel or to think...oh yes, even to wish to feel or to think, no one and nothing in the round of my body's toil and its nightmare sleep, only the eyes of others...unrelenting, etcetera., moving right along as if getting used to the lag of second thought, but still awkward, and slower than I remembered. I could see the Royal would be too erratic for any-thing now but the odd memo, or for drafting. Something with real finish, a public exhibit, would call for a more advanced machine. Still, the letters did line up on the page as unequivo-cally as ever, if a bit on the pale side, telling of a ration of idle-ness, the half-hour or more of unapportioned time before me, that made me laugh out loud.

Only those who have toiled long enough under duress that freedom requires a rehearsal can experience such lightness.

ii

Her laughter rolled—unembittered, I imagine—through that enormous, soft-toned room, rose through the light hues of the unencumbered expanse that was to have been her library, hung vibrant, and died as cleanly as sound at the bidding of the conduc-tor's hand. The wide-planked floor on which she sat cross-legged, hunched over the typewriter (still in work clothes for the final touches), glistened darkly around and away from her down to the other end where the dress for her drive back North was suspended from the refinished mantle, palely yellow fine-spun cotton catching the sun and, now and again, a little breeze from the open windows. She snapped out the page of type and dropped it whole into the trashbag slumped glossily in the middle of the floor, secured the Royal in its housing and clicked the hardboard case shut. A crack showed between top and bottom half, an old lack of alignment in the closure that needed a strap for a really snug fit.

iii

Pencil and clean sheet of paper in hand, she says, I climbed up into one of the high dormer windows and fell into a study of the striations of shadow the louvered shutter, the very one I'd had such a time with, was laying over me while I entertained my problem more, as they say, constructively. It was a matter of keeping the record straight, maintaining control of the point of view others might take on me—not to give out any particular image of myself, only to limit the range of them.

We've all received the message that as human media—for we're all projectors, aren't we?—we're responsible for our public face. It's up to us to regulate the flow of projections. The give, that is, and the take. The give-and-take. My love of truth (and the subjectivity of it never bothered me a whit, even before it became next to mandatory) is so strong I can paint myself as an old-fashioned intellectual without lifting eyebrows other than my own. But telling the truth is out of the question in the media realm; nobody's interested in that kind of detail for its own sake.

Slats of sunlight snuggled over my arms and legs, breezes whiffled, and here I sat serenely tackling the problematic character of private life existing under the force of public intercourse, the place that remains private because it cannot be shared in language or otherwise, the place that is, quite simply, your body. No matter what the strategies of possession, including identification, I can't be your body and you can't be mine—well, "tackling" gets in altogether the wrong picture and, as much as I like the idea, so does "dallying." Dawdling is more like what I was doing up in that oversized window seat a little past eight a.m. my last morning in Old Tarragona. Dawdling, incredible.

Privacy: the necessary material condition of all existence, not to be confused of course with "the right to privacy," which is a public matter to be talked about, talked to death and back again, and is. A political matter therefore. And public intercourse: that play of pure power whereby we are made, and made to love it, to hate it, to neuter and to neutralize it in accordance with sexualized specifications of feeling. I am certainly not alone in observing how words penetrate us, gathering like tumescence, proliferating like nuclear warheads ("nuke you" is bound to succeed "fuck you" on walls), collecting value like numismatic coins, pleasures promised like bathing in the ocean or drinking and eating and making love. As if to follow a natural law for merely being and continuing to be whatever we are now becoming, the repetitions of natural language worm their way to the very gut of privacy. Words: the communal wasteproducts of our privacies. I rapidly settled on: May–August 1977, A Critique of Signing in Historic Restorations. More or less a lie in the usual sense.

The unobtrusive fit of each piece, however, was still not all it should be. The lie ought to be as natural for the public as a good enough mother for her child. And with that I had a stroke of genius: insert "feminist" in front of "critique." Just as divorce with two children legitimized my female sexuality, so would a feminist project of any kind validate my female intellectuality. As irrelevancies go, not a bad *quid pro quo*. It had economy, and a state of the art machine would make a crisp job of it all in a single line. Outside, workmen arriving in their pickups rolled cautiously to a stop like trespassers, joviality a bit strained as befits a Monday morning in August, the weekend closed like a skimmed chapter behind them. Up in my niche I followed their rites over tool boxes and coffee and chitchat, as if seeing not from the vantage point of a second-story nineteenth-century window but through the moving perspective of my time—as if I were already looking back at it all from the evening of that day on the road somewhere, or from a moment in a week hence, or a year.

Next day, Tuesday, would be garbage day on Valencia Street—toward the very end I had after all timed things right. I folded the paper with my stroke of genius on it for saving. Called on to account for my time, I could; no holes showing.

iv

Within the hour, after closing the sale of her restored property in an elegantly cool lawyer's suite on Hernando Plaza, Harding will walk into the bright heat of Tarragona's rush hour tapering off, past the aggressive roar of office-bound automobiles, past a lumbering city bus or two carrying the black and white women who make their living a few blocks farther west, downtown, behind meal counters and at checkout lines of stores sapped by the smart shopping malls that ring the city now. Rehabilitation is nowhere imminent here on the margins of the Historic District; viability is elsewhere. In Tarragona's old commercial heart, municipal government, too, still churns its round of things scandalously running down. And I wonder even now, as I write this: driving back North where her children are, up the savage highways, would she be heading home or leaving it, here, at the edge of the moss-strung Plaza, the transfer point, where the women bound for their meager jobs in those unregenerate failing businesses get on and off the slow hot buses that lumber especially for them it seems?

The whereabouts of home. It's a question (among others) that all of Harding's stories pose. Going by the book, one way or another it would seem to be my job to answer them. It's what's expected. The buck, as those in authority like to say, stops here.

Quite so. I'm well aware, however, by virtue of training (and by inclination, too) that I'm not to intrude on you. I understand that your satisfaction depends on my discretion, my delicately nuanced absence—you know, those suggestive sounds of an author scuttling in the boards, the subtle judgments, modulations of tone and narrative angle that point you to the meaning in it all. Clearly, then, given my intentions, I should set the record straight immediately so as to foreclose the certainty of misunderstanding between us, ill feeling. I intend—as in the following—to make spaces for myself under the heading *psycheme*, the name tells all. Spot one and I'll be there. Everything else will show up in the text.

psycheme

In my utopian moments I imagine myself as part of the clutter that accumulates in your daily life, things getting out of place like the nail scissors, unanswered letters, bills, tax records, dark glasses, keys, throat lozenges, library cards, empty bottles, etc. Depending on how much it bothers you and how much time you've got, you stop every now and then and put it all away, make a clean sweep and start all over. Get rid of the clutter distracting you, place it all where you can use it, or not, as you prefer, and get on with your life. I envision myself, at such moments, releasing you from the distraction that builds up around the clutter of meaning, from your inevitable desire for something more revealing, from your expectations that I'll somehow clear up the mess. Suppose that, before desire intensifies, it were periodically allayed—nothing more. I'm here to amend the old contract between us: I'm coming out of the woodwork.

Psycheme: Call it a design for giving little close-ups of the author, self-epiphanies, let us say, rather than the usual fictional variety; self-offerings, my minimal units; the smallest parts of Jael B. Juba having any meaning. What I'm after is a kind of self-knowledge, and, so, instead of acting like God felt everywhere but nowhere visible, I want to be seen, seen along with Harding, but in a place of my own. The woman called Harding (a family name) tells non-stop about restoring an antebellum home on the Florida Gulf Coast, and as long as she's talking there's no room in her presence for me, Jael B. Juba, the author. I want to know where I, always in her shadow, am, to take a good look at myself—you might say I have a desire, not unlike yours, for authorial revelations. As author and reader ours is a problematic relationship, but all the more reason why bouncing the Dionysian pieces of an old, old world between us requires a new, more realistic fit between you, me, and Harding.

Suppose you were able to read her restoration stories with no more regard for me than if I had called the wrong number. Of course, I prefer to be something other than a minor irritant in your life, but, as Harding might put it, it takes two to tangle. Old habits die hard, I know.

This is the plan: As if installing a full-length glass, I'll stand here like this, wholly exposed for your inspection, let you see off and on precisely where I am and what I'm all about, at least at the moment I appear before you. You'll get used to these close encounters, and with enough little studies from all different sides, you'll come to know me as naturally as anybody else in your life. On my part, I'll curb all urges to repeat myself (since analysis of me is not our motive), but I mean to assume enough poses to allow you to form a kind of hologram of me. That, of course, is what I'm after: the hologram. Not exposure of myself piece by piece. Nor will I let only my best sides show (that would hardly be fair); you'll have enough shots of me to know me like a book. (An added bonus: There'll be no need to appear on talk shows or give public readings to promote my work; I won't even need my picture on the dust jacket, I'll be making appearances right here before your eyes.) Thus captured, transported as it were to your viewpoint, I can't fail to see my authorial identity from where I sit.

Remember: Another page, another psycheme. It's only me.

V

Self-removal, says Harding, comes as easily to me as though it were of my essence. Résumé tucked away again in folder with addendum clipped to it, blank paper in briefcase with writing implement, and me sliding out of my work clothes as confidently as if the graffiti of my summer in Tarragona could be moulted. Disposal of same in trashbag. Then, to my travel outfit: slipping on my yellow summer dress meant to double as the unquestionably successful woman's casual openness to Southern warmth. Last thing, I tied up the plastic trashbag and set it out front for next day's pick-up. Went back in for the typewriter and briefcase and wedged them into their allotted space in my car, every inch packed with tools, clothing, books (none opened), useful odds and ends: coils of rope, the polyfoam mat that had been my bed for the final weeks and was still good, surplus hardware, some old and quite interesting.

I crunched along the drive, new shells still shifting underfoot, to the back yard—nearing 8:30—and on out through the alley gate. No one about back there, not even a bird calling.

psycheme

Here I am. But what is "here"? Sooner or later these days that problem is bound to come up, if not "who is this author?" or "what is implied about her?", then "what are these traces? who leaves this track of herself?" Attempts, in so many words, to place an agent: godlike (even if Nobodyatall) when you desire authority; or not an author really, just a writer, merely somebody at work making marks on paper, when you don't. Regulator, or means of production, or something in between—the mystery of whodonit haunts every text.

Already I find I'm becoming as interested in you as in myself: In the drama of our interaction, what kind of character will you turn out to be? What can I, stepping out of our usual relationship, make of you? Being on such familiar footing with me—so personally involved—maybe you can work out a way to accept my presence somewhat as, say, the ongoing, piecemeal fulfillment of a child's need for his/her parents releases him/her to separation from them. Or, at a later age: as sexual gratification may spin a lover off to the heroics of eccentricity. All depends on what you do with my coming and going. The quality of intimacy from which we both shrink.

Such demystification puts us on the same level—you and me, me and Harding—all of us suspended in the same fictional medium. The odd thing is how my thoroughgoing knowledge of Harding's stories has resulted in no loss of interest on my part. My interest in them has changed, that's all, quieted, taken on a more distanced dimension. They have become a text for me, one I live with and, yes, love, and hate—hence my title, THE RESTORATIONIST: *Text One*. What began (long before circumstances brought Harding and me together) as a passion for stories, a world to lose myself in, hardened to a strange passion where I am ever present to myself, as solidly (if blindly) as if her shadow, taking in my substance, had disengaged from her. Passion either dies or fixes at the pitch of its strength. In the latter mold it becomes an intellectual passion.

Back to the text.

I

Taking Possession

"Can be a bit tricky getting in," my agent had scribbled in a p.s., "better let me come demonstrate."

Waiting, pacing about under the live oak that canopies the front yard and porch with its gnarled arms, looking over what I'd bought—keeping an eye out for her appearance every which way—I calculated my prospects for hiring a good demolition crew to gut the house and be out of there in under a week's time. After that, I figured, the trick would be to keep it all moving smoothly, and affordable. I had three months at the outside.

Maybe our appointment, made long distance, had slipped her enterprising mind—Margaret Avery was a busy woman; some say that real estate in the old Quarter makes no move without her, not up or down or any way at all. Or I myself might have slipped up in time somehow, and the nineteenth of May could already have vanished into the twentieth without trace. I'd lost sleep and braved more than a few speed traps to make it down there in record time, and all that chilly Northern spring I'd pushed myself to get things squared away or decently set aside so I could move right on to my summer project, into the thick of it without a moment wasted. A jangled part of me was still on the road topping sixty miles an hour.

I was reluctant to walk back down the alley to her office on the Plaza because if she came by car, the long way around, we were bound to miss each other.

Mine was, I'll be the first to admit, no ordinary impatience, that dangerous edge desire takes on, that wild push to walk straight in through the front door of that historic wreck vacated for me at the law's dependable, civilized, properly executed behest, signed and sealed and above all paid for (cancelled check in purse to prove it) complete with fine proportions, sound structure, authentic detailing galore. Potential, in short, so enticing that, in all its dereliction, I saw it all over again as I had the first time: whole, renascent, welcoming. Francis Claude Boullet House, 1857 is how they mark it in the little walking guide to Old Tarragona prepared for tourists.

Up close, the door jamb had a mangled look where the latch, when it still worked, struck into bare cypress a good two inches deep, a raggedness as of rats gnawing. Authentic shiplock, circa 1830, said the listing. Striker plate missing. Needs repair. A steel padlock secured the door now, a hefty galvanized one that meant business. I tried poking a pencil through the old keyhole the size of an eye wadded tight with pink tissue. The Wentworths—who can blame them?—placed a high value on halting visual access, however miniscule, to the interior. Closed shutters were doing their part for the floor-to-ceiling windows along the porch; terry cloth rags and yellowed polyethylene swathed the insides. It was a flawless May afternoon on the Gulf Coast, the bluest, most perfect and temperate day I can recall all that scorching, muggy summer, and the house wanted none of it. Nor of me, for sure.

Still, when I scraped a penny over the dirty scab of beige enamel around the keyhole, a soft bronze sheen spread outward from the clogged center like healing flesh. A good omen, if you take that view of things, or a cosmic prank if you don't, or a random event looking like either—a morsel flying out of nowhere for no reason into the maw of my impatience. Restorationist Lured by Chance Cosmic Morsel, in some otherworldly headline.

No apparent entry through the back either. Some steps lay in a rotten hunk under an upstairs addition sagging on clumsy piers of big old handmade bricks, rosy Spanish orange but cemented willy-nilly. Alongside them, the original ground-floor gallery, a beauty, weatherbeaten but intact, fronted the bedroom wing. I shook the sand out of my shoes and scrambled on up, scraped my elbow on the way. French doors bolted tight, and the panelled back door into the hall made a clatter when I pushed and pulled at the knob, like an old dog growling to be left alone. I tried a kitchen window next, with a couple of cracked panes at the top and a shutter dangling under it, and lo and behold! It moved.

Omens take on their character as such only after the fact,

which is why, even if you accept that account of reality, they are no earthly good to anyone in practice. Anything may signify, after all. The window sill was positively teeming—with signs of something or someone—and so were the sills of all the other ground floor windows in sight, studded with countless nails and tacks and spikey mega-staples that roughened my passage in. How to account for a niggling compulsion like that, for hammering, tapping, tacking? The thought did flit through my mind as I hoisted the wobbly sash up on my shoulder and stuck my head in, pulling first my purse then the rest of me over the sill (by which time Mrs. Avery was going on half an hour late, even by my perennially slow hand-wound watch), that this forcing of my way on and into the house was bound to have consequences, myself, at the least, rendered vulnerable to the perils of its decomposing structure. Already there was the scraped arm, and now the nailheads and sharp ends of steel gouging my kneecaps.

Those windows, I could see, were going to be quite a clean-up job, one I fully expected, however, to relegate to hands other than my own—some cheap laborer of the kind the old Quarter must be full of. Note: even if you're no innocent in any fundamental way, ignorance will snake a course in you; it's as though living itself, the sheer going on with it, spawns a certain amount of ignorance for its own blind subsistence so that the whole process can go hungrily on.

A whiplike crash, when I'd barely cleared the window sill, and the simultaneous shatter of glass stopped me cold—really quite frozen, as if my inner thermometer had plummeted back to March when this thing had started, or way before: coldest January, before it was even conceived, not so that I was aware of it anyway. Two panes gone, spilled out on the gallery. A single long vicious splinter lay near my left heel—one of those "consequences"—but not, you see, plunged into the ravening vampire's heart. Not yet. A sting in my mouth, a little nick inflicted by my teeth as I'd scrambled in, was salt-sweet with blood. Marvelous, how every tiniest escape gives further impetus to living.

To get your bearings you need light, and the power in the house was off, that stinking kitchen gloomy as a dirt cellar. I went to work, first thing, tearing rags from windows gracefully framed in their original trim, and where I couldn't reach I jumped and yanked—ridiculous, shoulderbag bouncing, bottoms of feet getting slapped hard through the thin soles of ladies' summer shoes, as all around me clouds of sour must were blending with the reek of old dinners ground into blotches of linoleum. What showed of the wooden floors was of lovely irregular pine filthy beyond belief, rims of grime where the new refrigerator had been, and the fancy new electric stove. Both gone now with the Wentworths as I'd suspected they would be. They'd left me the sink, pitted and layered with the slime of dishwater, beside a thirty gallon water heater whose predecessors I later found in a stranglehold of vines out back. The funky pungency underneath it all could only be a backed-up sewer. Items of restoration were pulling at me like hands—ruined windows, back steps, porches, locks, chewed-up woodwork, plumbing, wiring—more at every turn, and more. On top of a counter of sorts stood a blue Maxwell House coffee tin filled to the brim with grease and roaches gorged to a fat death, no doubt good to the last drop.

I was dead set against letting the house dominate me from the start. Groping my way out into the dim hall, recoiling from the stench, I found the back door and rammed aside the makeshift wooden bolt. Breezes puffed in wonderfully fresh and set dustballs skittering fleecily past my ankles down the wide central hall, an elongated garbage heap: refuse, left-overs, disposables, unusables, dregs, debris, rubbish, odds and ends, clutter, all the detritus of domesticity. When the door started to wheeze back to its jamb as if from a scared, sickly habit of shutting out light and air—guarding the gloom past the staircase and all the way to the indistinct form of the front entrance with its rag-muffled transom, its tissue-clogged keyhole—I swung it wide open again, then back and forth at arm's length listening for the wheeze, where it began and quit, till I found the steadying point of balance and it stayed uncertainly in place.

Nothing like enlisting the laws of physics on your side when you're about to appropriate your newly acquired historic property. I picked my way over the mounds and bundles of junk, the scatter, toothless combs, brushes fuzzy with flaxen hairs, listerine bottles and aspirin dropped like buttons that crunched into snowy smears underfoot, cardboard boxes spilling over with mildewed magazines, and behind them, around blind corners, old banana peels splayed darkly over cigarette butts, coffee grounds, tampons falling out of a brown paper bag—it goes on: Q-tips and cotton swabs and stained gauze amid TV guides in varying stages of dismemberment (the Wentworth baby's primer?), a headless pink doll in a dumptruck bereft of wheels, Dr. Pepper bottles aswarm with more roaches, some still straggling over lifeless others up the sticky necks, out the mouths. Never say die.

And, not to be missed in this helter skelter of family discards like the insides of trashbags scattered by a night-prowling scavenger, this Gehenna under lock and key and darkness: beer cans. Beer cans everywhere, punched into hourglass shapes, in a great catholicity of brands witnessing to the ingenuity of free enterprise at work. I'd already spotted a whole jerryrigged cupboard full out on the back veranda.

I barely sidestepped a scatalogical detail of some kind, along a baseboard in a little clearing, iridescent with flies. The likeliest explanation was that the Wentworths had kept their dogs, a pack of them, not wholly confined to the portion of back yard fenced off by chicken wire where I'd seen them in the spring. The flies were something else again. Had they found their way in just now through the broken panes in the kitchen, the back door open at last, or did they laze around indoors from season to season, on the most intimate terms with their human hosts? (Title for an essay, the kind that starts, say, with a fly-speck on a spoon and keeps on enlarging thematically: "On Sighting and Resisting the Familiar.")

A giant step brought me to the bathroom door, which I opened and instantly shut.

Rot. Abjection. Outrage added to outrage that the slum landlord who'd sold me the property should call itself "Committee for the Preservation of Historic Tarragona." Preserving what? Whose history? I tried another knob down the hall, a bulbous, battered one this time, decidedly inauthentic, that rolled off in my hand like a wormy apple. I tossed it aside, gave the door a circumspect push and squeezed through as it stopped against a mattress on the floor inside. They'd left their TV behind, a gigantic throwback of a console, the very bulkiest, ugliest imaginable, vintage family tyrannosaurus. And their orange vinyl couch, too. Slit all over and taped in several new spots, it was tilting to one side on a bad leg. On the hearth, all in a row, stood five half-gallon milk cartons crammed full of dirty pampers, provocative hints to those who drop in at inopportune moments. Omens, omens...everywhere, and not a sign of a message.

The Wentworths have a flaxen-haired, blue-eyed teenage daughter, Stephanie, already a mother and pregnant again that March when I'd first looked over the house. Has a mouthful of tiny rotting teeth between rather sweet lips in the sort of face one might, under other circumstances, meet in an eighteenth-century portrait: young Lady Somebody-or-Other with Pet Spaniel. Romney, maybe, or Reynolds, very English. Only this one had her chubby, pensive, indeterminately dusky baby on one arm, and the two of them, on my whirlwind tour, were in thrall to the TV. When Margaret Avery tried the door on the other side of the room, the one to the back bedroom wing, the mesmerized girl came to and leaped forward out of the orange couch nearly dropping her baby. Whatever was in there had the say-so in this house. She pleaded with us not to disturb *him*— real sick, she said, gets very upset when strangers barge in on him. Doesn't like strangers. Might even drag himself up and have one of his violent fits.

You could hear a rasping cough all right, and groans, and a bedstead creak, even through the swelling chords of "Days of Our Lives."

So my agent and I had pressed on to view the front rooms, where the husband kept his back to us the whole time and fiddled with a gas heater. The wife had a distinctly shamed look about her that she tried to hide by gazing into her can of Rheingold as if it contained archeological clues to a vanished civilization. And to get out of there as fast as possible—I'm touring the house, remember, prospective buyer already more than getting her feet wet running numbers and timetables through my mind, transforming it all in bold visions—I hurried up the stairs and over the whole second floor of empty, spacious, silent rooms musty as crypts, ravaged, and predictably beautiful. Alluring; tall ceilings, wonderful light, original cypress trim all over, old painted floors worn down to the wood, more random-width boards of heart pine. By the time we got to the library (I thought of it that way from the instant I stepped inside) I was far out over the deep, afloat, light as air. In it up to my neck. The room spans the entire front of the house, huge, with four oversized dormer windows, high-set alcoves in the boughs of the great live oak. Sunlight streamed in through them tinged with the faintest, most delicate of greens, a forest-shimmer of green.

But, back in March, there had been no pampers on the downstairs hearth, no soggy sack of a mattress lumped against the door. These and the vinyl couch I could understand: leave removal of the too-far-gone to somebody else. Why they'd left their giant-screen TV with its twenty-four hour appeal and its walnut finish in place, still reigning over one side of the room, was to be a mystery of short standing. I already had the answer on every side of me.

The door to the forbidden wing was pulled tight as before, with the same old dirty string coiled around two nails. As I unwound it, with just the tip of my forefinger and thumb, the weight of the door slowly opening pulled the string out of my fingers—so slowly, so very evenly, it might have been staged. My eyes finding their way through the swathed dimness in there met those of a skinny old man open-mouthed against a bank of pillows in a hospital bed.

I mumbled...something about being sorry, I think, "didn't realize anybody was still about   just stay where you are, sir...I'll shut the door again," and fumbled for the string, keeping an eye on him and backing out all at the same time, somewhat like a person in the presence of a dangerous beast kept from springing by the deception that nothing out of the ordinary is going on.

But something stopped me, something unnatural about his stare, his eyes, eyes like bluets on a patch of chalky ground. Something unanimal-like about him made me suspect that the joke was on me. It's all pure melodrama from this distance, of course, though in that moment anything but—even, when you think about it, an inevitability. The two of us alone at last, so quiet in that singular moment, so insulated and apart in that benighted old house, as if the breath of life personalizing my frantic spring had suddenly stopped. Although I certainly couldn't have expected to find him lying there, the instant I saw that look I should have known, as they say, all. Had he not been sprouting way back there in my northern garden while documents of sale shuttled duly back and forth, all through March and cruelest upstate New York April, riding down the breakneck highways with me, even getting there first? Already waiting for me.

Still in the doorway, I made myself pause calmly to watch the open mouth—didn't seem to be moving at all.

I let the string go, and the door swung open. The longer I looked—all of this couldn't have lasted more than ten, fifteen seconds at most—the more the mouth stayed unmoving, widened as if caught in preparing to scream his outrage. The fury of that mouth drew me to itself, closer in and closer, like an arresting canvas hung on the opposite wall of a gallery as you first go in. I padded up to the bed, balls of feet only, and stopped, waved my hand in front of the little fixed blue eyes, started to incline my ear toward the livid mouth.

Nothing. Silence and immobility so absolute they were not mere absence of sound and movement but presence of another kind, so palpable it closed in on me.

I heard a gurgle—mine—and my feet took off on their own, tripping clumsily over one end of the soggy mattress. I seemed to be knee-deep in it, wading through spongy funk, a hunted animal hard on my feet again and into the hall with life-or-death speed but without any sense of direction whatever, only a snapshot image of the lighted back doorway out.

Something rattled and thumped. Down the hall the back door wheezed once and slammed shut, and in that same instant, daylight illumined the staircase. I say "illumined" because of the way it all rose before me as if newly formed: the turned post, the wide treads bowed in the center from the weight and scuff of countless passings, up, down, spindles and banister splendidly ascending in a leafy diffusion of light.

Over the threshold of the front entrance a silhouette resolved itself into a dark-haired woman in elegant summer attire whose first words to me were unspeakably appropriate.

"Good Lord," she said, "you look as if you've seen a ghost!"

ii

Margaret Avery of Heritage Homes stepped in on Italian heels so fashionably high she seemed to glide on tip-toe. Even at that, says Harding, she was a good bit shorter than me, but every inch the professional Southern woman quite unruffled by the spectacle of the new owner stumbling out and shuddering uncontrollably against the nearest porch post.

She'd expected something like this, she said. "But it's worse than I thought—you already know. How did you get in?"

Gasping as you do when you've swallowed water the wrong way, I could barely stay upright let alone manage a dignified answer, rubbing my shins where they'd come in contact with that awful mattress. (What was I supposed to do with the revolting thing, advertise it in the local paper? Will trade one sweat-and-pee double.) "What is he," I finally got out, "part of this god-forsaken historic mess I bought?"

"That porch plank under you looks none too solid," she said, guiding me past danger by the elbow. Margaret Avery is a handsome woman despite an unseemly drift toward plumpness along the middle that she appears bent on keeping in check, shoulders back, diaphragm tensed to give the voice its assured sonority.

From her lizard handbag she produced an envelope of assorted keys, including one to the padlock. "No idea what the rest of these are good for, but don't think I haven't tried to find out." On the point of leaving her office well before two, meaning to do a little advance airing and checking around, she'd been stopped by the exterminator who was to have treated the house before my arrival. He startled her with the news that old Jeremy Wentworth lay in his room, stone dead. "Seemed like something for the police to handle, but you know what they're like—taking their sweet time, asking poky questions, putting you on hold. You'd think we've got all the time in the world. And then I thought I'd better see to it that word got to the family, you know—but, oh Lord, what a reception for you! This is not typical of how we do things around here, I assure you."

All this said in a cheerful though by no means unfeeling

tone, the kind considered appropriate for invalids whose recovery is in question.

"I should practice forbearance," I said, still pretty unsteady all right.

My agent gave a thoughtful pat to her auburn chignon too perfect to be the work of an amateur, figuring my reserves of forbearance, evidently, while wanting to know again, "But how in the world *did* you get in?"

"Window," I said and shifted to what was on my mind: garbage. If the Wentworths had managed to remove refrigerator and stove, they might have been expected to haul that off too. "What about the TV," I added, "is that for my trouble?"

"Broke down once too often, you can be sure."

And just as we were getting into the mattress, she obviously struggling between professional *sang-froid* and a hilarity she must have felt to be out of place, a car marked "Tarragona Police Department" rolled to a stop beside my agent's dove-grey Seville. An ambulance cruised discreetly behind like a chaperone on the lookout.

"The rescue team," she whispered, dark eyes betraying a habit of controlled irony, as the two officers ambled up the porch steps.

The squat middle-aged one with the sergeant's badge pinned to his shirt nodded his greeting, at a loss for words after "Miz Avery, ma'am...," and the world seemed to shake for a moment in his mirror glasses where I appeared in the foreground as a Boschian deformity. I caught a whiff of spearmint even before he addressed me, "You next of kin, ma'am?"

My companion took the situation tactfully in hand. "Professor Dumot is the new owner, gentlemen—the body belongs to her no more than it does to me." Margaret Avery has a way of giving utterances a little hermetic twist infinitely suggestive in the moment, elusive but with some exquisite point if only you know how to take it. The way of people who are always *on* to something but can never quite tell you what it is they're on to.

"You...unh...you're the one that bought this...unh...," the Sergeant traced a deprecating contour of the Boullet House with a folded handkerchief *en route* to wiping the sweat off his brow and completing his sentence, "...place."

The younger officer, who until then had stood by silently self-effacing, chuckled, hands folded at ease behind him.

"Sure I bought it," say I with a little flare-up of nerves.

"Well I'll be!" Both men laughed at Peaden's sudden witticism and more heartily yet at his confident follow-up: "What'cha gonna do with it now, burn it down and collect the inn-surance?"

Here my agent saved the day in a timely manner (which, says Harding, I as the daughter of a good Southern family could well appreciate). "It's a historic property," she explained, "one of the foremost in the Quarter, gentlemen. Miz Dumot is going to do the community a service it doesn't deserve by restoring it."

This caused the Sergeant to focus his twin mirrors on the altruistic Miz Dumot and smile wordlessly, an expression he managed with fair skill. The younger officer glanced sideways into the mirrors reflecting the bond of their certain knowledge.

To secure the dangling padlock while they carried on with their job, I snapped it together on the jamb and slipped the key into my pocket...making a point. "Just lean the door shut when you're done, please," I said.

"You from up Nawth, ma'am?" The instant he spoke, I registered the fact that the younger policeman had been looking me over from the start. Nothing tongue-tied about this one; he preferred to watch. And listen.

"No. Actually I'm not." His question, she says, surprised her, probably because, throughout all her years in the Northeast, Harding has never lost, has never bothered to modify (except when modification serves some tactical advantage) her Southern speech habits. Up here, she says, everyone approximately south of Philadelphia and west of Pittsburgh has an "accent." "I live there now, but I'm from Mississippi originally."

"You don't say."

"The Delta."

"That right!" from Peaden, "I got a friend lives in Cleveland." And the other one: "Thought you was a Yankee ma'am. I apologize."

Everyone laughed at that, more or less, and Margaret Avery seized on our shaky conviviality to tell the officers they could bring the ambulance right on in through the carriage gates.

"Just unwind that old chain," she said and tiptoed down

the cracked steps with me tripping after her to the front gate, the pedestrian way out.

From under the oak, whose horizontal mossy branches spread their shade summer and winter from the fence at the front all the way up over the porch to the second story dormers, she called out in native tones of command, "Y'all be sure to put everything back the way it was, hear?" And with the tact characteristic of old-style Southern courtesy, the owner-manager of the most prestigious real estate operation in Old Tarragona announced that she needed "something to soothe her nerves" and invited Harding to join her.

"While they take care of this," she said with a wink. "Keep your fingers crossed."

It was to be Harding's first—and, as things turned out that summer, her last—afternoon tea at the Bottomless Cup, a little turn-of-the-century warehouse on the Bay recently converted to a quaintly picturesque café—where the cups, she says, are anything but bottomless (though they are quite pretty unmatched English and American bone china), and the waitresses, a new breed, are more or less gracious until something better comes along.

psycheme

Warning: you may not be treated either to gripping insights into Harding's interior life or to inspirational changes in her outer one. These are of no interest to me.

And whether she acted in good faith or bad does not concern me either—certainly anyone suffering a compulsion keeps faith through all its permutations. Where the delusions of representation are no longer possible for a person to live out naturally (or, as is often heard: to lose herself in) she moves somewhere between the depths and the heights, emerging on that plane we call the surface of our experience, a function of its depths and heights. As the psychical terrain of our bodily pleasures and bodily survival, it may be valued for practical reasons and, by some, for the mystery of beauty tendered here and there.

It's at this surface that I would meet with Harding in

acknowledgement that her fifteen years ahead of me point directions for movement. She lives alone and by choice between this and that, accepting daily evidence that this middle ground she occupies is unclaimed, subject neither to laws of ownership nor to the stakes of power. No common good vies here with self-interest; her sphere of daily living is neither public nor private and so allows for a certain freedom from domination by the usual human concerns. No esoteric promise; one simply engages in making the familiar more familiar, as if somehow keeping the ground one steps on from car to supermarket at the center of attention.

Familiarity may breed contempt. Made more familiar it breeds uncannily. I come and go, and already it spawns.

iii

It's pleasant enough there, the clatter of cups and coffee spoons soothingly discreet. The voices seem to purr around you through cool flute and harpsichord strains of the French baroque, and, like a cat, they leave you alone.

Nothing at all, in other words, like the old Bottomless of my childhood, a long, low cinderblock structure with a giant marquee on top visible nearly all the way across the bridge from the Island, where we used to spend our summers back then. Out of the bottom of an enormous mug depicted on the marquee sloshed a coffee brown river in which the syllables bobbed like
buoys: B O
               T T O
                     M I, E S
                           S C U P

Icon of unending satisfaction. Inside, it was one of those clean, plain, crowded, gregarious Gulf Coast places where they served breakfast and lunch only, seven days a week, and where everything really was baked fresh early each morning, and they knew how to do all of it right.

Only the name, transposed to the Historic Quarter, remains. It has the appeal, now, of all such conversions, whether in Cambridge, Sante Fe, Charleston, Georgetown, and a host of smaller towns reviving all over the map, that feel of temporary refuge in the pleasantly receding background of a material environment made familiar by history. The eatery as artifact, aesthetized *mis-en-scène* of the bodily resolve to keep going.

Margaret Avery was busy drawing me out as far as courtesy allowed, being too well-bred for the really nosy inquisition you suspect she would relish. Also considerate enough to suppose that steering my mind off cadavers and garbage and wisecracking policemen would be just the thing to steady my nerves. But I'm an inveterate failure at polite small-talk. Those easy turns of speech that satisfy in brief and in general and without stirring things up are so many blind alleys to me; I seem to have evolved only imperfectly the particular organ that lets you be both sociable and a million miles away all at the same time. Relaxing, this is called. And that's what my table companion was after: ready formulations confirming how she thought things stood. When another finds her politenesses actually entertained rather than returned with politenesses that sustain a temperature precisely suitable to the occasion (even if she's too well-bred to let on), the disparity, the sense of indefinable excess, the discomfiture of things going out of kilter, reaches right across the table and stops you cold. ("Digresses from the point," turns up in my student evaluations like clockwork just when I've been thinking that we've managed, better than usual, to get to whatever's at stake.)

"Tell me the old ghost story," I say over our smoky glass-topped table for two. It had been weighing on my mind that part of the task I'd set for myself might involve working through a prejudice in local folklore against the Boullet House. Peaden must have been thinking of more than insurance fraud to get such a charge out of his little arson joke.

"Ghost?" The teapot paused in mid-air, and I acknowledged her signal by extending my cup.

"You warned me back in the spring. 'A ghost into the bargain,' you said, and I'm sure you couldn't have meant old Wentworth."

She laughed, "Just one of those sordid family chronicles," pouring herself a precise, well-sugared half cup, the flash of mischief in her dark blue eyes quite restored.

I confessed myself hooked on family chronicles, the more

sordid the better, but her face drew into a faintly ironic mask of distaste. Had Captain Boullet been a libertine or a swindler, I wondered aloud, or something so unmentionable even the passing of more than a century had failed to pale the old Victorian blush? But no, oh no—she set me straight there. The man was a kind of Errol Flynnish adventurer, loads of charm, great business sense. Put up the Hernando Inn first, which gave the town its first taste of social glamor and him a steady cash flow.

"Didn't stay home much, though, especially after the wife died giving birth."

"She's my ghost, then? Neglected young wife pining for errant husband?"

"The daughter, *Frances* Boullet—that's with an 'e'."

"Wouldn't you know," I said, picking up some coolness which spurred my curiosity, "a ghostly lady with the ghost of her father's name, an 'e' you can't hear, smell, or touch."

"He built the place for her."

"And she drifts up and down those stairs and all over the property swearing, under her breath of course, about the sanitary conditions there—things left rotting all over her patrimony. Is that the way it goes?"

She slipped a Bit O'Honey bar from her purse, daintily breaking off one of its bite-size segments. "Been tryin' to stop smoking," she muttered between chews.

I gave as my lay opinion that old Wentworth looked to me like he'd been half dead for a good long while, shut away in that room. "Must have been the ghost of Frances Boullet pulling him to the grave."

"Difficult as it may be to imagine, that half-dead old man's word was law in that household. The rest of them take whatever comes, good or bad."

"And leave whatever is so far gone they can't tell the difference—"

"They *did* take their dogs, yesterday afternoon in fact, when they moved themselves out of there. For that much you should at least be grateful."

Harding says she was trying to place what she was feeling about the Wentworths. Sympathy with their hopelessness, yes, but more: she was horrified. Despite purring voices and rococo airs, *still* horrified. And it was this that set the limits of her sympathy and left her wondering, yet again, at the range of what it can mean to be horrified.

"The husband came running into my office first thing this morning," Margaret was saying, "cold sober for a change, to drop off the keys, he said. Slipped in and out in a big hurry while I was on the phone with a client and mumbled something or other about not being responsible, and how he'd done his 'share.'"

"He's old Wentworth's son I suppose?"

She paused as if undecided, shook her head—"the wife"—apportioned a second bit of candy for herself and, wrapping up the remainder, tucked it furtively away in her expensive purse.

"Jeremy Wentworth was *her* father?"

An incidental nod—her anecdotal gusto is on the upsurge. "You should have seen it. The son's old pickup was piled down with their last load, some of the worst-looking junk you ever saw, blocked traffic up and down the Avenue right in the middle of morning rush hour. He was driving, and packed next to him like sardines were the wife, and the...large young woman with the colored baby, a good bit larger since you saw her last. Rumor has it the son is her brother—I mean, lover—along with the father of the child, whoever he was."

"Intricate set of relations," I said, picking away at the tangles.

"You can never be entirely sure in these families. The wife and husband are first cousins, both Wentworths, and it's the same with that crowd that runs the Hernando—they're all related a couple of times over."

Mock-salacious amusement belied a touch of prudery. If you savor the incongruous, the wayward, the perverse (and it would be small-minded not to), you do it from the propriety of a veiling distance; this is a fundamental condition of communal safety. You have certain obligations, what's more, if you're in the business of facilitating the exchange of choice plots in the communal terrain.

"Frances Boullet must be a free-wheeling kind of ghost to put up with all that irregularity," I ventured.

She had perfected the Southern woman's art of self-concealment. The reticence of one prompted by good breeding to be minimally forthcoming about a subject unworthy of her notice brought on a perfectly curtailed retort: "People here are old-fashioned."

"Maybe she didn't hold with majority opinion?"

"I'm sure any of the old colored gossips in the four-hundred block can tell you all about it." The last block of Valencia Street beyond Cadiz Boulevard, I understood from this, still a kind of outback, was an unregenerate fringe where rumors of my ghost and other foolishness could flutter irrepressibly from mouth to mouth. In an authentically rehabilitated building in the heart of the Quarter, one knew better.

I changed directions more or less on cue and asked Margaret where she was from.

The readiness of her answer assured me that it had been the right kind of question to ask. "My mother's people were from Mobile," she said, "Daddy's were planters in Louisiana cane before the War. They were burned out." Only Southerners still refer to the Civil War with such unquestionable ellipsis, as if two World Wars (not to mention the Spanish-American, Korea, and Vietnam) had never happened. In fact, I saw that what I'd come back to in Tarragona was a familiar milieu of communicative patterns where utterances often seem to issue without context on the assumption that it's the listener's obligation to supply it. Listening means closing the rift between words and the world.

"Made their way east along the Gulf Coast, to start over?" I said. I could still, quite comfortably, do my part as listener, even though as speaker, I realized, I'd developed an array of communicative restraints that virtually barred me from talking without myself providing the necessary context. There's academic training for you—if it takes hold, it will condition you to watch eternally for gaps and bridge every single one in sight. Know your audience. This, they say, makes for effective communication.

Grandparents had been headed for Leon County, or Suwannee, unclear which or whether it made a difference, when something beyond my grasp as listener (and marvelling, too, at this discovery of a whole new area of unsuspected repression in myself when I'd thought to have freely chosen my inhibitions) waylaid them in Tarragona, still a frontier then. "Never seems to get past it," she said, and I knew just what she meant: one of those places perpetually promising to boom. A

Clayborne home rose in due course on the Bayou, miles of woods and wetlands all around in those days. (The very kind of home I'd briefly fantasized about two months back as I watched coastal Tarragona approach from the new bridge that spans DeLuna Bay.) "Still lovely," she said, "still a private community" (with its gatehouse, says Harding, where they keep rosters of tradesmen and visitors expected and offer a convenient place to turn around). Margaret took a quick sip and glanced out into the green of the Plaza. Beyond the northern edge of it, above the treeline, rose the Spanish façade of the Hernando. From the café, you can't see how shabby, how run-down Captain Boullet's old goldmine of a hotel really is. "Guess I'll sell the place once the children are out on their own...too much trouble nowadays to keep up a big home by yourself."

Within arm's length of where we sat, on the other side of the Victorian bow window, a black teenager sauntered past, wrapped in the protective blare of his radio. "So the Claybornes," I summed up, fully attuned I thought, "were not one of the original families in Tarragona?"

She scrutinized me with the wry mirth I concluded was as much a social advantage as is tact, or the ability to give your interlocutor the slip when necessary. Context is listener's work.

The Claybornes, yes, they were an old family but not as original here as some. There was that Zamora woman next door—had I noticed her? "Goes straight back to the conquistadors and some anonymous Indian beauty on the beach."

It was the first I'd heard of any "Zamora woman," but I was on the lookout for the proper connections.

"She was born in the servants' quarters of the old Simmons home, and the family, no longer really able to afford it, let her stay on after her mother abandoned her there."

A dependent inherited from better days, I concluded.

"A shame the old homestead burned down," she was going on, "it was grander than the Boullet House even if it was post-War. He put up that cottage a room or two of it at a time over the years—that's why it doesn't seem to have the usual plan to it—and then he just up and quit in the late forties and hasn't touched it since. But I can tell you one thing: there's no way he can hold on to it once yours is restored, and the ones across the street."

Even on a frontier I don't like to be the only one risking my all—this was good news. "He" had to be my elderly neighbor whom I'd glimpsed earlier, on his side of the fence, as I paced back and forth, waiting.

"Being a Simmons, his mother would have fits if she could see how he lives openly with that woman, has now for over twenty years." Again, that incidental foregrounding of essentials which is also the speaker's prerogative.

"And the Boullets," I said—my ghost again—"were they one of the old families hereabouts?" Contrary to the *credo* of enlightened travellers that one must see a place through native eyes to appreciate it fully, I've found in going here and there that the chief value of that kind of looking lies in mapping out just exactly where the blind spots are.

"After people have a little money, nobody asks." The Captain had been smart enough to marry a Howard, which name I duly jotted down in my evolving Who's Who after "Simmons" and before "Zamora" (bracketed).

And now, to catapult things out of the hinting stage, "Considering her notoriety," I said, "Frances Boullet either didn't inherit her father's brains or squandered them, which comes to the same thing I guess."

"She was quite a reader."

"Oh? One of those eccentric female intellectuals society had no use for—back then—was she?"

"Books everywhere, all over the house they say, but mostly in that big room upstairs. Some of it you can see at the public library any time, just a fraction, they say, of what used to be her private collection, everything from psychology, and languages, philosophy, history, religion, music, to geography, medicine, botany, physics—what else is there?"

"Literature? Biology? Architecture?"

"Yeah, and just about everything ever written by and about women, books by people you never heard of or ever will."

I was only fleetingly stumped by what came next: "The Canes—they bequeathed the books to the library—never mention her name and haven't for as long as I can remember." I heard the lack of emphasis signalling a status so assured it makes elaboration indelicate. The Canes.

Tarragona is chock-full of pointers to help the ignorant and uninitiated see; in a flash I recalled how, on my March visit, sitting on a sunny bench in Hernando Plaza, my hand had strayed through the back slat to a little plaque fixing a Mrs. Randall (or was it Ransom?) Cane, Jr. in memory for any admirer of the rehabilitated cottages all around. "An inspiration to all." Could this Mrs. Cane have been responsible for excising my ghost from her family's exemplary lexicon, and no doubt from her guest list too? Or was it her namesake among the living, if she had one? "Mrs. Cane" is the name not of any particular woman but a succession, and sorting them out matters less than the fact of succession itself. In Tarragona you have to put things together fast. I summoned up an image of Mrs. Cane half-way between Athena Parthenos and Scarlett O'Hara.

"As if she'd never lived," came the afterthought from Margaret, while a passing waitress laid our check casually face down.

"But the persistence of her ghost would tend to prove otherwise."

"They say people used to cross over to the other side of the street when they saw her coming, or one of her associates." Her eyes went briefly naughty again.

"That dangerous?"

"She stepped out of line, and that's bound to come to a bad end."

"Exile," I noted, as I might a topic we'd met with in a class text.

Not a trace of counter-response as the word lengthened between us on an ensemble passage lilting from hidden speakers, only her rather shrewd appraising look at me. Even at my age, says Harding, I have to struggle not to overestimate the perspicacity of women like Margaret Avery. She and her kind weigh down memories of my early life with the awfulness of imagined discovery—"she sees me, she knows...." Exposure. Humiliation. But, I have to remind myself, *under*-estimating them and the sheer conviction of their judgments can be every bit as costly.

"But why would she care what anybody thought of her?" I added, even as I saw where this perverse dodge into naiveté would lead.

And so did she, of course, replying with easy good humor as if to a precocious younger sister who'll understand all by and by, though she can't be more than four or five years older than me at the outside: "Never knew anybody who didn't."

Not the kind of claim you can knock down with a little data to the contrary. A personal note won't do either, since it's presumed you may be on the defensive and don't know it. In over your head, younger sister.

"She wasn't one of us," said with such unassuming candor it sounded both original and wistful.

"But what could there have been for a woman like that...out there?"

She sat up straight at that, as though her back hurt, and smoothed an invisible stray hair away from her forehead. "She knew better—or should have. She had every opportunity."

What I'd meant by "out there" and thought my sweeping open-palmed gesture made plain enough was something more encompassing than Tarragona and its historic layering of attitudes. I'd meant to suggest an infinitely extended world. "So my ghost," I said, "is unquiet for all that she might have been?" Self-development foregone, shirked like a sacred duty, to her everlasting regret. Foreclosure; always that.

Glancing at her watch—calculating, I suspected, that the police had had more than enough time to do their job—she turned playful. Rumor had it that Frances Boullet died of an organic poison, some kind of toxic plant. Everybody knew "they" had been fooling with that kind of thing all along—Margaret Avery, I could see, had made one or two excursions to the outback where the old gossips lived—and, yes, the Boullet woman had a lot to regret.

"Maybe she finally just closed the book on herself," I offered.

"Yeah," she peered impishly over her teacup, "I never did hold with too much of a good thing"—more candy bits fished out of her purse—and, leaning across the table in melodramatic confidentiality, she whispered: "Some say she was murdered, all very hush-hush at the time. Poor old Jeremy Wentworth's corpse may not be all that's been left rotting in there, that's what they say." Candy wrapper crumpled a little guiltily into the clean ashtray next to the sugarbowl. "Oh well, it's just another twist in a long, complicated affair of no real interest anymore."

"Any suspects?" I felt myself entering into a joke I didn't understand.

Some mystery—might have known—about the housekeeper. Mulatto woman, something foreign...West Indian...Barbados, Haiti, one of those. She disappeared, and her niece too—or granddaughter, some female relative anyway—she might have done in both of them to get the house. What they say. Didn't work though.

"The housekeeper's niece...or whatever?" I repeat, just to keep my contexts straight.

She's no help at all, though the details do get more informative. "The hullabaloo about the will dragged on and on till the Canes ended up with the place as next of kin. It was pretty run down by then, but the Wentworths had no place of their own after old Jeremy's daddy drank up what they had, which wasn't much—most likely they think it amounted to more than it really did—and Randall did the charitable thing, although he was the kind of man who might have thought he owed it to them."

"*Randall* Cane," I say like a computer putting it all together. The indecipherable scratch of a signature on more than one document that has lately passed through my hands translates into "Randall Cane III." Of course.

But I don't know the half of it: the charitable one is "Randy's father," and that's the husband of the exemplary Mrs. Cane extolled on the plaque, hence Randall Cane, Jr., and that would make "Randy" the number III on my documents of sale. Self-explaining circle. The two of them, Randy's father, that is, and Jordan Wentworth ("old Jeremy's daddy") were law partners. And *he* (who else?) one of the best legal minds on the Coast back then, took after his father, the Judge.

Genealogy now in place going back to Judge Cane—the first Randall, I discover a bit farther on: Judge Randall Cane, father of Randall Cane, Jr., the charitable, who was father of Randy a.k.a. Randall Cane III. Dying, said Randy's father willed the house to the Old Tarragona Trust. And here the tale quickens, for the OTT turns out to be none other than the forebear of that slummy Committee of a landlord (alias Randall Cane III, indecipherable) who sold the property to me—strings of immediate rehabilitation attached—for quick cash. It's a case of dominoes: as the Boullet House goes, so goes the block, and so on down the street. With my purchase of the house, I've become a key figure in their historic project.

"I see," I can now say at last. "So the ghost in my house walks for vengeance on her murderer, or -ers, or maybe on Tarragona itself, for its treatment of her, however deserved, and her home. Is that about it?"

In the end, Margaret Avery simply cannot resist the local lore. "Actually," she says, "there's a whole raft of them, flitting back and forth along the iron fence under that big old tree out front, muttering and calling out to people on the other side."

"Oh?"

"Every age, shape, and color." The old gossips claim the Boullet woman and her kind had fearsome powers, like turning themselves into animals when they died, cats and snakes and God only knows what else—chickens even—the whole menagerie of them reputed to stalk the old Quarter and, of course, the house and its grounds.

"In human or in animal form?"

Her mysterious expression leaves it up to me. "Sometimes there's a white horse. No, not exactly white, it's supposed to shine like moonlight."

Just so, the Pale Horse of Death, I tell her.

She takes to the idea that Tarragona has spawned its own literary type and embraces the part of regional informant with authority. "The tree's definitely the hub of it all," she says, "and the horse—death horse, you say? There's a gorgeous young man astride him, sometimes with women behind, sometimes not." She used to hear a lot of that spooky talk as a child, all in gruesome detail. Even to this day she finds the Boullet House a tad distasteful if she lets imagination take hold—silly, but there it is.

"You know how those old colored women talked and what lies they could make up."

"Yes, oh yes," I say, "but I haven't thought about it in a long while." Her story, absurd as it was, had the intended soothing effect, there in that decorous little café on a May afternoon when what awaited me back on Valencia Street—three hundred block, about to take off—was the stink and bother of real garbage.

Mrs. Avery of Heritage Properties, who had been smiling to herself, said sheepishly, "Lord knows I shouldn't be telling *you* this stuff, should I? It's a handsome building, one of a kind, and you must realize you got some deal on it."

"Enter the shrewd investor: Elizabeth Dumot, Visionary. Lucky they moved the dogs out, or I might have had my trespassing heels snapped at." I drained the last of my coolly bitter tea, a smoky Earl Grey I'd never particularly had a taste for.

"It always pays to take the more traditional approach," was the hermetic reply as she zipped open the portfolio on the empty chair beside her. "Your papers," she said. "I nearly forgot—" words belying any suspicion that teatime might have been a tactfully orchestrated prelude to this official moment. "You'll want these for your records," a wad of documents the size of a hefty monograph, "closing statement, title abstract, and all the rest."

"'The Committee for the Preservation of Historic Tarragona,'" I read aloud, "'does bargain, sell, convey and grant to Elizabeth Harding Dumot—'"

"That's your warranty deed, let me see," interrupted my agent, settling a modish pair of spectacles on her nose, "'...does bargain, sell, convey and grant unto...*her* heirs...' yes, they had it wrong the first time, '...executors, administrators, successors, and assigns forever, the following real property, blah, blah, to wit: Lots 358 and 359, Old City Tract...according to...*her*...,' there it is again, 'To have and to hold unto the said grantee, *her* heirs, successors, and assigns forever...blah, blah....'"

"Reassuring, don't you think?" I noted without conviction.

"'...forever,'" Margaret was still checking, "'...free from encumbrances and...the said grantee, *her*, etcetera.... in the quiet and peaceful possession and enjoyment thereof.' Yes, that's got it." She passed the deed back over the empty teapot with a ritualistic flourish of being quit of her part in this transaction.

I leafed through the thick abstract documenting my legal title to the property all the way back to when the land itself had been part of a grant by the Spanish sovereign to one Jimenes Diaz, late sixteenth century.

"You'll find the entire history of Tarragona in there, in miniature," she said, as if to spur pride of ownership.

I took it as an opportunity to seize my prerogative as speaker: "They're going to hear from me," I said, and she seemed to know just who I meant. "I'm not having *their* history hauled off to the dump at my expense! Just because they're alcoholic and on welfare, I can't expect even minimal decencies? Not even a rudimentary clean sweep?"

Harding says she was prepared to stand on her rights, though she'd given no thought until that moment as to what precisely these might amount to in Tarragona. But Margaret Avery—on an afternoon when she might still be wanted at her office—proved as thorough in her courtesies as in business, a conjunction of attributes Harding knows how to value, along with all such vanishing rarities.

"Just to be sure you start on the right foot in dealing with people here," her agent explained, and set out to take charge of the new owner's garbage problem.

iv

With an understated hum the Seville rolled to a stop in front of a single-story cottage set back in the shade. Residential property is cheap here in the west end of town a good mile and centuries removed from the old Quarter's redolence of storied pasts, Spanish sovereigns, old families, ghosts. The four-lane two-way traffic along a central island of scrub palms is in a ruthless hurry both ways, with nothing to stop or slow it down for blocks in either direction. It's a harrowed crossing for the rare pedestrian. Farther west, after a tag-end of commercial sprawl, the road—sprucing itself up as it goes—passes by the Country Club, set back a good piece, and on to the Alabama beach resorts.

A chorus of barks from behind the cottage confirmed that we'd come to the right place, ordinary, domestic, as tidy as Mrs. Wentworth's hairdo, fresh disinfectant and paint agreeably giving way to the mellow specter of malt. Here was Mr. Wentworth, miraculously clean-shaven, sipping Coors in an easy chair as he contemplated a pamphlet on The Church of Christ Restored. There was the flaxen-haired daughter cooing to her boy who was trying out a few first discombobulated steps in snowy pampers. And—wonder of wonders—the sleek new state-of-the-art TV in the corner had its sound turned down all the way, projecting its mute technicolor spectacle without regard for its failure to captivate.

Mrs. Avery was glad to see the utilities had been switched on and sympathized with them again in their bereavement. Life must go on—and that was just the thing, she said: Mrs. Dumot had a big job to do and she would have an easier time of it without all they had left in the way over at the old house. "The odor there is certainly not improving," she said.

Mr. Wentworth broke off his spiritual pursuits with the laconic retort, "Weren't none of my doin'."

"Well, it's not mine either," I put in, maybe a bit precipitously, as is my unfortunate inclination, "and I can't start work until it's been cleared away."

"Don't take long for the odor to set in," he agreed, "in this weather. It's all been seen to, though."

"Couldn't be more'n a half hour ago," confirmed Mrs. Wentworth. "He signed all the papers, didn't you, Roy? The one in charge of it said he'd drive us out to the cemetary when they got ready to put him in the ground. He was just that nice and polite, real considerate and dressed up." With her look full of meaning shifting from her husband to Margaret Avery, she observed, "We don't have no way to get to the store from here."

I was on the point of caving in. Isn't there always some junk to dispose of when you take over a house?

But my agent, I could see, was of a tougher cast. "Your father's body has been removed, that's what I came here to tell you. It's the other items Mrs. Dumot wants hauled out of there."

Mr. Wentworth glowered at the Seville grey as fog from snout to tail light, inside and out. His wife and daughter watched him tilt the frosty can to his mouth and tip his head against the back of the easy chair without breaking his stare.

"There ain't nothin' in that old house we want," he muttered sideways into the wing, "we done took ours." The can crunched softly in one hand and clinked to the floor.

"Well I don't want any of it either," I chimed in with some spirit, hating the ensuing silence in which the wife fished up the beer can.

"The lady don't have no use for it neither, Roy," she prompted. "You'n Billy can pick up another truckload, first chance y'all get."

He muttered back that it was "just a lotta ole junk," with which I couldn't quarrel. Folks liking old things ought to appreciate a fine early model TV, "just needs a little fixin' is all," he said, lost in his pamphlet.

"Poor Poppa." The woman turned to me as if we were all alone in the white room, "Billy couldn't wait on accounta workin' afternoon shift, makes good money up at the plant, Billy does. And there was Poppa, you see, threatenin' to get up outta that bed and put a stop to us haulin' off his property. Don't know when I seen him so mad." She smoothed the can with her fingertips, absently, like a face in a photograph from another time. "Who'd have thought he could up and die like that? Poppa. I can't hardly believe it."

I expressed gratitude for what I'd taken as reassurance that they would haul at least their broken furniture out of the house.

"Why that's *all right*," she drawled, eyes very distant in their pouchy lids, still and blue as the dead man's, "don't think nothin' of it." It reached me as a condescension, my small spontaneous courtesy of the moment construed as defeat.

Not, I could see, a position into which Margaret Avery would ever permit herself to be maneuvered. In high heels like that, the last place you want to end up is on your knees. With an imperious parting look at the baby, she tiptoed out the door saying, "Do be sure you get to it by tomorrow morning, Mr. Wentworth, the earlier the better—and don't forget all those cans out back while you're at it, will you?" I could hear the Incredible Hulk roaring up behind us in state-of-the-art fury.

"That's a nice place they've got there," I said, settling back into the sculpted leather seat, push-button everything at my fingertips, trappings of this age when all, they say, is possible—or will be—every manner of body extension available to liberate the body itself for medical miracles and designer fashions, this and that-scans, transplants, coronary bypass, Calvin Klein on your backside. Quite a contrast to my old blue Chevy, flanks rusting from at least a half dozen Northern winters of corrosive slush, maps, newspapers, books scattered all over the back seat—probably one or two empty styrofoam cups on the floor, too, from my headlong drive down. In Tarragona, they would view it as just another junk car, with me in it simply an extension of the disreputable hulk herself. New York redneck.

"I wonder how they ever found it," I mused.

"Didn't," came her snappy reply as she pulled expertly into the traffic flow the way people do only on their own turf. "I did."

"That couldn't have been easy." I was starting to understand why I could depend on the Wentworths to haul off their junk one way or another.

"Well, you see," she explained in that older sister voice, "in what's left of our Great Republic, there's no end of breaks available for fixing up low income housing. Doesn't have to cost you a penny. When the tenants finish running it down again, you apply for some more. They say it stimulates the economy."

"And recycles your taxes," I added, playing my role of precocious sibling to the hilt.

I thought we'd finished with the Wentworths and everything to do with them when, entering the old Quarter, she pointed out in one of those apparent *non sequiturs* that "they weren't always like you see them today." Two prim toots of the horn shooed a pushy Datsun out of the way, and I learned that "old Jeremy" had been "Daddy's lawyer" for a time, in the old days. "Daddy" had been a judge. Judge Clayborne, contemporary of Randall Cane (Junior, the charitable).

Then she came up with something that took me a bit by surprise. She said: "I believe that everybody ought to have a chance to start with a clean slate now and then, don't you?"

Harding says she was turning over the possibility of asking, "Even the likes of Frances Boullet?" But just then, as if to spare her a gaffe, the Seville purred into a white-shelled drive between two impeccably restored eighteenth-century cottages on the east end of Hernando Plaza. "Here," said Margaret Avery—and their last two hours together, more or less, receded to the margin—"you can probably still catch him in."

V

She did, and tells of that eye-opening interview in as much detail as it deserves. But here, a last word about the corpse

Harding found on taking possession of the Boullet House that May afternoon. When she returned there late in the day, she says, she threw the French doors open wide in what had been old Jeremy Wentworth's room (the Captain's originally). The stained coverlet had been folded back toward the foot of the bed with some care, the officers, one on each side of the bed probably, lapping the cloth down between them till the last fold cleared the horny protuberances of the old man's toes, then lifting him whole, like a sack, onto the waiting stretcher, wheeling him out—bump-bump over the threshold—leaving the form of his body to be traced in the hollows of the mattress and the assorted cushions and rags on which he had lain propped. Scraps of paper scudded out from under the bed, nudged by invading breezes across the room and into the corner.

vi

He was working on a blueprint, a sun visor on his forehead below the line of close-trimmed sandy curls. "A real specialist," in Margaret's words, "someone you definitely should talk to before you plunge in and get yourself into a possible mess."

I got hold of this much: how a connection with Greeley Connor, architectural consultant to the Preservation Board, might be well nigh indispensable—he, the luminary of historic rehabilitation in Old Tarragona, me, an unknown quantity, giving out signals of intending to do my restoration on an improbable shoestring. "We were lucky to lure him down from Boston," said Margaret.

He laid aside his work as I came in, not like someone about to take a break but as if acknowledging, reluctantly, opportunity on the horizon. As a producer of mannerisms, Greeley makes a fine study; they fascinated me from the first. This one for example: rubbing shoulders and elbows with fingertips as he stands arms crossed in front of him, giving the impression of an aimless ascetic autoerotism gingerly at pains to brush away contact with others—apt to cling like cat hairs.

I came to my purpose without delay. "You know everybody in the trade," I said, "who in particular would you recommend?"

The fingers slowed over the freckled arms. Thought seemed to give them pause, with speech their activity quickened. "First off...second...third...," a man trained to itemize and prioritize. Names of contractors, good, middling, to be avoided at all cost "in a really serious restoration," passed at a wistful amble before the seat of his judgment, their coming and going slowed by the faintly elongated vowels striving for a convincing affinity to a generic Southern drawl.

I listened and nodded, and silently compared notes. After my purchase offer had gone through in March, I'd spent what was left of my spring break looking into the availability of workmen with experience in restoring old houses and had recorded every name in his inventory and more. An area under historic restoration, closed off and in on itself, I reasoned, is not unlike a village in an English detective novel: you have the greengrocer, the postmistress, the rector, the doctor, Major Somebody, Sir So-and-So, old Miss X, and their assorted spouses, offspring, nephews, aged parents, servants, weekend guests down from the city. They are on more or less friendly terms with each other; some don't speak except in direst circumstances (or when the plot needs advancing), and then ever so coolly. More to the point: everyone knows everyone else, so that if you strike up an acquaintance with any one of them, pretty soon you've got the whole village—from each other's perspective of course—none of which really tells you who's reliable and who isn't, not until it's too late generally, the murder committed, the roof leaking, your money and your time dwindling, but it does give you a pretty clear idea of what you may be up against if you should decide to take up residence.

Beside some of the names I had jotted question marks denoting reservations, among them "Thomas Evans & Son." Evans had been obliging and reassuring to the point where even so much as mentioning money seemed like a breach of trust.

"Tom's the salt of the earth," Greeley was saying, "well worth the extra cost, and a fine technician. Not many like him left nowadays." Had "a real commitment" to plumbing historic structures.

I find I don't hit it off well with people who have commitments to this and that, but said only that my main worry was locating a roofer who could install cedar shingles in accordance with what I understood were the requirements of the Preservation Board. On that one, I figured, I had better toe the line.

He settled into the adjustable chair behind his desk, pipe resting in an old Spanish ashtray, the façade of relaxation. "One or two of my colleagues on the Board would disagree, I'm sure, but I can tell you some to stay away from," he finally offered with a little smile like a prolonged twitch of the lips. "Bill Simmons is the only man down here I allow up on my roofs."

"Simmons," I said running down my list, "he's tied up all summer."

He could give me a few names to stay away from, the little smile repeated again—and again, as if under some arcane obligation to linger.

"The roof's going to be the tough one, I guess...." He really couldn't help me there, but if I was planning to do any demolition—I nodded, yes, there was that ugly addition at the back, for starters.

"You'll need a permit." He thumbed through his little blue diary and read off a phone number, practically whispered it lest the wrong people overhear him, a number I'd tried earlier that afternoon on my way to meet Margaret Avery. "Johnson Ware does all my wrecking," he said, still a bit hush-hush, "but you do have to keep an eye on him, especially the finer points. His people don't always grasp what you're after." Old Johnson was dependable though—even Greeley's particular brand of racism had been transported intact. Old Johnson would give me a good price, he said.

I'll say right here that he did, but at considerable cost. Like Greeley himself, Ware knows what's what and who's who.

"You'll want to submit plans to the Board right away." Distinctly this time the twitch tensed into a smile, but so inscrutable it communicated only with itself. (I came to believe eventually that it foretold some undeserved kindness, something like Greeley's secret pledge of impending grace.) I would need a good set of blueprints, he said; nothing could go forward until I knew exactly what structures I meant to demolish, what walls would come down inside, what additions were to be made, what changes—especially to the outside, exterior colors and all that.

Item, item, item. All of it would have to be approved in advance. By the Board. Was I aware that the Board had a reputation for inflexibility, and properly so? Only the genuinely authentic could be authorized. Did I understand that? "See if Greeley will do your drawings," Margaret, a member of the Board herself, had advised on our way out to the Wentworths, à propos of—I hardly knew what. Now I understood: since the non-specialist couldn't be expected to know what was "genuinely authentic" she would be obliged to seek out guidance in the matter. This business of restoration, I could see, had its deeper, spiritual side, its own *genius loci* to be appeased. Greeley was the uncompromising one, Margaret said proudly.

I asked him straight out how much these blueprints were likely to cost me.

He laughed, two closely spaced expulsions of breath with a pretense to joviality. "Well"—here the bowl of the pipe made a slow turn in its antique ashtray—"you probably don't realize how many charlatans and just plain gold-diggers a place like this attracts, all the birds around here out to commercialize it." And another turn, back again, as if he were examining the pipe for the first time, considering purchase. "Then there are the city inspectors. The Board works closely with them. You won't get by with anything that's not up to city code—can cost you more time and money than you ever imagined if you go wrong there." Again I remembered. Margaret Avery had said Greeley could handle the city for me too.

He was making an offering of himself, says Harding, no doubt about it, and I had the picture. I became quite an expert, by the end, in all of its emblematic detail.

"If you can stop by the house tomorrow, I'll show you exactly what I plan to do to it. Will that get the formalities started?"

"The Plans, yes," he said as if he'd been assumed into a higher sphere where words are pure ceremony betokening finalities—that it was time for me to go now, that my restoration was in his uncompromising hands, and that was that.

I was already at the door as he edged past me to oversee my exit. "The Boullet House...never have researched that one really except, of course, for that magnificent forged iron fence.

Lucky for you that the Trust had it in its care all those years."

"Spanish, I suppose?" The question concealed my realization that the Trust (alias Committee) evidently considered its commitment to preservation fulfilled in maintaining the fence without regard to what lay within its boundaries.

The little twitchy smile again: "Catalonian, seventeenth century. Not original in this location of course, shipped in and put up during Reconstruction." It was one of the very few artifacts of such age on the Coast, where not much survived hurricanes, tidal waves, fires, wars.

"All the catastrophes that destroy things down here?"

"Not everybody's cup of tea," he said, meaning, I concluded, the fence.

Traffic was thinning out on the Avenue as I walked out his front door and on past the Hernando. Close up, Captain Boullet's cash cow stands exposed for what it is: an entrepreneurial monument in reduced circumstances. Not exactly down and out—not the exterior anyway—but definitely straitened.

vii

Was I surprised to find him down there in Tarragona, comfortably situated, ensuring that right judgment and expertise might operate locally? "Greeley shows us just how important research can be in getting down to the nitty-gritty of history," Margaret had explained in a matter-of-fact tribute to her colleague, "the authentic details, you know."

Every Southern town of any size has for some time boasted a Greeley Connor or two, whole little expatriate cadres of them in some areas. He is one of the facts of demographic mobility, shifting job markets, slow regional blurring and assimilation. Greeley Connors wherever you go, establishing themselves as simulacra of gentlemen to authenticate their own reception into local society, barely disguising their contempt for what were so lately—and so long—backward provinces. There also to enjoy having their condescension mistaken for the authority of superior training in Northern academic citadels, by people for whom the open exhibition of condescension could be the mark only of an ill-bred boor. And that, of course, they could never suspect him of being, so his status is secure there.

God forbid if you should fail to enlist his cooperation, wherever you meet him; or succeeding, that you should dispute his fee and the price of his services all told. Your mode of appeasement must always be the same: things must be well done to get by him, but not too well, not outstandingly, not (in the etymological sense) egregiously well. I knew just what measure of excellence he would endure, down to every jot and tittle.

Oh yes, Greeley Connor is ever present, and so I am always on the lookout for him, North or South.

psycheme

I suppose we all feel there is some self or some part of ourselves that truly individuates us, some nebulous singularity of potentialities perhaps, to which accession does not come easily, if at all. There: Harding is for me an accession—in all senses of the word including, certainly, that of eruption. She restores something to me, something mine by virtue of a daily, onerous and humbling, brute and laughable experience.

My fierce tenderness toward her, my protectiveness, my delight—these may be explained in narcissistic terms. But the mode of narcissism that transcends itself in the sheer distance from which it details and, thus, subverts the activity of self-reflection, works always as an accession. For, the "I" Harding opens to me is the "we" of my Eastern European origins (every "I" she claims, begins its fictive existence in the pronominal we-form of myth), the original "we" I was when I took on my linguistic mask as an American. At nine years old I passed, in my first six months in this land, from a virtually non-English speaking status to that of winner of the essay prize in my elementary school. Winner: a message so powerful that the English language flowed in and out of me washing up ever more rewards from scholarships through the college of my choice to fellowships through the graduate Ivy League and Oxbridge—the strong, reassuring current of Anglo-American assimilation.

Linguistic precocity in my case was catalyzed by necessity.

("Go," my mother said in Hungarian three months after our arrival here, three bitter winter months in an unheated Bronx slum, "your brothers have no time. Find us another place to live.") I did, in Westchester, that affluent suburban band shielding New England from those "huddled masses" passing into and through the City. Do this, do that, my mother said. "How will I know where to go, what to say, who to see?" I asked. "Don't bother me with that. Go." And go I did. By the time I got to high school, crucible of assimilation, I had long lost even the slightest trace of an alien accent. Today, my standard Northeastern authorizes for me the luxury of occasional fatuities that, uttered by Harding in her deep Southern speech, would foreclose all escape from her provincial origins.

If language conceals my origins, it does so, I think, by proclaiming them at an ever farther reach. Western Europe, after all, carries the remains of more easterly beginnings; and Harding brings me, in her person, the Anglo-American version of Europe today—Harding with her French and English genealogy, and her Celtic face. I recently found myself reading some Englishman's attempt to distinguish America from Europe, this most ludicrous pastime of the European ego making itself feel good through opposition to a disavowed part of itself. We immigrants know, no matter how many generations away we are or how many turns and tributaries branch off, that the cultural current overdetermining our life's meaning here is still European. We immigrants know that the Americanization of Europe is not more nor less than a European necessity of self-expression. We know that the Europes mark off psychical places, and that the Americas are psychical extensions of the Europes as much as Portugal or Poland. We know that, as Europeans, we are not to admit as much and, as Americans, we are to relinquish our title to, if not to deny, our psychic birthplace and be born again under the red, white, and blue. Thus, it is under the conviction that I am more likely to spot myself, unsuspecting, emerging more intimately in what she weaves and designs than in any of the usual modes of self-revelation, that I throw the dice in a wager on Harding's narrative.

viii

Next morning I counted, behind stacked cartons of trash, four-teen green plastic bags all bundled in a row on the sidewalk in front of the Boullet fence. The inside was swept bare, the couch gone, along with the old man's bedstead, the funky mattress, the defunct TV. But the stench lingered.

Around the house at the back all remained as before. There were stumps of wood, old tires, assorted containers and utensils, rusted flanks of metal past recognition, all twined together in the delicate white and pink convolutions of bindweed. All prisoners now in a harmony of obsolescence. An oversized stove with a double oven witnessing to an era when compactness was not the prime criterion for an efficient use of space blocked what I dis-covered to be a gate into the alley. To the casual eye it was just another four-foot section of fence, its black spears reaching about eight feet, identical in form and height to the palings on either side, hinged to open and close without announcing its function. (A perfectly simple piece of camouflage, and not the last instance I was to encounter of the Boullet penchant for structural oddities.) Next to the stove, doing its part to defend against any ingress at this spot, stood a washing machine of the wringer type. A long claw-footed tub was jammed right up to the vine-entangled blocks it rested on, with three or four toilets sitting around in half-moon formation, hoppers verdant to the seats, porcelain bowls finely dusted to a dissimulating opaque grey. Dog droppings marked a path to the refuge of an old tin shed against the back wall, souring into the grainy soil.

It was a compromise, clearly their way of calling it quits with me—also my agent, their new landlord, and quite possibly the officers who'd had the trouble of looking after the patriarchal corpse, the polite and well-dressed funeral director, and the entire civic apparatus seeing Jeremy Wentworth decently and duly to his grave. For this, they'd done their "share" on the inside, with a far shrewder sense of equilibrium in such affairs than I'll ever possess. In ridding me of themselves, the Wentworths were rid of me; from either perspective, their remote respectability on the other side of town was now assured. They could begin again, and I—well, I could begin, doing whatever it was I'd come down there to do.

And, looking southward from the back gallery that Friday morning in May, with the jerry-built addition overhanging her, did not glints of color play even now through the summer lushness of her neighbor's garden like light scattered in the twirl and twist of each dark green leaf? It was the Bay lapping the southern edge of Hernando Plaza, sun-dazzled aquamarine waters glittering landward from the rim of DeLuna Island to Tarragona's deep, gentle harbor. And did not the old wall of hand-fashioned bricks—that sagged over cracks and crumbling joints and bulged over deformities of repair—rise to a sheltering ten feet or more, the solid rear boundary to her remnant of the Sovereign's grant? Wisteria clusters from the other side spilled picturesquely down one end and over a wizened fig tree where the pales of the Catalonian fence abutted the wall. In the clear morning light, the yard had that strangely stilled, distanced quality that characterizes scenes of places abandoned by humankind. I turned my back on it, she says, and went on in.

With the peculiar sense of trust that motor activity releases, she commenced now in earnest the list of things to be done to her new property, paper and pencil in hand, task after task presenting itself to her in formulae like incantation. Restore an old house, says Harding, and you're caught up in an exorcism—purging taints of the past, releasing uncorrupted spirit. That's what they mean by "authenticity," this purification by battering, eviscerating, flaying, then reconstructing and, finally, adorning, toiling over the minutiae, the catalogue of finish work. Well done, a restoration transforms not only textures and colors (and thus the quality of light and space in each room) but the very sound and smell of a house, the creak the floorboards make underfoot, the odor imparted to a hand by a doorknob or a light switch. No mere bedecking of the exorcised body, this, but a graft of new muscle, skin, nerve, tincture, to the osseous frame by which the whole stands articulated. Sometimes even pieces of bone must be excised, new bits wedged or hinged into place so that the load is borne more equably, more as one imagines it in its youth. In sum: all that has blocked or pulled the house away from realization of itself—its best—must be expelled, expunged, so as to free it at last to unite the strength of youth with the beauty and stability of age. All, of course, according to plan and with the guidance of people in the know—so says Harding, our restorationist.

She slipped on a pair of work gloves and surveyed the bare, wide-planked floors from the stairway going up, paused again at the library awesome in its ruin, walked from room to room along the upstairs hall, and down again. Was she smiling to herself as she went, that smile whose appropriateness is never quite grounded (I have seen her so, becoming engrossed in a problem with an expression curiously detached from the act itself, like the trace of an impetus to love), as she passed under the ghoulish light of windows still draped in their plastic tatters and rags?

I took the greatest satisfaction, she says, in ripping down every single one and piling it all on the trash out front. The strong revealing light of early Gulf Coast summer, reminiscent of Aegean light in its penetration, streamed through the house bearing something like pride of ownership from room to room. I propped open all the windows with lumber scraps from the site across the street and silently received the sense of heritage in the faint bite of the salty Gulf breeze. For better or for worse, it came to me.

II

The Reading Habit

psycheme

Once I offered a kind of closure to Harding's story by projecting
what went on that last morning in August when she stepped out
the alley gate into the old Quarter on her way to sell her restored
historic property. Saws would have been heard to rattle around
the Plaza, I reasoned, hammers to crack: other restorations-in-
progress. On the porches and balconies of the old Gulf Coast
homes turned offices, in their sidelong shade, amid the umbral
stir of foliage along Valencia Street at her back and the square
before her, cool morning begins its retreat before the sun. And
she, I knew, would be making herself walk more slowly than is
natural to her, because a lady (however obsolete such personages may be) does not arrive precisely on the dot for an appointment and, what is more, does not look as if she has been out
striding through steamy alleys on a late August morning. Taking
her time, making one last survey of things around her, hand lingering on the gate latch, she—

And on I gamboled with my vision (in a transport, perhaps,
of authorship) mistaking her silence and the thoughtfully arched
eyebrow for confirmation of imaginative insight on my part,
down to credible detail.

"But no," she said, "in those five or six minutes before I
signed on the dotted line and collected my check, I was passing,
for all practical purposes, through another time, another place.
What with the veil of equivocation over the house gone, lifted by
the Historic Preservation Board's new bronze plaque attached
to the entry gate, eye-level for those taking the walking tour—

Claude Francis Boullet House, 1857
Restored: 1977

—work done and so proved, I was already free of it when I
stepped into the brick alley that morning. No backward glances

55

at the house or, for that matter, at the Hernando Inn down the way. As I set out at snail's pace for the lawyer's office hardly more than a block around the corner—it was on Hernando Plaza in a two-story Victorian facing the Bay—I was not casting one last look around me, either of relief or longing, at 'the prison yard,' as you once put it, 'of a term of confinement."

"No, of course not," I said, put in my place, "that kind of retrospection is not your style. Your last walk in Old Tarragona is just not part of the main story because your mind was already on—"

"Strictly speaking," she interrupted, "I was not stepping into Old Tarragona at all. Moving around in the Historic Quarter had become such a geographic habit for me by then, you see, that the whole setting seemed to recede and take on the shape of a receptacle for my own personal past come out of oblivion to orient me passingly in the world where I'd made my first home. That's where I was, there with husband and children."

"Doing what?"

"Ambling through the old arcade to the vegetable and fruit stands. We're going to make market. I pick the ready ones by smell past prefigurations of spoilage, the girls pressing close, scanning all I pile in the pannier they hold between them, their critical vision searching out imperfections—there now, she runs ahead of me, six-year old Helen, golden blond, bearing little resemblance either to myself or her father beside her, certainly not Vanessa, four years old, black-haired, arms and legs wrapped tight around him, riding on his back. Memory intrudes flashes of my teen-aged daughters spending the summer with him, Helen still golden but with straight coppery hair, Vanessa's black curls cropped French style, both grown almost as tall as I.

"A blink—a turn at the corner of a shuttered house—scatters them into this past forming around me and I walk in its weathering, senses stroked and soothed by mellow discoloration, the gentling of decay, here in this moment before disintegration vents its finality: the St. Charles streetcar stops at Tulane and clangs off behind us as we cross over to Audubon Park.

"He walks with us a while along the lagoon talking about who owned the Park before it was one and how sugar was first granulated here when it was the Étienne de Boré Plantation, the lagoon forking off into winding little mysteries through islets of dense growth matted with Old-man's-beard. Ducks waddle out. Quickly, provocatively, Vanessa's hand darts into her paper sack and back out, fist spilling over with bread bits, quacks rising to the polluting pitch of radios. With perfect attunement to the thrill of living safely endangered Helen stiffens until Vanessa's fist opens to fling its hoard at the ducks converged on them, their cue to shriek in unison, and convulsed with the laughter of children practicing perils, to dash back into the circle of our protection. He leaves...we take a turn through the zoo, then over to Monkey Hill where the children run up and down while I watch tucked into the curve of a live oak branch as comfortably as if it were a brace especially fitted for me.... Gaiety, solemnity, hopefulness, cleanliness, ornament, anticipation of easy success, the very ordinariness of celebration with its accedence to the unbelievable: this, the Archbishop blessing the shrimp fleet. Only once-born believers, I note, play this one unencumbered.... I poke my paddle at the green face of the bayou, slice through the slime beneath. No solid ground—we push on to the rise of an Indian burial mound ahead. This is who I am, this place, made so by desire alone, the swamp-law of necessity, through the taupe veil of Spanish moss shimmying from cypress arms twisted over violet water hyacinths following the flight of a Louisiana heron, the first I have seen here, the pinkish streak of its neck snaked upward as it lights poised, expectant, and moves into the choreographed delicacy of its feeding A white egret eyes us and steps cautiously closer, in my nose a tingling spring-anticipation of swamp-body swarming in fetid warmth and in my mouth the taste of Delta orange wine. He reaches over their heads and takes the bottle from my hand...in the ruins of an old fort, looking up at the lighthouse on Grande Terre and over to the Baratarian headquarters at Grande Isle, calling to mind the Delta labyrinth of lakes, swamps, bayous, smuggling a cargo through it, neatly, efficiently...betrayed by a lifelong friend, made captive...rescued by Cuban refugees who enlist me in their struggle for independence against the Spanish.... We bring down sail, decide to stay at West End for lunch, platters of boiled crab and shrimp, gazing out over Lake Ponchartrain, and, with the smug certainty attached to experiences repeated from childhood, record once again this crowd-sound, easy gregariousness in the waterfront restaurants. Saturday: we continue his project for the family. He pokes a dollar toll out the window and we swing into the breeze of the Causeway intoning after him: Bernard-Xavier-Phillipe-de-Marigny-de-Mandeville...even from the sea wall we catch the faint whiff of St. Tammany's pines.... he swings on to Huey's bridge...at least he did not line his own pockets, he says, the old dictator did share the wealth...in the smooth-riding plenty of the American family castle I grieve, ensconced like a queen seeing her realm ravaged before the fallen magnificence of Magnolia, its structural integrity now in question, machine wreckage, old Fords, Studebakers, Frigidaires ringing its ruin in the technological amulet of their evil. But in the pirogue through the bayous of Westwego to the marsh-lake of lotus lily parasols, we float silently, yearning to see without it making any difference. Even the nutria continue their feeding. A great turtle the size of a small cart thrashes away with alarming speed—immediately an alligator, slithering indifferent motion, sinks into the mud, and we're cast out to go our way once more. Tony's Sunday session, right at the end of it, she shows up and sings that slow blues about a Delta woman that always makes me feel as if she is singing for me. Her body affirms an aged sensuality. Lizzie must be only a year or so from seventy now. He puts his mouth almost to my ear, we'll have an early dinner at Tujague's and catch a performance at Preservation Hall, all the old original Dixieland musicians to be there, not many left. I remember what Sally said last week when she was cleaning our house: her husband would be playing there tonight, and two or three years back some men from London cut a record of his group, she said, to sell in England, and they never got a penny of it.... Saturday nights in Bucktown eating oysters gathered by Tuckos. And the broiled busters...this land comes and goes in a lifetime. The cane fields of a century ago leave no mark on this my wetland, but the vegetables and fruits in our car smell of soaked-in swamp-sweetness. And Pilottown's whiteness. Who can say what it is that makes these shells the nowhere color of the Delta? Or the planes and angles of equipment engineered for oil production the no-place structures of the River's end? On the jetty at the end of the flow: the Deep Delta mouth dribbles its passes, splits itself for emptying out, the dying away into its Gulf grave. Force so desolated plays out in undistinguished passage. Yet even here where the separation between river and gulf narrows to this strip I stand on, the final twisted coursing of its energy clutches at the land. I turn away and look to the Gulf. A wind is blowing, hurricane season. They steady the boat, waiting for me. Here, before me, my country, in this joy of the body walking through a land ever shaping and reshaped by the force of the waters washing it. Wherever a delta crops, a river flows. And at this moment, even as I pass through, the reparation goes on, the blind mindless authoritarian energy that houses us. He pulls into the drive by our camelback shotgun on Bordeaux St. We get out on the brick walk and I watch the girls trail him inside. The door closes slowly, gently, and comes to rest, its double panels gone softly silver."

Even as her arm lifts to push it open she glances at her watch—8:30, it says—and goes no farther. She's immediately back in Old Tarragona at the water's edge and before her the tremor and shimmer of DeLuna Bay. Now for her appointment, and still no need to rush. That such time should be hers again puts yesterday far off, but not the fresh of morning, the sweetness in stepping off a distance that both shelters and frees.

i

Imagine this: Harding is stepping off the long front room on the second floor, the once and (she supposes) future library. It is the day after taking possession, Friday, May 20th. Front and back doors stand wide open downstairs, and she is waiting, in a skirt and blouse, for Greeley Connor, alert to any sign—footsteps, a presenting cough—that the dispenser of those indispensable "Plans" for restoring the Boullet House has come, as arranged, to insure that her enterprise will be launched on an authenticated course. Not an hour ago, Johnson Ware has set a price as reasonable as his reputation. What is more, he has promised to start the demolition the moment she has her permit in hand—a bureaucratic rigamarole, she understands, whose speedy consummation will necessitate the patronage of Greeley Connor, architect and historic regulator. But that's the kind of thing, she says, you have to put up with when you buy into history.

She reaches the opposite wall, pauses to open an ear out, makes the length of the room fifty feet and, turning to the front wall with its row of dormers, measures their deeply recessed sills by eye. Set in the wall at about shoulder level, they are a good five feet wide and at least as deep, their leaded casements sealed tight with old paint and rust. The reek here is intense. It is as if all the foulness of the house, fleeing before the scourge of open doors and windows downstairs, has taken refuge in ascension.

She manages to disregard it, concentrating on her business, delights in the room's handsome proportions, envisions tall bookcases along the back wall and sides. In the center, her medieval tavern table, acquired back in the 50's before such objects became fashionably expensive, catches a sheen from the faint light-dappled nooks above it. Chairs for conversation in twos and threes, and single ones for reading beside lamps on tables, some round and draped to the floor among the more solid English ones passed down by her mother, are set about in arrangements both pleasing and functional over old oriental rugs like self-contained, precisely ornate fields in faded recession.

Her things fall into place quite naturally, are quite at home in this room said to be Captain Boullet's library. Yet what little she knows of him does not suggest he was a literary man; his notorious daughter and namesake would seem to have a better, if unacknowledged, claim here in this space that accommodates the habits of her own life with such ease—as if they had originated here. The conviction is hard to dispel that it is the site of a deliberately conceived style of living: a design for the protection of freedom. (And what, asks Harding, is more protected, freer, than a woman fated, like Frances Boullet, to become a fiction?) In her seeing, a library ladder invites access to the window seats cozy with fat down cushions in a French cotton print. They furnish a private mezzanine for leisure, walled on two sides. They seem made for scanning life in the street below through slats of shutters that screen off a hiding place—shelter in the primitive sense that belongs to all living things, yet light, ample, beautiful.

And now consider this: it is late afternoon on Wednesday, almost the end of her third week in Tarragona. Still early June, but one of the hottest on record there. The demolition barely begun, Mr. Ware has come and gone; only just come the day before, gone now who knows where to more compelling business. No word about when he'll be back—when the work will continue, or even if it will. The grounds of the Boullet House and its lower story are strewn with what looks like the aftermath of a disaster that no one has had time or wit to attend to, jags and hunks of plaster everywhere tangled with splintering laths in mounds like rawly disgorged hills. Ruptured walls stand dangerously in place marking off zones of chaos that were rooms only yesterday, however disfigured.

The big one upstairs stinks more than ever of rats' nests and insects rotting behind the tall baseboards and in the cracks of the wide-planked floor, turning themselves into food for others of their kind, securing their arthropodal hold on the world's desolation. An age-old economy thrives on the fertility sustained by forgetting.

Here, now, is Harding: tools in hand. Hammer, prybar, chisel. She is dressed in an old pair of shorts and workshirt caked with plasterdust, seemingly disinterred from a crack in one of the walls, a survivor, perhaps, or a searcher after signs of others. The thick black coil of her hair is done up in a bun at the nape of her neck, out of the way.

She hoists herself up to the easternmost of the four dormer windows, in full shadow now, making do with the broken-backed chair that has been sitting, who knows how long, beside the hearth at one end of the library where it suggests nothing so much as a dubious gathering in some otherwise unrecorded and best-forgotten past. The palms of her hands are tender with splinters; when one of them thuds down on the massive lever of the casement, and down once more, harder, pain throbs through her wrist and up her forearm. The lever might be forged in its locked position for all the difference her blows make. She sighs. Weariness, of course—her workday is now in its tenth hour—but something more as the sigh lengthens: a hiss of unresigned acknowledgement that her course is plain, that chisel and hammer must go mincingly to work, scrape and chip away at the hardened paint until the sash has been worked loose.

Down in the street the last of the workmen drive off to their suburban homes more raucously and faster than necessary. She has observed that they seem to enjoy these little ritualistic exhibitions of what they suppose to be their freedom. The lanes and alleyways of the old Quarter are thick with their freedom's exhaust pumped into the heat and bustle of the day's end.

My summer, she says, my little bit of time, was dwindling fast.

What has happened? How does she account for these altered circumstances, this patent dimming of her prospects—so quickly—her fortunes, perhaps her destiny? These are not Harding's words, but the picture, she says, is accurate as far as it goes.

ii

There is, she explains, from one point of view precious little to tell about those early weeks of the restoration. The first one passed. And the second. Uneventfully, if an event is something that marches out and forward to an appointed end. But things were definitely happening, oh yes, a mile a minute, with me and the house as a kind of arena where anything and everything was contested, if nearly always without issue, even, it sometimes seemed to me, without the decency of rules and regulations. Though crawling with them—as full of creators of criteria as the Nietzschean future in post-modern mold—the place was lawless to the core.

Only muscle mattered, winning, losing. My purse was filling up with estimates for the biggest jobs. Exorbitant, most of them, non-committal, or both. The reputable contractors were always tied up or on vacation, and the rest didn't like fooling with old houses, or they did but strictly on their own terms ("Leave it to me"). Or they didn't show up when they said they would, or they couldn't say just when ("Soon's I can get to it").

Or I found myself having to send them away when they did come, reeking of alcohol—or apathy, or suspicion of one kind or another about working for an outsider, a woman to boot, who insisted, always just when a deal seemed in the offing, on things like writing time limits into the contract. "My rock bottom price?" they gasped, eyes like slits, incredulous to the point of seeming personally offended as well as professionally outdone. Since I appeared to lack all appreciation of first principles, one and all sooner or later took a didactic tone with me. "You get what you pay for," they liked to say, always as though claiming paternity to a uniquely incontrovertible law of Real Life in the Real World—the Machiavellian strain clipped from a branch in the primeval Garden.

They had me pegged: lady of leisure with more means than staying power, dilettantish to the core. Looking for a little excitement to relieve the boredoms of privilege. Pinching pennies for the novelty of it, or to prove a point maybe, like buying and wearing used but fashionable rags. Out to exploit and be deservedly hoodwinked by the workers of the world, just setting myself up to be outwaited, outwitted, outchatted, outdone, and above all, outbargained. Outexploited.

But as they came to suspect that I and my resources might not be all they seemed (or, judging by costume, that we might be precisely what we seemed), I receded almost overnight into a nobody to be dismissed or put off, which amounts to the same thing, certainly by the more respectable and the more established among them. "What you need is a good general contractor," became a favored refrain at parting, "somebody who'll see this thing through for you from start to finish."

Greeley Connor not surprisingly offered himself in this capacity, as I inferred one morning from a cryptic ripple of glances, hedges, and smiles followed by the observation that local banks were willing to lend large sums for restorations now. Soaring interest rates, yes, but worth it considering the expected appreciation of historic property. I figured his cut as general contractor would have indebted me well into retirement.

And when I wasn't fooling with regulators of one kind or another, not to mention just plain nosy people, all appointing themselves creators of criteria as thoughtlessly as any pagan, I was doing all the hard labor myself, every minute I could spare from morning till nightfall and later. Getting everything ready for Ware was how I framed it because that, certainly, was what it was; looking out for some of those "finer points" he couldn't be trusted with.

Ware, whose price was reasonable, you understand. The start of my second week, as I was tacking up a hard-won permit, he'd promised. "Oh yes'm, fust day I can git to it."

"Tomorrow?"

"Yes ma'am, I b'lieve I can." He'd even stashed the top half of an extension ladder in the kitchen that afternoon along with a battered wheelbarrow, as pledges, or so I wrongly supposed, of his intention to start the very next morning, Friday.

No Ware. And not Monday either, nor all through that second week. Mr. Ware, I kept telling myself had his faults ("You get what you pay for") but he always kept his word. Always. Not to worry.

Like those expert predictions that—eventually—interest rates will rise, or fall, or that inflation will moderate, or that it will heat up again, Mr. Ware's "word" was always reliable in the long run, but you were damned if you set any store by it for tomorrow or next week, or any date you could pin down on a calendar. Each morning, I would park my own car on the street and open up the carriage gates for his truck, raise all the windows in anticipation, put off errands till later so I'd be sure not to miss his arrival. So that he'd know me for a person of serious intent, on a tight schedule. What outmoded folly to imagine such readiness could be construed nowadays as anything but a sign of weakness and dependency, a streak of the loser.

The question isn't readiness anyway, but how adept you are at riding the tide of things you aren't ready for. By midday, the men at work on the houses all along Valencia Street would take refuge on the shady side, not, of course, as if they were doing anything of the kind, merely as if they'd timed things to fall out more or less this way. Not foresight so much as going with the good sense that flows from experience.

And so I kept after him. And he promised. Daily he promised, and I kept on waiting for him while I myself started the demolition—it was either that or nothing would get done at all, and there was no end of things to be done and an all too certain end of my time for doing it.

iii

"Not often you find it all still there," Greeley said, as though he meant to chastize me for my blind good luck, "all intact." The idea of course was to get it all down that way, all those moldings, mantles, window and door frames, room by room, all through the house, up and down, every inch caked with the paints and varnishes of over a century, so gobbed up with them in fact that you couldn't make out the detail anymore. You wouldn't dream of just painting over it; you have it sent out to be dipped, and once the walls are back up you remount it all. That's how you efficiently revive what's called "the texture." Ware's ladder, worthless as a pledge, revealed its rickety *raison d'être* in the delicate perils of this salvage operation.

Days and days of it—now *there's* a story. More than you ever wanted to know about working on an old house. How slow it is, how piecemeal; the prying, the wrenching, all the while keeping yourself balanced eight feet or so off the ground if necessary. How you weight stress against stress so that the force of square nails creaking out after generations won't split the dry wood—release pressure here, give it a pull there—hammer and crowbar passing from hand to hand. How after a while you go after the nails themselves, easing up each one a little at a time, evenly, all along the length of your original detail; that way the heads don't snap and leave the shafts embedded. There's the dust. The clouds and little avalanches of it as wood pulls away from plaster, settling grittily in your nostrils and eyes. The dank underneath molder of old things pried apart. How you finally scratch a number on the back of each piece you've managed to salvage whole—Detail Intact—cut your mark deep enough so the stripper's chemical bath won't erase it and make a shambles of remounting when the time comes, in some hypothetical future you no longer trust.

For, you tell yourself at night, before you sink into a dead sleep: there has to be an end to it, all this wangling and equilibrating, this maneuvering of armfuls awkwardly sideways through passages, doors; this bumbling and clattering down stairs and out back over planks wobbling on an incline where the steps have fallen off; this hauling, dragging your load out to the corrugated tin shed that will come down after details intact have been claimed by the Stripjoint (who remind you daily that your contract, their best price for your fussy job, has a time limit), making your way through vines and filth, offal, around heaps of junk waiting like all else for Mr. Ware who has promised…and now, back: how you start all over again at the next station of your punitive round, up the ladder, now down, to the next window, the next room, in the blazing sun, the heat.…

And where, says Harding, reflecting the restless stirring in such a question, where's the story in all this sheer grind of work turning the hours like a wheel? In these minutiae of sweat and deconstruction?

Hard labor's all much the same, she answers her own question at last with eyebrows drawn into an ascending curve, the left one a bit higher than the right. It all has much the same consistency—and the arch lifts higher, marking her wordplay—like gruel. Punishing, she means, exhausting, when all thought, all reflection, even hunger and thirst are absorbed into the round of what must be done, even the will to go on, till the slave of such a project has no will, till it is simply too dark for her to see.

But what we have here is a white woman of the educated American middle class who chose her situation, didn't she? It is not, after all, as if economic and/or political circumstances forced her to this pass, is it? She might have stayed comfortably at home merely by consenting to remain there. What can it matter, then, that by an augmentation of force as immutable, as obstructionist, as the building trade in Tarragona, late spring was roiling into high summer? That the sun's intensity during those first few weeks kept swelling through the ruined house and cast her out, again and again, on the bright hot expanse of the yard where everything lay waiting?

"Again and again" does not refer here to sameness but to the smallness of the differences that mark the increments of toil, and what this calls for, it occurs to me, is a calculus of description for the infinitesimal differences we live in.

iv

On the other side of the fence, my neighbor Doc Shibbles kept up his twice-daily routine of raking, sweeping, watering, as if to demonstrate an unwavering concern with the cleanliness of his grounds. He'd be at it early, just as soon as I arrived, and then again in the quiet spell about twilight. If I was out working in my chaos of a yard, he'd keep his back to me, whether filling his can at the spigot or down on his knees beside the steps of the cottage to tug at young sweetgum shoots invading his plot. And if he should happen to raise his head and catch my gaze, he'd lurch to his feet as if struck in the small of the back and start fiddling with whatever was handy, the garden hose or the tines of his rake or a shutter hook suddenly observed to be loose. The dark-haired woman who lived with him would run out with a hand towel and walk him over to the spigot to wash his hands, while she, leaning her head to his as if listening, would look over at me—a long unguarded survey by one who cannot be seen of a thing that cannot look back.

psycheme

Am I seeing something that simply, as her ex-husband Paul would have it, "isn't to be found in Harding's company"? If her stories are neither particularly touching, nor particularly insightful or moving or didactic or gripping, or any of the other epithets by which we designate what we believe to be at work in what we love, where is the mirage?

"Would there were a mirage," Paul complained last night when they were all sitting around the table after dinner listening to me read from my work in progress. Helen is home from college, Vanessa preparing to go soon, and he arrived a few days ago for his annual visit. Harding has invited me to stay on as long as I like. "If the bourgeois existential condition ever escapes consciousness, Harding's 'craft'" (he says this with a languorous wink) "manages to drag it back to its authentic *ennui*. Just when you think she might be going gothic, all terror and sentiment, she'll throw in something about money or dusting the furniture. Verging on a genuine mystery? Same thing: 'I have a short attention span for potboilers,' she'll tell you and snatch the mystery right out from under you with premature disclosures or mimetic distractions, like what the chief suspect had for lunch or how he tweaks his mustache. As for irony—can't be bothered with dissimulation; just when you least want her to, she comes right out and tells you where she stands. No regard for indirection, that woman, except of course when indirection is the last thing you want. Just try letting her get confessional, and she's wearing more masks than you can buy in a novelty store on Halloween. Rhetorical bric-à-brac, that's what her so-called 'stories' are— she likes junkshops, you know. Always wants all effects all the time I expect, and that's impossible, a sure way to get none, and she knows it. Or should. But mainly she's just plain perverse. Her one predictable pattern of self-expression is psychical polymorphous perversity, has to do with her silly notions of freedom."

She never bats an eyelash (they are long and dark like her hair) when he launches into what she calls "ill-bred discourses delivered in a well-bred voice." And she can, when she chooses, return as good as she gets. "Hardly surprising, is he, Jael?" she may say, murmured in response to his assessment of her narrative gifts, "After all, we're bred to our manner."

Harding, who delights in good food with exactly the same passion she has for the best in all its cultural modes, was, during this particular after-dinner tirade, giving her undivided attention to a bowl of fruit on the table somewhat in the manner of Mrs. Ramsay, until, breaking her own spell, she reached for a small locally grown nectarine swollen gold. Finding the smooth line of cleavage, she cut into it with a bonehandled fruitknife, one of a dozen we once found in a junkshop together. Even from where I sat across the table from her, the aroma was mouthwatering, and I wondered in a pique of child-like envy why I hadn't selected that particular nectarine myself.

She chewed slowly, inhaled deeply, and said, "*Oui*, Paul, *ennui*, who knows eet better than I, *moi-même*." Took another juicy mouthful, chewed, swallowed, closed her eyes in ecstasy and murmured in the soft distinct syllables of tenderest passion, "*Ennui, ennui, ennui....*"

I have witnessed any number of these little vignettes of family life in after-marriage. By inviting him to spend a week annually with her and their two daughters in Athena, she has for some years since the restoration managed to avoid leaving them alone with him for any extended period. His drinking, as we have all observed, is getting worse. Not the best solution in an ideal world, but it has satisfied to some extent his desire to see "his girls" and theirs for him without placing them in the position of caretakers when he takes to his bottle, she reasons.

And take to it he does, nightly, although I have yet to see him really drunk—I suspect he drinks himself into unconsciousness after the rest of us are asleep. An unusually attractive man still, though harboring the marks of dereliction for those who know how to decipher them in fashionable dress. All in all, I suppose, the critical stance he has adopted may not be without some value for me. (Certainly if I ever had any remote fantasy that my text would reach much of a wider audience, Paul successfully scuttles the likelihood—even, at moments, the will.)

Is he right about her? Is it mere perversity?

In my student days, it was just her gift for staying with a form, her ardor in seeing it through, that inspired love and admiration. Perhaps she hopes, now, to civilize her intellectual powers by holding back. For, what is loved and admired shall be hated and despised in equal measure. I have seen her move with terror and aversion between the Scylla of humanized mother-goddess and the Charybdis of scapegoat, swept and pulled, it seems to me, by infinitesimal degrees toward Charybdis as she ages.

v

Those first weeks, waiting for Ware to begin, crumble and fall together in my recollection like the old plaster grit along the baseboards of the Boullet House crunching under his ladder as I moved from detail to detail.

Recorded, during that phase, in the *Tarragona Sun & Sentinel*: two holdups in less than a week at a nearby convenience store, yielding the paltry loot of $23.97; police spokesman claims to discern pattern. Of paltriness? Participants in Right-

to-Life Sit-in at an Illinois Family Planning Center proclaim success in averting fetal murder, it says, for upwards of an hour.
Unspecified Arabs buying up Atlantic coastal property like mad,
amid local rumors of inequities in the tax assessor's rolls, allegations of kickbacks and bribes in the Department of Construction and Public Works. Perennial news. Officials blame comput-
erization and exhort Mayor Cleland "Hank" Tuttle to address
bugs, which he says he is fully prepared to do.

It's not every day you find a busy city official prepared to
talk to so broad a constituency.

Even in the shade, by mid-afternoon, perspiration no
longer brought relief but seemed an immersion in the very element of heat. And still, as elsewhere the hot light levelled all difference, the shadows of my neighbor's garden deepened into
richer greens like flora of the tropics and promised cooling sea
breezes, gentle nights yet a while.

vi

Every evening without fail, soon after the last glare of the sun
slips into the softening of first twilight, the Greek man would
come padding briskly along Valencia Street with his dog. It
would be their second outing for the day (their third, in the
moonlit darkness just before bedtime and the late news).
Steadily the two of them padded along, man and aging terrier,
he immaculate in sports shirt and linen trousers, at his ease in
European slip-on sandals, his confident no-nonsense gait followed with canine mimesis by his leashed dependent. They'd
look neither left nor right, nor, for that matter, up.

Descended from Aegean stock of Tarpon Springs, a lawyer
not long retired from a modest local practice now much transformed by his Yale-educated son, this man and his wife and
their Norwich terrier have occupied the corner shotgun cottage,
the first of a row on the four-hundred block of Valencia, as long
as anyone there can remember. They are, in that sense, one of
the "old" residents in the Quarter. The Stavros home has long
("always" in the local lingo) been "fixed up." Not restored in the
authenticated way, it's just an up-dated little cottage from before

Greeley Connor's regime. Snug with care, it strikes an incongruous note of bourgeois tidiness there at the edge of that unregenerate wasteland beyond Cadiz Boulevard. On the margin itself,
it stands as a sort of gatehouse to "the fringes"—or, depending
on which direction you're looking from, to the resurgent historic
district bounded by the three-hundred block of Valencia where
the Boullet House abides inside its remarkable Spanish fence.

vii

One morning the waiting was over, the demolition crew already
there when I arrived at seven. I counted, variously, two to four
of them, coming and going, but no Mr. Ware. Nobody, therefore,
to run the show or take the blame.

I had the downstairs (and some of the upstairs by then)
stripped of woodwork, not that they paid any notice one way or
another or made the slightest acknowledgement. Not a word
about all the time lost, the broken promises; no words at all, for
that matter, as they set to, ramming down hunks of plaster in
the hall and in the room where old Wentworth had made his
dying claim.

That was in the first hour or so, while they still appeared
driven by a furious energy, daring each other to knock out this
or that entire wall in two or three thunderous blows, with jibes
and challenges reverberating through the empty rooms and
loud cheers at each crash. Old Wentworth, I felt, would have
looked on with a certain grim satisfaction. But soon they were
huddling here and there in silence or idling pensively over
cracks with their crowbars and sledgehammers as though probing the contours of enormous scabs to assess the extent and
degree of the rawness underneath. Somebody produced a radio
and the wrecking turned into a raucous dance, with a slam here
and a poke there, as the spirit moved them.

After that, they migrated restlessly from room to room,
tried some of everything, finished nothing. Only the oldest of Mr.
Ware's teenage workers actually managed, on his own more or
less, to gut most of that disgrace of a kitchen before they quit
shortly after lunch next day, as unpredictably and uncommu-

nicatively as they'd started the day before. Nothing to allay my worries at their abrupt exit, the whimsical mutilations, rampages of destruction—that morning's cataclysm of wrecking out back where a great, ragged, gaping hole that had been the upstairs addition marked their passage. And the waiting started all over again.

viii

If you should happen to stop at the Hernando Inn on the Plaza and nobody has yet gotten around to fixing the place up, you'll see the marble treads of the main staircase spanned with frayed cocoa-matting that slips and bulges as Miss Annie goes up and down in her flip-flops. Originally, I'd thought of taking up residence there until the house was minimally fit to be lived in. The old Inn had seen better days, sure, but its convenience was hard to beat, cheap lodging just down the alley and around the corner, right on the Plaza with its vista of the Bay and its coin phone.

But people in the know—and that seemed to include practically everyone I had anything to do with—warned me off the place. "The clientèle," they said in that finicky way with words that signals a euphemism drawing suspicion on itself, "the conditions," meaning, I supposed among other things, the Hurds who lived there and ran it—that is, Miss Annie did. There was the old woman on the front gallery starting out of her catatonic dazes with alarms of invasion, and there was the boy lounging on the back porch or being dragged somewhere or other, screaming. "99% pure idiot," said Bill Simmons, the only man Greeley Connor would allow on his roofs. There was, too, the crooked Dollman and...well, they said, much, much more. "The things that go on in there," mumbled with an intimacy of signification I could mistake only at my peril. Somehow even the casual tourist knew better than to inquire about rooms at the Hernando.

In the end, it was the boy's tantrums that decided the matter for me. I call them that, though the word hardly begins to describe those chilling, shattering, sudden, groundless irruptions. Who could sleep through a sound like that, up close? Not so much like a child's rebellion against authority, something the Dollman or Miss Annie was making him do against his will, as a spasm of elemental frustration on the rampage, the world-monster bound from time immemorial rattling its chains. Premonitions of Ragnarok, right there in the heart of Historic Tarragona—in Captain Boullet's old hotel, where his daughter Frances, I found out, had lived as a child.

ix

I was in no mood for distractions, hardly in a frame of mind to entertain the quirks and turns of life in Tarragona shaping to its little climaxes (but, for Tarragonans, those things which make a big difference), least of all for a visit from Sergeant Peaden of the Tarragona Police Department—but there he stood at about four p.m. in the open doorway with the dust shimmering around him, mirror glasses and all, beaming silently at me across the devastation.

I'd just finished shovelling paths through it, hopeless, because I could see how more and more of the drudgery was going to fall on my own shoulders, and what with breezes through open doors and windows to stir up the old plaster, the stench was as pungent as a skunk's fear. If something can be both old and fresh, both wasted and vivid, it was the olfactory atmosphere of the Boullet House that bright hot Juno afternoon, with me still in shock over the demolition breaking off only a couple of hours before.

He cleared his throat so elaborately the shades bumped right down to the tip of his shiny nose, then asked if he might "have" a few minutes of my time—the last thing, of course, that I'm willing to turn over to him or anybody else in that town. The occasion, I see, calls for disinterested civility; firmness; presence, especially because mine is filthy dirty from my torn canvas shoes right up to my battered denim hat and exudes my surroundings. At this moment, my advent here back in May, in street clothes suitable for a woman of my station, seems as much a figment of our joint imaginations as does the ghost that gives my house its equivocal name.

In the spirit of his own buried metaphor, then, I ask what I can "do" for him.

Even this thin formula of *noblesse oblige* has an improbable ring. Eyes go skidding up the wall, out the back door to the debris mounded alp-like around the gallery, roll in again over the rubble and, furtively, skirt my grimy hand clenching one of Mr. Ware's prybars left in the wreckage, all in that unfocussed kind of survey formed by long habits of looking at something other than what you profess to be looking at. Finally, he thinks to slide the glasses back over his eyes and clears his throat some more, but *sotto voce*.

One fingertip lingers on the bridge of his wire frames, blunt, tense. Even under cover of the glasses, he looks uncomfortable. "Thought you might be able to give us some information, unh...ma'am." The hesitation audible at the end, over his mode of address, a dead giveaway of how things really stand between us, weakens his stab at professionalism.

"What about?" I ask, not wishing to seem uncooperative with the law, however inconvenient its appearance on my demolition site. And he—to render things legit, *à la* old-time TV cops—snaps spiral notebook from hip pocket, flips it open and dithers showily from page to page at arm's length, every bit as though he's putting on an act he doesn't understand well enough to keep from betraying its artifice.

"According to my, unh, records, here, you took possession of this property on about, unh, let's see, unh...."

"It was the nineteenth of May, three weeks ago tomorrow." Longer than I might wish, but he'd be uninterested in that.

The glasses flash me a quick blind look. "About that old man you found in here that day...remember him?"

"Finding a corpse in your house," I volunteer, truly arrested by his attempt to get to his point without calling attention to it, "is not an experience that simply passes out of memory—no matter how busy you are." It's a lame afterthought, and of course he ignores it; his is not an ear for subtle hints.

"Well, that old man, unh, ma'am, unh...corpse, like you say—anything you can tell me about his, unh, circumstances, unh ma'am?"

I am starting to think this interview will founder on gaps of hesitation and turn prematurely sanguine about seeing it to a swift close. "Not a thing, I never met the man."

He looks as if he's about to nod but has thought better of it. The silvery lenses catch everything in a minute shiver—the half-wrecked walls, the newel post between us, me in the foreground all puffed up—and mirror it all back stolidly in place. The nod is so tentative, the disturbance so brief, it may have been nothing more than the reflex of an involuntary tic, but when a man can hold his head as still on his burly shoulders as Sergeant Peaden, no movement is too slight to register a difference. The slighter the origin the smaller the difference that disturbs, and the more disturbing the smallness of the difference. Whoever thought up the accessory of the glasses has given this mild-mannered bungler a sly turn in the sinister accents of an alien tongue.

"He was dead." Can Peaden have forgotten to put that on record? "It didn't take his last murmured words to get the picture."

"How's 'at?"

"Just that the conditions here were so unnecessarily—ugly."

My shrug releases a spurt of personal conviction. "Well," he says, "folks like that, unh ma'am...." and the hearty voice trails off in uncertain speculation about how People-Like-That live the way they do by a choice incomprehensible to People-Like-Us.

"Is there some problem?" Irritation has gotten the better of me, probably because his ineptitude tugs at me like an impulse to help him along. Do I have nothing to do but sate their curiosity, official and unofficial, put up with their gawks and opinions all day long? Their habits and quirks and prejudices? Politely, patiently, evenly answer the asinine questions of this one and that one who's "heard" of a strange woman down in the Quarter single-handedly taking on the Boullet House?

"Surely you've found some way to dispose of the body by now," I say.

My irony opens a vein of pride. He hints broadly that police officials have come by new information, "unh, ma'am, that makes us suspect there could have been something funny about old Wentworth's death. We're checking into it—I am, that is."

Decrepitude *is* funny, leaps to the tip of my tongue. "What was it," I ask with exemplary restraint, "Drink? Criminal neglect, or just the ordinary kind?"

Couldn't say. I take it he's looking at me askance—everything slides laterally in his lenses to affirm the shiftiness of it all.

"Something else then?" It's *my* house, dammit, whatever he may think, and I'm going to have this thing out. And him.

He bounces the question back at me—"Any idea what else?"—as cagily as his uniformed status allows.

I turn the tables on him, "You say there's new information?"

"Confidential," he replies in a way that manages to be both brusque and smugly languid. He's learned that in tight spots where you suspect you're being coaxed to overstep some fine boundary of professionalism, the emblems of office—or their verbal equivalents—make the best defense.

"I see," I nod, "confidential. I see." Push the magic button and out slosh the proper formulae, ready-mixed.

"Any sign of forced entry?" he wants to know next, "when you arrived on the premises?"

"I myself had to make a forced entry, Sergeant"—can't see the eyes, but they're sure to be narrowing over the little notepad in his hand as he tenses it upward toward eyeglass level—"couldn't get in the regular way."

That seems to throw him off, and he burrows deeper in the notebook. "Says here there was a whole lot of junk laying around that day. *Old* junk. What about that now?"

"Hauled to the dump. But feel free to inspect any old junk you see lying about. Plenty of it left, all over the place." Ware's crowbar comes in handy for pointing out clogged doorways, half-demolished walls, hunks of plaster and splintered laths. "Here, you see? And there. Nothing but junk every place you look, and lots more where that came from." I continue recklessly jabbing the crowbar this way and that. Peaden's pursuit of the obvious has the peculiar effect of eroding any behavioristic controls hope engineers.

"See whatcha mean," he says, kicking at a heap of it as dissatisfied as if he'd been me. Some detail of his notes, though, prods him down the investigatory path he would perhaps just as soon not take. With a gyration of his jaw (that must be effecting a turnover of the spearmint gum almost surely wadded behind the crescent of his lower teeth) he changes his tack. "Anything... well, unusual?"

"What did you have in mind?"

"Maybe some stuff belonging to the old man, you know...any personal property, unh...records, things like that." He has taken a firm grip on the prime instrument of his profession at last, flashing it at the obscurest nooks of memory. (Later on, Harding was to discover that he had picked up his inquisitorial methods, however roughly, from a master.) "Maybe something you didn't expect to see?" Pressing on, spotting another nook.

"Every bit of it, Sergeant—none of it was expected." This might have been amusing if I'd had more time. "Go ahead," I insist, "have a look." A really *good* look. Let them all see just what a mess they'd handed over to me.

He did poke around a bit then, came back slapping dust off his rumpled uniform like it was Sunday Best, expression insinuating that a mess was, after all, what anybody with any sense would expect in an old-dump-like-this that ought to have been burned down long ago, on a has-been-street-like-this, inhabited by People-Like-That. And as for you, unh, ma'am, all the bustling and fussing and stomping might have said, you're right smack in the middle of it now in case you haven't figured it out. He looked as unyielding as a disgruntled two-year old.

Meanwhile Waro's crowbar was keeping me busy yanking rusty nails from the nearest hunk of wood which happened to be a partially exposed stud, a hefty one, as they are in old houses. Like insect hordes stopped in their tracks, those nails were everywhere, in all shapes and sizes, a whole hardware store full of them. Plenty to keep a nail-pulling robot busy puttering for days on end. If the fool was planning to sniff around after dead red herrings, I wasn't going to let him or any of them interfere with work—not as long as I was the only one doing any.

There was some fumbling in a shirt pocket. A poke or two with a toothpick between right upper biscuspids set him back on track. "One of the, unh, neighbors, unh, ma'am...thought they might have seen somebody entering this house through the rear door. After the fam'ly moved out, you see, next day."

Might have seen? Always these rhetorical tangents can tempt me, even from a resolute distance, no matter how clumsy— no matter how patently echoing the indirect discourse of prior instruction.

"That's what they said—I mean alleged. Do you recall if you spotted anybody, unh, suspicious hanging around the premises that afternoon?"

"If this neighbor saw anybody suspicious on these premises" (Echo to his Sherlock), "it was me, most likely."

"I reckon not." A gentle pat at his holster tells me that, despite my cleverness, I have missed the mark.

"Who'd have recognized me?" I point out.

"You don't fit the description. The person allegedly seen by this neighbor was a colored female."

"And what's so unusual about that? Isn't there a black neighborhood just the other side of the Boulevard?"

"It's our duty to check out any suspicious-sounding reports, unh, ma'am. That's our job." His profession is one to whose silent program others—especially questionable others like myself— must bend. Quite inexplicably he has risen to some authority of his office, some certification of an age-old right, and he smoothes the badge over his chest to prove it. "There was some old papers, you see"—this datum falls from his lips with stage directions clinging to it—"and the family, well they're not bein' a whole lot of he'p to us, so we can't establish to our satisfaction, unh, if anybody was with the old man when he died,or what...what the case may be."

Resources exhausted by this intricate summing up, note-book replaced at hip, twin mirrors give a final twist to the premises and my impassive gnome-like face up front. "If you think of anything more, unh, unh, ma'am," he suggests, "why the station is no piece from here, if you need us, unh...any time...."

If you need us. Any time—indeed. If you need. I needed Johnson Ware to return immediately, I needed to turn up some prospect of a roofer, I needed workmen skilled and unskilled— with permits up for all to inspect, the only one I could think of that I no longer needed was Greeley Connor.

Was there still time, I wondered, as I watched him go, for a little tussle in the contractual arena, a little give-and-take, a phone call or two to this one or that one who hadn't gotten around to whatever it was he'd promised to let me know "by midweek at the latest"?

Or was it to be on with the demolition, to take advantage of the few daylight hours left?

psycheme

Harding remarked not long ago that if a university course prepared and taught by God explaining all in its ultimacy were offered, she wouldn't bother to sign up. "I doubt," she said, "that any of it would matter." I agree. But, then, I had my suspicions about the existence of a Wise Author even in childhood; like you, I'll be bound, I've always felt I could do a better job, given that kind of power. Nor has the concept of an origin (or, if you prefer, a foundation) ever suggested to me a real thing or a place to be found and identified. The metaphysical quest was never on my agenda. I've always known as far back as when I started to use all such words that to search for origins is to weave an ideological fabric. And as I came along, I rapidly caught on to the fashion system. To sport mental-colored claims to originality, the many-colored cloak of knowledge, in fact to be caught doing anything more than playfully donning some native dress, intellectually embarrasses far more than flashes of the pieces and parts of meaning passed to each of us for designing our very own habits of self aggrandizement in omnipotent styles of good or evil, or in one of the victor-victim, winner-loser combinations.

Or, more recently, a little nothing of a g-string or jockey strap. You can show it all front and back nowadays as long as you don't dress it up and as long as you sustain the illusion that nothing making any difference has been shown. The modern law of metaphysical castration (Private Parts Shall Be Cut Down To Nothing) has its post-modern judiciary in epistemological puritanism (Thou Shalt Not Exhibit Thyself in Strong Colors). Dressing down whatever distinguishes you too much from the next person has so standardized what is said that private parts without even so much as a thread of gossamer over them fail to be recognized as such or to exert any charm. Flashers are taking over and nobody seems to notice. And as long as the philosophical status of flashing is repressed, Thou-Shalt-Not-Commit-Metaphysics will work about as well as the famous commandment against adultery; in fact, with equal access (if not to information, then to its technology) we can look forward to a future when all, under the rule of consent, shall exhibit their privates freely throughout the world at every moment without an ounce of self-consciousness.

A rational observer, knowing full well she cannot identify what she's looking at because her looking changes what she sees, may take statistical analysis as one fruitful approach: if nothing can be said about the parts, the appropriate mathematics can describe their movements as particles of a group of more or less like kind, i.e., naked metaphysical pieces. In the public domain, statistics remains the mathematics of choice (as distinct from consent in the popular domain, where we fall back on simple little arithmetical calculations—just yesterday, I received an unsolicited mail ad for 2 full color hardcore action videos featuring "80 fingers and 80 toes, 16 arms and 16 legs, 8 assholes and 8 tongues, 5 breasts, 4 cocks and 4 cunts").

Nonetheless, I would audit God's course and tape every word from first to last.

X

"Beggars can't be choosers" is an adage of long standing, tried and in that way true enough. But what it glosses over (conveniently all around perhaps) is this: that the condition of poverty, pure and simple, is precisely that of being so reduced that the power of choosing alone remains. This may indeed be our ultimate existential condition but, as such, not—notice—one we choose.

The options, once the realm of material advantage is withdrawn, can take on a rudimentary clarity. Daylight about to fade: I could start at one end or the other of that great stinking room, east or west, as I chose, or scramble on up into a dormer anywhere at random and get cracking on one of those immovable casements, or work outward from the middle—always remembering, of course, in that hot stench of staleness and decomposition, to take only the shallowest breaths and as few as possible.

But when there are four of anything, it becomes for practical purposes pointless to locate an exact arithmetical middle; and randomness merely defers the moment of choice, therefore the moment of beggary pure and simple. I am not against deferring things, not even pleasure if it comes to that—not necessarily— but the adventures of randomness hold no lure for me. I have never been much for throwing the dice and am suspicious of those who claim chance as their ally.

My dilemma came down to this: even though the window at the western end lay in deepest shadow, a little less stifling there- fore, it was quite possibly unsafe up on that ledge. Stained and moldering, the ceiling above it had sagged, and cracked, and dropped in heaps over the wide sill. Just how far the damage had worked its way into woodwork, roof, and rafters there was no telling. One more worry to gibber in my ear day and night: who will do it? when? what will it all cost? I decided to start with the window at the eastern end. No point bothering over what I could do nothing about, not that afternoon, not till I had a roofer.

So, up to the sill I struggled with my gaggle of tools as the chair wobbled under me, that broken-backed relic which was all I had left to climb on by then, Mr. Ware's pathetic excuse of a ladder having vanished after lunch with the crew. Even that. The left sash looked a little easier than the right and I started in on it keeping breath to a minimum—or rather, feeling that I did, with that aversive disengagement from the whole process that can fool you into disowning the habitat of your own body. Our durable adage leaves unsaid how the condition of beggary pure and simple narrows the scope of desire slowly but surely to a single, vitalizing breath. In the long run: to breathe or not to breathe is not the question.

The weather seemed to be turning—breezes would get started only to play out—and soon, I thought, unrelieved hot nights of summer would settle in. Everybody had closed up shop for the day, with the tired end of afternoon suspended like the slack leaves of the old oak tree dangling its moss at the locked window pane.

Nothing moved out there in the dead weight of that still- ness, but as I looked out again and down into the half-ruined, half-resurgent street, I saw a little procession rounding the corner from the alley into Valencia. It was the first time I'd seen all four of the Hurds together. Maybe the heat had driven them out, marching along with an air of being on their way to a picnic, though what travelled in the old Dollman's basket was hardly picnic delicacies (hardly even decent if it came to that), the two women in the lead stepping along side by side, setting that jerkily deliberate, dragging, solemn pace that kept them all heading in the same direction more or less as a unit. A kind of entourage for nobody. People said the Hurds spent their nights like a regular family watching re-runs on TV.

A family, actually, is what they were—too much of one, in the Shakespearian pith of local experts, e.g. Margaret Avery. A little more than kin. I never did get a straight answer from anybody, though, about whether the Hurds actually had title to Captain Boullet's old hotel, and I never had time to look it up. It was more as if they belonged to the place than the other way around, indentured to it through generations of absent or negligent or dead proprietors, Miss Annie more so than the rest. Old Mrs. Hurd was past ninety and senile as everybody would swear who'd seen her rocking like a wooden statue on the gallery, where her presence, it was felt, contributed to the decline of trade. One minute she'd be lost to the world, and the next she'd bolt out of her chair, highly agitated, and swoop up the closest thing, whatever it was—maybe one of the bedraggled kittens Miss Annie sheltered and fed by the dozens—and fling it down the stone steps, at the dry marble fountain out front.

"Go way, we don't want any, go way," she'd shriek, over and over like a stuck record till somebody stopped her, usually Miss Annie who kept an anxious eye on her between chores. When she wasn't whipping up and down the once grand staircase of the old Hernando, fetching and fixing and carrying who knows what at all hours, she'd be flip-flopping through the Quarter in her old pair of men's leather houseshoes on obscure errands for sundry businessmen.

Up in my nook I could hear her voice spiralling in through the open front door as the women passed along the fence. "No Momma...not thatta way...over here now...thissa way Momma, didn't I tell you...not now Momma...over there...," shrilling out lessons on the rudiments of perambulation to her nearly deaf mother, where to set each foot down and what to look at and when.

The boy, tow-headed and wearing his usual khaki cut-offs, broke away from the family procession and limped up to my fence. Sometimes when he saw me working outdoors, he'd stand somewhere alongside it with his head stuck between two of the palings and just stare. Upwards of an hour at a time he'd stand around like that, with most of the fingers of one hand, as many as he could manage, stuffed in his mouth in what could have passed for the peace of inner contentment that so many strive for. When he wasn't having one of his awful screaming fits he was often like this: very still, very quiet, eyes never moving, hardly blinking. The old man in his bright pink shirt slowed alongside the boy, grinning, hump-backed and atilt. He wedged the basket more firmly into the crook of his arm as if putting the finishing touches to a tableau—Allegory of Dementia: Youth and Age Bound in their Destiny of Blood.

Jimmy Hurd was said to be so severely retarded that the school special ed programs were at a loss to place him, so he slouched away his mornings on the back porch of the Hernando with a great big boom-box to his ear, or watched the old woman pace behind the latched screen when Miss Annie wouldn't let her out. Occasionally, he'd find some way of riling the Dollman as he contemplated and rearranged the junk inside his basket, the trash he spent most of his days collecting on the water-front curbs of Historic Tarragona—bottle caps, shells, scraps of rag, twisted shreds of cork and other bits of litter he decked out his shoddy little figurines with. His "folk art" people called it, when they were striving to be non-judgmental. He had no small success pawning it off season after season on indulgent tourists who couldn't escape his grin and his claim to be one of the disadvantaged gainfully employed. Downtrodden maybe, but not without initiative. I was to have more than a suspicion later that some of his folk art was bought for the kick to be found inside.

"Jim-my! Jim-my-y!" Miss Annie's voice came piercing back along Valencia Street, mother, grandmother, jailor, whatever she was to him—or he to her, or the Dollman to any of them. Toothless and stubble-faced, he'd fixed on me as if I were a freak mounted behind glass for his entertainment. He could be less than kind to the boy, and Miss Annie would have to come flying to the rescue.

At the sound of her voice, he jabbed his basket into Jimmy's ribs without effect and hobbled off after the women, spritely despite his deformity and his sixty-five years take or leave a couple. Where Miss Annie was concerned, life seemed to have conspired to make chronological age a matter of indifference. Forty-eight, fifty-six, sixty-two? Old enough to be the old woman's daughter, which she certainly was, young enough to have borne the boy, or to take him on as her own to watch over with her rough, fervent attentions while she served the needs of that one and this one in the Inn, the Quarter, on demand. "Would you check on it for me Miss Annie?" "Sure thing Mr. Bob...." You could catch bits of their interchanges drifting along porches and doorways at almost any business address in the Quarter on almost any afternoon of the week. Trusted with their extra sets of keys and the special delivery mail that arrives off-hours on the premises of upscale entrepreneurs, she was treated by one and all with that mix of familiarity and condescension accorded to useful, grateful dependents with the husk of life squeezed dry in them at everybody's beck and call.

"Jimmy, Jimmy!" The boy was still there staring up at me with the blind irises of a subterranean creature that framed me without calculation, without any effort at scrutiny or recognition, eyes that merely confirmed objective facts of my existence. Mild, strangely restful eyes. Then came Miss Annie herself, flippety-flop past the black bars of the Boullet fence. "Jimmy! Git along here boy! This minute, hear!" Jimmy had his hands pried loose, one from the fence, the other from his mouth, finger by finger, and limped away, head craned backwards as if it had been severed and reset in the wrong direction. In his skewed stare, the horrible scream was imminent, trailing from his white face like an invisible effluvium. But no sound issued as her hand jerked him, stumbling and tripping over his own bare feet, out of my sight.

If anybody ever buys that old place to restore it—as someone with unlimited funds surely will one of these days, the Hernando is an important historic landmark—Miss Annie will get thrown into the deal one way or another. The family is the real problem.

xi

The first time I saw Miss Mary Louise was from the window, when the casement I was chipping away at sprang without warning from its frame and out, nearly pulling me along with it, giddy and unbalanced, into the leafy mass of the tree. Clean fresh air was in my mouth and nostrils and over my damp skin. And in that split-second loss of equilibrium I spotted her down below, a slenderness in motion crowned by something green that might have been only a shifting concentration of the tree's foliage as a breeze sighed through it. It was as if everything for that instant became foreground with me suspended in it, a richly textured surface without depths or distances, only that sweet, soothing fresh air.

I leaned unsteadily back against the wall of my recess letting the coolness wash over me. In the street, on the other side, robed in a print of earth tones with a dark green scarf wound turban-like around her head, she walked straight on and undistracted. Three black girls in late adolescence jostled alongside her, chattering in high spirits as they headed towards town, their bright synthetic summer dresses, softly delineated in the tenuous neutrality of light that spreads there before dark, glowing past the patient, ravaged houses like the brilliant taffetas and silks of a bygone era.

"Evenin' Miss Mary Louise," they called out as they passed, and she stopped to look after them. She was well past middle age, on into her seventies, skin with the patina of pale old wood, so light it seemed merely to mirror a shimmering undertone of swarthiness. In the exact usages of an older racism, Miss Mary Louise would have been a "quadroon" or perhaps an "octoroon."

Alone, she scanned the Boullet House, first the yard behind the fence, the porch, the raised windows downstairs, the old cypress door propped open with a brick. Calmly, as though she were taking stock of how the work was progressing, she turned to the upper story, the window where I stood absurdly pressed into the wall, peering down. Unsurprised violet eyes came to rest straight in my own. Almost imperceptibly, she nodded—in greeting or in confirmation of some private expectation—then

turned, walked on, no hurry or huff, but, as before, with the measured grace and purposefulness of one trained from childhood in the art of movement.

psycheme

Family, class, wealth, nationality, race, religion, all the old ways of establishing who we are, have suffered, if not demise, decline. The function of the fundament or theoretical bottom (what are family, class and the rest but the buttocks of power upholding permissible times and places of psychical movement without question?) is to keep us all in line, in good form, habits regularized. To decline from the bottom is not an oxymoron, therefore; it points rather flagrantly, I should think, to where our fundamental values accrue their power. If you can follow me from one end to the other: what displaces such rock-bottom values (and does so even as I speak) is talk—talk about anything enough and you bring it into question, bring it to a higher level of consciousness as the saying goes. Once it reaches the top and you can hear about it anytime on TV, our mouthpiece of collective consciousness, a rock-bottom value loses not its appeal necessarily but its natural force, its power to compel us by the necessity with which we respond to nature's calls.

I ask myself what, at the fundament, reigns supreme today, unquestioned, in the nature of things, what indisputably defines me. The answer is unequivocal: my own talk. How, what, and when I speak put me in my place. In this new era, each of us produces herself in her own speech; the signs I make make me what I am. Each submits to the linguistic laws of her own body—one hell of a position to be in frankly, especially since enough talk about my own talk, i.e., consciousness of this new master, works, as one might expect, to void the law and institute linguistic anarchy, a phenomenon increasingly familiar on a global scale.

Given the truism that one cannot reasonably expect the reigning power to topple itself, must I not then fall silent?

As an alternative, I am in the experimental stages of designing a machine to do my talking for me. (With my strong entrepreneurial bent, I always keep an eye on technology and its possibil-

ities.) I call this machine the Surrogate Talking Subject or STS. My projections are that demand for such personal talking machines will be instant and worldwide, and, in light of uncontrolled population growth, unlimited. Most exciting is the prospect of STSs for small children, a model especially designed for positioning new talkers; what such a device might achieve in the educational field alone could make going to school, as we know it, obsolete.

When all have their talking machines turned on, grown-ups and juveniles, every STS establishing the status of its very own program—all the machines, in other words, talking to each other—we can each go on with our lives as usual. Think of it.

xii

"OOOOhh...lookit the baby, shhhh...," crooned old Mrs. Hurd, wagging her head like a dignitary sweeping the multitudes with her gaze. And when it seemed she had their eyes, she intoned, "Go way, go way, go way...," softly, like a tune to lull a child to sleep. The Dollman turned his head over his flaming pink hump and spat past the boy into the gutter.

Straight blond hair down her shoulders, wheeling her little boy (Hispanic? Vietnamese?) in a Lil' Junior shopping cart with a big sign tacked to it that said "DO NOT REMOVE FROM PARKING LOT, Penalty $50," swelling belly pressed into its grid of chrome—I recognized her at once.

"What you doin' in this part of town Stephanie Wentworth? You oughtta know better'n to show your face over here," yelled Miss Annie between herding her old mother along with "Come on Momma, keep your mind on your feet," and backing up for one of her slippers stopped dead in its tracks on the edge of the curb as if unwilling to take another step.

The girl kept right on pushing the cart at the Hurds, straight down the sidewalk ("Like she owns it," Miss Annie complained to me on another occasion). At the last moment, Miss Annie made her mother step down from the curb, out of the cart's way, but the old man and the boy let it rattle along between them barely missing the basket and Jimmy's toes.

"You too boy! Where's 'em sneakers I got you last week? If that Co-cola ain't cold enough to suit y'all by the time we git home don't come cryin' to me 'bout it, hear?" The Dollman snickered and shifted the basket to his other arm as Jimmy handed him the six-pack. In all my time in Tarragona, I never heard Miss Annie address the old man or acknowledge his presence in any way beyond speaking to Jimmy in the plural when he was around.

Just then a smallish man who was something of a fixture in the neighborhood, with the look of stepping out for an evening of important business, cut a neat path down the sidewalk between the Dollman and his adolescent facsimile. At the wave of his hand, which, on account of the slender cigar poised in it, came across as a fillip of dismissal, old Mrs. Hurd yanked her arm out of Miss Annie's and screeched her litany of terror, "Go way, we don't want nothin', not today, go way, we don't want nothin', go way, go way, we don't want nothin'...." She looked set to keep it up, indefinitely this time, loud enough to be heard up and down the block, and I was holding my breath for the boy to chime in. Miss Annie's hand flew to the old woman's mouth just in time to forestall *götterdämmerung*.

"I ain't forgot about your new lock, Mr. Jake," she called out after the man. "Mr. Jake—"

But he, cigar in mouth, with his infuriating air of being too busy and important to listen, chose not to condescend.

One of those late nights, in my exhaustion, I would have bumped into Jake on my way to my car if I hadn't caught a whiff of his panatella in time. I smelled it well before the round of its stub glowed towards me in the dark and just managed to step back and let him pass. He greeted me by name as if we had been neighbors short-cutting through each other's yards since time immemorial.

xiii

Harding's nose is remarkably acute.

Having given up the idea, she says, of lodging at the Hernando, I took a room in an inconveniently located guesthouse halfway across town which offered reasonable accommodations with spongy mattresses of the kind I loathe, that hold you like an unwanted all-night embrace from a vaguely unclean stranger. Everything down to the lampshades has soaked up the smoke of your predecessors; only the bathroom window opens, barely, and the misnamed air-conditioner whirrs mustily all through your sleep. But I can report that they change your sheets there more or less dependably twice a week. The towels are sent out, stark white and threadbare, and quickly absorb the prevailing ambience. No phone, of course, and TV if wanted is extra, but there's marginal respectability—God knows I could never hope for anything like a convincing demonstration of mine to any Tarragonan. The place being out of the way, though, where people-in-the-know would be unlikely to pick up my scent, I never had to put it to the test. And that was, of course, the whole idea. I didn't have much choice at that point.

Paul calls this her "evolutionary atavism." She claims she can smell the lather if one of the girls is taking a bath upstairs when she comes in; it has always been a way for her to know where they are, whether they are safely back at home. "Plain old regression, like all the oral joys of passivity or even outright schizophrenic immobilization, doesn't reach back far enough for her," he says. "They're both far enough," she tells him, "but no earthly use to anybody over the age of six—six months, that is."

psycheme

Which reminds me. To insure your future in the global world of talk, you may want to place an early order for your STS. Prepayment by credit card will guarantee availability. To be sure, software is still somewhat of a problem but long-term plans for expansion call for intensive R&D with the aim of providing individualized talking programs in a one-minute to a one-year frame, depending on the client's need for and investment in release time. Venture capitalists may contact me directly concerning STS, the IBM of tomorrow and tomorrow and tomorrow.

I have already named my personal STS "Harding" in her honor.

xiv

Ware's truck was nowhere in sight after that fitful start at wrecking, for more days than I care to number. Reported sometimes "around the block," or "just back from the dump and on its way," or "parked along the Plaza no more than fifteen minutes ago," it was as elusive as the terms of our word-of-mouth agreement. Ware refused to put anything in writing, mumbling disagreeably, "since I can't read nohow, a contract don't mean nothin'."

Neither, it seemed, did no contract. History had left him with a fine grasp of the no-win situation, and he knew how to make the best of it. Giving chase on rumors, I had visions of myself going the way of Miss Annie in short order, aging not with years (like a tree, or wine in the bottle) but with the unnatural fever of crisis succeeding crisis. The breath of life to some and a pure horror to me.

Ware ran his business, to the extent that he did, out of his home where sometimes, they said, you might catch him in. Keep on trying. The line there stayed busy all day long and well into the night when it becomes past decent to call. If your dime should happen to hit a break in the household's conversations-with-the-world, you'd get: "He gone," and if you pressed the matter, "He not here now." Nobody could say just where he was at—"Could be over to Mr. Greeley's place." Or Mr. Somebody's place. Home for lunch? "He might." This evening? "He could." Laconic replies served up with as little savor and civility as possible.

One thing Ware's business was not was a family concern, though all seemed to have the same fine grasp of the situation.

His neglect of me looked, if not calculated, opportune. "Ware's a good ole Uncle Tom," said Bill Simmons, "cheap too," meaning thereby to keep my spirits up and my perspective clear. Most of that summer, Bill was busy with the carpentry on the house across the street where I had to put up with him almost daily without being able to enlist his services. He kept his own hours—sunrise to early afternoon, just about when the other men would come straggling back from their late lunches—and because of his unexcelled reputation as a craftsman, he could afford to take his time. Everybody in the Quarter, he'd point out, "used Ware," and then remind me of the old refrain: "Pays your money, takes your choice." I never explained to any of them what *my* experience taught: the chanciness of getting even remotely what you pay for, in money or any other coin.

Written contract or no, Ware had me locked in. Forced to pursue him if I didn't want to be forced to carry on without him with whatever chance labor might make itself available, some time or other, for hard cash. As a reader, you get into the habit of absolute engagement, which is nothing if not an act of subjection, the act, *par excellence*, of the slave. (Be it remembered that the nitty-gritty work of aspiring civilizations has always demanded something like a slave class.) He would have had me bound to him in either case, contract or no, but marks on a piece of paper are at least testimony of a kind, even if only in the lip service of reciprocity.

I concluded that this laxity in the matter of our agreement fell right in with the prevailing attitude down there as I seemed to pick it up on winds of patronage, back-talk, evasions-in-the-moment, expediencies of one kind or another. They all reeked of it—the odor was as unmistakable as the aftermath of asparagus—all of them, from Ware's phone-bound clan shoving bits of stale information at me, right up to those fine old Tarragona families and their agents, official and unofficial, presiding over the daily scene. One and all, high and low, snickering (so went the drift of my paranoia) in concert, no doubt, about that woman come from who knows where at such an outlandish time of year, hottest summer in memory, to restore one of *their* historic homes, ripping the guts out of it with her own two hands no less! They could at once claim it as theirs and go right on despising it in my person. I was history's answer to their ambivalence, a walking example of metonymy. The Boullet House now object of renovation, I, as life-bringing agent, quite naturally took unto and into myself the odor of its past—I in my metonymic identity as a pit for waste management. Wasn't the house in a literal sense working its way into me tooth and nail, all ten of them black-ridged, ragged? Also nostrils, hair follicles, pores under the suntan, eyelids, etc.? I didn't need Peaden's mirror glasses to document the changes.

To sustain its pull, the whirlpool of the paranoid position had only to gather these physical data into its momentum. One ineffectual morning—might have been the Monday after Ware's crew walked out on me—my dime clinking back time and again like solid proof that the phone company itself has now joined against me, I kicked the door of the booth shut so hard it spooked a stray dog and set it snarling down Hernando alley, where it caught Bill's grinning attention, me trying not to hobble too obviously behind. Last thing I wanted any of them to think was that I'm accident-prone. Explosive Personality Type.

XV

Ready for his first coffee-break, half past seven like clockwork, Bill assures me yet again that "it's just a matter of time" with Ware. We'd had our morning coffee together once or twice, a satisfying little interlude for him, apparently, that left me rattled well into the morning. With Bill, once or twice engrains a habit. His expertise illustrates, in a new context for me, the hazard of life-long overspecialization: personality mined hollow and raw to produce the single disciplined skill. Just as there are academic specialists, urbane and learned in print, whose conversation on the everyday topics of life can make the average fourth grader sound like a well-rounded individual, so Bill, when he isn't actually tinkering with wood in the profoundest concentration, is deaf to anything but his own internal clamor. He's nosy, demanding, self-centered, and as inflexible as a galvanized twenty-penny nail.

"Time. Just what I haven't got any of." I hadn't slept at all well and my arms were loaded down with a carton of tools. What I meant was that I wished he would let the gate click shut behind me and stay on the other side of it—let me get started on my day, collect myself by myself—wondering, too, how I had once come to the conclusion (in a youthful lecture on existential-ist poetics) that the defining experience of inauthenticity is never having any time.

But for sure, I think, as his arm prickly with sawdust reaches past mine to give the gate a shove, for sure I haven't got time to think about it now. The rest of him, past middle age but spare and quick as a youngster always on the move, with his big silver-topped thermos already unscrewed and wafting aromas of coffee my way, looks poised to follow the arm in through the gate at the slightest sign of weakening on my part. He means well, but that isn't the point. I add forbiddingly that I have to finish the house by the middle of August, "no matter what. Or I'm out of a job." Perfectly true, my obligations to the college lacking the elusiveness of Ware's to me.

"And now," I say—a desperate subterfuge—"now I have to run right back out and track him down." Through the hall to drop off my load, over the backyard litter packed down chalkily by a recent rain, out into the alley through the side gate and straight to the Plaza, the phone booth, sour and disgusting as I left it moments before—that's what I *want* him to think stranded at the front gate shaking his head and fretting his goatee, mouth puckered into the caricature of an "O."

"August?" a gasp: "Did you say August? Why that's hardly eight weeks!" As if I didn't know. "Not a chance, dear, not in Tarragona. Not unless you've been speaking the Unknown Tongue to D-O-G spelled backwards. Hey, that reminds me of the one about...." Voice going strong for a bit, then tapering off by the time I've reached the back yard. Out there, where I can hide at least some of my movements from watchful eyes along Valencia Street, I settle down as I do each morning for twenty minutes or so at my makeshift breakfast table, two hunks of a cracked garden seat, original from the Boullet era I would imagine. Precious seclusion.

I have my first quiet look at the folded quarter of the front page that happens to lie uppermost. WOMAN KILLS GIRLFRIEND resolves its ambiguity into the usual:...shortly before midnight...shots through the ground floor window of the Starlight Motel...Mrs. June Radley, maintenance worker at M. Larue Pulpwood Enterprises, Inc.,...wounding Josie Anne Johnston..."never meant to harm that Johnston girl"...live-in girlfriend of Mr. Daryl J. Radley...unlocated...four children. Such stories tell themselves by heart. Spread out in front of me, the contents of my old canvas bag, an easy bargain struck years ago on the fringe of the Athens flea market where, across from Aeolus' Tower, remember, it meets the mute, ruined, grassy tranquillity of the Roman Agora.

Mingled with plasterdust and the lingering wastes of the Wentworths' dogs come whiffs of the Bay. And such is the power of ceremony, even this meager homely ritual of peeling a boiled egg, an orange, unfolding, with the shadow arm of hibiscus gesticulating feebly over my shoulder, the morning paper; such is its assurance of life rebounding that these whiffs seem to rekindle, for the time being, sparks of the old enthusiasm. Ware in recession, Bill in his banished silence is soon hammering cleanly beyond the rooftops, getting it all done for Dr. Cane in good time—breezes of desire as I sit sucking a pungent strip of orange peel in the morning sun amid ravages of demolition abandoned. The light of morning reveals yet again the nightmare work of an Anglo-Saxon darkness, and I must have my moment of repose.

At the periphery of vision among the forged iron pales of the Boullet fence, the blues of chicory and rampion straggle low into Doc Shibbles' yard where the ground lies finely crisscrossed by the ever vigilant prongs of the old man's rake, a crinkled apron spread out between his half-derelict cottage and my fence. And farther in, at the back, spangles of sunlight jingle deep in the dense ramification of magnolia, citrus, evergreen, live oak, motionless saurian limbs trailing Florida moss. The breeze carries the scent of ligustrum past its prime. Coffee streams down into my yellow cup, its fragrance for the moment obliterating all else, shivers and flattens like the pale brown mud-face of the River, and I settle down to the news. Like a coming-to, after exile, in familiar terrain.

xvi

Ware, who had no use for written contracts because he could not read, reported to be having trouble with his transmission; dumptruck stopped cold somewhere on its way to city dump. Spotted one day, nonetheless, in front of Mr. Greeley's office.

Ware clearly has no urge to do business with an outsider in the way he does so officiously (managing all the while to give the impression of an invisible whip lashing him to action) for the likes of Mr. G., whose technical grasp of what is authentic has been such a boon to the town. Just a matter of time though.

psycheme

I've been reading George Steiner. About a kind of Jew, assimilated to the Western heritage by blood, who, appraising daily its architectural tilt toward holocaust, survives to inhabit "the house of civilization." This is not altogether an ethnic matter. Among those come to be thus dubiously housed is Harding, and her voice recounting the daily perils of historic restoration breaks the silence. Homeless, I wake and sleep amidst the babel of holocaustic afterthought. Unintegrated eruptions denying the very possibility of enlightenment. And how, I might ask, does one survive where I live, here in the wilds of intellectualization?

xvii

...a judicious desire on our part to wait until all the facts are in..., it said in *The Sentinel*, June 14th. Editorial page. No rush to judgment here; just a timely review of an issue impacting on the entire community.

The facts were few and, after about a week, thoroughly rehearsed: untenured literature professor at Community College; female; contemporary novel of dubious moral value on syllabus the previous term. Doesn't anybody oversee these people? Waywardness in the classroom might have passed unnoticed (and evidently did for a time, as she'd assigned the same text the year before with the bookstore complaining of unsold copies) or been contained as the centuries of literary indecencies usually are, had not the daughter of Tarragona's Chief of Police, J. Winston Fleming, been enrolled in the course. She not only bought a copy (one early article identified her as a straight-A student) but brought it home to read, thus perturbing the domestic tranquillity. Impacting unfavorably. Pandora's box ajar, cries for censorship under the banner of public accountability were rising quite beyond all attempts at containment.

The more responsible of these were alluded to in paragraph two (...academic freedom...divergent views...nevertheless...) but, one had the feeling, only as the most cursory warm-up to paragraph three which, taking a deep editorial breath, embraced the principle of the general welfare in a notably long sentence:

> Our public institutions are accountable, first and last, to the community that supports them...that community being shortchanged and dishonored by educational commodities which are, at best, in questionable taste...at worst, an offense to the morals and beliefs of American families.

It is easy to overlook the bottom line of this whole educational enterprise: as a teacher, you're a dealer in "commodities." Lest you forget. I wonder: is there a futures market here? options? warrants? indices? Might there be an instrument for upping the returns on your long-term investment in the profession without treating yourself like a psychical excavation from which truth, goodness, and beauty are to be mined, each purified of the others and exhibited in its pristine artificiality? Always the problem seems to be the same: how to go about the business of mining the crude ore while you're being set the professional task of developing packaging techniques bound to change the product's quality. One might follow this view of intellectuality to the conclusion that a professor of the liberal arts functions largely as a kind of quality control expert.

A letter to the editor cut through it all: Novels? Is that what my kid's tuition money is paying for?

Virtually the entire town, as far as I'd been able to determine, failed to make any fundamental distinctions among writings of sexual signs. Margaret Avery said, with that ironic modulation that throws up its genial smoke screen as much for self-protection as for propitiation: "Their defense is always that it's art." (This, you remember, before it became politically correct to undercut such distinctions.) And Bill Simmons claimed, in fact insisted, that the town's preoccupation with the whole "porno business" at the College was suspicious—he, at least, did distinguish that much—but he felt that a novel about perversion, so he'd heard, didn't belong in a classroom where people were supposed to be learning how to read, not till it became a classic anyhow.

"Where then *does* it belong?" I said in that way typical of the quality control expert momentarily spinning out of control.

That set off an avalanche of anecdotes the gist of which

seemed to be that anybody who wanted to indulge their depraved tastes could always catch one of the local peep shows, it was a free country. Of the former, I'd found by scanning my very first Friday's *Sentinel*, there seemed to be a half a dozen or more up front, counting drive-ins. The entertainments always appeared in the special weekend supplement near houses of worship. "Enough of both," said Bill, never one to miss a chance for an anti-religious quip, "to cater to all the faiths and fancies." Personally, his favorite author was Chaucer. Bill had his standards.

psycheme

The rash of movies I've seen lately: they appear at first not to place you anywhere, perhaps because they don't permit identification with any of the characters. But upon closer attention to where I am while watching them, I realize only too well where they put me, there in the depth of my gut, too familiar and too close for recognition. It's the marketplace. *Agora*: popular assembly for exchange of ideas and commodities. Time-space for sexual exchanges of power. The marketplace of sexual desire with no trace of love, compassion, decency, or bonding of any kind—psychical movement within the space of this desire, this gut-deep place, unfolding the world outside has the effect of rendering all but trickery and violence illusory. If I don't myself quite go through with the specifics enacted on the screen, if I don't blow their bloody brains out—if I don't fully become the imago of this sexual desire, I am fully in its grip as onlooker. *Voyeur*: there is nothing to interpret or decode here, only the excitement of watching imagoes of pure sexual desire execute their preferences, or be executed.

   I am not confessing a secret fascination with hard-core pornography; even the ingenious Marquis fails to hold me for long. I am acknowledging the pure sexuality of the marketplace in all its multiple forms. And I am experiencing myself in its grip, myself being purchased by consent, eagerly receiving its coin, admiring the artfulness of a truth confounded in realistic images—this in order never to forget again, I tell myself, the

worldly transformations of sado-masochism. I record myself
standing under your gaze in order never to forget.

xviii

On the face of it, *The Sentinel* is merely a fatter, bigger, updated
version of the paper that, during my childhood, the postman
rattling along country roads at five a.m. dropped off at our
place, the Fondeur Plantation, about an hour before I'd fetch it
out of the big metal box. From the first grade on, I'd imbibe the
world of grown-ups each morning while I leaned against a
water oak waiting for the school bus, then neatly shot the paper
back in the box the instant the yellow hulk appeared on the flat
landscape.

No special training or instrument, therefore, was necessary for those short spells of morning leisure in back of the
Boullet house, if you can call "leisure" something that has to be
so deviously appropriated as those little breakfasts of mine
under the withered hibiscus, with the prospect of just about
anybody or anything breaking in at any second. I needed no
bearing there but this unreflective ambience of my own past.

Not quite the same news—not as literate by a long shot as
the old local paper—but absorbing in something of the same
way, in the typicality of its shootings, stabbings, nabbings,
wrecks, rapes, luncheons, improprieties, feuds, phobias, *faux
pas*, snatchings, causes, rumors, Acts of God. And the thinness,
some days, of it all, over the bare bones of comics, puzzles, obits
and legal notices in small print—that too was familiar. There
were the announcements of who was coming to town and who
departing, the engagements, marriages, passages of one kind or
another, the prizes, the social events both grand and wishfully
grand, with hardly any perceptible difference except to the ear
alerted to such distinctions by long habits of attunement; and,
then, at week's end, the rich spill of classifieds, personals, sporting events, auctions, recipes, spiritual resources—anything and
everything whether you wanted it or not. Not to be forgotten: the
daily integrated column (so they were still sometimes spoken of
in the seventies), with its solidly black news items headed by a

small photo of its Afro-American columnist who could always be relied on not to overstep any lines worth bothering about.

Though *The Sentinel* is thicker and laid out with more of the ad man's flair than the paper of my childhood, on the face of it the two are kin, tirelessly glossing the commonplace in its quotidian violence and puffery, organs not so much for disseminating information as for reaffirming, in print, with the regularity of the sun's rising, the community's sense of perpetuity amid perpetual danger. Readers could always count on a smattering of spin-offs and follow-ups to earlier *causes célèbres* gauging the public appetite. If Tarragonans seemed addicted to weekly features like Roland B. Markit's "Then and Now" (Wednesdays) and "Face to Face with Ellen Rappaport" (Fridays), it must be because their reappearance dependably by the week played so crucial a part in keeping the whole story going, on and on. Markit was *the* rising young staffer on the paper, had the best credentials and a knack for celebrating prominent names and rehabilitating forgotten ones (though not, of course, *best*-forgotten ones, e.g. Frances Boullet and her ilk). Brought it all off in the spirit of a respectful newcomer, too, which he was, testing the communal waters and already savvier than thou about how deep was deep enough for everybody's own good. Rappaport's interviews, complete with "candid" photos at home and at work, made a nice match, said to grip readers with the instant authority of one who knows just how to "get at the real person." What every interviewer strives for and some few are perceived to achieve. Week after week she "got at" real men and women about town in an interminable scenario of Who-we-are, Where-we-come-from, What-truths-we-hold-to-be-self-evident, etc.

Even the Elks' Friday night dinner menu did its vital bit here for perpetuity with: Ribs of Beef, Seafood Potpourri Special, Barbecue Chicken, Pompano en Papillote or Grilled Shark if available, Bucket-O'-Crabs, Broasted Oysters, Various Sandwiches and Salads from our Buffet for those with smaller appetites...a treat for the entire family. Varying only slightly from week to week.

But when you fold back the glossings of things as such, *The Sentinel* is not at all the same paper I read as a child. Under the skin, it's as different as can be, this product of a technologically expanded communication; no regional limitations here to bind or to charm. For, no place on earth—no place in the information cosmos in fact—lies any longer beyond immediate comprehension; this news has absorbed every place and every thing into its radius beyond which there is no place, nothing. The ways of Beijing's underground economy, of Tanzanian chimps, or black holes are now as immediately accessible as the doings of hooligans in the Historic Quarter, or shifting shorelines on DeLuna Island just across the Bay. New evidence here, too, of how difference arises from the extension of sameness. Neither regional nor cosmopolitan in the old sense, this new kind of local paper gives the impression of One World jammed into whatever region you happen to be located in—wherever your Honda or your Friendly Skies or Greyhound can transport you—any diversity being rather like some decorative variation in structures of violence and our ways of living in and with them.

And yet *The Sentinel* purported still to be a Southern paper in the old style, more or less the kind that turned up on front porches and in mailboxes all through my childhood and youth in the Yazoo-Mississippi Delta. And Tarragonans seemed to read it as just what it purported to be—this despite the paper's immersion in the age of telecommunications, not to mention, of course, the town's bloated city limits, its mall-bound thoroughfares, its Community College soon to go four-year, its intimations of tourist gloss. If it purported to be what it no longer is or can be, this fiction sustained the very ease of my reading, and made it work for me as so peculiarly my own that it brought me quite without effort to something like self-possession.

Only the smallest shift of consciousness, only the finest attunement of feeling, and I would locate myself.

psycheme

I had resolved to reveal myself to you fully by showing up in enough of my different moods to convey the range of what it is like to be me.

I had trust in your empathy, your capacity to move with me and to suspend judgment, your compassion, your flexibility, and above all, your humor, your playfulness—these are, after all, merely the attributes one might expect. All these come to the surface and go into operation when I read. Reading brings out the best in me, I think. I think it does.

Understand, I'm not reneging on my promise to withhold no part of myself from you—I've said what I would do and I'll do what I said. I always do, or try to, at least when I give my word. I want you to be able to depend on my word. But something unforeseen, something terribly familiar is closing me in, as if I cannot be myself or, rather, as if I've been constricted to a me I don't want to be, not the best or most interesting or pleasing me at that. Quite the opposite, I can't even think straight; that is, I can, but not with the usual interest and joy I have in the movement and strength and charm of my own thought. I feel like screaming at you that I'm not usually like this. It's sickening.

Of course, I know you have nothing to do with it in any personal sense. Obviously, I can't see you at all, so how could anything personal be happening? Or is this how personal matters come up between us? It takes enormous courage to do what I'm doing: standing here without being able to look back at you, knowing that the moment will pass and thus seal off all possibility of my ever seeing you seeing me this very moment.

xix

The old man kept on dogging me.

How could it have happened that *The Sentinel* with its reportorial nose for all the grotesqueries of life, all its calculated and inadvertent iniquities, caught no whiff of what might have befallen Mr. Jeremy Wentworth, formerly of Cane & Wentworth, as he lay stinking and abandoned on Valencia Street? Not a word then or since, and as an avid consumer of the daily news I would have known. What a front page scoop it would have made: skinny old cadaver with staring little eyes, propped on pillows, surrounded by panic and emptiness. Even more eloquent, bordering on artistic in fact: the bedding all by itself with the dents and hollows of the departed, Jeremy Wentworth *in absentia*. A post-structuralist trope of the first rank, this, to be clipped and filed for posterity.

xx

Ware did come back, just as they all assured me he would, in time, and chaos broke out all around me again.

xxi

Everybody else had called it quits, the contractors and the real estate agents, and the smart young businessmen hunched over their wheels as if getting set to compete in a race for weekend gains. Even the last of their obliging secretaries had gratefully vacated the old Quarter, and I was just gearing up for a final push of uninterrupted work while the light lasted, when a car ground to a stop across the street—and, immediately, another, brakes squealing.

"...really had no idea...coincidence!" a melodious female voice called over the whirring idle of their motors. Then a man's: "...Miss Amy, so respectable...," hearty laughter wrenched by an onset of coughing like a wall of plaster giving way.

The blur of their voices drifted up to me through the open dormers of Captain Boullet's library. Engines switched off. In the restored interstitial quiet I could hear the soft plash of water next door at Shibbles' place (the evening round), and a catbird mewing.

I bumped down the stairs with my load of woodwork and paused at the open front door undecided.

"Doesn't want me to, I told you."

"...tell that turkey husband of yours a thing or two about how to handle a woman, sweetie." Voices distinctly more robust at street level.

One of those constant small organizational decisions: with the shed crammed full, whether to try the porch, due to have its floor torn up shortly, or the messy back yard, after all.

"...opportunities for his...you call it? Pursuits? Chasing his nurse's ass..."

"...improve your vocabulary."

A nail gouged into my skin propelled me without further

deliberation out the front door where my load crashed to the porch floor.

Voices went still. In front of the house Bill was working on, a dusty brown and white El Camino piled high with bundles of roofing cedar crowded a sporty white Jaguar the color of Devonshire clotted cream. The woman waved eagerly in my direction as if that would cancel all association of any significance with the two parked vehicles and the bearded man slumped against the smooth haunch of her Jaguar. Even as I nodded back, she was already on her way toward me, her long-legged stride choreographed in its easy economy, shoulder-length hair blonde and glossy under a floppy summer hat.

"So *you're* the one," she called up from the walk as the gate swung shut for her at the merest brush of a backward trailing hand, the kind of entrance that never seems to take gates, or hinges, or their maintenance into the slightest account. Her smile was warm with surprise, face and throat tanned, not so much an addition of color as a deepening enrichment of her skin's own translucence. It's the golden lushness most often associated with very young women, but most often seen in those well past youth.

After all, though, she was not really pretty, just a trick of the sun's lowering softness. Too bony at the throat and shoulders when she's right up in front of you, hips disproportionately wide in their creamy white linen slacks—something roughly put together about Aimée that she knows how to bring to an artful finish.

"This is the most marvelous house in the Quarter, absolutely," she bubbled in accents comfortably somewhere between New England boarding school and Southern gentry. "I'm Amanda Hulin." In a diffusion of perfume I recognized—Madame Rochas, one of my old favorites—the hand that commands seventeenth-century Catalonian gates and, one presumes, much else besides, reached out to the owner of the marvelous house.

"You want to be careful what you touch around here," I said, pointing the way in.

"Elizabeth? Why that was the name of my dearest childhood friend. I called her Elissa, such a lovely name." An unsought intimacy in the making. She paused in wonder between the door-jambs: the wrecked hall picturesque in the fading light framed by the open back door, Gulf Coast genre scene awaiting its Vermeer. "Uncle Randy was mad to get rid of this house, absolutely out of his mind! Actually I suppose it was that prissy Committee that sold it to you—amounts to the same thing." Creamy espadrilles cut a reckless path across the plaster-strewn floor. Ware's crew had had a more than ordinarily energetic day.

"Careful, you can fall off the back gallery if you don't watch it," I said, "steps are gone."

If she'd come to Valencia Street on a late Friday afternoon with the express aim of touring the Boullet House—maybe even collaborating on the restoration with me—she couldn't have been more taken up with the possibilities of it all. Is it "sour-faced old Greeley" who's doing my architectural plans? Not that anybody with any brains can't see exactly what there is to be done, plans or no plans, but, then, these things do entail a certain "historical consciousness" (here she brought off a rather nice mockery of his cadences complete with labial twitch). Isn't the cypress stairway splendid (said over her shoulder as I follow her upstairs), a domesticated version of the one at the Hernando. Fantastic building. And this absolutely incredible front room, and, oh, those fabulous window seats like little rooms—she can't resist climbing up into one of them, kicking off her espadrilles on the way. A crime to have let the place run down so, just goes to show the narrow-mindedness of people in Tarragona really is beyond everything. She's heard that I plan to live in the house—if I don't, she just might start a residential trend in the Quarter. She knows just what she'd do with the Captain's library.

There is that about Aimée that can speak so directly to one's naive responsiveness—she never seems more artlessly sincere than when she is at her most disingenuous—that I found myself falling right in with unaccustomed frankness, indulging aloud my worries about time passing, the demolition still far from over, even going on a bit about my original fantasy of living and dying in the Boullet House, my return after exile up East, etc., all of which she understands perfectly.

But candor rang hollow—only your own sincere words can transmit this echo of such nothingness to your own ear—as if in promoting such a view of myself I was nurturing an enormous, absurd falsehood.

With that echo still in my head, I got hyperconscious of my watch ticking away the minutes, not to mention the fact that I'd come to the end of yet another frustrating week with the doors and their frames still in place. I was already past due on those, an easy job for two of Ware's crew working in tandem, but slow, cumbersome going for me alone—another one of those stories grueling with detail, Harding warns, and offers to tell it, in full, upon request. A story without charm of any kind; a story, she says, by, for, and of slaves only. And yet in spite of it all, she says, I loved the house, loved it, if anything, even more than before my hands had literally and laboriously started taking it apart. Loved it even in the face of that looming question: What for? Having already invested more than was safe of my money and time and nerve, I let it stand—loom. There's only one direction for movement when you're at the point of no return: forward. Beggars can't be choosers.

"Tarragona can be a real bore, and depressing beyond words," Aimée sighed as if my unexpressed worries had cast a shadow over her enthusiasm, artless eyes shining across to mine, "the secret is, you have to meet the right people, Elissa."

How well I knew her—the charm as well as its falsity, the self-dramatizing poses and what they conceal. Even now, they never fail to stir a peculiar anguish in me. "The right people rarely have that effect on me," I laughed, but remembering how others often find my reactions strange if not outright hostile, I took an earnest tone with her, the kind that can't possibly be mistaken for anything but itself. "Honestly, I don't have the time," I said, "not with all this."

She knew just what I meant. "Listen," she said, as we strolled along the walk to the gate, the words springing out of her with the spontaneity of one struck by illumination, "you need a roofer, right? Well I've got a perfectly marvelous one for you!" Whereupon she linked one pale peachy silken arm in mine and swept me out along with her into the deserted street. My need offering a convenient alibi for what could have been an awkward situation.

"I'm bringing you business, Tony," she called out to the bearded man, a cue that the action, now, is to take a sensible turn.

In that roguish pose of striking his match—the swarthy face, tight dark curls barely streaked with grey—he might have been thought handsome, devilishly handsome, with all its amorous, piratical connotations. A plunderer on the high seas of amatory pleasures with a perfect disregard for the civilities of introduction. The first inhalation of his Lucky Strike (I'd no idea you could still buy them) tore through his chest like a coarse-cut file. As the cough eased, he said in a voice made deliberately, irresistibly gravelly, "I'm always open for business, dear." He would let you take him as you pleased, but if you took him at face value for a mere fool trying to come off as a man of the world, a cad, that was your problem. ("That's *your* problem, lady," he would say to me later on, in that blasé tone I learned to hate.)

From a styrofoam cooler tucked among drums of roofing tar in the hold of his El Camino emerged a frosty beer can which he hoisted above Aimée's head at tempting arm's length with a sing-songy "Party, anyone, par-teee!" She started to make like a dog on its hind legs to sniff it, but immediately lost interest in his routine. "I could kill for a drink," she rasped with the moody exaggeration of Hollywood vamps. "It ain't the country club, dah-ling," he drawled, peeling off the tab for her, "but it's wet and cooh-ool!"

He offered beers all around, perhaps interpreting my scrutiny of his cedar shingles as feeling left out. "No thanks," I said, "not while I'm working." Having drained his own can appreciatively, he flung it on a pile of rubbish and, with thoughtful pats to the slight swell of his paunch (not long ago, I would have said, he was still trimly muscular) fell to inspecting the roof of the Boullet House with what I came to recognize as his professional eye. Not a bad one as they go.

"Tony's good, he really does know what he's doing," Aimée vouched, adding in an aside to me, "Uncle Randy hired him even though old Sourpuss Greeley doesn't consider anybody except Bill Simmons worthy of *his* roofs." She gave an offhanded nod to Bill's fine handiwork, the rebuilt porch, as easy as if she were idling in the artistic and philosophical concerns of the cocktail hour. "You'd think that getting up there to nail down a few shingles was a spiritual quest of some kind."

Krasner gave her a flirty glance intimating a whole range of competences having nothing to do with roofs, or spirituality. I could see him fingering a calculator in his shirt pocket.

"See that you don't go running off now, Tony, to do the Boullet House till you've finished this one, hear?" This with a plaintive grimace, evidently over the quality of Krasner's beer.

"Am I a man of my word...?"

Ignoring him, her look to me said: it is clear that only *you* follow me in the truly serious concern of the moment. "My husband has an option to buy this house from Uncle Randy if I consider it suitable for a business," she said. "I'm considering. What do you think?"

Krasner's cough rasped through her question: "Doctor Sweet Baby James needs a write-off, gee. A little artsy-fartsy boo-teek would go nice, put little wifey to work saving hard-gouged tax dollars instead of loafing around at the country club." The tail-end of his second beer produced a hollow burp.

"Your Mr. Crass-and-Vulgar act is *not* amusing!" It sounded like a flicker of genuine annoyance. "Men, honestly. It never occurs to one of you that a woman might want to *do* something with herself that has nothing to do with your little tax schemes and your other—"

"Benefits? How's that for vocabulary, dear?" Yawn expelling a series of neatly formed smoke rings.

Her eyes sought mine—she seemed about to enter a plea, artless again, wholly sincere. "I wanted desperately to get into a graduate program at the University this fall, but James doesn't hold with commuting that far, and of course he wouldn't hear of me taking an apartment there and coming home on weekends. He says anybody with a Master's degree certainly doesn't need more courses. But just *everyone* has a Master's now, don't they, and I want to go on, you know?"

Krasner cocking one handsome eyebrow over his pocket calculator, leaned toward her in a stage whisper, "Dumb of the old s.o.b. Could have made..."

"In what?" I asked.

"Fiction—creative writing. Not theory. I'm more interested in doing it than just thinking about it. What do *you* think?" Krasner's index finger was clicking out numbers a mile a minute. "Really," she said, "I think James is afraid I might get too literate for comfort—that's not how he'd put it, but it's what he means. Remember that thing Mill says about education being disastrous for women?"

"Bill who? You never *told* me."

"Well, James couldn't agree more, only—" with a chuckle, as if making, or making again, some out of the way discovery that places all in a predictably absurd perspective, "he doesn't seem to realize that John Stuart was being ironic. That's *Mill*, Tony, for your information. 'M' as in misogynist." Then quickly, in defense of her husband, "Of course, James does have a marvelous mind, but purely scientific. You know these deep, rational brains—like the Grand Canyon, and all around there's nothing but desert as far as the eye can see." This, clearly, was wicked and meant to be.

"And that, for *your* information"—Krasner looked hard at me from his calculator display—"is where dear old Uncle Randy Cane comes in."

"It's true. It was his idea. He says he finds what I've done in our house 'devastatingly charming.' But honestly, I do have a small knack for interiors, a special way of bringing the outside in and the inside out as they say in the trade. I think it would go, here in the Quarter, don't you?"

Krasner interposed that it would suit her to a tee, not to mention all the business that would come her way from the loafing artsy-fartsy set. They engaged in a little round of mock-fighting about "Uncle Randy," he exaggerating her coquetry with mincing prissiness, "wants his little Amy to have ever' li'l thaing her teensy-weensy heart desires. Ain't that the truth, old turkey has the hots for her." Translated for my comprehension: "In this town they keep everything in the family as much as possible, in case you haven't noticed."

She rolled her eyes at me to signal our mutual understanding of and tolerance for this adolescent masculine ribaldry, even a teensy-weensy bit lovable when it came to that.

"Well sweetie, you tell me why he goes on listening to all those frigid rich females laying and laid on his couch all day. Is it the de-icing that turns him on, or just the cold cash?"

"Randall Cane is the most decent man in the world and a first-rate psychiatrist, neither of which *you* would know anything about. Couches suggest only one thing to *your* squalid little pea-brain."

Krasner cocked his ear, "Did you say 'little'?"

"Just for that I'm leaving." And she marched over to her creamy Jaguar with every appearance of having been deeply wounded, or perhaps just ineffably bored after all, and slid into its eloquent curves. "Let's have lunch, Elissa—tomorrow? Or is later in the week better for you?"

"Neither, I'm afraid. I never leave my work here to eat lunch." If there was a look of anything like hurt in Aimée's face, it was so fleeting it might have signalled no more than a shift in the leaf shadow overhead. "Maybe," I amended reluctantly, "maybe coffee some morning, when you're down this way—if you don't mind the dirt."

"I'll be around to check on things for Uncle Randy—" her gold-flecked eyes refused to let mine go, just as only moments before I had seen them lock into Krasner's in the duplicitous signing of their erotic contretemps—"and I, I need a friend like you, I really do."

Krasner tossed his calculator into the air and caught it close to his chest like a fragile football. "Toodloo," he said, "*ciao* baby," with a discreet cough behind one hand.

"I have some marvelous ideas for stories I would love to get your opinion on, Elissa," and she was off in a smooth, gliding start without so much as a glance in his direction.

"You gonna put cedar up there?" He shook another cigarette out of the pack, lighting it from the stub of his last. "Smoke? Or is that another no-no?"

"Do I have a choice?" I said, turning down the Lucky. "That's what the Board tells me I have to put up there. What's cedar cost now?" I already knew the answer. Or rather, three or four of them.

"The top quality stuff, which is what those bastards call for, don't come cheap," and the figure flashed on his display midway between the top and bottom amounts I'd been quoted.

"That's per square, huh?"

"Just for the material, mind you. You'll need upwards of, unh, this many squares, but I'll have to get some measurements on the old crone, to be sure."

"That much?"

More figures, and he handed me the calculator. "Installed, you can just about double that price if you get one of those tight-assed s.o.b.'s like Simmons to do it. He'll drag it out like a fucking funeral, charge you top dollar for his time, and slap another twenty or thirty percent on top of whatever it costs him, and then he'll act like he's doing you a big favor just for being who he is."

I punched in some figures myself, studied them while he smoked down his cigarette, handed the calculator back to him without comment and waited.

"Tell you what," he said a little edgily into my silence, "I can pick up the stuff a little cheaper, got some special sources, and I'll pass it along to you at cost because, well, I'm a nice guy—that's providing *I* do the work. No two-timing, see?"

"*You* do the work," I said, nodding, "personally."

"None other. Just don't blab it around too much." He leaned closer, "I don't want those other turkeys draining off my supply. You gotta watch who you deal with in this town, bunch a cut-throat crackers around here." The native Tarragonan in his modified accents colored by all that risqué flippancy (so at variance with the puritanical habits of the locals I had become used to) is not hard to detect.

"Let's see," I thought out loud, to get our deal straight, "You'll tear down the old roof, haul it off—"

"Yeah yeah, babe, not your problem." What's more, he can read—a blank contract on a clip-board to prove it.

"How much, then, start to finish, necessary repairs included? And what kind of a calendar are we talking about?"

He picked little bits of tobacco off his tongue like lice and wiped his fingers down the side of a tight jeans leg before resuming his calculation. "I'm tied up right now, did I tell you?"

"How long?"

"You'll have to work me in right after Miss Amy's job here, at the end of the month, or it's no deal." I kept my silence, alternately studying his figures and my roof across the street. "Here's my rock-bottom price—that includes it all, chimney flashings too and all the trimmings. But that's only if you're ready for me, no loafing, and no damned interruptions while I'm up there. I like to keep things moving and get the hell out."

It beat my other estimates by a considerable sum (including that of a company that Greeley Connor had, in a rare jest, described as "the K-Mart of the trade, their hearts are in vinyl all the way"). Krasner might be an unknown quantity, but at that price I was not unwilling to ride the eminent Doctor's coattails, especially with the eminent Doctor's charming niece so prominently in the picture.

"You want me to take down that old whatever-the-hell it is up there? Wind turbine? Probably vented your attic at one time."

"That's one of the historic features of the house. Can you work around it?"

"Hell, why not. Just one more pain in the ass when you're up there. Wouldn't want to mess up any grand old useless artsy-fartsy historical features." The cough wracked him again, really hard this time. "Tell you what," he croaked, "you time this thing so your job doesn't get in the way of anything else I've got lined up and I'll give you a bargain you can't refuse." Calculator flashing past my eyes one last time on its way to the passenger's seat of the El Camino.

Another five percent off! It was a real break, my first and only one. "No interruptions, you said, from start to finish?"

"Love it or leave it," he said, clinking his keys in my ear like coins in a beggar's cup.

Did the man matter? What if he revelled in the part of irresistible boor, says Harding, with the autoerotism of a boy enthralled by his own bodily functions? If he played himself with an ironic detachment from his own blustering act, it was an irony that never subdued, never escaped further elaboration of the show itself. Harding knew intuitively just what he had vested in exposing the conventional stance of Southern males so that he could make himself an embarrassment to the more sophisticated among them—perhaps the scientific Dr. James Hulin, if not his admirable father-in-law (who, if there was anything to him at all, was surely beyond such posturings and mockeries of posturing). For Amanda Hulin, the act seemed to hold a passing fascination, even if she was, above all, a product of her class, flirting just at the moment with one of the more accommodating feminisms.

Slouched at his ease beside me, says Harding, arms folded across his chest, he was silent to my silence, patently not a man holding his breath for an answer, but surveying her sideways with what she describes as "a multiple dare." Had she not known from the outset that the project would involve risk all the way? Every variety of risk? He offered competence—on the face of it—and price, and she couldn't afford the luxury of refusing the risk of the man.

She reached past her reluctance and took his outstretched hand in playful imitation of a big merger. "It's a deal, then," she said, concisely reviewing the terms of their agreement to the dollar, "and that's the bottom line, right?"

"Done partner, bring it to you in writing Monday." He linked his arm in hers then and stood solemnly beside her facing the Boullet House—joint venturers in a good cause, being photographed for the social pages. "The bottom line," he chuckled in apparent answer to an imaginary reporter's inquiry, "but strictly on my time scale, remember."

Any time scale at all, even Krasner's, seemed like progress.

A southwesterly breeze picked up the satiating sweetness of confederate jasmine and carried it through the dimming afternoon until the exhaust from the El Camino, roaring off to its nightly berth on DeLuna Island, overpowered it.

xxii

Through the foliage at the very back of my neighbor's yard, where branches sagged low into an empty lot on Hernando Avenue, the waters of DeLuna Bay showed soft iridescent green and so near in that spreading twilight that it seemed you could have reached your hand through the leaves and dipped it in, cool, motionless. Among clumps of late-blooming atamasco lilies, their single white corollas flushed with rose, Maria Zamora stood with hands folded primly behind her back, turned, and passed with Indian quietness through the dense undergrowth, receding as if she might disappear into the still shimmering scroll of the Bay.

psycheme

You think you can't be seen as if you have a one-way mirror to watch without anyone knowing. So much for begetting as-ifs on my image while forgetting me in theirs. Sorry to interrupt social reality; it's not resentment pure and simple you're hearing, more like past frustrations multiplied and complex, more like the extravagance of impatience. Come spring and little pure white flowers rend the garden ground.

xxiii

"That old shit" was Krasner's term for the rubble Ware should have been trucking to the dump as it came down. The yard, near the end of June, lay buried under great musty mounds of it, front, back, sides, right up to the fence and spilling through. Just about impassable, with even my breakfast site swallowed up, one afternoon, by the wrecked innards of the house.

It better all be out of his way or—Krasner was not a man to mince words and proud of it—no deal. Meaning no roof. He'd rip up the contract right in front of my eyes and that would be that. He could put up with a lot (he said) but he was very particular about what he would or would not haul off as part of our bargain.

"Your bargain," he'd remind me. The debris from the old roof, nasty though it was bound to be (and only time would tell), he was fully prepared to take, but under no circumstances would he run the risk of having transported—on his time, by his driver, in his vehicle—so much as an ounce of anybody else's shit that might have gotten mixed up with his. How it is that such scatalogical refinements become second nature to some never ceases to fascinate me. Can it be that the psyche hangs, for such men, suspended over an abyss of fecal chaos, the Great Chain of Being collapsed into a Vast Unity of Waste, that distinctions of "I" and "Thou" persist only by virtue of absolute separation between "Mine" and "Thine"? Is this some primordium of paternity in a being condemned to surrender its seed to another? An arrested infant's anality etching its little template of selfhood? And so on...she who gazes long into the abyss must be prepared to have her gaze returned, paraphrased.

The trouble was that Mr. Ware, whenever he did manage to stop around to cart away the odd truckload, transmission permitting, was always just passing through, always on the run to some other job more pressing than mine ("Mr. Greeley he...Miz So-and-So she..."). At the critical point, walls down, skeleton gutted, he considered his obligation to me technically at an end; clean-up as you can get it, and lucky to get it at all, because I'm reliable. He never said any of this of course, not in so many words, but Ware is a good enough communicator in his own way. He'd attuned himself so finely to the letter of the law (even if he himself couldn't read or write, he knew full well what it means to live in a land of scribes) that he became for me a touchstone by which to test the accuracy of my vision and, in particular, my eye for the fine print in the strategics of restoration in Old Tarragona. At this late date, he had me stalled more than ever at his convenience, with Krasner's ultimatum to my head—or to my house, or my purse, which came to much the same thing—and holdups all down the line: plumbing, electrical work, insulation, walls, painting, and the rest, meaning those countless "minor jobs" so-called, for which I could find no reasonable takers and had just about stopped expecting any.

The last part of June passed this way, me frantically repairing windows all over the house with utter indifference to the problem of "mine" and "thine." For it had become perfectly and painfully obvious that I myself was to be left holding all the shit, without regard to origin or kind.

Saturdays, kids from the Project trouped past on their way to town and back all day long, looking sidelong at me in my dirty outfit, out-of-town white woman on a ladder, none too steady, doing who knows what. The youngest ones liked to start up games of hide-and-go-seek on one of the demolition sites nearby where I'd be sure to see them crawl in and out of gaping doors and windows. Through these apertures they scurried like ants out the eye and nose holes of a picked carcass. Shouts and giggles were calculated to keep me noticing. A contractor there let it be known he'd already found the remnants of more than one fire inside an empty shell of a home—but nobody worried now, he laughed, because "she" was always there to watch the kids.

xxiv

Back in May when I'd first taken up reading *The Sentinel*, I came in on the middle of one of those stories of local goings-on that cannot be allowed to die a natural death. In one of many follow-ups to a drawn out trial that had ended in acquittal, a prominent local psychiatrist (so prominent the epithet functioned even then for me as a manifest allusion to the missing name) had been quoted as describing charges of sexual misconduct brought against an established dentist in the area as fantasies probably stimulated by orthodontic manipulation of the oral region. Acted out, presumably, with the aid of anaesthesia.

Beginning of July, the story resurfaced, yet again recapitulating the issues of this much publicized case with a disregard for blanks here and there equal to any experimental fiction. One either reads this kind of labyrinthine account with the diligence of an insider (the story naturalized) or, like some of my students, takes incoherence unreflectively as a norm (the un-story naturalized). Those among us who consider themselves advanced regard the latter as a kind of post-literate sophistication born of the mass media, and the former as the old bourgeois bag of tricks privileging its own practices—two more ways to trump up the *status quo* as the human condition.

The upshot of all this was yet another happy ending, and that seemed to be the whole reason for bringing the affair back into the news. This very orthodontist acquitted back in April with the help of said expert testimony was quoted as stating at a well-attended Chamber of Commerce luncheon, where he led a seminar on "Profiling Your Business for Success," that all the publicity had been worth a million in advertising: confidence in him had been amply demonstrated by a doubling in the number of his female patients. The ladies, God bless 'em. Nothing succeeds like the success story.

xxv

Sundays were best, everybody and their cars at church in the morning, drowsy hot summertime all afternoon long and nothing much going on in the Quarter. Everything shut down, rehabilitation at a standstill.

True, the odd detachment of tourists might be seen cruising the quiet streets in their air-conditioned transport, but nobody else who didn't have to would set foot in Old Tarragona, dozing, wheezing with satiety over the stagnant weekend—streets, shops, buildings, from rehabilitated to derelict, rank with untended growth, from derelict to gutted and all the way to reproduced (yes, we had one or two of those already, conforming to code and way over-priced), all one, all members, membranes, of a single, supine, barely stirring organism like a somnolent old dragon with a patch of antique glitter here and there restored along its sinuosities, around the Plaza and environs, along the winding blue-green Bay to all the fringes, East and West, and North through the alley by the Boullet fence into Valencia Street itself where I alone made such an incongruous, such an unseemly commotion about tending, who knows why, to a nick in the old renegade's back.

The heat had taken over, summer at its height. Under the shelter of the great arching oak, I had to keep a rag slung on one shoulder to catch sweat running down my forehead and to wipe my palms dry for rolling balls of window glaze.

xxvi

In the minutiae of restoration one passes through all manner of old yet familiar places: the *topoi* of the project. Nuances of self-composition by chancily layered debris from the cultural memory. Nightmare rampages; dragons. Surreal landscapes with carcasses in foreground. Apollonian clearings, Dionysian frenzy. Orifices.

xxvii

A rhythmic squeak made me turn.

Jimmy Hurd was discovering how to give himself a ride on one half of the carriage gate by hopping on one foot and pushing off with the other, a major accomplishment for him, which was obvious from the fact that he would keep stopping and starting with an importunate "awee!" meant to attract the complicity of my approval. And maybe, too, to start up another conversation. In the broken sounds of his language, the shards of words in elusive curves of utterance, he was calling out my name, brashly, to impress me with his recent mastery of it, "awee, awee, awee!" in a bossy sing-song with the squeaky gate for back-up.

I was on the point of giving in when he took off down the alley toward the Hernando at a wobbly trot.

"Been tellin' Miz Hurd for I don't know how long," said a voice directly behind me, "boy like 'at don't b'long out in public." The voice knew how to interpose itself without introductions, with its air of unquestioned intimacy like a thermometer registering the state of your insides. Pitter-patter around the concrete jags I'd cracked off the front steps that morning with a sledge hammer, the blows already stiffening in my shoulders and back like the onset of *terribilitas*. Beige patent leather shoes atop one of the hunks, settling in for a visit. "But she ain't right herse'f, so what can you expeck?" Face slick as a shaving commercial; pencil line mustache.

One sultry afternoon a couple of weeks earlier, I'd dropped a door on my foot and nearly blacked out just as he was passing by—happen' to be, he said. Nobody there to look after me, so he'd let himself in the gate. Kept snooping around after that, exactly like somebody who's been told he doesn't need an invitation to come on in, any time, making a demonstrative show of appreciation.

"Claims he got weak lungs. Kinneys too. But that ain't the half of it if you as't me."

Or if you didn't. Above all, the voice gave itself airs of assurance and of self-assurance, citizen in the civic thick assuming the type of communal talebearer. Between nostrils and thin bloodless lips, the diacritic of a mustache marked the distance exactly half-way.

"It don't take but one look from me to straighten him out though." Such a busy, wide-awake look, hue of shallow ocean water trapped in little tepid sand-indentations along a breezy shore. Vigilant little eyes; one might almost imagine they stayed pried open by a habit of reconnaissance, even in the natural repose of sleep.

Antipathy made my hands fly and old hardened window glaze spattered out around him.

"Looked to me like he mighta been innerferin' with your work ma'am, am I right? So I took the liberty." "Libbedy."

"Not at all," said I, catching as I did so my unintended ambiguity. But with Jake, always on the lookout for signs of capitulation, you didn't set things straight after the fact. Talk was a treacherous incline for slips of the tongue, and he kept score. I tapped in my pane, set the points, whipped out a lump of glaze, spinning it rapidly into a slender foot-long rope, and squeezed it around the corners of mullions with a thumb become deft through repetition. I smoothed it flat and cut it away clean and fast with my utility knife.

His look encompassed my well-being with tentacles of benign concern as he flattened back his grey-streaked hair, just so, over a bald patch. "After that fallin' out spell you had, I'd a thought for sure you was gonna ease up some—lady like you doin' such heavy work. My, my."

"That wasn't any kind of a spell," I said testily. Whiffs of panatella in silence told me who'd won the first round. The next time I glanced his way, the oversized notebook he always carried lay open in one arm, cigar in hand, and the other was moving across the page in tentative strokes, at its ease, as the eyes measured me.

"Never sketched a woman doin' this kine a labor," he said, "edjicated too. Good subject, don't often get the opportunity."

"Just don't expect me to pose for you."

"Portraits are not in my line atall ma'am, not as a rule. I like to catch folks right inny act." That's "ack." "'In may-dias rays,' like they used to say inny old Roman days, am I right?"

A police car came coasting down the alley practically sideswiping my fence. "How you, Jake?" Sergeant Peaden called out his window, fixing his mirror eyes on our *tête-à-tête*. Jake's hand kept up its swift, fluent strokes undistracted, informed only by occasional glances up at me. Past the Boullet House, the car rolled to a stop on the wrong side of the street in front of Doc Shibbles' dilapidated cottage. "Never here this time on a Saired'y," Jake murmured, "drives out to the cemetair' with that woman a his. Mother's buried out there, big vault, fam'ly name a Simmons, fancy old-style lettering." In one of his books, he had a drawing of it, couple of the other big ones too—Canes, Howards, Hightowers. Some day he'd bring his cemetery book to show me. The Shibbles side wasn't much count. "Never made a picture of that one," he said.

If I had any doubts as to what he knew about *my* routine, he put them to rest. "You must get awful sore an' wore out," he said shortly, "workin' like you do, foe-teen, fifteen, some days even sixteen hours a day ever' day non-stop, right on through Sund'y, am I right? I can see it in the line of your back, ma'am." Instantly I straightened. Under Jake's scrutiny one ought to have been cut from stone, with thoughts of stone as impenetrable as a Precambrian fossil, stonily serene as an armless, headless god in a processional of stone. A granite angel in the grassy shadow of a vault belonging to one of the fine old families with their English names. What you could never escape in Jake's presence was the too, too solid flesh of your own resistance.

And for all the world as if I were burning with curiosity, he volunteered smugly: "You might say it's my bidness to know what goes on around this Quarter, keep an eye on things."

"What exactly is your business?" I asked with a mild ironic emphasis on the standard form. These rhetorical retrenchments were not lost on Jake, though he might let one pass in the moment. Peaden and his sidekick, Pat Gorrie, sat in their patrol car smoking, the voices from their radio crackling out on the weekend somnolence, as he paused to fuss over his cold cigar. "Fack is," he said and paused some more, "fack is, I got me a *bunch* a lines, ma'am, an' I got a hook an' a worm at the end of each one of 'em." Chuckling at his conceit in a way doubtless calculated to be disarming, he scrutinized his work in progress, nodding in confirmation of what he saw.

Some word for him had been eluding me for weeks. It came to me now with all the laughable omnipotence of childlike cunning: slimy. "And on weekends," I said (not entirely in good faith, for what I offered as conciliation sprang from an irrepressible urge to prick his composure) "on weekends you do a little recreational sketching." That I should act on such an urge, even have it, was most irritating of all.

"Fack is"—he was not even grazed—"what's recreation to me might just turn out to be a service to the community." Turns out he was not only the people's eyes, ears, hands, but their conscience as well. "Now let's take a for instance," he said, eagerly flipping through his notebook till he came to a sketch of a burly man in a hardhat bearing down on a jackhammer: big hunched shoulders, thickset torso, broad face with overhanging brow and a deep scar down one cheek paralleling the aquiline nose over an emphatic fullness of lips strained back to bare a set of boldly crooked teeth. By exploiting the figure's sheer physical power for its potential of menace, in a few energetically drawn details, the sketch managed to be an accusation. Unfocussed, unspecific, but as ripe for snatching up off the page at the opportune moment as a fat billfold from a bulging back pocket.

"Would you b'lieve this here drawin' he'ped bring a criminal to justice?" I pressed my putty knife into the glaze, angling it just so, with steady, concentrated unconcern. "I declare," was his comment, "I never seen a woman hannel tools like you do, big ones, lil ones...." No, I decided, that sensibility impressing its insinuating purpose on the craft of eye and hand wasn't harmless, anything but.

"'Bout a week after I finished that sketch," he bragged, "police sent out a composite of some dark-skinned Hispanic they was lookin' for at the time. Robbed an old woman's house, they said, beat and raped her. Turned out I had him right here in my book—didn't think nothin' when I made it, though, just like I'm standin' here now doin' you."

Doc Shibbles' white sedan of uncertain sixtyish vintage chugged to a halt grille to grille with the waiting patrol car. Peaden and Gorrie propped elbows on opposite flanks while the old man sat mopping his face at the wheel and Maria Zamora wore a smile suggesting visions of another world.

"Scared ole man," muttered Jake, too absorbed in his likeness of me even to acknowledge the policemen's farewell when they rode off a few moments later. "Fine ole fam'ly on his Momma's side like I said, doctorin' folk from way back. Had ti'le to most a this here districk clear on down to the Bay inny ole days, use to be known as the Ole Diaz Tract. Should say so in your papers, if you got inny."

"Transfer of title is customary when you buy property," I said.

Silence, savory clouds of new smoke drifting briskly my way. "Lawyers," he said after a bit more puffing, "lotta them tryin' to buy up that proppity over there. Speckulators. But the ole man ain't got the sense to turn a profit. Not like you ma'am— must take a heapa cash to haul off an' buy an ole place like this. Edjicated woman like you knows what's what, am I right?"

I jerked the rag off my neck, wiped my hands on it, and gave him my silent back.

"Didn't have what it takes, you might say, Doctor Gregory Shibbles, MD, of Hightower, Shibbles & Dawson, Pediatricians. That was inny old days." He reached around with his pad to flash me a sketch of Bill Simmons, instantly recognizable as a triangulated rump with a jutting goatee at the top, one exacting hand stretched over closely set sawhorses as if it meant to measure the span between them. "He's part a that same ole fam'ly if you go back a coupla generations. Went to college. Bet you ain't never guessed that just from listenin' to the ole cuss."

"Never would have suspected it," I said, moving on up my ladder where I could put some distance between us.

"Big talker—used to be a big drinker too, bad blood. What they call 'genies' now'days. Don't think I don't keep up with today's science, ma'am, that's where the action is, like they say, am I right? Science. All 'mounts to the same thing though, fam'ly, blood, genies, don't it? Words, words, words, like they say, that's my philosophy. Am I in your light, ma'am?"

"No matter," I said.

"Ever seen a nice clear stream pick up muddy water from some dirty little crick feedin' into it? Ever notice 'at, ma'am?"

"I don't look at nature that way." Walden Pond, despite its reigning spirit, even the mosquito-infested swamps of Audubon's

Florida, in the company of that egomaniac, beckoned like Elysium just then—anywhere, as long as it was away from the ramble and rant of this one, who made dissimulation as necessary and as automatic as taking breath.

"That's just exackly what happen' to that Simmons blood somewhere down the line, don't nobody know just where or when. Now you take ole Shibbles. Man's crazy as a hootowl, soft 'n the head, reckon you must of noticed. Way I look at it, a man might get accused of somethin'—happens alla time don't it? Might even be dragged out in the public eye, but it don't necessarily have to break him for life, am I right? Not necessarily. Why I seen some of 'em rise to the top twice as fast."

"The cream," I said.

There was a snap, a soft cluck of annoyance like an overridden oath, and the sound of a pencil point being honed with a knife. Four, five, six fast snips.

"You musta known some like that yourse'f, roamin' 'round the country like you do, am I right?" The blade sprang back into its sheath.

"I've read about them." For a while there was only the scratch-scratch of his moving pencil and the scrape and squeal of my tool down the rim of the pane where old glaze stuck hard as nails.

"Shibbles plain shrivelled up, his kind always do," he said as though we were whiling away the summer afternoon in a front porch reverie, seeing the pitiful state of the world eye to eye. "After the grand jury wouldn't indict him, he shacked up for good—'scuse my language, ma'am, but it's a fack ain't it? Fack of life. Woman's some kine a Creole mix, been hangin' on to him all her life." Crack! went the window pane under the force of my knife prying out old glaze. "Don't know if I should be tellin' a lady like you what they charged him with."

It was a relief to go off in search of a new pane from my shrinking supply.

"Couldn't keep his hands offa little girls, that's what." He'd been saving it up for me. "Guess you can figure out why he never went to trial, smart as you are—an' a mother too, am I right? What kine a mother would let her lil girl stand up in the public eye and tell things like 'at to a bunch a strangers an' muck-rakin' newspaper reporters? Didn't make no difference though, wasn't a soul back then didn't b'lieve he was guilty." Sketching up a storm, Jake was.

Carefully, I tapped loose what remained of the broken pane, catching the fragments as they slipped out. "Know what innerests me," he said—pausing motionless over the delicacy of my task—"what innerests me is what they call 'human sigh-chology'," and he fell back to it exactly as if pressed by a dead-line. "Way the mind works, thass what. Whether he done it or not you see, that ain't the importance of it, y'unnerstand my meanin'? Fack is, all his over-confessions kept gettin' him off, don't nobody pay no attention to Shibbles now when he takes off down to the station and blabs it out all over again like it just happened yesterday. Way I see it, it don't matter what the truth is, only what folks b'lieve it is, right? Like they say on the TV, 'perception'—that's the whole thing right there. Perception. You don't need a college diploma for that and no fancy words nei-ther, if you got eyes and common sense."

"And a vocation," I said carelessly.

"You are so right there ma'am. Most important thing you got to have, though, is what you might call 'magination. Comes natchral to some. You got to put yourse'f in the other fella's shoes and that ain't easy, but I don't need to tell you that. Takes all your concentration an' more. First thing you got to unner-stand is what scares a man and how he's liable to start actin' when he gits *good* 'n scared, y'unnerstand what I'm trying to say? 'Phobia' is what they call it, folks always scared somethin' might catch up with 'em. Lock 'em up, they git scared, put 'em out on the street, same thing. Scared. Give in too easy. But fear ain't all like that, you got to look deeper, a whole lot deeper. Why sometimes a man—or a woman, of course—will rush right at the ver' thaing that scares the livin' daylights outta him—or her, of course—and they'll go all to pieces on it, like a ship smashin' up on a rock."

Behind me the pencil was still, perhaps suspended in midair by the force of simile. "Now that's your *cuntra*-phobia," he said quietly amid a whole battery of puffs, "what they call a phobia makin' out like it ain't one," he finished in apparent dis-traction.

When I turned calmly to face him, the alert little eyes grabbed at mine, then dropped down to my image. Broodingly, as if it and old Shibbles had converged to lead him to some troubling synthesis, he muttered, "Trick is, you got to know which kind you're up against."

"Phobic or counter," I proposed.

The cigar butt flew over thirty feet through the air to the other side of the fence, Jake nodding vehemently in assent, "And that's where 'magination makes all the difference." He clapped the pencil between his teeth and surveyed his handiwork in a smug estimate of his powers. "I do b'lieve this is the best I can do with you, since you won't hardly turn my way. Yep, best I can do."

xxviii

Jake's drawing shows me from the right, rolling a bead of glaze as if in animated prayer, head down and to the side over a partially hidden left shoulder. No part of the face shows behind the hat rim. The nape of the neck is vulnerable, wisps of hair escaped from the loose bun I had made of it that morning. Curve of the back—mine, definitely, the arch of it incised in my aching muscles—and, an infuriating detail (since my old shorts, a relic of some years ago when I'd been nearly fifteen pounds heavier, were notably baggy and unrevealing): more than a hint of cleavage between the buttocks, curves so exactly suggestive, however, that I would have hesitated to call them pure fantasy.

He'd managed to capture what I had struggled to deny by single-minded concentration on my glazing work: he had me in a crouch of averted rage. Distinctly, a hostile feline crouch.

And perhaps it was all true. Perhaps a woman has no business fooling with an old house—sledge hammers, broken glass, plaster walls, contracts, dismembering the place with her own hands and fancying herself in charge of its reconstruction. Is not her peculiar genius, after all, one of adorning the world others have made, hacked out, spattered with their virile blood? Consider Hrothgar's queen, treasure among treasures, bearing the jewelled cup on soft feet from warrior to warrior flushed with

accomplishment! Consider Grendel's vengeance-driven dam biting off more than she should and getting her comeuppance. The
enthusiasm of Agave wrenching off the head of her son Pentheus.

psycheme

Have you any idea what it's like to be stared at without being
able to look back, without even the slightest glimpse of who's
staring? Like a door opening without warning on to the mastur-
batory care of the body's orifices, a page turns and you're there
gaping an arm's length away, holding the margins steady for
eyes to eat off the snot of sinuous sinuses, a clammy breath
vaporizing the surface of letters spun out convulsively pushing
and thrusting interrupted by moans and sighs and laughter bitterly accused, laughter without cause, autistic spasms flattened
across a space glossed by idiot outsight. Flattened between
leaves for all time. A figleaf for your thoughts.

You make the assertion that absence is merely the farther
limit of presence an experimental fact for me. And all that can
never return, in one way or another, is this very passing
moment; for even if all eternally returns just as it is now, it still
would not be this passing moment. All else is show and representation indexing its own presence, diverting attention from
the temporal dimension, from the gift with no return, the gift
without meaning.

Meaning. Now there's the issue. Meaning gathers and
maintains power by its threat of absence; bring any meaning
close enough, under sufficient analysis, and it is not lost, as we
often say—what we mean is that it loses its power. What is lost
is the feeling-of-meaning, that vaguely delineated sense of
something half-there joined to us without force, by our consent
as it were. Seduction is never more than the promise of meaning, and meaning become familiar, as it must in time, continues
to seduce only by threatening to go away.

Are you afraid I'll take Harding from you and you'll be left
alone with me?

Is the feeling-of-meaning what you miss here? That fullness charging our rituals of absence with the suggestive cur-

rents of lived myth? Think of the fixed dramas of insects and other animals at their breeding and feeding rituals, the inflexible carnival of nature. Have you noticed how people will clamp on some chain of meaning, however horrible, shuffle around in it, rather than live without it? Rather than live without the experience of seduction? I concede that all of this is quite natural to *homo sapiens*, so much so that I'm confident I could still seduce you; I could take you even now away from Harding, but that, you see, is what I refuse to do. I have neither the heart nor the head for it.

You in your absence: if you are not perceptible as you slouch there staring, you are conceivable. You can be conceptualized and analyzed, and thus the distance between us closed in a kind of familiarity. Those searching, judging eyes with which you can see no more than I—"you can see no more than I"— shall become as familiar as this always passing moment. And when all has been said and done, only this—"only this"—cannot be repeated. For in this business of provocative invitations to a sharing of meaning, you and your desires pull at me, suggesting all manner of commerce between us while I'm finding it far easier to adopt an ethical position, to give up the power of seduction—no, to rid myself of this nauseating power—than to resist falling into your hands, coming under your spell.

Unilateral disarmament, this. I can't get you off my mind.

xxix

"Letcha in on a secret, ma'am," the fresh, unlit cigar inclined to his ear like a tuning fork, "I got me a big projeck here." It was a day or two later, another hot, sultry afternoon.

Having captured (for all to see) the contours of my unsociability, caught me "in the act" and snatched it from me, my work, my time, estranged my body and by the very accuracy of the representation disaffirmed and denied what had been lost— having done all that, he was going to sound me out, today, at closer range. My escape this time was to be achieved, if at all, only by encountering him head-on. Naturally.

"Everybody's got a project nowadays, what's yours?" I said.

Mine, that afternoon, was tearing off the old porch floor. "You've got a real flair, and it looks to me like you might do something with it besides—" I wanted to say "snoop" but managed a somewhat less regressed "waste it on the vagaries of police work."

He flicked away a splinter of wood that had landed in his mustache and drew nearer. "Vay-garies," he mimed in perfect auditory slow motion, on the brink of lighting up, pausing, pausing ostentatiously with another long, almost longing, gaze at the image of me in his sketchpad, "Don't b'lieve I ever heard that one before." Stringing me along, no doubt, so I might fully take in the ambitious character of his enterprise. "I know you bein' a college professor with two or three high degrees can unnerstand this type of a projeck," he said at last, "and it's a pleasure, ma'am, a real pleasure talking to somebody that don't gimme no problems in communication." Rings of satisfaction from his initial puff thinned gauzily over my head.

He flipped me out of sight and turned to the back of the notebook. "Fack is, I got a record of what ever'body in this here Quarter is up to, in black and white."

"What for?"

"History, ma'am. A livin' history of this here community is what I call it, and that's why I like to catch folks without no posin' atall, just like I did you the other day. You ever want to check up on anybody, I got it right here," he said, patting his sketchpad. "This here's my real bidness, capturin' history in the makin'."

One way or another he had done about everybody, starting with the Hurds on their ramshackle porch out back. Jimmy was splayed rubber-like on the Wentworths' old couch, taped-over slits and all; the Dollman leered down at him like his very own Picture of Dorian Gray ("Don't either of 'em b'long out in the street if you as't me"). Old Mrs. Hurd had her scarecrow arms on the ruined balustrade ("Her mind's gone you know") with Miss Annie flying out the door at her, all mouth.

"Yes ma'am, had my own studio right here on this very proppity in that addition you up an' tore down. No hard feelings, I got better resources now and I ain't used it in many a year—that was back in what I call my 'early period.' Why, up in my studio room out back I could see more 'n half of ever'thing goin' on in Old Tarragona."

Jake flipped, with quick, fastidious puffs, over two successive pages crowded with figures at various angles. "Some a the local winos over where I live," he explained, "I got so I like to capture ever'body up close." Jake as Pollaiolo anatomizing the body degenerate. Men slumped over chairs or on the floor lay propped against dishevelled bedding; others tilted down the curved staircase of the Hernando into its lobby, or flopped like sacks alongside the Boullet fence with bottles half-poking out pockets and shirts. "They're kine a like the walkin' dead of Old Tarragona," he said with a smirk and a neat flick of his ash sideways. His was not the open ridicule of the caricaturist who renders laughable by exaggerating what he sees, certainly not the social conscience of the satirist; it was more as if a hidden imaging device, a special sort of absorptive mirror perhaps, or lens, or robotic eyeball, had been devised to drain the subject of self-possession by appropriating identifying marks of the body, its essentials, so as to turn its very material individuality into a technological datum for timely use.

"Don't you think it don't keep me busy," he said. "Gennelman friend of mine that's edjicated like you, ma'am, says that what I got here is kine a like a sigh-chological diss-play."

There were full-page displays of workmen active in the Quarter, caught, like Bill Simmons, "inny ack" one and all, hammering, measuring, hauling, figuring, blundering—Mr. Ware and company slouched beetle-browed on simian limbs ("All 'em civil rights ain't done nery one of 'em a bit a good and has just made things worse for us"); Aubrey Evans in a drizzle of sweat, welding a pipejoint under the pot-bellied disapproval of his father; old Mr. Livingstone in from the country—I seemed, in fact, to recognize in Jake's pencilled possession of them just about everybody I'd had anything to do with since my arrival in Tarragona.

"Vay-garies," he muttered again as though to feel it glide out between his teeth, listening as he flipped forward through the pages for the phantom of a meaning in the amble of the Latin syllables—or as if, in the mere acoustic registers documenting the long cultural deadening of their roots, to decipher what he supposed to be some trace of my aberrant mind's working ("She won't never look your way for love or money").

"Fine stud, ain't he?" said Jake with the ash of his cigar

pointed at one of a pair of facing sketches. Except that the man's skin was a dull ebony, he might have made a study for Grettir the Strong straddling a roof; the slimness of waist and hips were so pronounced that his torso seemed to rise out of them into shoulders of mythic strength. "Fancy foreign nigger, name of Martin Kingston."

Who, I could have told him, was standing just Friday afternoon where you are now, Slimy Eyes, looking down at the smoky pink of his ridged palms, rather indifferently entertaining my offer of weekend work. "Doing what?" The words had seemed to issue from a little chuckle, like an afterthought, the second thought of amused reserve. I gave him a tour through the wreckage, Ware's "shit" still waiting to be trucked away, and he had laughed outright, not at all a derisive laugh, though, but a kind of unrestrained delectation of life's infinite absurdities. "After I take *that* lot to the dump," he said, nodding at the truck across the street he'd just finished loading for Krasner, "I'm off to the beach. It's too hot for this kind of nonsense." A West Indian languor slowed his Englishman's drawl. "If it makes any difference," I said, "I could make it worth your while to put off your shore-leave for a couple of days." But he was uninterested, moved neither by my plight nor my cash; couldn't be tempted, he said, by the prospect of pyramiding his assets, hadn't left home to pursue the American dream. More chuckling. "And I don't suppose industry itself holds any lure for you," I said. "Afraid not, dear lady—laziness is my lure. Sheer la-ziness." He made a flat monophthong of the root vowel, drawing it out pointedly for ironic effect as if to say, "Isn't that it? Isn't that what you always say about us?" In the end, he surprised me with another second thought: "I'll come around Monday afternoon and we'll see about it. It's still a long time till Wednesday." Wednesday, as Krasner kept reminding me, my roof work was supposed to start, or else.

"Can't hardly trust 'em when they git like 'at," sighed Jake over his display, "No matter how strong and healthy they might be." He had Krasner opposite Martin Kingston, lighting a cigarette inside cupped hands as in a storm at sea. Curly-haired rogue responsible for nobody's shit but his own. If I'd been putting a caption to it as they used to do on engravings in old novels, it would have been a snatch from our conversation just the day before à propos of why he used Kingston on his jobs: "Can't stand one of those shuffling Uncle Toms working around me, gives me the creeps," ejaculated Mr. Krasner with a visible shudder, "no balls."

"Not bad," Jake said, taking a measure of who knows what, his artistic skill, my appreciation, Krasner's devil-may-care pose. His declining cigar.

A few pages later he uncovered a courtroom sketch, the kind televised on the news ("One of the clerks down there calls me 'The Eye'"): Margaret Avery on the stand, unmistakable even with her hair done up under a dark scarf, hollow-eyed as I had never seen her, stricken.

"Still not a bad looker," he said with clinical neutrality. "Should have seen her inny ole days, though, like a movie star…Guess you'll be readin' about the custody fight soon, keepin' up with the news like you do ever' day bright an' early. Reckon you an' me got lots of innerests in common, am I right?"

I made him turn back to the sketch of Krasner, but it told me nothing about the man I didn't already know. You had to hand it to Jake, though: even at his kindest he went straight for the chink, in this case the bulge of self-indulgence over Krasner's beltline, and something else—a slight contraction, like hidden alarm, around the eyes.

"Grew up right over yonder," the cigar pointed vaguely in the direction of Cadiz Boulevard, "where the City put up a parkin' lot for all 'em new bidnesses. Always in some kine a trouble with the ladies, that boy was, and just between you an' me ma'am—lady been around as much as you—that Clayborne girl got what she was askin' for, if you know what I mean an' I think you do, hunh? Bill Simmons had his eye on her too, but they say she hooted him off the place. 'Why don't you immortalize me in one of your plays instead?' That's just the way she talked in them days, Miss High-an'-Mighty." Jake had a knack for vocal mimicry as cunning as the strokes of his pencil. "Ole cuss wanted to be somethin' hoity-toity at one time…whatchama call it? Somebody that makes up them plays for the thee-ayter—we got us a right li'l active thee-ayter here in Tarragona 'case you ain't been down there yet—what's the name again?"

"A playwright," I said.

"An' that oughtta tell you how them plays was meant to be, but now'days some of 'em are just plain dirty if you as't me. What was I tellin' you about?"

"The Clayborne girl," I said pointing at the sketch.

"Tony used to work up there on the Bayou, for the Judge—that was her daddy. Dead now. Big place, nobody much to keep an eye on the two of 'em, like I said, an' she turned up pregnant. Got married off to a broker name of Avery from around Jacksonville, Palatka if you know the place. Bidness arrangement her Daddy made...well, you can figure it out yourse'f, smart woman like you. That female liberation ain't all bad, way I see it...."

Jake had even managed to catch the obliging Mr. Avery ("went broke an' drug most of the Clayborne money down with him, but Judge Clayborne's daughter don't let nobody get the advannage over her when it comes right down to it").

"What about Krasner—back then?"

"Tony went outta here like a shot, fa-ast!" The hand with the cigar flew out in simulation of a jet plane taking off, ash streaking away over the porch rail.

He was well into the top half of his book and it was all getting to be quite predictable stuff: Shibbles as Paedophilia, Zamora woman in attendance; some hasty sketches of Sergeant Peaden and other officers more or less on the job. Resemblances seemed to flit from page to page in Jake's living history as the tell-tale pencil compiled its extended family's album, a family joined not by blood in the slant of features and expressions ("genies" as Jake might have said) but by apprehension, the maker's mark in the mold of each of them. With a bit of practice, I thought, one could get hold of the letter, if not the spirit, of Jake's art; one could become, so to speak, his reproductionist.

"Never did know what the Judge paid Tony," Jake muttered dispiritedly, rushing over pages of stiff, stylish men and women posturing in an emptiness reminiscent of nineteenth-century fashion plates. "Way I see it, he could of had the money and the girl, too, but he always would take a fast buck instead, hasn't got the idea of hangin' on in for the big kill. Says he don't take to folks tyin' him down. Sometimes he just marries 'em an' leaves 'em—smart as a whip Tony is, don't get me wrong, but he never would take the time to unnerstand the way the human mind works. Not like you an' me ma'am. He coulda had it all, that's my philosophy."

One might even have improved on his cursory yet oddly finicky attempts at Aimée Hulin, her doctor husband, Greeley Connor, their social set. The technique of the identifying voyeuristic line had somehow gone amiss in these drawings, as if the lens were sufficiently dazzled by its subjects to blur just what "caught" them and in what act—Jake himself caught between zeal in his craft on the one hand and a temptation to idealize on the other. Neither tendency came off well.

"Picnic," he muttered, "benefit," pushing the pages back in vexation, "Founders Day Festival is what they call it. Can't hardly see the nose in front a your face." He stopped at a full-page picture, male, seated, three-piece suit nicely fitted to a long aristocratic body. "That's the one," he said, and gently rolled the cold stub between thumb and fingertips. Here was a drawing of an altogether different kind, a tribute to authority in repose, relaxed manliness in the crossed legs, wisdom's equanimity in an open volume steadied over the knee by one fine hand while from the other hung a pair of wire-rimmed spectacles, functional, ageless, made for eyes skilled, like these calm eyes, in coming to rest on some receptive object—the viewer, perhaps, of this very likeness—eyes that shattered all pretense, predicted that any disguise of secret hurts or shames would lift like gossamer before their steady, deep-seeing, accepting gaze. Behind him, the vista of flowering shrubs through the open casement lengthened away to water and horizon.

"Dr. Randall Cane III, At Home" was neatly printed along the bottom. "'Case you ain't met the gennelman yet," Jake offered with an uncharacteristic regard for the social forms. "Did him all from memory, right up here," he said, with the stub of the cigar to his right temple. This was an art eager to please, patient as a mirror to catch what it can of the man most fully, most naturally, himself. Jake seemed inclined to linger over it, perhaps to compare it detail by detail against the image he carried about in his head, gratified by the rightness of the correspondence.

I'd seen enough of his transfigured alter ego and reached in through the window for the big crowbar. But he wasn't done with me yet.

"Now this one right here," he turned down a page at the front and set the pad beside me on a joist like an easel, "this one's what I call a genuwine portrait. Took me a good long while, bein' around the Doctor's place so much an' what not, on a li'l job I did for him a while back." It was a pastel and, while showing up his lack of expertise in the medium, succeeded in portraying a woman strikingly beautiful by any standards—*in medias res* like the others, but as if stilled at her ritual by the stillness of the objects surrounding her, the cane-bottom Sheraton love seat strewn with cushions, the corner of a figured rug under her foot, the black lacquered Chinese teapoy at her right knee holding a bullet-shaped silver pot and creamer beside a French *trembleuse* cup, an Elizabethan armorial tapestry stretched on a back wall.

"She didn't pose for me or nothin'"—hands at rest in her lap, right palm cupped like a full-blown tulip—"just caught her settin' the way she always does for an hour or so ever' day havin' her tea, sometimes with visitors, sometimes by herse'f."

A Southern type much admired when I was growing up, she had the pale creamy complexion, the eyes of amber green, the dark, nearly black glossy hair, posture firmly erect but nothing if not graceful (as it were, nature's grace—"genies"), definitely a Scarlett O'Hara type, yet lacking that seductive vivacity. Such aloofness in one of lesser surroundings might have been taken for sullen withdrawal; in Mrs. Randall Cane III, it signalled distance as of royalty, her identity emerging not, as was usual in Jake's work, from that relentless pursuit of the telling feature, but delineated and composed as a function of the setting itself.

Not that he seemed the slightest bit aware of what he had done, how he had managed to render the feminine as *mise-en-scène*. By calling this a portrait, he meant only to emphasize how slow it had been, how painstaking to lavish such attention on the minutiae, almost touching to the extent that it betrayed the strain on his craft. The forms, textures, colors of the space she occupied drew the eye initially away from the face, led it back there only by way of a great emerald suspended in the fine hollow of her neck, brilliantly inanimate as the green eyes.

And why, if the woman amounted to nothing other than her setting (and this says Harding, pleased me well enough), why, then, should she herself be so distasteful?

"Can't hardly unnerstand it myse'f," Jake said, after a look back at his drawing of me, "First day you come into town I thought for a minute you was Miz Cane here."

"All tallish, dark-haired women look alike in ordinary dress," I said carelessly as I popped loose one end of a plank he was standing on. "When you've seen one you've seen them all."

"Like you say, ma'am, musta been the way you was fixed up that day...my, my, how time flies, don't it?" Just as if he'd glimpsed, in the display of his digital wrist watch extended over Miz Cane at tea, an opportune moment to slip away, he clapped the pages down over her with a great air of finality.

"You skipped one. There, I said, lifting the cover off the pad lightly with the tip of my instrument. He's set me up for this, and I know it but am past caring. Not phobic but "cuntra," I remind myself. "Who has the honor of being on the front page?"

I'd just about concluded that the sketches were arranged in an order reflecting the degree of contempt he had for his subjects; starting at the back, most contempt. That would account for why he'd placed me not with the Hernando's habituées but on a clean page farther in, among the workmen, close to but not quite up with Tony Krasner. As you moved forward, those less and less deserving of contempt would be featured, culminating in Dr. and Mrs. Cane, both, in their different ways, entirely free of intended derogation. Jake's hierarchy was bound to open yet another telling perspective to an interloper like me.

His response disconfirmed my hypothesis. "Nothin' much...ole colored woman."

African witch, he should have said, as dangerous as she was marginal—for an instant only, I drew a blank.

"Looks pretty outlandish to me."

"You mean you ain't seen her sneakin' down the alley and all over your yard? I know for a fack she hangs around this place alla time, acks like it's hers—sure you ain't seen her?"

"Excuse me," I said putting my crowbar back to work on the board his feet were still occupying.

Absently, he tweaked one end of his mustache, thrown off by my indifference which rather neatly mimicked a ploy of his own. "Lives right down on the next block in one of them beat-up ole shacks. Nigras call her Miss Mary Louise."

"Mary Louise what?"

"Used to teach in the colored school when we still had one. Never did know how to make a fittin' place for herse'f an' stay put."

As a corrective to all such failures, he secured the sketch-pad under one arm and embraced the gravity of his subject. "Fack is, I been thinkin' about bringin' up her problem to my friend Dr. Cane. He might be able to put her up in one of them state asylums where they can look after her, you know, way she keeps carryin' on, makin' a public nuisance of herse'f, and endangerin' the public welfare with all that witch stuff."

"You've got a point there"—and I whacked away at a head-less nail, "superstition *is* dangerous."

"Took the words right outta my mouth ma'am. Woman's a clear and present danger to the community, like they say—calls herse'f Bernard."

"Excuse me again."

He had to take another step back. "Heck, you can see her most ever' day trampin' around down by the Bay an' all over this here Quarter, trespassin' on folkses proppity like I said...why she doctors the colored with all 'at mess she cooks up from berries an' greens an' who knows what. Them people are just as superstitious, like you say, and just as backward as they was a hunnerd years ago when my granddaddy, rest his soul, was alive. Worked three or four hunnerd head in his day over in Leon County, on the old Howard plantation."

My crowbar had forced him on to the hunks of concrete, and he looked down at them as if they'd been lately placed there by his care. "Way I see it, they shouldn't never have been allowed to step outta their natchral place, that's my philosophy, an ole one an' a good 'un too. Even them Evanses knew their place back in that generation...them sure was the days, am I right?"

"Wouldn't know," I said, "but barring the prospect of nuclear disaster or environmental collapse, and judging from my own experience, immediate and otherwise, I'd say they were not significantly better or worse than our own." This was superfluous and smacked of Jake's own harangues. I really put myself into my work then, straining the crowbar hard against a rusty spike which slid out with an ugly, agonized creak.

Jake shifted his weight to his lower foot, edging on down. "My, my, my...wherever did a lady with your class, an' edjicated too, learn to hannel tools like 'at?" He was reaching the end of his repertoire, falling back on old strategems—and here it was three o'clock already, time flying, he said. "Ought to buy yourse'f one of these here digital wrist watches, modern woman like you. Tells you ever'thing you wanna know, from the date right on down to the second, ticks 'em off one by one before your eyes...but I reckon you would have held up real good in them ole pioneerin' days, too, strong as you are," picking his way nervously over my broken hunks down to the walk, all smiles.

Now, it flashed through my mind, he'll get really nasty.

"Vay-garies...," he mumbled, as if he were already attending to more important business elsewhere, "that's the word, ain't it?" And he strolled off without further ado, all of us hoisted in readiness under his armpit, his whole collection of blunderers, suspects, victims, jackasses, spooks, idols—the useless and the fashionable. Dr. Cane, eminent psychiatrist who sees and understands all. Miz Cane who fills her rightful place with taste and tact—and, on the evidence, does not read; has no need to. Miss Mary Louise, the enemy who endangers the order of things. Me.

xxx

When Krasner arrived on the appointed day, Ware's shit was on its way out thanks partly to Martin Kingston; and on the guarantee that Ware would not be back, and after only a little bickering, he climbed up on the roof of the Boullet House and proceeded, more or less steadily, to make a very large mess of his own.

xxxi

And just as the Greek man and his terrier came padding along on their pre-vespertine outing, Dr. Cane's Austen-Healey sports car, well-groomed as a prize stallion, doubtless a classic, pulled smartly through the carriage gates and stopped short of the ruts made by Ware's dumptruck in the last rain. The British racing green of its deeply polished flanks darkened with the umbral play of oak leaves overhanging it and its two riders, in their cool tennis whites, stepped out.

If I'd been a fashionably attired guest at his table, Randall Cane could not have greeted me more warmly. So good to see the historic Boullet House under restoration, and in such capable hands.

We made the tour, Aimée fluttering ahead golden-haired, golden-limbed, he giving an intent ear to my plans—a sympathetic caution here, an appreciative inquiry there. No unwanted expertise flaunting itself in the petty postures of approval or disapproval (and, he, a member of the all-powerful Preservation Board). No mere chitchat taking up your time either, but the conversation of someone entering into a thing with you entirely without presumption, not appropriating what is yours but surveying it as *you* would, for its own sake—in short: the quality of his attention, the easy absorption in the concern of the moment, had an effect both solacing and satisfying.

And, yes, he was a distinguished-looking man. Tall, though not overbearing, as slender of limb as a man in his best years habituated to regular disciplined activity. Frank of expression, clear of eye—oh yes. Clean ascetic features, greying but ample hair; sixtyish, a man about Shibbles' age, or Jake's. Old enough to be Grooley Connor's father.

Poor Greeley did suffer in the comparison. He was, in all kindness, callow beside this model of manly deportment in whom those characteristics marking off members of the "old families" seemed to acquire some kind of immediate validity. Where Greeley assumed a finicky self-importance derived from his MIT degree and his stint in the public sector, Randall Cane occupied his worldly place as though only the grace flowing from generations of good breeding could certify so privileged a status. He wholly convinced you of it, in the moment. Where the technician could speak only from the biases of his training, the doctor (not unlike his counterparts in the plays of Ibsen or Chekhov) expressed the liberal breadth of the educated man. Greeley— evasive, indirect—was always stalking some ulterior prey, a deal, an extension of his résumé, a reputation; Randall Cane radiated candor, trust, understanding—all, in fact, as Jake's drawing had so faithfully foretold: boundless understanding, intellect, a reassuring scope of experience in the world, that seemingly unconditional acceptance of, yes, human vagaries; if he towered above the foibles he looked on so compassionately, it was because he himself was wholly certain where he stood—Harding can wax ardent on Dr. Cane's qualities once she gets going, and the line between ardor and irony can blur. It is, she says, only in grasping the power of their appeal that one can begin to appreciate the dangers of such men.

Before leaving, he tendered his help in any way I might require, even to suggesting that his carpenter, Bill Simmons, might take off a few days to help with my finish work when the time came—when he said "my carpenter," one heard the phrase as such only in its afterglow. For this offer I expressed my gratitude, sincerely (and never more so than later on, in August, when Bill did help me out a couple of mornings, near the very end).

"Now you see why I'm so crazy about Uncle Randy," whispered Aimée, having insinuated a golden arm behind my elbow as we neared the car.

One had to agree. Only a churl would do otherwise and, says Harding, I can be accused of many things, and am, but churlishness seems not to be one of them—though, granted, it may no longer even count as a viable category.

Dr. Cane laid a protective hand briefly on the other golden arm linked with his own. What a display for Jake's pencil, the three of us there, fraternizing. "My wife and I have practically adopted Aimée since her father passed away," he said, adding with a twinkle in his fine eyes, "She's a wonderful role model for our daughter Julia, home from Radcliffe for the summer." All the best with my tremendous venture, delighted to have met Dr. Dumot at last. The hand that clasped mine conferred trust upon our civilities, upon time, upon touch itself. Even a minimal contact with Dr. Cane carries an assurance that he moves in a sphere not to be shaken.

"Oh don't be so stuffy, Randy—her name's Elizabeth, and you're certainly old enough and eminent enough to call her that," was Aimée's teasing salvo. He smiled inquisitively, I nodding assent. "Good-bye, then, Elizabeth."

Amid waves, the sleek green sports car reared and straightened, and sped out of my sight. Here we had been wandering through Frances Boullet's old home, talking about bringing it all back, and not the remotest allusion to her had passed his lips, silence confirming that he had chosen to sever all public ties between himself and the elderly relative whom he must have known in his youth. Time brings death; but Dr. Cane's legacy, from his father, Randall Jr., and Judge Randall before him, is the power to confer non-existence pure and simple. And this is what the supple hand had assured me of in its brief hold on mine.

xxxii

Mind you, she says, wasting time with contractors day in day out was bad enough, the haggling, posturing, positioning, but on top of that there was the constant coming and going of one kind or another, the just passing by, the visiting, dropping in to see, standing around to stare, time sapped by the living histories of the local Jakes—and, now, time relaxed in the easy, warm, everyday balm of civilized good taste. I had come to the point where I wanted none of it, could afford the latter no more than the rest, till my project could go forward, if ever, without the whole of my energies turned to it ("foe-teen, fifteen, sometimes *sixteen* hours a day," as I'd been reminded).

Wandering through the house in that dimming afternoon, crunching along trails of its fragmented insides, retracing alone the tour we had made together (as if, she says, to gather the psychical traces of it in myself), I crossed to the ell, finally, old Wentworth's room, looking for nothing but what seclusion the house might yet afford in its hindmost quarters. There, she leaned against the one wall still intact, unable, in the twilight, to recall or project which of the multiplicity of things to be done was to have come next, energies drained and frittered, my presence, she says, reduced to a receptor working an incessant probe of stimuli, specialized to prick away from inside, pattern fractures chink by chink...almost spiritual, this...so spiritual that the body in its slow solipsistic innocence knows its shattered condition too late. Too late to whisper: enough now. Enough. I shall not, must not, go to pieces. Too late, she means, this suspicion of the body's claim to ignorance of its limitations. I imagine her backing away from the wall, reaching out her hand to it for balance against all inclination to relax into the shattering, feel herself falling, floating, falling, pulled smoothly, weightlessly apart.

She was to hold the line after that, firmly refusing all, even kind, brief, sociable episodes, so that, shortly and predictably, she was left quite alone to the harsh necessities of demolition's aftermath while Krasner's roof gradually closed them in.

xxxiii

With the aid of his chronometer, Jake was set to compute his scrutiny of my life at the Boullet House in exact cycles of toil, so many daily hours and fractions of: scraping, sweeping, dredging, hauling things out of the way, in between wheeling and dealing (and wheedling and making do). Had I been working by the hour, at somebody else's expense, such a tally would have been a great aid; as things were, it could serve only to highlight the inadequacy of any likely compensation to me, then or later. The days of summer slid over each other flat as cards, back over back. I could no more slow their recession, or—which came to the same thing—speed the progress of this job or that, than I could control the weather.

The utility of a calendar is to help keep track of time passing; I had only to situate myself in my round to mark a calendar. When the weight of everything yet again left unfinished or bungled beyond remedy pressed like lead on my prospects and my routine, it had to be Saturn's day; and the sense of everything lightening up gratuitously like hope reawakened was Sunday, a bright desert of sorts, when nobody as a rule stopped by. Monday was sure to come crashing in like a lunatic all right, everybody more than likely showing up at once to prove their reliability or collect payment, blustering and bumping elbows. Or else, one of them might be mooning about, waiting, nothing at all materializing for hours while vacancy stared from the drive and equipment stayed idle, monumentally in the way. Monday morning catatonia—out to lunch, and then some. Already over the rim of dreaming you could hear the gods of war on the march—Tuesday, Wednesday approaching with a vengeance; gods of mutilation, old shape-shifters not to be trusted, above all, to be appeased. Tuesday, obscure and therefore terrible. Would they make good yesterday's failed promise to deliver? Would there be strategems to cut corners? extra charges? Wednesday, the mercurial middle of the week shifting the limits of what might or might not, after all, get accomplished before the weekend, day of decisions about where to accommodate, where to force the issue. But, it being Woden's day, god of runes, god of the hanged, of riddles, mystification, you may of course be way off the mark in your reckoning. As for Thursday, you could always count on blows and rumblings of one kind or another to make it live up to its name, what with the prod of the weekend in the offing. And the day of the goddess tended to be noteworthy mainly for the poignant absence of all she was said, once upon a time, to lavish on the earth: pleasure, peace, plenty. She could snatch the dead out of battle as well as anybody, remember, and lead them home. Friday the workmen quit early and anything half-shapen or misshapen stayed that way till the next week—or until I myself could get to it.

Here's a curious fact, says Harding: one's capacity for being astonished by the ways of the world does not diminish with experience. Though I was past endurance by then, I was not past astonishment—at Aubrey Evans, for instance, stopping by to confer with Krasner, flinging his cigarette butt on the clean-swept threshold and grinding it viciously underfoot, fuming about "the old man's" faults of character. That's Tom Evans, master plumber, salt of the earth. Was there no end to their slovenliness? Their stomping, spitting, trashing, all in the line of work? The roar of their pickups gouging up the soft sand of my drive? Their ever-present junk food wrappers dumped all over my floors, stairs, shrubbery—whatever space any one of them could appropriate for his refuse of the moment?

It's knowledge not ignorance that opens the mind to astonishment; perfect ignorance, it stands to reason, would practically insure a life as placid and unsurprising as a blue June sky. The more I know, the vaster my capacity for astonishment grows. The ways of the world neither jade nor sate it; they hollow it out, widen and deepen it until, finally, I suppose it may be of astonishment that one dies—the self in its capaciousness stretched so luminously thin at last it just pops. *Finis*.

At the sodden boundary of my skin, time and temperature meeting fed on each other and in their symbiosis grew each day, hot and long. The brief first cool of morning swelled with the hours into sultry midday, and swelter distended the afternoons well past the approach of dark—time, heat, always the crowding circumference of my drudgery. Night expelled its sultriness in a single unmeasured breath while I slept—and dreamed. And what dreams, what processions of limbless, headless, flayed pulsations of flesh, lumps shrunken beyond recognition, hard and scaly to the touch, resembling self-transformations in the course of my daily activities and, in turn, imprinting on waking thought the riddle language of my dream-life: pig's head/flayed mare/crab-claw/I am baked, I am raw, I am relished/carried cunt-canyoned/my mother flung me far from her to sea/adrift I simmer in the din/butchered/bartered/bought/I am cow's lip, cattooth, ear of pachyderm/serve me skewed/tended/tendered/I am rare sucked cerebrum/razor-licked bone/I am live meat listening/watch the dead eat the living and the living come sated on the dead/dare to say what I am/. Monday, Tuesday, Wednesday, on and back again relentlessly to Monday, and around again like the old serpent said to ring the human habitat.

In short, it seemed as though the long supplanted pantheon hypostasized in the rubble of those diurnal names still has power to turn human affairs this way and that. Is it any wonder that toil unabated takes on this mythic momentum—when you don't see it as sheer trivia, that is? Or perhaps precisely because you do.

xxxiv

A Tuesday: watching me test a kind of dull reddish paint I planned to use, Tom Evans, relaxing inhibition in view of our common historic motives, described it with a wink as "titty color." To which I reparteed, coolly, that as a matter of fact nature was not an important source of color schemes on the old Gulf Coast, going by my research.

Click, click, went the blue and red ballpoint pen inscribed

with the firm's name, as he countered with some facts of his own, to wit: recent increases in the cost of plumbing supplies; he'd been meaning to tell me, maybe more on the way. Round dark figures lined up as proof on the little pad resting in his fleshy palm. We'd have to wait and see—wait and see. The placid voice promised to take care of you.

Or then again, maybe it was Wednesday. Woden's day: day of wrath. "Careful, careful," his slightest movement gave warning, "Cross me and you release depths beyond your control in every way."

Tom Evans, salt of the earth, a man to be trifled with strictly on his own terms.

XXXV

"Just gimme a call, shuga, we'll be there the minute you're ready for us." This he assured me of one of those grim afternoons early on, way back when we'd struck our deal.

No sooner have I got the house ready for plumbing, however—everything hauled out, finally, even the back yard clean and clear—and I give him that call. "Soon's I can get to it, li'l lady, what's the rush?" He agreed, in the end, to make it "Monday," day of all promises that turn out to be arrant lies.

About ten days and as many phonecalls later: the cedar roof is neatly up over the stripped house—Krasner getting the hell out as per contract—July is moving right along, and enter Aubrey Evans, unaccompanied, at about nine. "T. Evans & Son, Master Plumber, *we see to all your plumbing needs*," runs the professionally exact white lettering over the shiny blue doors of their trucks. On the snowy ground of the son's tee shirt the message blazed again in red. Effective advertising requires reduplication of lies. Judging by the slouch, furthermore, I see it is going to be a struggle of heroic proportions to get him fired up.

"I expected you yesterday—'for sure.' What happened?" Never mind that it had been a lost day all around, me licking my wounds after my weekend ordeal of cleaning out the attic in temperatures over a hundred. A shattered day, a slow groping to orient myself in a world again.

"My, my my....," Aubrey crooned in honeyed evasion as he thumped the newly floored porch, which I'd put down the week before while waiting for their promise to materialize. "I'm crazy about that baby pink color."

"It's not." Nerves, too, still raw. Ware's shaky ladder remnant under me, which he has discarded for good at the Boullet House, doesn't make things any better.

"Hunh?"

"If you really look," I say without taking my eyes from my brushwork, "it's three slightly different shades of a sort of dusky salmon. This part right here's the darkest, see? Hardly more than a shadow of this other."

"Sho nuff? How'd you happen to think that up?"

"Didn't. Found little patches of it scraping the frames. Original coat, most likely."

Aubrey's damp chin scratches past my extended elbow—he has a knack for timing such intimacies, a part of his attention always alert to opportunity. "Damned if I can see them three shades! What's the point?"

"Step back—there." A single shade of any strong accent color, I explain, gives a garish, flat look. But this elicits only a skeptical "unh-hunh," as he lounges against the banister to pick at oversized teeth with a stalk.

"What's the rest of it gonna be? Pink blush, I bet—kind of like a baby's bottom, hunh?" He's genuinely struggling with the subtleties and plainly shocked to hear that the weatherboards will be the palest of creamy applegreens and the shutters a dull greyish bronze.

"Like a rich dry mud." My stab at graphic communication. Greeley Connor, granting the Preservation Board's approval, had noted with rude surprise that my scheme was "quite appropriate, a bit unusual but authentic." And my imp of the perverse had replied, "It isn't really, but pretends to be successfully enough."

"Tell you the truth, that there brown mud—well, ever seen what comes out of a sewer line?"

Like father like son, however reluctantly making a marginally obedient living in Daddy's business at thirty-some-odd and hating his well-greased guts for it. His own too, most likely, and mine—for the moment, Daddy's *fiat* has us tied up here together, just him and me.

"The idea is," I say, circumventing his excremental imagination, "to get just the right shade of everything. You want it to come out being more the old house than the old house was, if anything—or so much the old house it isn't the old house anymore. Get it?"

I can tell he's losing interest in my aesthetic problem, straddling the doorless threshold, puffing down his stub of cigarette with a peculiar intake of breath like a quick, hard sucking. Maybe he fancies it's something else. Evans & Son make a tricky combination, the father's no doubt long memory for details of insubordination and the son's short attention span, his quick reversals of mood.

"Ole man can really get to you sometimes. Whatever you do, it ain't never right," he complains. "Screw that."

"Too demanding, is he? Everybody says he's the best in the business."

"Shit! 'Scuse my mouth, but shi-it! Who in hell do you think does his dirty work? And that's all it is, honey, take it from me. He's supposed to be here right now, and where in the you-know-where is he? Where is the old so-and-so when you need him?"

Where indeed. Done efficiently, my rough-in plumbing was at most a two-day job. What will it take to get this one going on it?

"You know shuga"—he's gazing off into space and, as if to soothe the pangs of desertion, massages his inscribed chest, hollow over a potbelly of the kind narrowly built, skinny men get when they take to excessive beer drinking—"one good hard rain and that drive out there is gonna look like a swamp. You oughtta get you a load of cee-ment and spread it over the whole mess, right up to your fence. Give you a good hard surface, easy up-keep."

Tired, utterly bruised, I shoved the tattered ladder aside. "You keeping bankers' hours?" I quipped, "it's close to nine-thirty by my watch. Always thought you plumbers like to 'get down to it first'—didn't I see you cruising around in a tee shirt to that effect just last week?"

Slouched in the doorway, lips softly compressing the still unlit cigarette, he's waiting for something. My firm touch has been premature. One way or another, a woman's work always seems to bring her right back up against the synecdoche of the breast—suggestively draped, seductively glossy in the cleavage of the centerfold, bathed in the sepia softness of suckling. A versatile, dependable organ, the breast. Feeding is definitely the operative metaphor here. Chattily, in a non-pressuring way, I explain that I've got the electricians lined up for the next afternoon, and the insulation crew is due Saturday, special off-hours deal (no deal if Evans & Son can't finish their job on time). "The walls are going up next week, that's the plan."

"Ain't got no doors, what'cha gonna do with walls?"

"The doors," I reply in the muted, assured cadences of a lady transmitting the word from her finishing expert, "are ready for delivery any time." This mask of the lady in all her subtle permutations has been the hardest of all for me to cultivate: the very sign he can read as his own potency, the graceful replication of his authority.

"So—" I give it my last shot, "when do you think you'll be through here? What's the schedule?"

That would be for the old man to decide.

There's a great crash in the hall, a few minutes later, of copper piping and vinyl tubing—machinery clanging off to a start with something of the feel of the last train out of the depot. "Water closet, lavatories...," he's disgustedly grumbling over Greeley's blueprints laid out for his inspection on a window ledge. The father, by contrast, has a way with the names of plumbing fixtures that is impossible to render, so lovingly, so possessively does he linger over the syllables: "Here's where we're gonna set your lav-a-dores honey," I can still hear him croon.

"Sure you ain't got too damn many toilets in this place?"

Blueprints sailing to the floor, underfoot; more trips out to his truck, rummaging noisily through supplies. Cartons and armfuls of things dumped on the porch all around me like impetuously offered gifts, the intricacies of his métier, "...pipe wrench, spud wrenches, blades, drill...where in blazes did I put them extra long bits? T-branches, y-branches, reducers, traps, joint compound...almost out of this shit...epoxy, plenty of that, but no solder, great! Ole bastard always carries a lotta that in his truck...ball cocks, gaskets, washers—hell, I don't need all this stuff now. Get it ready, though, just in case...all kinds a nuts and bushin's, clamps and sleeves, adapters...couplin's and nipples—no offense, shug, plumbin' talk is straight talk ain't it? Last but not least, this here's the real nitty- gritty: tube cutter, bender, flarin' tool, flux, flux applicator...That's all of it I reckon. 'Orr-ganize your tools, son,'" and he pretends to hitch up his trousers like a fat man.

All work has its aesthetic, every aesthetic its own toil.

"See what I mean about who does the work in this outfit?" he brags. Then, again, in that puffily altered voice hard to mistake, "'If you don't know how to solder a sweat-joint, boy, you might as well forget this bizness and find yourself a job at Mc Donalds.'"

"Gee, looks complicated."

He tightens his belt a notch to mark an evident beginning, and none too soon; the day is heating up furiously. "Now first thing I'm gonna do for you," he says, "is rip out all your holes for your new feeder lines and your drains and stacks. You were one smart lady to get this place cleaned out like you did. Don't everybody go to all that trouble."

"Makes things easier?" Against the scraped boards framing the open window, door to ceiling, my three shades of dusky salmon were a gaudy smear. The look is commonplace throughout the Quarter: raw dabs of trial color on the hides of eviscerated hulks enduring their clumsy latter-day beautifications, telltale stains of life returning to the wink and jangle of the street. The fact that this particular revenant was mine seemed to entitle me, at that particular moment, shaky and frayed as I was, only to a stake in its gutted shame, its availability to any passerby.

"Easier?" he shot out through the window at me, "why shuga, I can run the whole system right up between your nekked studs—whole thing shouldn't take over two and a half days, three at most if the ole man ever gets his fat you-know-what over here and sends me a decent helper."

Next thing, I was hearing the high-pitched screech of his drill and jigsaw.

xxxvi

In Jake's living history, the firm's senior member is shown inspecting Aubrey's cuts and joints at such close range he might be sniffing at them, while the latter glares brow-beaten accusations at his immaculate progenitor. Thick sandy hair slicked back from his broad face, short-sleeved sportshirt so fresh and white you can imagine it still exuding a faint whiff of Bounce, the extra poundage only seems to enhance his general aura of vigor.

When he finally appeared that morning, he had me on tenterhooks with the casual prediction that the lines would be roughed in "by the end of next week." Teasing, I figured—if that's what it was—like a sleight-of-hand, could show itself to be in the hard practical nature of things if necessary. Careful, careful. He paced around sniffing and commandeering Aubrey for a good quarter of an hour, as in Jake's picture, with me getting into a state meanwhile about our timetable.

"Golly," I said, "I was hoping...well, that we might be able to finish up this part of the job in a couple of days...I've got electricians coming...your son said...any chance, Mr. Evans?" That voice should have made me about three feet tall, on my way to "going out," as Alice says, "like a candle."

More sniffing and commandeering, even lending an expert hand, with lots of groaning and behind-the-back theatrics from Aubrey, trying to get me in on his act. No answer, though, from the old so-and-so, till he was out the door and halfway to his truck.

"Just pullin' your leg shuga," he said in that soft, fatherly way, "we'll do right by you, don't you worry. You take things too serious—how 'bout comin' out to dinner at our place, take a little time off, enjoy yourself for a change? Been tellin' the wife, Leona, all about you."

Not the first time I'd heard this. Leona Evans, you got the idea, was more than ordinarily persistent. She was one person, though, that never made it into Jake's picture book as far as I know.

xxxvii

"Bitch!"

"Giving you trouble?"

Thud on hall floor, Aubrey stomping down the stairs and back up with a new drill bit, steely bright in the socket tightening around it.

"Women! I tell you, they're a big pain in the you-know-where, on the job or off." Cigarette butt hitting floor like spit; two neat new holes, one for the hot the other for the cold water line leading to the sink. "This the right spot?"

"That's it," I say supportively.

Aubrey's cut-out for the toilet to the new powder room downstairs had turned out to be about four feet off the mark; he had my guests relieving themselves smack up against the door-to-be.

"Well, if you want it some other place," he'd yelled, "it's your damn house!"

Damn right. Rip, roar, a second hole through my "X" drawn in the fresh sawdust, the first one now joining my list of small repairs.

Holes in place on the ground floor, we'd moved on upstairs to the other baths.

"I'm tellin' you," said Aubrey, drill taking hungry nips out of a stud, spraying shreds of aromatic old wood to all sides, "you're lucky Daddy didn't send that girl he hired last week. All you'd be hearin' is 'I don't fee-eel good, my stomach hurts.' Says plumbin' upsets her digestion. I can tell you she ain't gonna last a month—why she don't even make as good a helper as you. Between that girl and my ex...know what that bitch did?"

"Your ex-wife?"

"Dumped the little girl on me Friday night, without no notice or howdy-do. Said she was leavin' town to find her some work."

"Hm." Probably slammed the door behind her.

"Just like that." Sawdust blown out of drill socket, drifting over into my eyes. "If it wasn't for me, that child would be in a heap of trouble by now." A coughing fit has him braced against a stud, eyeing me as if to appraise my potential as a successor to his ex.

To get better leverage for chiselling out the damaged floor board I'm replacing, I spin away from him. "How old is your little girl?" I ask.

Just the right spur, it turns out, monologue and handiwork rattling along briskly again, "Adele" this and "Adele" that, eighth birthday coming up, a child of many charms, taking after her daddy thank the Lord—going places too. Got picked to ride down Hernando Avenue in the Mini Miss Bikini float, right after the Pre-teens and just before the Tiny Misses—new category in this year's Founder's Day Parade. His little princess is so excited about riding on a real float, she makes her daddy or her grandpa lift her on the counter top in her brand new bikini— pink blush, he adds with a twinkle—to rehearse her posture, every bit like a grown-up beauty queen.

"Don't get me wrong now. My little girl knows who's boss." No sooner home from her Grandma's, where she spends the day, than she runs straight to the icebox without even being asked and gets him his cold beer. "Takes a father for some things."

"For sure."

He'd tried to gain custody of the girl, but "those damn judges always take the woman's part, like Daddy says, even when she's just this side of bein' a real slut." Man's talk bothering me? Forgets himself when he's busy. "Old man says lawyers ain't nothin' but leeches on decent workin' folks," but he might have to get himself one anyway, now that she's run off and left them both high and dry, which was certainly going to be a hardship for a working man like him.

"What the hell's the bitch good for, you tell me." Aubrey is at his most authoritative when posing unanswerable questions to the universe—everything gliding along as if streamlined, the screech of his saw hard against the floor of the second upstairs bathroom.

"Shit 'n damnation!"

"Now what?"

"Looks like you've got one hell of a double floor up here, must be more'n foot between 'em. Did you know that?"

"That's what makes these old homes so solid, good insulation too."

Groans and execrations amid measuring, sawing, more drilling. "Catch the bottom side later on."

"Good idea." I snatch up the thread of little Adele, "It's not easy to bring up children, I know—brought up two myself."

This autobiographical detail (whose consequences for his future treatment of me will, I hope, prove favorable) revives volubility with the presumption of shared concerns, mutual understanding, and he throws himself into his task again like one driven to avoid punishment.

"I bet you'd love to know," he says, "how I keep my little princess in line."

I say I'd certainly be interested to hear about it.

Tools get shoved aside all of a sudden—to my consternation—cigarette balanced on the edge of a board. "That child," slapping the sawdust off his clothes, top to bottom, "that child understands her Daddy one hundred percent. I taught her. When she gets outta hand, all I have to do is stand in front of her just like this." In his straddling stance, a yard or so in front of me sitting down on the floor, he looms as he might over little Adele, though Aubrey Evans is not a big man, hardly an inch or so taller than me.

"I look her straight in the eyes," he explains, "and I don't say one word, like this," fixing his own cats' eyes penetratingly on me, lips drawn away from the strangely lupine teeth. "When she starts showin' a little respect for her Daddy, I unbuckle this here belt—like this," legs spread in gendarme fashion, eyes continuing to fix on mine, the thick leather strap at his waist coming undone so slowly it is hard to discern motion in the tautly controlled hands, the belt sliding out through the loops of his waistband, hanging at full length between his knees. A few precise snaps of the wrist, a whiplike snake in the air—

I jumped up, my movement shattering the fixity of his gaze, fetched my bag of square nails, and set to fastening down the piece of flooring I had replaced. Aubrey's face relaxed into a grin. He replaced the belt and jerked it tighter than must have been comfortable, with an ostentatious flourish attesting to his boyish good nature.

"Works, too. She's got so much respect for this here belt I never have to lay a finger on that child. Not a finger, mind you."

Here's yet another expert in the psychology of fear. What would Jake's imagination predict about little Adele—phobic or "cuntra"? And exactly how would his theory accommodate the paternal whip? Swift hammerblows drive down my nails, but the last one goes in askew and splits the dry old wood fashioned so painstakingly for a snug fit.

"That's about it for your holes up here," says Aubrey kicking his tools into a tangled heap in the middle of the upstairs hall. "Next thing, I'm going under the house to lay your sewer lines. It's all dug up, ain't it? But first I'm gonna go get me a nice cool drink. Want to go?"

Sawdust and chips of wood and cigarette butts litter the swept floors. "You go on." No choice now but to rip up my splintered board and start all over. One good thing about the nasty addition I had torn down was that its innards made a practically inexhaustible supply of patching material.

"It's a wonder that housing project over there don't worry you, bein' so close. You ever thought about that, a white woman all alone down here?"

"I'm afraid I'll miss your father if I leave—he said he'd be back."

"Don't hold your breath, baby," laughs the self-confident offspring slapping himself all over to shake off any particles of sawdust still clinging to him. "You don't know the old s.o.b. like I do." And he's off and away with a jagged little tune on his lips formed by the intake and expulsion of smoke from a brand new Winston Light.

psycheme

(Pressed against the glass wall of a well-maintained architecturally significant public building, I squint into the darkness outside dotted here and there with faint candle flames. My arms reach up and my fingernails scratch the glass as if I wish to climb out. A glaring overhead light prevents me from seeing you and Harding seated in the outdoor cafe just in front of and below me. Tree branches darken your table so that I can't even distinguish the candle flame marking it out. I know you're there because I've arranged this meeting, judging it's time to get a real dialogue started, express ourselves. I have also arranged to listen in on and record your conversation without your knowledge, although Harding may suspect. Already I'm incredulous— I can't believe I'm doing this. Appalled at the mistake I'm making, I momentarily step back to consider whether it's yet possible to sneak quietly away. Too late, I'm trapped. I've been seen.)

YOU THE READER: There she stands, in that contorted position. Is this really necessary? I think we might be a great deal more comfortable elsewhere.

HARDING THE NARRATOR: She doesn't bother me in the least, really. Pay no attention to her, she means well.

YOU THE READER: Well, between you and me, whatever desire I might have had to get to know her has...cooled, shall we say. It's *you* I'm interested in.

ME THE AUTHOR: (muttering, since I can't be heard anyway) Am I to blame if you don't like what's going on? Is it my fault if our meetings are not what you expected? Did we sign some kind of a contract? Did I? Did I promise you anything? (The fierce light is giving me a terrible headache and I want to scream, but I shut up and listen—somebody's talking.)

HARDING THE NARRATOR: (slowly and very thoughtfully) Still...still, it's *her* resolve that gives *me* audience, it's she who's hearing me out. Without her, you would never even have heard of me.

YOU THE READER: (sounding both resigned and impatient) It's some kind of a compulsion she has to repeat your story, endlessly maybe, but I do wish she'd get on with it. (An audible sigh follows.)

HARDING THE NARRATOR: (still thoughtful and speaking very gently) A compulsion? I see it more as a way she grooms her experience, as habitually as the natural bristle of toothbrush, then hairbrush, early each morning prepares us for the day. She's telling a story not hers set in a world not hers.

YOU THE READER: That's putting the best face on it...

(I feel I can clearly see, blinded as I am, the admiring smile you bestow on Harding. I have a surge of tenderness for you and speak as softly to you as you to her.)

ME THE AUTHOR: As far as we—you and I—are concerned, I bear you no ill will. In fact, I'm just as sensitive to you as you are...

(I have entirely forgotten for the moment that neither of you can hear me. I consider having a line run out to your table so I can enter in but I don't want to miss what you are saying.)

YOU THE READER:…but (you glance uneasily up at me clawing again at the glass, while Harding regards my behavior as a fact of life she has accepted like night and day—my blindness has become a screen for the moving images of the two of you) let's talk about *you*. How do you feel about all this, our present situation, for instance?

HARDING THE NARRATOR: You could look at it as a social problem.

YOU THE READER: (disgustedly) No kidding—that's about how it feels.

HARDING THE NARRATOR: And who wants social problems, right? But like it or not, they always coil in our collective dreams, collective plans, collective beliefs, all the endless variations on collectives: family, tribe, worker, colleague, church, state, nation, empire, congressing and parliament, the rich and the poor, the literati and the illiterate, unions and management, movements and support groups, friend and foe, Africans, Austrians, Europeans, minorities, the People, capitalists, the University…

YOU THE READER: (blithely interrupting) Gays and Mercedes-Benz lovers, heteros and opera lovers, the starving and cat-feeders, the media, the military, ladies and gentlemen, realists and idealists, nailbiters and vegetarians, Americans and…

(I'm coming up with my more extended list: bats and battering rams, guts, gutters, gutturals and the gutted plus the rotters, rotten, rotted, I-beams and blinders—but I'm cut off)

HARDING THE NARRATOR: (chirping in) …even you and your computer and you and your feelings—you name it and you can hatch a collectivity, something or other that can be regarded as a unit. Whether it's saying your prayers or paying your dues… you get the idea.

YOU THE READER: Covers just about the whole range of our values, right?

HARDING THE NARRATOR: Or reduces them all to one. Think of it as survival, served by the fiction of collectives. What's survival all about if not what groups we join, create, support? What's survival depend on if not access to the right group? Collectives gird you or somebody—or else the fiction's of no use—with work, support, protection, ego-affirmation, comforts, status, love, money, entertainment, whatever helps us in some way through the day, whatever staves off, if nothing more, our destruction.

YOU THE READER: Fictions, you say?

HARDING THE NARRATOR: What else?

YOU THE READER: (smilingly suggesting a contradiction may be afoot) Not exactly benign, these fictions, if that's what they are. Nations bomb each other to rubble, street gangs gun and knife and dismember each other, terrorists mangle the innocent... need I go on?

HARDING THE NARRATOR: All such violence is intent on proving that some one collective or another is *more* than just a fiction, that it's an agency operating at an indisputable level, the level, that is, of material reality—the body.

YOU THE READER: (smiling in disbelief but leading her on like a good interviewer, a good listener) People commit atrocities to prove that one or another of their collectives is no mere fiction?

HARDING THE NARRATOR: Can you think of a better reason? What lays bare the fictionality of your enemy's claim to be a unit, to have survival power, more definitively than the fact that you've managed to tear him to shreds? Dismember him: this will demonstrate that you and yours have a *real* claim to be a unit, precisely because you *do* survive. He and his are mere parts with nothing to hold them together.

YOU THE READER: I see, but it seems to me that you're collapsing a cardinal distinction, between human survival activities and terrorism.

HARDING THE NARRATOR: Not at all. I'm looking at the angle of their connection. No unit, no collective, including the cells that compose your body, survives without its terrorist activities—witness the somatic devastations by which you or I persist right through to the end, the nuclear, chemical, and biological weaponry like fever, muscle spasms, inflammation, runny nose and dry eyes, on and on right to the finish with never a sign of truce.

YOU THE READER: A novel if somewhat morbid view. But aren't you mixing up the collectives we create, like, say, the Republican Party, with material collectives we did not create, like our own bodies? Frankly, you're starting to sound like your friend up there (indicating me with a backward flip of the hand), the author, your former student. Incidentally, have you noticed she no longer looks demented (you glance up at me and away, as if your eyes had been casually detained in passing). Just keeps standing there looking and listening as if she can see us clearly and hear every word we're saying. Makes me feel like she'll break into our conversation any time now. (Revulsion, seemingly, causes you to shiver.) What kind of past do you suppose hatched her? Family life or lack of it?

HARDING THE NARRATOR: Not as unusual as you might think—nor as ordinary either. According to her, like most people when they're growing up only more so, she made enemies from sheer ignorance—again, like most people. She says she couldn't understand how and why she so quickly became an irritant to others, even a threat. I never realized, she once told me, that I kept pointing at the fictionality founding their collectives, and I had no idea, of course, that was like calling them liars. "Gangs" is the word she tends to prefer, probably because the idea of the collective solidified for her in a Bronx ghetto as she was learning English.

YOU THE READER: (uneasily) Look at her, she's nodding and smiling.

HARDING THE NARRATOR: According to her, she readily understood that things like cars, boats, houses, planes, clothes, computers, the usual, were all signs and proofs of a person having access to the right gangs, but something was amiss. Material objects never seemed to her the be-all and end-all of what people were really working for. And then she discovered spirit, or felt it. We're talking about her at an early age now, like between five and twelve years old, when she paid special attention to the spirit of different gangs—all kinds: political, ethnic, religious, from social clubs to lovers. You'll find she has the consummate knowledge of gang-spirit that you can only get from long concentrated study. A specialist. (Harding stops just when she should be starting and gets that deeply thoughtful look. I'm clenching both hands in front of me, urging her on till I see you the reader observing me again, narrowly, or something like that. But she continues as I knew she would, dear Harding.) She has a particular interest in the way gang-spirit won't let you go if it ever lays a claim on you. As long as a gang is a gang moved by its spirit, you're either for or against. Either one with them or an enemy. Try to get out of a gang, unless its founding fiction is so weak it's falling apart, and you're calling for big trouble.

YOU THE READER: (primly, with a yawn) Best not to go along with them in the first place if you're going to want out. But what kind of social life do *you* have?

HARDING THE NARRATOR: *My* social life? Why, I suppose this is a good example of it, being here with you discussing her. I guess figuring out what moves all the sub-gangs composing the human community-gang became second nature for her—and that's how she got so interested in abstractions, not of course in the usual sense but as ways of making real what has no other existence. Abstractions, she once told me—freedom, pride, truth, dignity, above all, love of this, love of that—are something I understand, and I'm not talking about semantics. I mean spirit-talk, she said, passing through your limbs to pull your body into its collective work, into social action. She thinks people make their biggest mistake, blinding them for life, when they're young, and keep on making it either by treating abstractions like empty talk or by latching on to them as if they're plugged into some transcendent source, as if they have nothing to do with our everyday world, our gang-bangs. Once I got a little spirit, she said, and realized what was driving every action we think we have any control over, I developed a healthy fear of abstractions and got to thinking about strategies for coping. Become a weak enemy, not worth dismemberment: that's her advice. Willful weak spirits live a fraction beyond the domination of survival power, she claims, and says life is best when your time is not put into holding on to it.

YOU THE READER: How about...(you stop as if struck by insight)... we can't be comfortable here really...(dark as it is out there I'm sure I'm staring directly at those eyes of yours looking meaningly at me)...no way for us to feel alone together, you and me, know what I mean? What say we move on, get to know each other under more favorable circumstances...probably be good for her to get away from us anyway.

   (I'm shaking my head, gritting my teeth, scratching at the glass again.)

HARDING THE NARRATOR: If you prefer. Would it put you more at ease to know that she's conducting a kind of small-scale experiment using us and herself as subjects? A testing ground for what happens to us without the survival power of our literary gang: I the narrator, you the reader, she the author, can we live together, come and go, each in our own right? In plain English, she wants to see what happens when we stop setting so much store by collectivities, starting with our own, let it fade into a history where once in bygone times we regarded ourselves, quite unthinkingly, as a unit. Suppose we take her at her word, let her scratch at the glass, and go on with what we're doing....

YOU THE READER: Reminds me of a relationship I once got into—not unpleasant, but it didn't do much for either one of us. We both let it go on far too long, seemed easier to let things be, make no fuss. But it went nowhere and finally it just petered out, died a natural death I guess. Wasn't worth the time put into it any way you look at it.

HARDING THE NARRATOR: I suspect she would like that, the death of our gang. Obviously you want out. So why not let it die, be done with the obligation of keeping it alive and well, get liberated from our commitment to each other? I'm ready to move on too.

YOU THE READER: (eagerly springing out of your chair, reaching for her hand, pulling her up half-playfully but decisively) Come on then, I can show you much better places to get acquainted. Music, fun, food, somewhere to dance.

> (I'm screaming, clawing at the glass: Harding, wait, wait. They're glancing back at me, I know they are. I straighten up, tall, proud, and belt out my freedom song:

> > Hail, hail freedom's here
> > The gang's all gone
> > The gang's all gone

> Hail...They're moving off, she with that half-smile and murmuring something in your ear. I strain to hear, missing the first part.)

HARDING THE NARRATOR:...freedom from spirit.

> (That's *my* line. You anxiously tug at her, pull her away into a night on the town, fun and phantasy. She looks back over her shoulder, I change my tune and sing with absolute conviction:

It don't worry me none
It don't worry me
You may say that I ain't free
But it don't worry me

None, hear? Not none. I plaster myself against the glass in full view
stretched out like Kafka's beetle, but you've gone, the two of you out
there alone together.)

xxxviii

It has become with-it to say, in a trendy confrontation with the
mind-body problem, that we are what we eat. I am a mouth on a
food-chain; that's one version. In the great national monotype
revealed at last as The Consumer, we are known by where on the
foodchain we hunt and gather, earn and purchase, and, lastly,
dine.

More telling in the end, as Hamlet observed in the case of
Polonius at supper: we are what eats us. "We fat all creatures
else to fat us, and we fat ourselves for maggots." In my case: for
the whims and trifling coercions of others. For what winks and
grabs at us (in our diaphanous, tattered solitude) from the
street—in the ancient sense, therefore, for trivia. Time was not
mine, and human existence depends on having your space and
time—without these you get as close to experiencing body without mind as is possible.

Trivia was eating me up; it consumed my time. (Ingestion
equals possession; what consumes owns. Corollary: fatting
yourself for trivia equals dispossession.) It wasn't just that the
unpredictability of workmen and contractors made planning
anything at all pointless—what with the coddling, the waiting,
and breaking-off, and jockeying for advantage all day long.
There's more to it than that. Trivialization of your time amounts
to a leeching away of your world as the round of places you
inhabit by virtue of desire, intention, memory, sensibility, gives
way to the pressures of the moment. What was a private room
of your own becomes the marketplace.

Even in sleep I was mapping contingencies. "If this one,
then that...if that one, then some other thing," on and on down

the labyrinthine speedways of circumstance. Time was a centrifugal chimera, perpetually elsewhere—not flux in the old way, impersonal and chartless, gathering all life, all action and being, into itself; merely someone else's. That's how it is in the marketplace: the buyer's when you're selling, or the other way around.

Jake's digital chronometer, infinitely reproducible in the high-tech sweatshops of the latest cheap labor mecca, bore testimony to how little difference time and the passing of it made in the progress of my restoration as the materialization of my intent. A silent palpitation of perfectly regular signals—here now was the ultimate perpetual motion machine tracking the Age of the Consumer. A gadget for all wrists and seasons. Only a precision instrument so mindlessly attuned to the revolutions of the public domain could measure the sheer trivia that appropriated my every thought and prompted my every act.

With the marketplace moving in on me like that, thought and act had, truly, become one. And yes—we are what we do.

xxxix

"You could use a stepladder there, missy," he said, watching me scramble up and down Ware's leftover. "Got a spare one out in my shed, eight footer, nice 'n light, just the thing for a lady. S'pose we take a run out there, see if you can use it."

A "no thank you" was liable to produce the scratchpad again, numbers lining up to my detriment—maybe even having my leg pulled again, or both of them, in earnest this time. Then again, I was in no position to have said anything like "Why don't you drop it off here, or one of your men, when they come in next time?" You don't accept one favor by exacting a second. Miz Cane might, but then she wouldn't be having this problem in the first place. I must clearly demonstrate at all times my castrated position.

Nothing short of riding out to the old homestead would do, to meet Leona, he reminded me encouragingly. One of my own kind, I understood, a paradigm of castration. It was that or accepting, sooner or later, Leona's repeated invitation to dinner, meaning hours of forced conviviality with the Evanses, and the very idea of that made *angst* so real I experienced something like a momentary paralysis—not of the will, just the plain inanition of it in the offing. Imagination can be trained to identify, in advance, those few experiences of life from which absolutely nothing is to be learned after the first go-around.

So I agreed that, yes, it *would* be nice to get away for a bit, "won't take very long, will it?"

"Why it's no piece, shuga, five minutes out there, five back. Do you good." Joviality beamed over the paternal visage once more. "I'll introduce you to my babies, too. You like dogs I bet."

"Oh yes," I said and climbed into the cab of Evans' immaculate pickup. Other people's animals can be a godsend when you're being overloaded with social contact. "Have one myself—for the children, you know."

Some years before, I'd seen a news story about former police dogs gone berserk in a remote village somewhere in West Virginia. They were reported to have set on a group of kindergartners at play; when it was all over, identification could be made only on the basis of clothing stuck to bloody human scraps. The instant I laid eyes on them, Evans' "babies" tore that image fresh out of whatever corner of my memory I'd buried it in, one of those dim crannies full of emaciated children's faces buzzing with flies, or locked in cages from infancy, and reports of solitary octogenarian women raped and beaten to a pulp and stuffed into a closet to die—daily happenings too terrible to acknowledge and go on living as before. No sooner had I set foot on Evans' drive, when what could only be his "babies" lunged at furious speed out from under the covered patio and hurled themselves at the chain link fence enclosing the property, two full-grown Doberman Pinschers with teeth bared, attack machines at his command.

But I'm jumping ahead here, letting myself get distracted down the more dramatic turns of my outing with Tom Evans. Even in narrative form, it's hard to stick to pure trivia once it's privatized.

Fifteen minutes later, then—an eternity it seemed of careening at a cocky pace through the moribund downtown, whizzing out Western Boulevard sizzling in the fumes of midday past the Wentworths' new place (windows already draped with variegated odds and ends), swinging high up in Evans' air-conditioned cab redolent of the master plumber's toilette, down quiet side streets in neigh-

borhoods turning newer and flatter—I was having a phantasmago-
ria of second thoughts about the whole ridiculous expedition. The
idea of accepting favors from Evans & Son didn't sit at all well,
though God knows their plumbing fee should have come with an
entire assortment of ladders (and scratchpads) thrown in *gratis*.

I was curbing impulses to jump out at the next Stop sign
when we angled smartly into the drive of a single-story home on a
big treeless lot at the corner of Laurel Walk and Park Lane. So
smartly, in fact, and so unexpectedly, I went flying across the slick
vinyl seat right up against the master plumber's resilient shoulder.

"Home sweet Home," said he and reached one arm across
me to flip up the latch. It had green and pink striped aluminum
awnings, close-trimmed shrubbery pressing against the foundation, and one of those lawns shorn to approximate indoor-
outdoor carpeting. Nature imitating technology, the new folk
aesthetic. "We keep things nice around here, shuga, you can see
for yourself," he said. "All working families in this neighborhood." In all directions were similar houses on similar lawns,
concrete drives with their clean-washed sedans and pickups
and campers in cozy mobile clusters. Not a soul on foot anywhere, not the whole length of Laurel Walk and Park Lane. Not
even the mockingbird seemed to have made a roost here.

"Down Donner! Down Blitzen!" brought the elegant pair
sharply to heel on trembling haunches, soft red tongues laid
between fangs of snowy white. Enthralled by the master's hand
unlatching the gate, the prattling and cooing as he entered,
theirs was the tensed readiness of perfect dependency, unqualified obedience. He grinned at me over his shoulder with half-
closed eyes that knew why I held back, knew, too, perhaps, how
the pop-culture absurdity of their names would render his mastery, in my eyes, the more absolute. "Good Donner, good
Blitzen," he murmured, "good babies."

I had no objection to waiting in the truck, I said.

"Heck no, honey, come on in and look around!" The dogs'
eyes followed in perfect synchrony the robust arm waving me to
the azaleas on either side of the front door, a gift from the
church ladies to Leona, "real pretty when they're all in bloom,"
he said with a round-eyed benevolence aimed straight at the
heart. The toothy muzzles at my calves were less terrible than

that look which told of his power to protect or to withhold protection, as he pleased, and to prattle on however long or much he pleased about the wrought iron umbrella stand Leona had redeemed with green stamps (to keep visitors from dribbling water all over her new carpeting), and about the redwood picnic table under the covered patio with its overhead bug lights (where the family ate supper on coolish nights when you could do without the air-conditioning), and the row of oversized plastic bowls alongside the table—"where my babies eat theirs"—and the coil of hose he washed them down with once a week.

The low cinderblock structure behind the patio, a sort of miniature of the homestead itself, with its own shower and toilet and the master plumber's supplies was the new doghouse. "Where I keep the little stepladder, honey."

The dogs sat back beatifically still, open-mouthed sentinels of his desire that the outside be a mere preliminary to what waited behind colonial door and venetian blind, a preface to linger over so that the initiate might be all the more prepared for what lay within. I threatened to break off the ceremony by eyeing the shed with undisguised eagerness.

"Now watch this!" In Evans' fingers a ratty rubber toy wheezed like an emphysemic old man, and the performing duo were on all fours cocking tiny angular ears. Up whirled the toy in a lofty arc over a sudden play of water, a leaping and whirring of droplets five or six feet high over the cropped stretch of lawn before us, a fine drizzle dancing with all the colors of the rainbow. The whole thing was so unexpected I grasped only belatedly that I was witnessing an elaborate sprinkler system with which Donner and Blitzen showed every sign of being very much at home, chasing each other through the iridescent spectacle, cavorting wildly on the wet grass with the omnipotence of children who take all that comes to pass as theirs by the *fiat* of desire alone.

"Cute, ain't they?"

Up and forward, their overbred heads tracked the motion of the toy flung from Evans' hand, bodies breaking into a sleek, high-speed race to retrieve it. A snap of the fingers brought them to heel, statuesque, precise, shreds of toy laid between slender forepaws. "Good boys," Evans crooned, "good babies," patting each perfunctorily on the nose.

And as if the brush with his hand conveyed some secret command to them, the dogs resumed their tense sniffing of my parts, Evans fingering his ample key chain in proprietary languor. "Look up, honey." Those two giant spots under the roofline were installed, he explained, to discourage troublemakers.

"In this safe-looking neighborhood?"

"Coupla months ago one of 'em forced a white girl—just pull the door shut behind you, shuga—we got 'im though." Ever since, Leona had been carrying a little snub-nosed pistol in her purse,.38 Colt Cobra Special, just in case, indoors and out. He'd taught her to use it.

"You got who?" Outside, muffled squeals of frustration; inside, it was damply cool behind drawn blinds under fiberglass drapes, a surprising diffusion of pink light revealing a hall and, just beside me, his plump well-groomed hand cupping the noiseless switch.

"Why the colored boy, darlin'—this way, shuga. The fucker that tried to force himself on her. You can't depend on the law, ain't no justice in the law. Never has been."

For an instant only, the bright kitchen, spotless from its no-wax vinyl floor to its color-coordinated formica countertops framing a gigantic stainless steel double sink, promised asylum.

"Where's Mrs. Evans?" I said. Even her woman's spirit which, I had thought, might reside here in this glossy, ordered laboratory of nurturance, was nowhere in evidence, no coffee cup left standing out unwashed, no apron or old cardigan drooped over the back of a chair.

"Must have gone shopping with the little girl. Car's gone." Only my surprise at the two "babies" could have made me overlook a detail like that; now they were whining and scratching at the door to be let in. "Don't do to spoil 'em too much."

He swung open one of the color-coordinated refrigerator doors and withdrew a family-sized bottle of cherry soda. "Care for a drink? We got Co-Colas too." With a low sigh when I declined, he scooped up a handful of limpid ice cubes from the automatic icemaker, clinked them one by one in a fat-bellied plastic tumbler, poured himself a drink and downed it in one long draught, watching me over the rim of his glass.

I wandered over to the stainless steel sink weighing my

chances against his guard dogs—not seriously, of course, but I have always been one for entertaining what TV anchormen and Defense Department spokesmen and other experts in risk-management call "worst-case scenarios," on the general principle that it's essential, in a tight spot, to assess your limits. Know what and where they are. I may be given to desperate impulses, but I'm not one for the grand gesture, preferring, on the whole, to wait things out. (Harding's ex-husband Paul makes light of what he calls her indulgence in endurance, discounting, of course, the fact of limits.)

Evans hooked his thumbs inside the waistband of his trousers as the hips rolled forward flattening his ample stomach more than one might have thought possible, hoisted the low-slung trousers up to his emergent midriff, and rolled his hips back again so that his stomach spilled slowly over the waist-band as it slid down into place once more—all this with the smooth continuity of a grotesque but perfectly executed dance movement. I had seen this done as far back as I could remember, but never with such natural skill.

"Try out my spray hose here, shuga, go ahead—finest plumbin' fixture money can buy." The rubber slid out of its socket like a wand materializing from the ends of his fingertips.

"Not on my budget," I said as though we were having a perfectly ordinary business talk on neutral ground, and ambled on out into the hall where pink lights went up, then down, then half-way up again under the urging of his fleshy palm.

"Dimmer switch. Now there's a real money saver, honey. Them utility comp'nies is suckin' people dry—hold it, just there shuga, you'll appreciate this!" A lurid panoply of black and red appeared under a fluorescent ceiling of corrugated plastic: black kidney-shaped tub and toilet, red sink with gilded repoussé water tap and faucets, red and white and black tile on the floor and two-thirds of the way up the walls, fuzzy red-embossed wall-paper above that, monogrammed towels thick as fake fur, and a long-haired shag rug that harmonized with the toilet cover.

I caught myself blinking in the imitation French provincial mirror at my own startled gaudy green eyes. An exhaust fan came on with a powerful rush.

"We don't scrimp on the extras," he said, sure he had

trapped in my reflection the surprise of complicity in his vision of things. Deft fingers ran down the row of make-up lights that framed the mirror. "Had these installed the same time as my out-side spots—that's how we caught sight of the boy slippin' away."

"Didn't I hear a car door slamming?" I said, but Evans' steady gaze into the mirror advised against false hope. His tat-tooed arm reaching around me steered me firmly out into the hall.

"You could use some of them spots in that big old house of yours, not all that safe down there. Why they're so strong we could see her layin' on the ground with her legs spread, honey, all the way from across the street. Me and Aubrey set out after that motherfucker but we lost 'im. Afterwards, some of us went lookin' for him down at the Villas, over your way."

"What about the woman?"

"Wasn't nothin' the matter there that a little soap and water couldn't fix." He was testing my responses, finding out how my limits lay. "You know as well as I do, honey, a girl that really cares about herself wouldn't be walkin' around like that at night, without a dog or nothin', now would she?" Salaciousness modu-lated by the clear-eyed vision of the righteous man in full knowl-edge of the world. "Besides," he pointed out, "she wasn't from around here. In this neighborhood, shuga, we know folks by the church they go to." Above all, a god-fearing family man.

"How could you be sure about her—or him? Or even what color he was?" My outrage was under control, but barely. ("Was I not," Harding says with that quizzical eyebrow that never quite manages to belie the gravity of her words, "a visitor in his home?") Just barely enough to maintain my distance, in his eyes if not my own.

With a smile that I recognized as an expression of his solic-itude for me—the one he wore when he was pulling my leg—he whispered, "Now shuga, ain't that always the way?"

I'd seen more than enough of the Evans homestead to imagine the rest in vivid detail and headed back towards what I thought was the front door.

But the lights had me at a disadvantage. "Go on down," he nodded as I stopped unbalanced over a short flight of steps, "might as well go on out through the basement, straight over to the doghouse, honey."

Again, the sudden miracle of illumination—a purplish glow this time, not so much revealing as suffusing a long, darkly panelled sunken room. Midnight blue fiberglass drapes rigid against the world. Vinyl recliners and plush easy chairs, and a velveteen sofa sectioned around a ponderous coffee table in a style I might, on a lighter occasion, have dubbed Rustic Formica Mediterranean; matching side tables galore and coordinated lamps on bulbously lustrous bases, knickknacks and coasters and giant ashtrays at every conceivable angle of convenience. Turneresque seascapes churning grandly along the walls like primal energy, amid distantly brooding Himalayan peaks and pale Keene-eyed children of both sexes with adoring kittens and puppies of the same physical type.

"Down at the end yonder, honey, in the big cabinet," said Evans with a little wink, "is our refreshment center. Leona calls it that, and little Adele copies her, cute as a button. Care for a sample?"

The Evans family room clamps over you like a dark sack. "You have such a nice home," I lied, realizing in the same moment that now—if ever—he was going to bare his soul to me.

"It's this kind of life we're trying to save, honey, just a decent Christian family life."

An image flashed unbidden before my eyes—my far-away study in Athena, New York, the comforts of its worn beauties peacefully self-contained as it seemed to me then, sheltering the diurnal cycles of morning sun, afternoon, dusk, midnight, the early crepuscular hours when one feels safely alone in the world—so that I was flooded, unexpectedly, with a great longing for my Northeastern exile. Any vision of the good, however deformed, had power—in that moment—to touch me. When it comes right down to it, he said, he doesn't mind those people any more than I do; live and let live. Even tries to give them work when he can. "But you can't have 'em interferin' with our way of life—black, red, commie, queer, or any other kind." That's all he's trying to tell me.

And he tells it to me up very close. My presence here with him, away from others, away from daylight, proves all, even as my accedence to the business of the ladder marks me, beyond all doubt, as one already compromised. My subjection, after all, was entered into voluntarily—a free trade. I get the stepladder, he gets to draw me into his world; that's how things work under the street rule of Trivia. The obscenities uttered in the darkling privacy of his own home—these rites of our intimacy—are the signs of our commerce, our common vision. As Evans himself might put it, "Ain't that always the way?"

The room went pitch dark, blank and dead as only interiors can be that never see daylight. Beside me, his breathing was like a profound sigh.

"Watch your step, shuga—" My foot bumped against something rough and hard as he caught me to the round softness of his belly. "Look out for my conversation piece down there," the rim of his glasses pressed against my temple, the detergent freshness of his shirt mingled with sweat.

I grabbled free of him to the handrail, as he switched on an overhead light.

"There," pointing to an object at my feet, some fifteen inches high, an upturned pair of hairy buttocks spread to reveal two shallow indentations down the center slit, gruesomely distinct in the white light. "Don't it make you wonder how it came to look like...well, like it does?" Low suspirations of excitement, and Donner and Blitzen yipping like a couple of nervous puppies behind the door.

"How ugly," I gasped, so that the hand reaching out to support me froze.

With an awkward formality straining for everyday good-humor he slid the damp rim of his spectacles up the bridge of his nose. "What they call a Siamese coconut, honey," his voice awash in the din of my ears.

Two giant coconut shells, he means, grown together. "Parabiosis," I remember mumbling nonsensically as I drew my feet out of the mire of the carpet and up the landing towards the exit as fast as I could. Keys rattled and the white light faded into hot, lowering afternoon. The dogs nuzzled joyfully against their master with a sidelong gnarring at me, but at his harsh "Lie down!" retreated to their patio in slinks of punishment.

He motioned me to the pickup without a word, swung it around and to the storage building at the back, where, dispensing with any invitation for me to inspect it, he flung the ladder on the bed of the truck. I was not to mistake the new coolness in him for the reserve of one who feels he's been rebuffed in a secret, vulnerable place; our business together had simply taken a no-nonsense turn unmodulated by the play of fatherly kindnesses—no more than I'd asked for, was it? "I'll keep my end of this bargain," said the crash of the ladder, "but don't expect any extras from here on in." Back to the Quarter we sped like that, just as fast as the impatient flow of early rush-hour traffic would allow. Back to the old hulks, the old whores, authentically rehabilitated and revivified, or just old.

As I jumped out of his air-conditioned cab, the torrid afternoon came at me like blows, a rainstorm in the offing. Aubrey stood wringing his tee-shirt out over the porch rail. "It's almost quitting time," he whined, mopping his pink chest.

"Get your shirt back on, boy!" Evans snapped out the window, "we ain't got time for horsin' around." Adele's daddy shambled off, with a backward glance of puzzlement, toward his own truck as Evans roared away down Valencia Street, taking the corner of Cadiz at a reeling shriek, hot-rod style.

This, then, was to be the start of my punishment: work deferred, left off and resumed at his pleasure. Possibly tomorrow, or next week, or some other season entirely.

Nothing to do but march down the alley to the phone booth on the Plaza where I dialed Greeley Connor's number, viewing the façade of his rehabilitated historic office through the open door of the booth. As a matter of policy, I never set foot there dressed in my work clothes; Greeley has such an eye for the little things.

In the breezy style of the smart business woman, a pose so exacting just then my rebellious hand nearly dropped the receiver in mid-conversation, I explained my Evans problem— the part of it having to do with their unexpected departure and the other workmen already lined up. As someone with an interest in her project, could he persuade Evans & Son to be back on the job first thing tomorrow?

He certainly does understand, however...

I wait, breathe in silence for a full five or six seconds. The reek of urine in public telephone booths ripens in hot weather, a trivial phenomenon familiar to all who must resort to them.

As it happens, he is supposed to be getting together with Tom some time soon, on another matter.

I mention a name he approves of thoroughly, my electrician slated for tomorrow afternoon—a man who has only the nicest things to say about Greeley Connor.

Tom has always been especially good about timing, he says, coordinating his work with others, you know. Very dependable in that way—no reason to hold up my electrician, or the insulation crew. He'll look into it.

Certainly is a relief...muddling along quite well otherwise, yes.

I timed the conversation. How does Greeley Connor, I wondered, calculate his fee for slightly under one-thirtieth of an hour? Such a very busy man can't be expected to exercise himself for the sheer love of history, can he? Far less to come to the aid of a lady in distress.

Especially when it was probably she who precipitated her own distress in the first place—isn't that always the way?

xl

Thursday (almost certainly): the single painted window frame has a curiously wounded look in the darkening air, the dusky salmon still a bit sticky to the touch. She leans over the porchrail of the Boullet House and listens for the roll of thunder. It comes first on irregular spasms of lightning like the clatter of barrels down a cobbled lane, some distance away. Soon it rumbles louder, angrier, a bound monster's growl rebounding in the sky from flash to flash, then a continuous crashing like the pandemonium of battle.

When the rain arrives, it smashes down in a tumult as if someone had slit open the bottom of a vast overhead skin— Thor's sack, if he had one. The downpour does not happen everywhere all at once; it plunges down first at one end of the street, then lunges greedily along the hot pavement lashed by lightning until the whole length of the street, as far as can be seen down both ends, falls under its drenching fury. Valencia Street may be about to be washed back into the sea from whence its earliest procurers came.

She rushes down the porch steps to the soggy drive and her

parked car whose front windows gape wide open. Her hand reaches out toward the door—a great sliver of lightning sinks through her and down into the earth in a deafening crack of thunder.

Or, so, for an instant, she imagines. It is as if the mass that is herself has been sundered in a final flash of astonishment. She finds herself stooping to pick up her car keys as somewhere nearby a fire siren screams for passage. Her body still one, drenched and quaking, fingers automatically work the handle that controls the window pane. The glass slides up and closes her in like an uncaused event. Her head sinks back to rest and she watches the great gush of water spill its force on the windshield, blinding her to all else.

psycheme

From high school English, recall Silas Marner and his mysterious fits. He returns to me now as a man transfixed in the spell of pure sexual desire, a victim for whom the spell is gradually broken by years of love, companionship, decency. But that was a traditional story and the saviors of Silas were a simple folk. Who among us is not Silas gone rigid under the power of phallic desire and hopeless in the knowledge of it? And what saves us now from this fetishistic fit if not our voyeuristic penetration of it?

xli

Yes, says Harding, that was definitely a Thursday, about the middle of July.

III

Acts of Violence

i

On a blaze of sunlight a round tray floated toward me at eye level: a fat glass pitcher nearly full of an amber liquid with lemon wedges suspended in it, two tumblers frosty on the outside, loaded up with ice cubes to the rim. August had arrived in a stretch of blistering days, violent rains alternating with skies of unrelenting Aegean blue. My throat was parched.

It had to be desire creating its own fantasy—or lightheadedness from bending over and coming up too fast. A mirage. But the hand that powered the tray down to the end of the sawhorse, beside the shutter I was painting, palely freckled with a tiny tremor ticking through the fingers, looked real enough. A gold signet ring twinkled along the rim of the tray. "Hi neighbor," said—of all people—Doc Shibbles, coming into focus as a synaesthetic sequence of pressed cotton, medicinal soap, and grey hair streaked with the tines of a wide-toothed comb.

"You took me by surprise...the sun...." My own voice like a stranger's, forming raspily in my throat, was surely inaudible.

But he had leaned close, eager to hear me. "Essential to stay cool on a day like this." His was hollow without resonance, distinctly clinical. "Drink plenty of liquids, avoid dehydration. Careful not to over-exert yourself." He poured tea and offered a glass on a cocktail napkin imprinted with tiny floral sprays. I tipped it obligingly (drinking only makes you want more), taking decent sips instead of the greedy gulps my thirst craved. There had been other hot days all the way back to early June, and he'd avoided even the most casual exchange, he and Maria Zamora both—why today?

"Said to Marie when I saw her making tea, 'Here's my chance. I'll just take some of this next door,' I said, 'explain things to the gentleman.' And she fixed me this pitcher and said in the sweet way natural to her, 'Yes indeed, Doctor, this is some very nice refreshment for a hot day like today.'" He swept the empty glass from my hands—dark rivulets streaking down its sides—and held the jug poised as if for a signal about to issue from the silent, sun-drenched back of the Boullet House. A spasm of the ring finger spilled glints of gold down the frosty handle. "Don't let me interrupt," he said, as he eyed the open door.

I was trying to do just that, the bristles of my paintbrush gummy over the bottom slats. It had been the trickiest of all the house colors to mix, a kind of tarnished pewter appearing at some angles murky grey tinged with green, at others a cool darkly drab brown—what in the seventeenth century might have been dubbed "mungy." Deep river mud. Four times I'd gone back to the store to try a drop more of black, or green, or brown, until the salesman was so fed up with the whole fussy business he turned to another customer with the warning that more drops of anything at all would cause the color to "float." A color bordering on unstable, I understood him to mean. The painters, just finishing with the exterior trim and slated to start on the shutters next, would more than likely take Aubrey's scatalogical view of my choice of colors, though they might be too polite—or too much in a hurry—to mention it. For sure, they were not going to appreciate its unstable subtleties, not even with my sample shutter all ready to prove it worked.

"You're not drinking yours," I said, lightly sanding over a rough spot.

My neighbor's gaze passed anxiously over the second glass, cool and undisturbed beside my smeared one, the little soiled napkin under it puffy with moisture. Lips compressed in readiness for speech parted narrowly and froze, deferring—what? I gave my tricky paint a stir, softened the bristles with a splatter of mineral spirits and dipped them into the can with the reassuring precision of workaday gestures. In heat like that, you feel a seepage of elemental matter; inside and out, surface and depth, self and other lose their difference, escape definition.

"That one is for *him*," he returned at last. Perfectly ordinary words whose utterance might decide, perhaps yet alter, all, disseminating their contagion in the brilliant air between us.

"Someone in—in my house?"

He nodded impatiently at the open back door, "There," the roar coming out of it. "He's waiting."

Old Mr. Livingstone was doing my floors. He'd been at it since Monday while painters clambered like gymnasts all over the outside on their scaffolding. His ear-splitting Clark sander that must have weighed a couple of hundred pounds droned all through the house, roaring at my back as I stayed just far enough ahead to give walls and woodwork their final touch-up coat of paint, the spots the workmen had missed in their impatience to be done with the inside. The mysterious "gentleman" for whom tea and who knows what else had been prepared seemed to be none other than my deaf old Mr. Livingstone— who has never heard of Greeley Connor, and vice versa, which is just as well. Mr. Livingstone would fasten his brilliantly blue eyes on me and shake his head in disbelief at the idea that run-down old houses should have attracted so much notice all of a sudden, not to mention capital. "Historic?" He'd snort. "Greed, that's what's behind all this. Borrowed money. Connections."

"He must be made to understand," said my strangely agitated visitor. Raised eyebrows and parted lips approached me in disembodied fatefulness, a mask of skin tacked to bone. "He is my only hope now."

"You know Mr. Livingstone, then?" Promptly at noon every day, he switched the sander off for half an hour, never more, and sat down to his lunch of crackers and white meat tuna or sardines straight from the can, washed down by a whole quart of grapefruit juice. He didn't consort with the other workmen, if any were about, but seemed to welcome my company in piecemeal conversations, laconic stop-and-start affairs, him for a while, then me, on favorite topics like dietary excess, machinery and how nobody could fix things anymore, what computers did to your bank statements and doctors' bills, what a mess Social Security was in and would be if they didn't do something about it soon, and what a shame it was I never would get any when my turn came. The sanders had made him hard of hearing. He'd pushed around generations of them screaming as they licked up old paints and varnish and encrusted grime like day-old chocolate icing. That afternoon he was fine-sanding the downstairs, and the weekend continuing hot and dry I spent on my knees brushing three thin films of satin finish over the smooth planks, with a light surface sanding between coats.

It was one of the few jobs, by then, for which I'd had no acceptable takers. As the house took on the look and air of a viable restoration, it attracted more and more hands willing, even eager, to have a part in it, once the filthy, unrewarding, killing phase of heavy labor was over and a credible end to it all lay in sight. It was as if the previously shunned old wreck had begun to hold out some universally compelling prospect for gain—money, reputation, a spot in local history. Workmen pressed themselves on me right and left, now that my project had started to exude its new odor of success in the offing.

Yet for me the days still stretched from dawn past dusk, more harried, if anything, by the necessity not only to keep it all going in some sort of harmony but also to pick up, clean up, touch up, dream up—in short, make up for whatever others botched or bungled or avoided or missed. Always, to the very end, it seemed purely accidental if any of them showed on the day and hour promised, with the result that I had to be there prepared to start, and perhaps finish, or somehow work around, any job anyone else had agreed to do. No matter how competent, even elegant, their work, none of them considered schedules binding. Never would I become more conscious of how a project—any project of living—shackles whoever under-takes it to the clock, the only seeming escape to join chain gangs rattling time's manacles in the delusions of equality offered by mutual consent. Or else to do nothing—give up projects alto-gether. For once in my life, doing nothing presented itself as a genuinely practical, if not desirable, alternative.

"You've met?" I inquired again of the mask, "you and Mr. Livingstone?"

A flash of the signet ring dismissed my question as vapid irrelevance, quite possibly (strange to say) as pretense of some kind. Eyes peered into my own, bony spatulate fingers drying my used glass with the rumpled napkin till it squeaked. "Marie was away," he said, "things were not what they seemed. She rode the bus to Mobile to see her sister in the hospital and I drove on to Mother's grave, as we always do."

"Saturday?" I asked, consulting Jake's calendar of goings-on in the old Quarter.

"You saw me—there—raking leaves beside the fence where the bricks are. You looked at me when he spoke, and then you went inside to him. Why?"

What to do but go on dipping my brush, stroking it evenly over the sticky slats, smoothing it with a counterstroke? Saving monotony in the face of such dire, such dreamlike portent, the workaday gesture making a difference.

"I did what was expected of me. What else could I do, tell me? I took three of them, to show her." He pointed. "Only three. They were clean, ready for her."

"Oh," I said, working away at my demonstration shutter, "the old slave-made Spanish bricks. They came from the piers under that jack-legged addition I tore down. Where did they get them, I wonder?" About half had gone into building new porch steps out front which were getting more than their share of notice from passersby used to seeing only wooden steps throughout the Quarter. "Take all you want, Doctor, any time, please...."

"No need," he said with an edge of chastisement in his hollow voice. "You above all know whose blood I carry in my veins. And the gentleman...but what is important now is that he must be told. That's the thing. I couldn't find my way to her grave alone because of the old interference, you see."

"It was sweltering hot on Saturday, before the rain started."

"The demon blood was pounding in my ears, such a pounding I could hardly hear, but he spoke distinctly, to make sure." My startled pause goaded him on. "She said she would protect me—like a child herself, and some of the others, too. He came on his white horse the first time the day Father died. I needed her and she would not get up from her bed...all that she left," he nodded at the neat stack of bricks on my side of the fence. "All ashes."

"The fire," I said, astonished at my own leap into this coalescence of fact with the preternatural.

"I was a young man, just beginning, and there was nothing left, nothing, only piers and chimneys." Beyond the fence, Doc

Shibbles' Depression era cottage sprawled in its haphazard domestic ruin. "But it can still be stopped, *if* he can be made to understand."

Maybe the salesman at the paintstore had been right. Why go to all that trouble working up just the right color when there were two or three nice pre-mixed shades so close you could hardly tell the difference? In his opinion. And the advantage was you could always buy more when you needed it.

"This act," he said, taking a deep breath, "it was...a mere technicality.'

"Of course, sir, none of it matters now." I had visions of myself hopping this way and that to stir shutter paint for disgruntled workmen so it wouldn't "float" right there in front of their eyes and make them walk off the job in disgust.

"Nonsense." The mask of skin inclined slightly, distantly, toward me in the manner of one transmitting, to his peril, things of deep consequence. "All of it matters, oh yes. But I tell you it need not happen this time—the bricks were not a factor, not like the others, surely you see that."

"What," I asked hesitantly, "are the other...factors?"

"No, no, no! Listen. As I approached your fence, I noticed her in the alley. I recognized her of course, right off. Poor child. Humming, she was, and wearing her little blue dress—too young for her now in that condition. Shameful. She turned into the street and passed in front of your house, then mine, and just then she looked back over her shoulder and smiled straight at me through the veil of her long blond hair. Like pale cornsilk." The mask invited me to appreciate the significant links—"Do you understand?"—of what may pass, for all the world, as casual and therefore meaningless occurrences. Mere circumstance. But such naiveté, such literal reading, it warned, is doomed, its loss foretold. One may be blind and deaf to the fatal utterance, but only a fool thinks eyes and ears are made for understanding.

"Yes," I managed, "Stephanie Wentworth. I saw her too."

"She lived here before...before you began this."

"She didn't have the boy with her."

"Exactly. She came by herself. I knew without a moment's doubt what she was: bait. *And* the other business too...."

"Which? What other business?"

"To a disinterested passerby it might have appeared that there were three things, for at the very moment, you see, as I was pulling Mother's bricks into my arms through the fence palings, she turned to me, swinging her blond hair to the side, and from the sand pile across the street—there, do you see?—a Negro child was watching. That, if you wish to view it so, was the other 'factor.'" He gave the word a fastidiously scornful emphasis. "But this apparent third—the bricks, you know..." The mask seemed almost sure of me, "a technicality, nothing more. Nothing."

"Wait," I mobilized myself against his certainty and, in that crazy resistance, saw myself already drawn in, "the child in the sand pile, and the Wentworth girl...are you saying those two were somehow implicated in a plot intended—"

"Not *intended*, of course not. No." The voice trembled with disappointment, and something darker. Horror. Shame. Even chosen with the weariest care, it implied, words inevitably betray, always telling the wrong story, bearing false messages, exposing the flesh to every kind of mortification. Words are nothing but the simulacra of desire's chaos titillating our rage for order, closure, definition.

"Of course not," I agreed uncertainly. "How could they be?"

"You're not schooled in the problem of intention I see. The children participated un-witting-ly." He would speak more slowly, more distinctly still, to give me every chance. "They were innocent threads in the web of things, ignorant actors in the momentum of the situation. Now do you follow?"

I stirred my paint some more, watching the dark swirl thin and fade into the dully even pewter I was after.

"You know Greek tragedy I presume? *The Bacchae*? *Oedipus*?" He paused searchingly to assess whether this fresh attempt at final clarity, by suggesting a useful frame of reference, had met with even a glimmer of understanding from one so wholly unschooled in the problem of intention, one who has, inexplicably, turned out to be nothing but a novice, or wickedly, sadistically, pretends to be.

"Yes I do, I—I do, do." It was only the tip of the silent gibberish mounting in me. "Is it the old gentleman sanding my floors you suspect? Mr. Livingstone?"

The mask wagged from side to side in the pangs of hopeless negation. Fool, oh fool—my silent voice, says Harding, projecting his viewpoint—even a half-literate undergraduate knows ancient tragedy doesn't work like that, not a case of an Iago malevolently shaping ends or society throttling the individual spirit. Did somebody put Oedipus up to killing his father and coupling with his mother? Was he manipulated? Of course not. Even the Oracle merely told what was to be: Oedipus being Oedipus would do what Oedipus does, what Oedipus, to *be* Oedipus, must. Character is fate. And the Sphinx's riddle merely mystifies the glaringly self-evident progression of man (and of course woman, too) from his first to his final debility. To wit: Oedipus Swollen-Foot lives to be old Oedipus tapping his way with a stick. So it goes. So it must.

The eyes maintained that he knew me now beyond all doubt: Manticora. Devourer of men's flesh, unfeeling to the old agonies—but hear me you will, once and for all: "Remember, they were all she left, all. And I understood I was to save them for her. *I* stacked them, just like *you*, in the same place except on my side of the fence. Then *he* came, I tell you, years ago when I was a young man. How could I have known then that they must be protected? He made pillars out of them for his lookout; he said my friend Randall Cane told him to, and he stood up there watching me, drawing me, keeping the record on me. *You* tore it down. *Now* do you see? *He* watched *you* stack Mother's bricks. *You* cleaned them and *you* put them in their place again, within my reach, one by one." What you pretend not to grasp even now, the eyes said, is as self-evident as the Sphinx's riddle, the nose on your face, as inescapable as the Oracle's prophecy. Truth is an axiom.

"But who—"

"Who, when, where, how, why—the one who watches and questions me."

"Not on the white horse then?"

Flatly, dispiritedly, he said: "Not his time yet, you should know. The little man who took the bricks. The one who draws our pictures. He always has instructions."

"I see." And of course I did. "Pay no attention to that meddler. He thinks he's an expert on everybody's life. A nuisance."

"Can it be you don't know him?" The question suggested that I might be acting as unwittingly as Stephanie Wentworth.

"As for Mr. Livingstone," I passed over his question despite a shabby sense of spinning out the kind of drivel one can make up only with solid facts, "he was not even here last Saturday, I assure you." I had a firm grip on my paint-stirrer, in pursuit of evidence triumphant and incontrovertible: "Mr. Livingstone never set foot in my house before Sunday afternoon, early, right after church he said, and then only very briefly to discuss the job he would begin next morning. So, he definitely could not have had anything whatever to do with the events you're describing." Q.E.D. and so on, rattled the machinery of solid facts. (Aha, whispered my questioner: was the Oracle present when Oedipus killed Laius? Of course not. Did the old Babbler instigate, witness, the primal incestuous scene from behind an arras? Caught again.)

"He's an elderly man, you know," I added. Incontrovertibly a fact.

"Of course," returned my neighbor, eyes averted, "his age is necessary for his knowledge, but you and I know he never dies."

The sanding machine had stopped; from the back door came an irregular tap-tap. "Nails," Mr. Livingstone warned on his first inspection of the floors at the Boullet House, like one thoroughly conversant with the enemy, "got to watch for 'em, got to sink 'em so's they won't chew up your paper. Yep, that's the biggest nuisance of refinishing these old floors, nails."

Doc Shibbles raised his tray with a fearful look at the house, listening for the code tapped out inside. "I've been watchful," he said in a voice strained to breaking, "I've been careful. But now...the gentleman's words...the words...." The sander sprang into action with a terrific roar. "Can you still doubt me?"

"Whatever it was you heard, sir, and whoever said it, I'm sure no one here means to harm or offend you," I said, balancing the shutter on its side to reach behind the slats.

In their mask, the eyes drifted to check who else might be around, listening. Shame, anguish, despair, the whole vortex of mortal suffering attenuated the voice to a rasp like newspaper scraped on edge over concrete. "He said I would commit—he said I was bound to do it again, because it is time." Setting the tray back down he wiped his forehead and lips with a folded napkin, then resolutely swept it up and made straight for the new back entrance of the Boullet House like a waiter in great demand.

I caught up with him in the hall swirling with fine dust. "...he said I would commit an act...of violence involving—" His voice gave out.

"Yes?"

The rustle in my ear was distinctly "sex." And he bolted away from me into the screaming reaches of the house.

In the front room where Mr. Livingstone guided his machine with singular concentration slowly back and forth the noise was deafening, then faded into a mechanical whine. The lively eyes passed over me and Doc Shibbles to the idle Clark sander as he reached out a gnarled hand huge for its fragile old wrist and tipped the proffered glass to his mouth for a token sip.

"Never drink 'cept with my meals," and he set the glass politely back on its tray.

Doc Shibbles administered quick wipes to glass and pitcher as breath trying to form itself into voice scratched in his throat before the words came out exactly formed, predetermined: "Here, sir, is how the matter stands between us. When you addressed me, you saw what you saw. But the bricks, you must understand, were not for myself. I fully intended to take them to Mother, believe me. But I could not find my way there without Marie...they are still in my car in exactly the same condition, unused, clean as they were. You may look for yourself, sir. This lady is a witness. I rest my case, sir, on this distinction between reality and appearance. The technicality alters all."

Mr. Livingstone, whose sharp profile was turned to Doc Shibbles while both hands rested on the machine as on the shoulders of a child, stared out the window like a farmer absorbed in deducing tomorrow's weather from the blue sky out there. But the flush spreading up his cheeks and into his pendulous earlobes gave him away; he tugged a handkerchief and blew his nose in a loud snort lengthening out to a wheeze of which my distraught neighbor, straining forward, tried to catch the meaning.

A sign, sir, a sign. Mr. Livingstone undid the dustbag attached to his machine to look inside, patted its fat sides to make the dust settle, and closed it back up for the next go around.

One final time Doc Shibbles made the momentous effort at speech, a desperate clarity to hold off the coming dark, ruin, chaos on the march again: "I understood your words perfectly. The thing returns, sir, we know that, you and I. The girl looked at me through the veil of her hair...the Negro child...as if all of it were beginning again. But the bricks are an old matter, between Mother and me. Nothing to do with it at all. Surely you see that I am doing all I can to prevent it this time: *prevenio*, I go before. Hear me, change your words, sir...I am doing all I can this time, all, all...."

Mr. Livingstone rolled his apparatus on its side to tighten the sanding belt, a precaution. The stricken eyes witnessed the old gentleman's detachment with anguished acceptance of what they alone envisaged; fingers cramped along the edge of the tray. When Mr. Livingstone's hand moved, unrelentingly, to the switch, Doc Shibbles, with a quick, submissive bow from the waist, like a schoolboy before the headmaster, rushed off to his fate. Mr. Livingstone touched two fingers to his head, commenting by way of ineluctable diagnosis: "Fella's not right in the head, 'magines things," and let the machine roar into action.

Outdoors, I cleaned my brush, making a poor job of it with the few dribbles of mineral spirits remaining in the jug. Everything around me, no matter what, was constantly running out. Or it was the wrong color. Or it had nylon bristles instead of natural. Or it was white pine instead of number two utility yellow. Or it cost twice as much as last time, or it wasn't where I'd put it— and the extra gallon of mineral spirits wasn't where I'd put it, just that morning. Or it was out front, under the porch—maybe I'd left the top off, and one of them, disposing of his infernal cigarette butt or cigar, would set fire to himself. Or my house. Then Doc Shibbles could haul away every last brick in the place without a qualm, including the ones I'd just built the front steps out of, if he could manage to pull the hardening new mortar apart. No trace of my neighbor out back, not even a cocktail napkin recording his visit, and the afternoon, well past its midpoint, was slack with heat and the burden of all I had left to do.

psycheme

Always something more. Should I host another crop?

There comes a time when exits frame within the frenzy of meaning: language parts its limbs to the Real. Brutal of me, it was, to speak as I did to my mother as she lay dying. "Mother," I said, "don't you want anything at all, don't you want to live?" She looked at me as if, at thirty, I had become the *idiot savant* of our species. "You always want to live—it is to live you want—but there comes a time when you don't have that choice. Wanting counts for nothing now." She closed her eyes but opened them briefly to direct a more kindly focus on me. "I have to deal with what's real," she said. Except for scant indication of her immediate needs she never spoke again during the days of her dying. But all in all, weighing only fifty-four pounds and looking no different from the Auschwitz victim she had barely escaped becoming some forty years earlier, she made, I think, a splendid exit of it.

ii

The sandy soil out there, back of the Boullet House, after all the ripping and hauling, and raking, with its straggle of stubborn grasses and vines, looked more than ever like a neglected old garden plot waiting to be revived—dug up and tended, cooled in growing oases of shade, made green and fertile again. "Zula's garden" was how I'd come to think of it.

For, among predecessors of questionable status having inhabited the house in Frances Boullet's time, "Zula," explains Harding, figured notoriously in local folklore for her demonic powers, derived from mixing foreign tropical plants with ordinary herbs and garden vegetables. Ambiguous, like all such possessors of special powers: terrible and benign. Dark Destroyer and Healer. Lady of green things, of the bitter cup: Kore.

psycheme

Reconstructed from memory and old seminar notes:

"Where do archetypes come from?" She was repeating the student's question.

"You're asking about the creation of a certain kind of idealized image: how a perceptible form, be it person, thing, or event, accumulates feeling and takes on the power and configuration of that feeling, and how, legitimated by perceptible form, that feeling returns to us as an archetype open to intelligent response, interpretation. Archetypes, I suggest, swirl out of the feelings of people in groups, which would make them the imagoes of group feelings believed by the group to be incarnated. Humbled by their power, we modestly disown them. Let belief in the archetype be verified in some person, some human body we can see and touch (and, it must always be one enlivened by a power beyond itself, namely, of course, the power of our own feelings inflated and obscured by coalescence beyond all recognition), then, heil and amen, we can disclaim ourselves as its creative source, this verified archetype who is now, you see, a human body personalized with the turns and convolutions of a group feeling, a human sign of what we had already felt in some fainter, less concrete way was going on, a living, breathing index of a feeling-text we can deny we collaborated to author. Authors are always two-faced, one face demanding creative recognition, the other busy doing away with itself—effacing itself, as we say."

"What's the point?"

"The purpose of archetypes, you mean?"

We all knew the question had been put to her to elicit more of the same. She took the bait.

"Depends—depends on what kind of answer you're looking for. A way people living together have of sharing feelings, of giving them a formal focus, thus informing themselves as a group? A way they can all refer to pools of feeling with a sense of being always understood? Of ritualizing the referential use of language—of having the feeling, the thereness, of meaning? A way groups have of purging individuals of their feelings, and, so, of controlling them for the benefit of the group? The aesthetic satisfaction of perceiving the form of feelings? The residual work of triangular psychodynamics? Or a religious answer: the archetype as our embodiment of a transcendent order? (Or of writing the iconography of that order?) Maybe you're looking for a biological answer: Why do culturally joined members of our species create archetypes? That's like asking me why humankind projects its own feelings into things, why this mythicizing process of making meanings that can interact with other meanings evolved. Why? Because. Because we are what we are, condemned to meaning, producing it, criticizing it, correcting it, on and on *ad nauseam.* Because we *can,* we each get what little power we have by way of our place in the meaning industry. Because we routinely make meaning with as little purpose—or as great a purpose—as an Argus cock displaying his eye spots to an Argus hen. Answer it yourself: start by trying to live without all these projections of feeling into things and the consequent meanings that evolve. Your question is a bit like asking me what the survival value of fictionalizing is. My own experience of this biological pass of ours is that we are a tragic species, flawed by this absurd, comic excess of feeling ritualized in perpetual imagoes of meaning.

Try a little experiment. Breathe the life of a powerful communal feeling into a human form and you get an archetype. Now drain the life out of this cultural creation and you get a stereotype: reproduction marked by nature's impersonal machinery. The archetype serves to reinforce the feelings of people and promote more such constructions, more archetypes, and the behaviors they call up and for; the other, the stereotype, serves either to kill the very thing it reproduces or—playing on that part of our mentality that wonders at mass-production—to make addicts of us, cultural vampires hungering after signs of life in the bloodless. Surrender to the bite of the stereotype."

"Maybe," I remember saying, "the life we hunger after in the stereotype is that of the archetype, the original of an acquired taste."

"Precisely," said Harding. "Only the taste of archetypal blood fully satisfies. That's why stereotypes may appropriately compose the *dramatis personae* of a poetics of alienation—or is this reality in the making?"

"Yes, but what difference does any of it make? Who cares about stereotypes?" There was a unanimity of nods and "yeahs" from the class.

"Precisely again," said Harding and gathered up books and papers, her habitual signal for ending the session, "what's the difference, and who cares?"

iii

"Oh wah?" Jimmy Hurd shouted, loping with unaccustomed energy through the alley gate.

I braced myself against the post and heaved hard. Nothing. It was all that remained of the Wentworths' unsightly chicken wire fence, last of the excrescences once rife over the yard from the back of the house to the old wall. I'd yanked out the others, half-rotted, one at a time, whenever I had a minute to spare. This one reached to my chin, and it was sound. A vine had it in a lush, strangulating hold. I locked both arms around the other side and strained the post towards me. Infinitesimal movement, at best.

Jimmy took his fingers out of his mouth, all ten of them, curled one hand inside the other and reposed them, so folded, against his left thigh. As usual, he was naked except for his khaki cutoffs.

"Oh wah?" he repeated with a bolder emphasis.

"What?" It was anchored deep down, deeper than you'd think any Wentworth would have had the energy to drive it. I wanted the thing out—out of my yard, out of my life.

"A ho goo maw."

I got a spade from under the house, hacked through the stem of the vine, ripped away the mangled pieces and dug in. Under the top layer, the soil was packed dry.

Again: "A ho goo maw." A beatific grin was chiselled into his skewed face. "Dionysus as a Youth Appearing to a Maenad," if we had been a sculptural tableau—late Hellenistic, portraying the corruptions of Nature more tellingly than Nature herself.

"You're going to school tomorrow." I pushed against the post, and I pulled. I groaned, arms, back, soles of shoes braced harder at every try—yes, it was starting to give. I kept on digging as the dirt loosened, arms trembling like Doc Shibbles' little finger curled along its tray, and watched the vine disappear under mounded earth. "That's nice," I said, "You'll learn to read and write." I'd heard this before, many, many times.

"Unh-unh! Doa ler ly, ler wawk." He was mighty pleased with himself no doubt about it—proof he couldn't mean reading and writing.

"Walk? What for? You already know how to walk." My trench sloped down to three feet nearest the post; still deeper. "Well, hop along, anyway."

This made him giggle and he obliged me with some sample hops. "Unh-unh!" he shouted. "Wawk. Waw-wawk! Go wawk, may may-yi!" Hands and torso gyrated in a series of clumsy gestures that evoked digging, hammering, painting.

"I get it. Work. You're gonna learn to work and make money. Join the party." There was a plan afoot to place Jimmy in a program for the trainably retarded, Miss Annie told me later, but as far as I know, nothing ever came of that one either.

"When are you gonna start?" I said.

"Hab dja' maw." Jimmy, for one, was sure the moment was at hand. Tomorrow, tomorrow. "Ma'yi. Me wawk. Dja, hab djah. Awn may-yi." Zany jubilation gave way to sly pride as the upper lip drew itself down over the top row of teeth and the jaw tilted upward.

With a final surge of strength that seemed not my own, I wrestled the post out of the ground. End of *agon*. I heaved it on the scrap pile and filled the hole back up, stamping the earth down with both feet. Jimmy smoothed the soil behind me with his soft bare soles. The new patch was darker—the deepest earth, rich and damp, lay on top.

"Awn ma-yi," he said again to stress his rising status.

"You'll earn money, that's fine, Jimmy. Fine." What a staff of comfort the handle of a spade can be when every ounce of strength seems to have been wrung out of you.

"You plee," he said, without altering the set of his mouth.

"Yes, I'm pleased for you."

Again, I had it wrong. "Plee! Plee!" he squealed, pointing both index fingers at me like a gunslinger. He drew a curvaceous shape in the air with both hands, ending with a thrust of a finger at me and an oddly impudent forward-jutting grin I'd never observed before. Could be that the prospect of earning his own money opened whole new paths of feeling in young Jimmy Hurd that gave him all at once a vision of his true place in the world, a place from which to grin and stare and point and whatever else, at his pleasure, and to experience impudence diffuse itself over the body of another and assimilate her to the alien mass of his own. Could be.

iv

And people, I thought bitterly, are still attempting to settle in this god-forsaken excuse for a town. Madmen all, as deluded as the Spanish conquistadors and the likes of Raoul Boullet—an ancestor of the Captain's said to have lived and died under the profound conviction that Tarragona was the hub of the New World's historical destiny.

v

My, my my...see you been livin' here goin' on two weeks now. Reckon you got alla comforts of home inside, ain'tcha?" Cluck, cluck, cluck, one twinkling patent leather toe at a proprietary angle on the mellow brick steps, neck craned to peer in through the open door. "Got yourse'f a workin' bathroom and a coupla lights, too, I see. Kitchen comin' along?" The mustache looked just trimmed, the upswept sides of his thinning hair—that revolting depression down the center—freshly pommaded into place.

I jerked the three-pronged plug from its socket in the temporary utility pole out front and dragged the power line up to the porch.

"Looks to me like a hunnerd-foot heavy-weight cord, a real handful—but you ladies wanna be equal in ever'thing, am I right?" This theme still had the roughness of the untried in Jake's repertoire, a new leaf in his book portraying modernist imagination tossed between wishful fantasy and hard reality. Provocatively at ease, raised foot tapping the old Spanish bricks to an eccentric rhythm, he flicked his ash onto the step above.

"This isn't a garbage dump," I snapped, dropping the looped cord with a loud thud. *My* wishful fantasy, I was thinking, is to get to the point in this restoration when I can just slam the door in the face of *your* hard reality, Mister.

"Easy to forget this place ain't the old wreck it used to be," making himself entirely at home, sketchpad in lap, getting down more living history before the dinner hour.

My arm tensed in control of an impulse to pick up all one hundred feet of cord and pitch it at his face. In a split-second vision, I saw him reel back from the blow, his skull smash open on the brick walk.

Jimmy Hurd and the Dollman came slouching through the open carriage gates, but stopped at a cautious distance from Jake. "Guess you know the police is after that ole colored woman," he said, puff puff, sketching as though his life depended on it. Superficially, at least, Jake at his work always made me think of those evangelists in the Ebbo Gospels awhirl with the Carolingian fervor of penning their Good News for posterity.

"I don't have time to worry about all the shenanigans around here."

"I know you stay real busy, ma'am. But I do b'lieve you might be innerested in this particklar case—you know the one." Produced in evidence: the image on the first page of his book. Jimmy and the Dollman basked in the proximity of Jake's exceptional acumen.

I shrugged, bedded a stray hammer in the center of the coiled power line with measured precision, saw again the skull crack open on the walk, the watery green eyes roll back, the cigar going out on the blood-spattered grass, the idle pencil. "What could they want from that old woman?"

"Might know a thing or two."

I glared indifferently at the notebook in passing (Harding can make you want to shrivel up when her eyes deliberately refuse any expression of interest or understanding), and got on with sweeping off the porch. In the frenzy of work, day after day, the one thing nobody ever bothered about was cleaning up. Wisps of insulation, bits of wood, sawdust, packing materials, turpentine-soaked rags, and the perpetual junkfood wrappers and remains of cigarettes—all stayed just where they fell. Some days the disorder at the Boullet House recalled nothing so much as the look of it when I'd taken possession that first day.

"So what?" I said.

He was sketching—as if it had appeared in Valencia Street overnight, a sudden historic miracle—the Boullet fence, paling after black paling, a whole iron legion of lances marching over the white page.

"Opium, thass what. Growin' poppies right unner everybody's nose. In her back yard, b'lieve it or not."

"Shocking. I wouldn't wonder if she was growing hyssop and bergamot and woodruff and anise, and God knows what else. Hemlock. Such blatant criminality ought to be checked in the interest of the public safety." The Dollman cocked his head at attention like a barnyard rooster, and Jimmy burst out in the number one hit, thumping an empty bottle against the palm of his hand for accompaniment.

"Thought you might like to know, ma'am." He clapped the book shut, rebuffed in the disinterested pursuit of justice. "Tell you the truth though, there might be more to it than you think. Might have somethin' to do with ole Wentworth's death— remember?" His unlit cigar end tapped the notepad with what I could see was meant as delicacy.

"That old nonsense again! If emphysema and sclerosis didn't kill him outright, he more than likely had a weak heart, or high blood pressure. Why keep making a mystery out of it?"

"Police cain't jump to no conclusion where a man's life is concerned. Ain't ever'body equal 'fore the law?"

"Does that apply to your exhibit on page one?"

"You think about it, ma'am—edjicated professor lady like you don't need no lessons in logic: if somebody seen somebody else comin' on this proppity that don't have no bidness bein' here atall, any time, and if this first somebody noticed this other somebody actin' peculiar, mind you—what the police call 'suspicious behavior'—it stands to reason, don't it, that this somebody else was prob'ly up to no good. Am I right? It's a clear an' simple case of what you might call raddio-sin-ation. Thass the word ain't it?"

"Acting peculiar, you say? How's that?"

"I'm not at libbedy to comment on what they call the technicalities of the case, ma'am, y'unnerstand." Complacency oozed from him and attached itself to the old Dollman's face.

"Technicalities," I echoed, "yes I see."

"Aw, do i' agay...." Jimmy bellowed at the top of his voice to a clumsy shuffle of bare feet. Jake spun around like a top and the bottle burst in murderous shards on the bricks.

"Pi' i' uh!" came the Dollman's glottal command between uncontrollable guffaws. Jimmy glanced furtively at me from his harvest of glass slivers as he dropped them into a brown paper bag foraged from the old man's basket.

"What will they do with her?"

"Well now, that depends...."

"On what?" I said, sweeping refuse over the lip of the top step.

"There's one thing I *can* tell you, Miz Dumot ma'am, and that's a fack"—he had no choice but to move out of my way—"it ain't hardly pleasant down in that city jail this time a year, hot as it's been.' The Hurds chuckled appreciatively and backed off, keeping their proportional distance.

"Unless they have some real basis for holding her, your 'fact' doesn't amount to a hill of beans." Voice as steady and flat as they come.

Wordlessly, he occupied himself with his ritual of trimming and lighting a fresh panatella, drew it out with finicky precision even longer than usual, not exactly in my way but not quite out of it either. The woman, his silence warned, was in trouble, facts or no facts. The only question: how long her troubles might last and just how tangled up in them she would get—if, that is, she couldn't give a good enough accounting of her peculiar behavior, and not likely she could.

"Like I said," he allowed, having launched the cigar to his entire satisfaction, "you do have a fine head for logic, ma'am." His eyes lingered appraisingly over the brick steps, the firm, newly set porch rail (dusky salmon against the creamy pale green spindles and weatherboards behind them), the cypress entrance door waiting ajar for its last coat of finish to dry to a soft glow. "Ole man would rise up outta his grave if he knew what you done to his place, ma'am."

Seems to me like he never really had a chance to settle down into it, I had a mind to say, not with the living dragging him up all the time.

On second thought Jake turned around with: "Who knows,

maybe that colored woman can hoodoo her way outta this lil spot she's in. They say that's her speciality."

Just then a police car cruised to a halt in front of Doc Shibbles' cottage, and the familiar duo banged loudly on his door.

psycheme

If I am obsessed with Harding (and in some way I obviously am, although not even slightly titillated by the Lawrencian allusions Paul has lately begun to drop) it is perhaps because I, like her, have no ruler and anticipate none to dictate my path. Does it take courage to live like Harding? Will?

Sometimes I sense a more than historical affinity between woman and the lesser literary forms. Take the gothic: bizarre, pathetic, overblown and predictable horrors codifying her routine sex acts, which is to say her daily life. Where man as such symbolizes his world and experience in it by reference to his sex, woman's ordinary living, moment by moment, blow by blow, bears the tale of hers. What does it take? Not courage, neither that of the hero nor that of the martyr, or even of the eccentric or the recluse—courage is not what it takes. Nor (though Harding obviously has plenty of it) will, either. It does, however, require a certain turn of being, a trope of consciousness from which something like her sensibility evolves in spatializing the formations and dissolutions of horror pervading it as naturally as the weather. A kind of psychical weather box. And this force working so pervasively through the days as to function like gravity in our every moment has the color of joy, not a lust for life, the quest, the bliss we are all advised to follow, but a love for the moment-by-moment, year-by-year, century-by-century details stretching our living places to millenia. In this bizarre landscape where the loveliness of life peeks ever so briefly, if at all, through its horror, its pathos, I too must live if I would keep my integrity, if I would acknowledge the range and character of my womanly sex acts.

I mark the labyrinth of her sexual satisfaction, the power of passion without its license, like the energy of life without its ugliness so threading joy along its course as to restore me to mine. Ariadne? Used, deserted—married in the end, to a god. A gothic tale, if ever there was one.

vi

One might, says Harding, come to oneself having sliced out an eye with a jagged edge or knocked out brains as handily as old plaster. Do not the moments by and through which one lives gather terror as they roll, one into the next? Words, looks, intonations leave their contexts like vapors swelling into ominous formations: signification auguring ultimate meaning, ineluctable judgment. One might, in the fullness of time, be oneself torn limb from limb. Contrary to current critical opinion, there *is* an origin—the beginning of meaning—but you never have to look for it; you're always in it. Always.

vii

Jimmy sucked his thumb and the Dollman with legs astraddle took up Jake's position on the bottom step as though there might be some special power in that stance. The old man's hump tilted sideways, the rim of his stained fedora touching the boy's arm. At that angle he gave off an air of rakish perspicacity, and his smile, close up, revealed itself as an encirclement of yellow tooth remnants in a brown sea of tobacco juice. Amiable and foul, it offered itself up as a seduction, a phantasm of a smile around stalagmites crumbling over the putrid face of the deep. Maw of Greed.

The pink-shirted arm popped into the basket and swung back out in a flourish that brushed the top steps and my ankle, a gestural sign for me to take note: demonstration about to begin. In one open palm, on her back, lay a dark-nippled coppery figurine with a miniscule bird feather stuck in her hair. The other hand held a Spanish conquistador doll decked out with a dented thimble for a helmet and a shiny bottle cap for a shield. Out of the old man's mouth came something uncannily resembling speech. "What?" I said, "what?" Jimmy offered a translation

choked off by laughter and more gibbering from the Dollman as
the hand with the conquistador doll came down and bounced
rhythmically, hard and fast, on top of the other one. My broom
swung out so suddenly the dolls were bumping down the ends
of the steps, bits of their frippery bouncing off even before I got
hold of what had happened, before I registered my wild impulse
to swing, to smash his pornographic puppet show and all the
sleaze in creation with it.

The Dollman was down on his knees in the bushes piecing
together what he could find there in the dirt and twigs, whining
like an injured animal. Jimmy had vanished, gone as if my fury
had swept him away somewhere into an out-of-the-way corner
of the world where things hide and wait till it's safe again, business as usual.

I rummaged in my back pocket and found a couple of dollar bills. "For the damage," I said, "take it, please…your broken
things."

The smile tilted up at me again, and, without getting off his
knees, he tucked the bills one after the other inside a handsome
maroon leather billfold, where he fanned them, along with several others, like cards, and calmly counted the lot. This done, he
sprang lithely to his feet and ambled off, basket and all, stopping from time to time with a smile and a nod over his humped
shoulder.

I gasped for air, once, twice, then deliberately slowed my
breathing, relaxed my shoulders, swallowed. Doc Shibbles was
scrubbing his hands at the tap and wrung them away from his
body in a slow daze. I told myself that he was certifiably paranoid, as though by giving a name to his condition, I might—at
least in the moment—separate myself from it and him.

viii

Maria Zamora turned off the tap and slipped the soap into a
plastic dish, took the scrub brush from his hands and dried
them gently in her apron. With both arms steadying him, she
led him up the steps to a rocker flaked with green paint. Wrapping his hands around the glass she had brought out, the way

you teach a child to drink, she guided it to his lips, and when he'd had a quick frightened sip, she took it back, delicately, like the stem of a parasol.

His arms jerked into the air when he saw me coming, hairs stuck damply to his glass-like scalp.

"The doctor is having one of his spells," said Maria Zamora wiping his forehead gently with one of the flowery napkins. Hers was the face of a Byzantine angel mindless with serenity.

"I wanted to thank you—" Another glass made its appearance, for me.

"Cold tea always makes him feel better," she said and rocked his chair with one hand, softly, like a cradle. A thin breeze shivered through the tropical foliage to the accompanying crack-crack of the rocker. From a thicket of magnolia and palmetto, a bird chirped through the earthy muskiness of decayed vines and was still, as still as if something in its shadowed sanctuary had triggered the wisdom of muteness. No street sounds reached us back there. The old man, in his private agony, started to mutter.

"Here," she said, "have a sip of this nice cool tea I brought you, Doctor, here. Always picks him up on a warm night."

He pushed her offering aside with no outward change of expression, answering, it seemed, the same question yet again, giving each syllable its exact, separate emphasis—trance-like, eyes blank as a zombie's. "She came down the sidewalk with a sack and entered through the front gate. I saw her coming, old like me but she still has her power. I watched her. I saw. She walked around the side of the house to the back—there. The dogs barked at first, but they know her and crept away into the shade with their tails under. They fear her kind. At the foot of the steps she squatted and strewed something over the ground from her sack by the handfuls, back and forth, over the ground, so." He made the motion with his hands. "Then she took the rattle from her pocket, as always, and entered the house."

"Through the back?" I asked.

"Up the steps."

"Did you say the dogs barked, Doctor Shibbles?"

"At first. They barked loudly and ran up to her as to an intruder, and when they smelled her they crept off."

"And you say she knelt where?"

"At the foot of the steps. She squatted, her back as straight as a dancer's—from girlhood she has been like that. Through the bushes I watched her dance, around the gallery and into the garden, singing, till Mother called me away and warned me. It's the demon that pulls me to her."

"Who is she, sir?"

But he was far away, rapt in the fatalities of memory's tragic closure. "I know where you come from," he said, gazing at the Boullet House, still as if seeing a garden abloom there and a figure winding her way through it, dancing. Then his eyes turned back to me and deepened beyond vacancy into terror.

"Where?"

"You and the other one, both of you dead these many years. You're the one that looks at me from the window, and she walks the streets, day and night—I see her." He trembled with weeping. Maria Zamora raised his head and tipped the glass to his pale lips again, and this time, he took a deep, greedy swallow.

"Who is it you think I am?"

She rubbed the folded napkin serenely over the old man's brow, he looking at me, eyes suddenly going into focus, seeing— looking from me to the house and back again at me, shaking his head, "I thought...but that was long ago. She died long ago. They died together, both of them. Still, I thought she...you had come to—" With an immense effort he nodded at the house as if its original form slowly emerging from my work on it made everything clear. "From the first you made me think of her...this heat and all the questions. The police. That man again. But I see you are a stranger, come to take her place—is that it?"

"I'm Elizabeth Dumot and I'm here to restore the Boullet House, nothing more."

Like one gripped all of a sudden by the need to have the truth out, once and for all, Maria Zamora cried, "It's nothin' but that old colored woman's voodoo. She got the knowledge from the others and put this hex on him, but I'll never let any of them in. Never!" As suddenly, her face relapsed, without a trace of passion, into its former repose, a face that the smallest knowledge might crack irreparably. She took the glass from his hands and wiped the beads of sweat from it with her apron.

"Marie," he said in his toneless, spent voice, "don't excite yourself. No need. There is no such thing as voodoo or hexing, I've told you. Nothing like that exists in this world. There is only...only...terror and all that can't be stopped." His chest heaved in a throttled sob that sank him down into his chair.

And just when it seemed that he must have gone to sleep, he raised his eyes to me again. "They made me tell all I know about her," he said.

"Miss Mary Louise?"

"'Everything,' they said, 'everything you remember.'"

"When was it, Doctor? When did you see her?"

"When *he* came to me the first time, I told him...but it was the demon I heard, it must have been because he—but that's something else. Something...no...too many things happening now, too much, slowly, but always coming together until it can no longer be undone."

Maria Zamora placed her hand protectively on his shoulder and looked down at her feet.

"But you were kind," he said, "kind to come." His eyes met mine briefly in a commonality of knowledge, "Kind like her."

"Please—do you remember exactly when you saw her, there, in the back?"

"I see her after I sweep the porch down and I see her at other times, after dark. The days are all alike now." He gazed blankly into the lush green shadows where the silence was thicker, closer in than before—muted, like a bird just alighting with its tongue cut out. "She started it again when you came, and now he questions me and watches, and he comes back and back...It's you who began it again." No reproof, only a hopeless, terrible sorrow at the fatedness of it.

"You told the police...all this? That you couldn't recall when it was you saw her by the back steps?"

"He gets dizzy spells sometimes," Maria said in a sing-songy voice, not a communication so much as a memory voiced to no one in passing, saying it out loud to hold on to it like the old man's half-drunk glass of tea.

"It was a day like any other. I told him that. He always comes in the early mornings and tells me it is my duty as a citizen to divulge all I know to the police. My duty, he says. He says it is wrong for someone to withhold information of that kind in a case such as this. To protect the innocent, he says. The public interest. I explain over and over about the demon, and the danger, but they will not listen. They say they want another kind of information from me. Facts, they say, plain facts."

"It was Jake Landry who pressed you to tell the police?"

"He knows and he waits. He's patient, more patient than the sand out there and he has just as many eyes. Now he watches you too."

"You're sure, sir, that the dogs barked when you saw her over there, on the back steps?"

"Yes, yes," he said, "they frighten Marie, she never liked them."

The tea she had poured out for me was sweet, a dark strong sweetness edged with the bitter of tannin and a faint citric tang. I drank it up with the elation of new knowledge. "Thank you," I said, "Thank you," and, then, more telling her than asking, "The woman everybody calls Miss Mary Louise, she lived in...my house, the one I'm restoring." Ratiocination, as Jake would say, pure and simple.

"Why surely ma'am. Didn't I see her myself when I was a little one, and them two old ones that disappeared? And other things." The apron alone, neat and practical, showed she belonged to this world still.

"Maria-Louisa Bernard," the old man enunciated precisely. And more softly, "Maria-Louisa."

I had taken several steps back to the Boullet property when his voice reached my back, clear and matter-of-fact: "Of course the house should have gone to her when they died."

psycheme

If, on going about my business, I'd happen to leave the bedroom door even slightly cracked, my old dog Bella, a mutt with the dignified girth and curled tail of an elkhound on funny spindly legs, would nose her way inside, ease up onto the bed and under the covers, head finely laid on my down pillow. I would surprise her there in a deep, snoring sleep, eyes fluttering lazily open as I neared. In an instant, she was out and slithering away mortified. Earlier on, I used to punish her, even, I now think, cruelly. Nothing worked; the habit firmed the more I apprehended her in it; the more comfortably I outfitted her own cozy sleeping place, the greater her shame at being evicted from mine. About everything else in our domestic coexistence she was singularly respectful and intelligent, eminently teachable as dogs go; but this business of burrowing down into my bed when I wasn't in it was something she could never get past till her dying day. Shame, the residue of exposure, is intransigent. It may be soothed and smoothed away momentarily, but, like insensate things—rocks, lumps of iron—it never learns. I decided she simply couldn't help herself. The door left hastily ajar set off in Bella's yearning, passionate dog-brain the idea, perhaps, of being me, taking my place in the bed.

Although both dogs and children give trouble, dogs on the whole are to be preferred. Dogs feel they're off. You can see it in their eyes—you can see they can't understand how and why they get carried away.

Unlike dogs, when children look you in the face they make up a lot of nonsense about it. Dog-ignorance gives less trouble than child-innocence. We all know what it is to lead both a dog's life and a child's; but those among us targeted for weakness, be it on grounds of sex, age, race, class, or what have you, lose dog-advantages precisely to the extent that infantile nonsense must target a receptacle as surely as the premises of a valid argument entail a conclusion. Although you can always see in their eyes their attraction to and for dogs, women as receptacles for the world's nonsense cannot escape the child's lot. The neutral-to-cheerful media voice reports daily, it seems, from desert, from city, pole to pole: "As conditions worsen, women and children here...." And dogs—dogs run wild again.

ix

Came a time, finally, about the second week in August, when the accident rate on county highways shot up an amazing sixty-nine percent as compared with June—report in *The Sentinel*. Police officials note, in addition, a surge in acts of wanton destruction and point the finger at abnormally high temperatures.

Workmen were always coming and going now at the Boullet House, delivering and installing all day long, hanging and checking up, or in, venting and correcting (there was a lot of that), and inspecting. And calling up, now that I had a phone. Between them and ruination of the pine floor's lustrous patina lay only the rolls of brown paper I'd tape down before even *The Sentinel* arrived new-minted on my porch. (By the end of the day, my protective paper runners were so torn up I'd simply discard the shreds and start all over next morning.) Atmospheric phenomena were on everybody's tongue and getting under everybody's skin. "Hot again." "Hotter 'n blazes." "Rain didn't help much, sure didn't. Muggier 'n ever, and s'posed to get even worse tomorrow." The check of good manners—maintaining that unruffled, mildly congenial surface once so common in the South—began to be expressed as strained amiability, by turns snappish or overly talkative, protesting too much. "Heat botherin' you? Don't bother me atall...why you should have been here when...." Everybody appeared to put a lot of energy into sustaining a borderline decency. As a result, everyone, even in the briefest interchange, gave the impression of having a high opinion of himself and others throughout the town, since all shared the secret knowledge of caging the lusts that possessed them.

The thinner it stretched, the more I experienced this parochial veil of minimal courtesies as crucial to maintaining life in its rudimentary civilized forms. *The Sentinel.* After months of deadlocked negotiations between the KKK and concerned officials, Klan spokesmen have released their program of what is billed as a public "teach-in" to be held this week at the Community College. Slated, it said in Section B, for Saturday night at 7:30. Had to be the weather again; atmospherics. How else to explain the perversity of a group famed for clandestine terror not only going public—*negotiating* to go public, no less—but doing so in the interest of raising everybody's consciousness? Little did I realize back then that Tarragona was on the cutting edge of a global strategy for justifying acts of terrorism. There were to be speakers, a question-and-answer period, exhibits of locally manufactured robes and other authentic handcrafted artifacts on loan from generous patrons, to illustrate (bring vividly back to life) the early history of the Klan in DeLuna County. You'd think they were talking about an organization founded to promote the twin virtues of free inquiry and homespun industry. Record crowds predicted. Marxist professor travelling abroad said to be considering resignation from Speakers' Committee in protest; black cleaning woman on campus known to have walked off job that morning, leaving mop and bucket stranded in hallway. No groundswell of opposition expected, though. Ample parking at specially designated campus locations. Public welcome.

More news-about-town: the porno scandal so-called, quiescent through several torrid weeks, (one could only guess at what intricate *quid pro quos* might be at work in all this) reaches influential ears at high levels of government. Official investigation reported imminent, prompting editorial concern over what is said to be widely available in any one of half a dozen book stores and theatres in the area. Local traffic in pornographic materials showing configuration of an iceberg of unknown depths, prompting level heads to call for cleaning house, mixed metaphors suggesting as much the conveniences of euphemism as the spirit of things getting quite simply out of hand.

So much of everything was now a matter of luck, what with all that was going on at so strained a pitch, it was as if the restoration had acquired a life of its own quite apart from me. Luck would only count if all else was under control. Case in point: the Evans men had assumed an air of inscrutability since my unmentionable visit to their homestead back in July, Aubrey mute but testy, Tom coldly standoffish to the point of seeming as dangerous as I, for one, knew for certain he was. Would they have it all in good working order by the end of the week? Would I hit it lucky? There was no telling, and you wouldn't dare ask.

In a wanton act of destruction, Aubrey smeared long greasy fingers over the front of his baby-blue teeshirt stamped with "My Plumbing Works All The Way Down." This after the inspector, having blessed the various lines, joints, and hookups—"all but one or two little things"—sped away with "sure is hot, ain't it" and a macho squeal of the wheels to put his good friend Tom Evans to shame, but without signing off on the permit. That was Tuesday.

Aubrey, I thought for sure, would grab at the chance to unburden himself to me while I mounted shutter hooks on the front porch, when none other than Tony Krasner drove up in his El Camino, washed and waxed.

"Heard you been looking for me, babe," in his most winning manner from the driver's seat.

"Have I!" For over a month I'd been waiting for him to seal the flashing around the chimneys and attic vents, worrying about it through one downpour after another. Would he show up before the next one? His delays had been trying my patience and threatening the ruin of my whole project from the top down—now that I'd spent nearly my all.

"Bet you thought I forgot." He wasn't budging from his car, which left me no choice but to yell back, "Knew you'd show, sooner or later." I'd paid him in full upon his insistence and knew no such thing. ("For a bargain like you got off me, baby, I ain't including any interest-free loan.")

Every day, three or four times a day after the stains appeared in the freshly painted upstairs wall where the back chimney runs down from the attic, I'd called his number, only to be put off by a snippy answering service, or by one of a string of unobliging females who, when pressed, maintained that he was either at work, or out of town, or "busy."

Agreeing that he was an unreliable bastard, Aimée Hulin offered to employ what lingered of her charms. Maybe they'd cast their spell one last time, or possibly what brought him back to Valencia Street was the whimsy he liked to call his "word." It was sacred, of course, and, like everything sacred, past human understanding.

"Can't handle this mob scene," he shouted, racing his engine. "I'll be back by here about two o'clock. Toodloo baby. Lookin' good."

Aubrey stomped around the house yelling at his underling that not everybody had time to horse around like some. "Leaves me holdin' all the shit!" he muttered, loudly enough so I'd be sure to get it. And for once, it was easy to agree with him all the way.

psycheme

A promise kept is a kept promise. Thus do keepers of promises get carried away, not for lack of keeping the faith but precisely *in* keeping faith.

Resolved: not to get carried away. When the deed has already been done, you might conclude it can't be undone. And perhaps so, if a deed is ever done. Standing here before you where the deed is still being done, I'm still being carried away. As if I am not who I am, or more accurately, as if there is no way for me to be seen, as if every eye always sees another in my place— always that as-if person. But their as-if is not mine. I am in the habit of standing whole and intact under the pornographic focus that serves up my parts whether on billboard or platter. But without this habitual imprisonment of eye cells, each protected from his/her own confinement by the very ignorance of where he/she is as he/she busily locks others into his/her own eye cells, I stand defenseless; I cannot look back; I share none of the ignorance of their own looking. This defenseless position sometimes passes for self-consciousness in the ordinary sense and sometimes for self-consciousness in the philosophical sense. In their eyes, I'm trying to be like them, to act appropriately—jail and be jailed. But the gaze I return you in my deliberate blindness always misses its mark; in short, I always fail. Always, if only a bit off.

I'm trying to explain to you why you can't quite focus on me. Try it—try focussing on my blind gaze.

x

And just as I'm mulling over the fact that the sand and oyster shells for the drive and parking area, due first thing that morning, haven't arrived, two shirtless men, one fat, the other tall and skinny, amble in through the gate. The two I'd finally hired for the reasonable fee of twenty dollars. All summer long they'd been stopping by to offer their services, and, desperate as I'd been for help at first, I kept turning them down. I didn't trust them an inch.

The fat one gleamed with sweat and came on like a promoter, all talk. The other one, approaching middle age and slouching along with his colleague in a detached reverie, had quite possibly seen better days, and definitely worse. Whether above it all or just out of it, he'd never said a thing, not in my hearing. They lived in one of the last unrehabilitated cottages on Cadiz Boulevard (suffered uneasily through a scrappy hedge by Hinckney & Jones on one side and Solar Ideas on the other) with a rough-mannered, foul-talking, stringy-haired woman and a chubby baby with never a thing on but pampers. The baby looked stridently healthy, tan all over and always trying to climb out of someplace and up onto something.

They'd carouse drunkenly through the neighborhood whenever the mood took them, squealing around corners in their tarpaulin-covered pickup in which they purported to "haul" things of an unspecified nature, "wherever." One steamy morning, while the house stood gutted and wide open, I found the woman calmly rifling a box I'd stowed out of sight under the porch, like a shopper come early to sort through the merchandise on the clearance rack. "Still good for somethin', these here ole doorknobs an' things," she informed me in a patent rebuke to my bourgeois wastefulness. After that, I suspected them of removing a number of not especially valuable but useful articles from the house—a spade, an old wooden level, a good coil of rope, an iron coal bucket I used for trash, and an extra door. "Wanton acts of appropriation," was how that read in my book.

When the restoration entered its visibly constructive phase—walls going up and doors, stripped woodwork, new paint appearing inside and out—they'd insisted on getting in on it. As the fat one put it, "You been givin' jobs to all kine a other people, just ahandin' 'em out, even niggers, an' we're just as willin' to work as inny an' cheaper than some, so what's wrong with *us*?" He had a point there, and I finally contracted to pay them the twenty to spread the sand and shells. And now he demanded, with a flush of resentment and a swipe of his pudgy hand under his sweaty chin, that I call up the company, right then and there, on my new phone.

"We don't stand for no jivin'," he said. "We come over here ready to work this mornin', took the day off special, me an' Rail here."

I held the receiver out to let him hear the clerk at the other end explain that the delivery truck slated for my job had broken down, and all the other heavy company vehicles were already scheduled elsewhere for the day. They'd be sure to catch me next morning, though—an old story, of course, but one I was by no means eager to discuss with the fat man.

He bit his lip, demanded a tenner up front because they could have had "plinny other jobs," he said, if it hadn't been for trying to help me out with mine.

"No." I recognize the small-time shakedown. "I don't pay for work till it's all finished"—which is, of course, not strictly speaking so, but good in principle.

"You would if you trusted us, lady. But since you don't, let's just say that ten bucks ain't too much to keep you an' your place lookin' good."

"Wrong boys!" Was there anyone, says Harding, in any social stratum of Tarragona who hadn't misjudged me? "To pay you anything at all is too much," I add hotly, "and if you're contemplating any damage to me or my property, I advise you to leave me dead, because I won't let you get away with it if I'm not. And *if* you leave me dead, be prepared to face a murder charge, because I intend to report this little shakedown to the police right now." He has taken the toothpick out of his mouth which hangs wide open. "If you want my twenty dollars," I say, "stop by again tomorrow; if not, there's nothing here for you."

At that, the one called Rail comes out of his reverie and whispers to the fat one who laughs out loud with surprising good humor. "My friend got a lil proposition," he says. "You see, he really takes to a tough, high-class woman, Rail does."

"Oh?" Is this some kind of a new turn, or just a seeming new turn on an old one?

"We wuz thinkin' you might like to go with us, an' our woman, to the meetin' this afternoon."

"What kind of meeting?"

"Mean as we are, we can stand a lil Holy Ghost gittin' into us ever' now 'n 'en. Why you don't know what fun is till you been to a revival! Holy Ghost comes in at your head—first you git all tensed up an' you kin feel it comin', an' soon as it hits you your head snaps up and you kin feel it rollin' right down into your neck an' your arms, an' then the jerkin' starts, an' when the goin' gits real good it goes all through you an' you git to shoutin', an' the jerkin' goes all regglar like so you juss cain't stand still no longer—bet you ain't never been to one."

"Not in a long time." Not since childhood, I remember, astonished at witnessing just such goings-on among grown people most of whom had seemed to me more than ordinarily staid.

"Ain't nothin' equal to the Holy Ghost, lady, for showin' a body a good time, not drinkin', or smokin', or shootin' up neither. Nothin'. But you prob'ly don't unnerstand 'at, do you?"

"Yes," I say, "as a matter of fact I prob'ly do." In fact, it is just the kind of hysterical phenomenon I like to observe.

"That right?" He's momentarily disappointed not to be able to introduce me to a new experience, but the proffer of an extraordinary variation on it, one that's sure to be news to me, inspires him afresh.

"But lady, you ain't never seen how the Holy Ghost can take a man till you seen Rail here, all six foot. When it comes on 'im, his head gits to rollin', arms an' legs git this lil churnin' motion an' his mouth opens up an' his tongue starts just awhippin' in an' out. It's wild. Pretty soon he's talkin' like you never heard nobody talk in your life—speakin' the Unknown Tongue they call it, same as our Lord Jesus did, just atalkin' that ole Hebrew language that cain't nobody, not even Rail here an' the others sayin' it, unnerstand no more. Rail says he knows it ain't him doin' it cause he don't never say nothin' atall if he don't have to, an' that goes to prove it muss be Jee-sus gittin' in his tongue an' flippin' it around like 'at. You wanna come?"

"Thanks, but I'm not here for a good time. You boys get the Holy Ghost for me too, and I'll see you tomorrow, bright 'n early."

"All right," said the fat one with a backward grin at the house that left me harboring some second thoughts about my twenty dollar bargain.

xi

"Coupla punks," Jake muttered. Always somewhere nearby, he was, turning the corner, or just behind you, or slipping his shadow over the work in front of you. Cool as a cucumber, as if neither heat waves nor fraying tempers could rattle a mind so steadfast in its own designs.

In fact, he seemed to grow increasingly complacent and sparing of words the more the rest of us betrayed our signs of wear and tear. He made an irritating contrast to the sweaty, grumpy workmen muddling, at my expense, through their chores and only with the frequent succor of cigarettes and iced drinks, and a good bit of inessential gab. Aubrey Evans was already taking his pre-lunch break in the patchy shade of the old hibiscus next to Doc Shibbles' yard, availing himself of the comforts of my breakfast nook. With an avid interest in work not his own, he kept his eyes peeled on the electrician's apprentice propping his extension ladder against the west side of the house at a dangerously steep pitch.

What business anybody besides Krasner could have on my new cedar roof at this late date was a mystery to me, but even before I got my question out, something struck me hard above the left eye, something that seemed to catapult itself at me from the fence the instant I stepped over to have a look. My fingers, touching my temple, came away bloody.

"Hey shuga...all right?" Somebody taking hold of my arm, "...see...?" Words buzzed by me like flies..." "did...hunk...fence."

I sank down in the shade of the house waiting for my head to clear, the electrician pressing an icy dixie cup to my forehead. "Seems that a hunk of two-by-four Junior was taking up the ladder there slipped away from him and bounced off the top of those spikes," he explained. Rough-cut and heavy, an old piece of heart pine studding from my scrap pile—a prop of some kind, he said disgustedly, for wedging my attic vent in tight. "Wouldn't have worked anyway. Boy's new on the job, or he would have left that for your roofer."

"I'm orderin' you to clean out that cut, hear?" This was Aubrey in his paternal mode, "right this minute, hear?"

"Just a scratch," I objected, but did as I was told (at the new sink in the new powder room, in front of the pleasant old mirror with its mustard lacquered frame—dry, just). It stung, the skin angry and raised along the fine cut like a bit of clipped copper wire.

Afterwards, he insisted on inspecting my band-aid under solicitous clouds of smoke as though in compensation for weeks of sulky silence.

"I'll be fine," I assured him, rummaging for my shopping list. I could see several of the workmen tugging at their watch-bands and shoelaces as if getting set to join the race for lunch—as safe a time as any for me to vacate the scene. There was the flat black paint I needed for the locks, more triple zero steel wool, machine oil, and still the problem of the molding: a piece to replace a rotted strip under the eaves where anything short of a perfect match would stick out like an odd button on a coat. There were things on that order still to be done all over the house, inside and out, adding up to a list of small but salient cosmetic improvements nearly two pages long.

If it hadn't been for the many junk piles I'd methodically scavenged in those past two months every time I got the chance, I might have agreed with Jake, about an hour later, that turning up the sixteen feet of molding, old and sound, just the pattern I was looking for, was a piece of good luck. "A godsend," he suggested with a self-satisfied, abstracted air.

An *ignis fatuus* of the end.

psycheme

The greatest aggravation here is not knowing who you're talking to. It could be no one, or anybody any place any time, the world at large, some group in particular, some specific person, all and sundry, phrases tumbled sideways, sentences half-lifting off into space, half-collapsing at my feet. Trying to communicate with you here just proves that my place is outside, out on the street where you can step out of my way the second you notice that I'm one of those there's something wrong with. An unfortunate. Another homeless person not to be messed with—best to leave them to the authorities, they say whatever occurs to them, nothing to do with real people, no way to carry on a dialogue with them, attempts to make contact could be dangerous, you never know. Now that I've scanned the street, getting used to where you've put me, I kind of like it out here. A little outing. I can talk to others wrapping the flight of their own ideas around them like recycled overcoats breeding lice. How're ya makin' it man? *Are* you makin' it yet? Turned up any good reading lately? What, nothing but scraps of this and that? Can't tell the end from the beginning? I can speak naively here, freely and from the heart, say whatever pops into my head—follow my nose, and God knows I'm in a position to understand both to whom and whereof I speak when I address my fellow readers out here, the functionally literate. The thinking man on the street. Huddle on up—a little closer to the fire, street-readers, just watch that over-coat—I've got a lead on what will best serve our self-interest and make us feel good about doing it at the same time. The rest of you go bug off to your own deals. Me, jive? Not on your grandmother's flea bag.

Tell me, do we or don't we all share one big problem, the problem of how to get along in the world, how to con a living from day to day? All right then. You may be very savvy when it comes to the details but if you don't mind my saying so, you're probably missing the forest for the trees. I bet you are—I should know, I've been there. Aren't we all so wrapped up in conning our way from one minute to the next we hardly notice that we're playing a hit-or-miss game? When was the last time you thought about picking a really good con job and sticking to it, huh? Would you even know how? It takes a certain eye. Training. That's where my expertise as a generalist can be useful—I can tell you a thing or two about the artistry of conning that'll change the whole way you go about it, your entire con-ception of it if I may say so. I don't think I'm overstating the case when I say that knowing how to pick your con (rather than taking whatever comes along) is bound to improve the quality of street life exponentially by helping you to proceed 1) more knowledgeably and 2) more predictably. Feel you're a little too rusty upstairs, too set in your daily habits, to go at it from scratch? Remember, street-readers, this is our wealth and welfare we're talking about. Slide those glass eyes a little farther down your nose and listen. Fact #1: You can't develop the intuition of a good con artist without going into history. Don't groan, there's no getting around it—but here's where I can offer my services. You see it's not enough just to get hold of the do's and don'ts of a job, you have to go where the action is, get a feel for who the experts are (given such a mob claiming to be experts), and which ones to start with considering your limited time. In short: the winners. Having made a hands-on study of conning throughout time, I'm happy to report that there's only one master con job. That's right, *one*, pulled off by that old aristocratic Greek dude we've heard about since we were knee-high: name of Plato. The very one, took lessons from a great gang of earlier cons, but only *he* got together a job that always comes off.

Backtrack with me a bit, street-readers, for a look at the ground rules of all this so you can fully appreciate the genius of the old con master's achievement—pared down, you understand, to my own words. Here's the gist: wherever you go throughout the world, you never meet a soul who doesn't consider himself (whether he ever does anything or not) to be a locus of activity—what I call *psychical movement*. That's the movement making the psychical reality that's you-in-the-moment or me-in-the-moment. It's always performative, meaning that our psychical moves make us who we are at every moment as surely as saying "I do," under appropriate authorizing conditions, locks us into the wedded state. What authorizes our psychical movement is membership in our species: what you spin out as you move about fastens you into the situation of being as human as the next man. Well, now. Suppose you could have some prior knowledge of all the regions of possible psychical movement, and suppose there's one region tough to reach but containing everything you want, everything you could even conceive of wanting—say you have your doubts about the existence of such a place? Sounds too much like the El Dorado that tempted early explorers of Florida? Granted, but you can see the benefits of exploration *per se*, can't you, getting to know your way around better in psychical reality by virtue of sheer mileage, maybe even getting the jump on other travelers, who knows? Also, just on the slim chance that there should be anything to reports of a psychical El Dorado after all, you wouldn't want to miss out on it for sure, not on the ultimate golden opportunity, man!

Listen: the original, the master con job I was telling you about—you won't believe this, an enterprising sixth grader could have come up with the gimmick: the grand old con ties right into this El Dorado business by nothing short of marketing a travel guide, to the entire psychical terrain. Talk about shifting the odds, you bet.

And, street-readers, this is one item you can't do without, not if you really want to get on top of things, so stop throwing away those hard-hustled quarters on shitty little crap-games. Go for it. This guide tells you what the real goods are and where to find them, shows you the stacks and stacks of fakes in region after region, what fakes are worth more than others, how to appraise them yourself in a pinch, and really critical of course, how to know where you are at all times because different regions have fakes of different value in them. I figured that would appeal to you, street-wise as you are. You wouldn't want to get mixed up and confuse one bunch of fakes with another, or strike out in the wrong direction expecting a better quality of fakes only to find out that what you might have mistaken for the very best of counterfeit goods is the very worst. (Sounds all too familiar, I'm sure.) My point is that everything you'll ever need to know to move along with your fellow travelers in Psycheland can be had out of this one-of-a-kind guide, along with judiciously placed warnings (every con job plays on fear) that if you don't follow instructions to the tee, the odds are just about 100% you'll get gypped. BUT, if you don't mess up (and all but a few aristocons do, so if at first you don't succeed....), you'll make the biggest haul of your life, what you've travelled so far and so long for: the real McCoy, nothing fake about it.

Are you still with me street-readers? The practical problems of travel never do go away, of course. For instance, this trip takes most all your time and energy, and even then you probably will not have gone very far. Can be discouraging. Also, you'll inevitably give in to the temptation to just rest every now and then, curl up in your overcoat and forget the whole scam. And there's one major drawback for sure: the very gauge you need for measuring how good each region's fakes are is not available until you reach your destination, so all along you're proceeding blindly. Hit-or-miss again.

Here's where you're going to need this travel guide like an addict needs his fix. It may not be all that specific (and so leaves a lot to be desired) but it does keep pointing you in the direction of your desire and no two ways about it. For sure all of us want something, but few if any know what. This one minute, that the next, darting off here, running off there with barely a scrap of a travel plan, never finding what we want or turning up with another fake worse than the last, the merest shadow of a hope...hustling in the dark, we get so desperate there's no listening to reason. Sheer anarchy; whatever convinces us that it might be or might provide what we want, that's the thing we'll dash after, stumbling into and over each other on the way. You've seen it, friends, every day of your lives, I don't need to spell it out. As practicing cons yourselves, you can appreciate how planting the idea that there's a place with everything desirable in it (even if no one knows what they desire) and then actually supplying a plan of how to get there, with general instructions about routes of transport from region to region (specifics to be figured out by the individual traveler, as well as correct filling out of forms, on which more later), can con the pants and everything else people might have accumulated right off them! And that's just exactly what happens. In simple terms: Plato's con job roots in the hard reality that psychical movement expresses desire. How could he miss?

Always keep in mind: to the very extent that you yourself follow this old and irreplaceable travel guide, I guarantee you'll con yourself. You'll discover that you're putting all you've got into filling out travel forms to get from one region to another under the conviction that if you don't mess up you'll either get what you want or something close to it. Self-conning, you must realize by now, isn't all bad; in fact, it's necessary (though not of course sufficient) for any kind of genuine knowledge. As you fill out more and more of these forms, you get intimations of, a little participation in, what you're after, and then somewhere along the way it hits you that if you could just get hold of the form of all forms, the perfect, complete FORM to fill out, you'd have it all: full participation in what you desire, everything you ever wanted, El Dorado! And since we're all after this one form (there's equal opportunity for all to have a go at it, although practically speaking most either can't or don't and so lose the benefits of equal opportunity), you might ask how we're to be satisfied if we all have to share it, especially since it's not something that can be cut up in pieces. In fact, it's the *only* thing not cut up, not missing something but always a complete whole. Here, you can see the real genius of conning at work in the original: all during our trip, what we wanted keeps turning out to be fake, amounts to nothing much, so what keeps us moving, what we desire passionately all the time, we finally realize, is *nothing*. Nothing in all its different forms: the Form of all forms, the Nothing of all nothingness. You can see why it can't be cut up and dished out like a pie. Complete and perfect forms, says Plato in so many words, can't be any *thing*. Your travelling will bring you to this conclusion by way of induction from the fact that everything you encounter has a flaw, and if that's so, then whatever is complete and perfect simply can't be a thing. No thing, no being. How're you going to assay the value of this, your heart's desire, i.e. the value of nothing?

I make a big point of showing you how the power of this original con—this paradigm of all good cons—*lies in telling the truth*: the return we're going to get on our investment is nothing. Zilch. But notice what has happened in the course of this con: these nothings—the jewels in Plato's con crown—have been demonstrated to us to be just what we yearn for.

I could throw in some pointers here for those of you thinking of specializing in how to rip off Plato's jewels—there's some real opportunities here, though, mind you, they won't last forever. As a general principle, always look as if you have no use for his guide book, as if you've broken away from the con-father and are striking out on your own. All cons have a stake in believing a con-son is better than his papa. (Could be an Oedipal thing, I wouldn't be surprised.) Don't be subtle, make a ruckus about it, pick out something from Papa Plato's job, anything will do, then say everything he said as if he himself never even dreamed of it, and all the while steadfastly refuse to acknowledge even the possibility of Papa having gotten there before you. This is not as easy as it sounds, but you can always take your cue from the French; after you get hold of the time-honored Plato-bashing strategy for making your name as a con-son, you'll want to emulate them for sure. Here's how: take Plato's con crown and show how its jewels amount to nothing (never mind that he already made all that so crystal clear you can see right through it). You then argue that they're the biggest fakes of all while implying that what you have to offer is little nothings, too, but genuinely precious little nothings, having been transformed from deceptive and worthless nothings into truly precious nothings *by the nature of your assay*, a sophisticated alchemy for laundering Plato's jewels insured by passing them through the inspection of German con authorities (ask for Nietzsche if you need help). What you're actually doing is doctoring Plato's guidebook in such a way as to pass it off as yours (which is, of course, the whole point). To assure a global market for your product, take a multi-cultural approach by repeating in as many different languages and ethnic guises as possible what Plato has already said, remembering to emphasize how radically different your inspection process is— how detailed, fine, missing nothing, revealing what none other has or can, etc. In the con game all's fair game. And only the odd kook here and there will notice that you're just appropriating for yourself what you've delegitimated. Very resourceful job, that.

Back to the original. It may not have escaped you street-critics that you can never have what you want—how can you ever *have* nothing?—but you can have the next best: you can get closer to having nothing than you ever dreamed, close enough maybe to get a glimpse of your heart's desire, a peep at all you ever wanted rolled into one. To reach the realm of peepshows, keep moving in the right direction as indicated, careful not to be misled or get distracted or waylaid. Once there, you'll have to use all your wits to hang on, all you've learned along the way, because this is a swinging region and you're apt to lose your place, get jostled right out of it just when you're peeping or getting set to. If you do manage to stick it out— remember this is a long con—you may even catch the Peepshow of all peepshows, billed as THE IDEA OF THE GOOD (the most desirable of all nothings). One flash of this one and you'll never want anything else again. You'd rather hang out there hoping for another peep than take possession of all the goodies available elsewhere because you'll know beyond a shadow of a doubt now that they're all fakes; they're all something or other, and not fully nothing. Now that you've spied the genuine article, you can judge the measure of fakery at work in absolutely everything else there is.

I wish you success in all your future endeavors, street-readers, wherever they may take you, and, in conclusion, let me say this is the first time I've enjoyed being here. It's a real relief to have someone to talk to.

xii

The predicted downpour came a little after two o'clock and was over minutes later, no more than if someone had carelessly rolled up the close air we all breathed, like a soggy rag, and wrung it out over our heads. A steamy haze shimmered briefly along rooftops as the clouds lit up from above, then that too dried off and all was as it had been. Maybe a few degrees sultrier, and distinctly quieter. Again the sky dimmed and sagged over the town.

All the installing and inspecting and correcting had come to a halt at the first drop; work was pronounced "rained out" for the day with much pious head-shaking and premature loading up of equipment. Since everybody, in the tenuity of maintaining civilized life as we all knew it, seemed perpetually ready to break off whatever they were doing the instant a drop of rain was observed to land anywhere, being rained out, for me, meant delays down the line, more phone calls and more waiting. Most particularly, it meant I was back where I'd started with Krasner, no cure in sight, even as the chimney leak got worse with every downpour.

But, if the day had been short and chaotic, the sheer volume of activity at the house had yielded results. Heating vents and air-conditioning grilles had appeared. The kitchen, with its new sink and a few cabinets already in place, was starting to look like a proper space of domestication instead of a big empty room with plumbing outlets roughed-in. And the upstairs baths had their tubs, sinks, and toilets neatly fitted over sixteen inch squares of marble tile, although most of it wasn't hooked up. An antique chandelier, rewired and refinished, hung resplendently from the tall ceiling of the downstairs hall, and worked. Old brass plates, scrounged piecemeal from sundry junkshops or forgotten corners of moribund hardware stores and polished to a soft gold, waited to cover plugs and wall switches. Freshly painted lattice sat snug between rows of piers, lending the outside of the house a breezy holiday air.

With any luck, the major installations would be complete in the next few days and, after that, the house would be all mine. My list of finish work lengthened by the hour.

At about half past four, just as I'd checked the installation of the lattice frames (still brooding over the sacredness of Krasner's "word"), what should come rolling into my rutted drive but the El Camino.

"On wet shingles you have to wear ice skates, baby," he explained, "so I waited a couple of hours," making much of how he'd driven all the way back downtown—in traffic—just to accommodate a lady. (What a way the man must have of persuading others to his view of things, when even Harding, who disliked and feared him from the first, could be momentarily lulled by heartfelt gratitude!) No time wasted as his extension ladder rattled up the side of the house, the outdoor spigot squeaked on and off, a trowel scraped against a mortar board—there was that bit of pointing to be done on the leaky chimney. Unlike the other workmen, who required coddling or goading or just plain watching in varying degrees, Krasner could be left entirely to himself. In fact, he discouraged attention of any kind while he worked. He ran a tight ship—his very words.

Sharp, loud blows of a hammer: a toe-board going down to steady his equipment. Before me on the kitchen counter, one of the old rimlocks that refused to catch when the door was pulled shut lay in pieces. In his offhand way, Bill Simmons had shown me how their insides worked, and after oiling and reassembling a dozen or more, my hands were growing deft, my eye as shrewd as his at detecting the source of the trouble: a tiny part one could lose hours searching for all over town had snapped in two. Better to junk this one and pay the extra dollars for a fully repaired lock from the local business in antique hardware.

A thumping rumble overhead like a stick rattling over a boardwalk—then silence. I knew the noises of construction and this one didn't fit.

Krasner, leaning against the side of the house under his ladder, was trying to light up with shaking hands. "Jesus Christ!" He flipped me the matchbook and presented his unlit cigarette. "I could have been stuck on top of that fence like a pig for Chrissake!"

"What happened?"

"Goddamn spikes. Jesus! Or if I'm lucky enough to miss the fuckin' fence I can bust my skull open, or break my back on this charming brick walk of yours," arms huddled against chest and stomach as though shielding them still, "son of a bitch." He took a deep drag and spilled the smoke my way. "If I hadn't nailed down that toe-hold, I'd be a goner—slowed me up just enough so I could swing on to the ladder."

"Shingles still wet?"

"My ass," he snapped between clenched teeth, "they were fuckin' loose!"

"But how could that be? You nailed them down yourself."

"That's what I wanna know, babe, because if I get to that son of a bitch...who's been up there since I laid that roof? And I don't mean just on top, I mean in the attic, the goddamn house!"

Nobody had actually walked on the roof since early July when he'd closed it in, I'd seen to that. And the electrician's ill-advised attempt earlier that day had been cut short. But half the building trade in Tarragona had, for one reason or another, been inside the attic, running ducts and wires of one kind or another. "I myself go up there almost daily," I said, "to clean up everybody's junk. And, of course, there's been that leak—last time I checked was about two hours ago."

"Well sweetie—" soft sarcastic eyes surveyed me, asserting that right of appraisal that makes you want to spit in his face, slap and kick him below the belt all in one satisfying coordinated sweep—"I've had my little suspicions that you're not just crazy about me, but I don't think you have the balls, frankly my dear, to do me in. Besides, you don't owe me any money."

"*Kill* you? Is that what you think?"

"I ain't the kind that plays guitar under a full moon or writes poetry—I don't make things up, honey, and when I nail down a row of shingles, it stays put, you know? This little 'accident' was some kind of prearranged surprise *bon voyage* party, only the character that thought it up doesn't have too much going on upstairs—that don't narrow the field much, mind you, but it helps."

"How do you figure that?"

"A guy that has his shit together doesn't try to take you on your own turf, get me?"

"Well, whatever the intelligence quotient of your assailant—if there was one—we'd better report this immediately."

"The hell you don't! I'll handle this myself...a little personal matter between me and some screwball. Shouldn't be too much of a challenge, dear."

"Personal or not, if there's somebody around using my property to endanger people's lives, I'm not holding out any more invitations. I'm going in to call the police."

He was in the doorway before me straddling it. "You know lady, this place has one hell of a weird reputation, from way back."

"So?"

"So why don't you just cool it, *capisci*? Forget it. Keep a low profile till you finish up your little decorating job here, put a wad in your pocket, and mosey on back up Noh-th to your fat-ass professors, and your hubby and kids, and whatever else you got up there. Your lit-era-ture." The syllables wormed their way sneeringly from between his handsome whiskers.

"Damn right! I do intend to sell this place (I made up my mind, she says, right then and there), and I also intend to go to the police, on foot if necessary."

"Sweetie..." he cooed after me, "you know dear, I've got about, oh, an hour's work up there, tarring that flashing you're so upset about and nailing those shingles back down. And as much as you want this little job done—right?—I sure would love to oblige a lady."

"Is that supposed to make me feel over a barrel?" The oldest feeling in the world it seemed at that moment, practically the prototype of all feeling.

"Let's just say that if I see one of those bozo cops showing up here, I'll tell 'em I'm fixing a lit-tle bitty leak around your chimney. No problem, I'll say, everything hunky-dory, wee oversight—nobody's perfect." He lit another cigarette, steady as can be, plucked tiny bits of tobacco off his tongue, smiling his craggy smile. Disarming. "This grand old historic home of yours, dear,

has a way of touching folks in the head, especially the weaker—
oops! second sex. High-strung system like yours is bound to
snap when you take on more than you can handle. Whacko!
Those redneck cops know all about thaings-like-'at, honey."

Holding the gate open for me with mock courtesy he
added, "If I keep mum about this, and I will, they won't believe
your story and you know it. Your word against mine, dear, no
contest. They've all seen how nervous and techy you can get,
and, what with that muggy weather we're havin', gettin' techier
all the time. Read me?"

I could have sworn at that moment that the voice mimicked by those beard-fringed lips, animating those dark-green
eyes, was Jake's: sly innuendo greased with Krasner's special
brand of flirty insolence.

I shrugged and picked bits of trash off the walk. "Have it
your way. It wasn't *me* that fell off the roof and nearly broke my
neck, and just for the record: I couldn't care less about what you
do, Mr. Krasner, or don't do—or anybody else in this silly town.
You can rip each other into lit-tle bitty shreds and cook up a great
big bah-be-que out of the whole mess for all I care. It's your
party." And I made my way nonchalantly back up the porchsteps
and shut the door, leaning against it while the extension ladder
squeaked with the weight of Krasner on his way back up.

A hammer-throb behind my left temple pulsed through the
cut at the surface with a dull sting. My very right to the work I
was doing, my right even to its daily torture, had been chal-
lenged. Even it no longer belonged to me. But finish it I would,
no matter who might lay claim to it.

psycheme

Welcome back.

Friends and colleagues, my research shows there's only
one true antagonist pitted against us cons: the kook. And she
can turn up on any corner. Laps up conning like mother's milk,
digests it, regurgitates a mess of it, but is never absorbed by it.
Contrary to nature, she never becomes what she eats. You think
you've found a perfect gull but what you're harboring is a real

live skeptic, your one and only true enemy. Easy to overlook. The problem is lack of submission—even as she gorges herself on what you want her to believe, she's digesting it all the time and will eliminate it as if beliefs about hard reality work their way as naturally through her as roast beef and potatoes. In short, never holding on to any belief long enough to be thoroughly conned, the skeptic spells failure for your job (plus doing her own anal transformations and variations on it).

What to do? On the trusty principle that the enemy should always be hit where it hurts most, take advantage of their one great weakness, namely that these skeptics, never sharing a common bond with anybody, tend not to run in packs and so lose the advantages of collective strength and its systems. So to get these kooks on your side, form passing alliances with them: they *are* subject to temporary cons. The best example of how to do this can be checked out in that modern master strategist, Descartes (French, as you might expect).

This classic con begins with the claim that you can doubt anything running through your head (every skeptic starts nodding in agreement right away), but you can't doubt that *something* is running through it. Try it and you'll see you can't. All this tells you is that *if* you want to pay attention—systematically test it out—to whether or not something is going on in your head (following Descartes, we'll call this "thinking") you'll find 1) you're thinking something or other even if what you're thinking shows there's not much going on in your head and 2) you can't catch yourself doing no thinking at all. Using this ploy to get in with the skeptics, Monsieur D. then makes a lot more out of it than necessary, which is to say he moves right along with his job.

The case of Descartes has a further instructive side as a caution against self-conning even if you're really top-notch. As you know, every good con starts by hooking you on something real—and the reality, as in the old Greek master con I was telling you about, may be nothing but your own desire. Once partaking of desire, though, just a shot of it, you can be led to believe anything that follows; you're hooked on the stuff. Or, in the turn of the trick, you're placed where the only way to proceed is by conning yourself, and that's what happened to Descartes—he thoroughly duped himself, forgetting where he started. In telling about his discovery—one we can all get hooked on, by the way, because we can all say, yeah, I'm aware of something or other going on in my head now that you mention it—he was so moved as to say "therefore." Watch out when you hear that word. "I think," Descartes said, "*therefore* I exist." *Ergo* in his parlance. The first time I heard this it blew my mind. It didn't make any sense (always check into these first reactions if you don't want to con yourself). It didn't make sense until I got caught up in listening to Descartes explain himself—damned if I wasn't going along with the guy. All good con jobs have this effect, they leave the reasoning up to the sucker in order to be sure that he's conned by his own reasoning (i.e. he becomes a consenting adult). In fact, all that Descartes said does follow if you follow him. But when I don't, this stuff going on in my head doesn't tell me whether I exist or not—not that I tend to have any doubt about it as a rule, let me assure you, I don't—but I see plenty of others who do, and thinking, in their case, rather than assuring them that they are real people, is more apt to have the opposite effect, ever notice that? Descartes himself finally hauled in God as the only one with enough power to tie his own thinking in with real things going on, an old but great strategic move that switches the responsibility for D's conning (as well as any self-conning you may be doing) over to the divine Father-Con who guarantees whatever is real in your thinking. As any good psychotic suspects all along, a big part if not all of this stuff in your head comes from a power outside, so it's not really yours.

Let me assure you again I don't believe a word of this any more than you do, I'm no nut.

But let's look briefly at the positive aspect of Cartesian conning. What it calls to our attention is that we *think*, whether we want to or not; we're duped no matter what it is we're thinking about (and in the final analysis, don't even know where it all comes from). Given the Cartesian dilemma that you can't turn thinking off although you know it dupes you, it makes plain sense to keep tabs on what's happening in your head, not so you'll know you exist (for reasons already adverted to) but so you'll smarten up. I know you're streetwise already—that's why I can talk to you like this—you're hip to the fact that the biggest sucker is he who collaborates in his own suckering, right? If you don't keep up with what's in your own head and you suspect I'm calling you a sucker, I am; that thinking you're doing, that's the man, the con man you are—nothing personal intended, it's a universal structure. Everybody's got his own con man lodged where he calls him his thinking.

Look at it this way: to call yourself a thinking thing is to refer to yourself as your thinking, so, to say "I think" is to say "I I" sir. Or to indicate what's going on this very second, you might say more precisely "I'm thinking," which is the equivalent of "I'm Iing." Granted this translation gets you no place, it has the virtue of lending a different function to your *Is* (also your *is* as in "I is") or, as in one woman's beginnings, the eye of your story.

That's about it, friends, except for pointing out that to say we all want our Idea of the Good expresses in grand old con style an equally fundamental tautology of psychical reality: we all want what we want, I want myself wanting, better known as "Platonic love." Not that I propose cancelling any trips through regions of Platonic desire, for such psychical movement can only bring us continuing satisfaction in being who we are wanting nothing. Hang on to your travel guides, street-critics—this has been the merest peep at our common ground. It's no substitute for the original.

As for me, my desire is intransitive: I want nothing more than I want. Me-wanting. To be left alone in my wanting, my desire, now *that's* life well-lived. Never more let it be said that you have not been fully informed about what a woman wants.

xiii

"What's your name?" she asks the fat one, pen ready.

"Whaddya wanna know for?"

"So I can write out this check to you for spreading the shells, and a good job you did too." It's true—there, before them, the level expanse of oyster shells, deeply bedded, still grey with mud as they had come off the delivery truck. A good rain would wash them clean and hot sun bleach them pearly white.

"No checks. We made this deal for cash." He turns for confirmation to the gaunt one gazing through the fence in disinterested silence.

She replies that, as a matter of fact, absolutely nothing was said about the mode of payment and that, besides, she doesn't have over a dollar or two on her, "never do."

"You can go to the bank. We'll wait."

"Not today, car's in the garage." She watches him crane his short fleshy neck to make a confirmatory survey of the street. "Drop by tomorrow and I'll have the cash ready for you."

"No deal, lady! We get paid when we finish a job, and we don't accept nothin' but greenbacks. We don't bother with no receipts neither," said with a sly wink. He worries the gap between his upper front teeth with a pick and shifts his considerable bulk from his left side to his right on the crunchy shelled surface. You bluffed me once, don't push your luck, his eyes say.

Accustomed to keeping up with my money down to a few cents, I knew perfectly well, she says, what I had in my purse, but I didn't want those two, above all, to think I kept any ready cash around even in small amounts. "I'll have to borrow from the accountants down the block," she said, pointing to the nineteenth-century raised cottage three doors down, decked out in fully sanctioned Charlestonian tints—one of those old Gulf Coast homes rambling deep into its city lot, offering the careless ease of its sturdy survival, the first building on the block to have been converted into rehabilitated office space.

The fat one nods distrustfully as he works over his teeth, and strolls along behind with his cohort. Up into the gallery she marches and swings open the fine cypress door with a backward wave at them to wait at the bottom of the steps. In the empty hall, electric typewriters clacking behind doors, she fishes out two tens from her wallet, peeps down at them a few moments through the wavy leaded sidelight, and emerges with the bills ostentatiously thrust toward the fat one. He takes them and promptly passes them on to the other one, hitches up his trousers and struts off, mission accomplished.

"Heard you had an accident on your property yesterday." The one called Rail, addressing her in the quick, clipped drawl of a Gulf Coast gentleman. "It's gratifying to see, ma'am, that the report of your injury was exaggerated."

"Oh that…it was nothing. A scrap of wood grazed my forehead."

"One of the perils of restoring an old home, I suppose?"

"How did you know?"

"Not much goes on in the old Quarter that doesn't get around within minutes, hours at most. It's like a community network, not as high-tech as CBS of course, but a lot more local color."

"Hardly sensational news, though."

"Could have been—I'd advise you to steer clear of flying objects, Miz Dumot." A thoughtful smile softens the gaunt cheeks—the gauntness, no mistaking it, of debauch, not asceticism. "Easy for anything at all to fly out of control in your situation, if I may say so."

Conceivably, she reflects, I was losing my ability to judge with any degree of accuracy those I was encountering daily. This abrupt geniality over something of no consequence to him: no more, perhaps, than an expression of ordinary passing concern?

Even Tom Evans, who arrived during the lunch hour to collect his final payment (not in his pickup but in the family Delta Royale, maroon inside and out), even he seemed another man—the old Evans again, expansive as Jove, admiring woodwork and walls and hardware without a ghost of meanness. "You certainly have done yourse'f proud here, shuga," etcetera. Just the fulsome fatherly type with old-fashioned ideas about the inferior sex. Well-meaning, of course; a man who is good with children and pets. Sorry to hear about the accident, "Too many bunglers in the trade nowadays…kids don't have the craft no more." Sure enough.

"See you don't go off without sayin' goodbye to your friends, hear?" he said. A huge first piece of Tarragona seemed to break away from her in that moment, she says. The longed-for diminishment, relief. And, not unforeseen even in the longing, loss. What drew her once, back in March, what gripped her and drove her through all the permutations of infatuation running its course, had entered its terminal phase.

About four o'clock, still feeling the end beginning as she stopped to finger the narrow blades of white oleander (just behind the big down-curving branch of the live oak), the pickup with its tribe from Cadiz Boulevard rolled leisurely past, like a carnival float. All of them, the woman with the baby in the middle and the fat one driving, leaned forward, eyes almost closed in laughter. Staring after them from behind the iron pales, in the shadow, she was caught off guard when the gaunt one stuck his head out the window, looked straight back at her over his shoulder and briskly tilted his chin and nose upward: the nod the Greeks make when they are saying "No."

In the step or two she instantly took toward the house and her business there, an involuntary tension closed her fingers over the oleander leaves. Their rumpled feel in her fist (leathery, she says, as the skin of old paper dollars my father kept wadded in his pocket when I was a child) brought back a long-forgotten spell, stories about how a powerful poison could be made from them, quickening in her, like an answer to the ancient call for insight, the resolve to move on, on and through the finish work before her—to move on unmoved in her refusal to justify either existence or its suffering, to stake out claims to either knowledge or power.

Or, even more perverse, says Harding, to love. On the porch, she opened her fist and watched the little crushed green mass flex limply back into her palm before she flung it, out, over the cool blue-green heads of the hydrangeas. There it caught and hung untidily. No matter, she says, the Gulf breeze would blow it free sooner or later.

psycheme

He shall not speak from the grave in my voice nor any of his cult, neither those before 1900 nor those after. That is not what I meant at all. That is not it, at all.

xiv

"Hello there...anybody home?"

Restoration of historic properties seems to give the public, or so they imagine, something like the unquestioned right of entry belonging to ownership. They ramble in, even perfect strangers, and wander and poke about at their pleasure. Lately, this tendency to go on treating the Boullet House as if it were still a demolition site open to all had become tiresome, to say the least, but I myself was so inured to earlier conditions, and there was now always so much legitimate coming and going, that the door stayed open, sometimes wide open, much of the day.

"Elizabeth?" Randall Cane's voice from below. A seafaring man had built the house (as the Old Tarragona walking guide informed the public), and up in his library, under one of the four great dormer sills doing double duty as a hatch, he'd had a sort of hold installed the full depth and length of the sill, lined with cedar; intended, one supposed, for special safekeeping. That's where I was when I heard my name called, giving the hold a final wipedown with a damp sponge.

Why, I wondered, had I never noticed that peremptory, wheedling insistence on being heard? On being heeded—in all its cultivated difference, so gentle, so hedged by decorum, a voice reminiscent of the Evans voice. "Elizabeth?"

A summons is a summons; but one can refuse. Quicker than you can say "wanton acts of secretion" I pulled the hatch down over my head (I'd just oiled the hinge and the descent was smooth as ice cream) and hunkered down. It was like any cedar closet except horizontal, aromatic and roomy.

Steps creaked up the stairs. Pacing slowly, like someone taking in the sights, Randall Cane advanced along the upper hall stopping at each room, clicking doors shut and open, open and shut, testing, sampling the reconditioned locks

A soft humming and, again, the call for me to come forth, once, twice, as he entered the Captain's library. "Hmmmm...." Quiet, irregular pacing up and down the room—a room made for pacing, to help thought find its stride.

And back out into the hall, to make his presence known once more: "Is that you, Elizabeth? It's Randall Cane."

I'd heard it, too, the light quick step on the stair.

"...saw your car, sir, front door...don't seem...car's gone." Is it possible that, for once, he'd overlooked a detail of my routine? My trip to the repair shop that morning, my ride back a bit later in one of the company vans? Digital chronometer recording five p.m. and he not know where I was? (Was this my triumph at last?)

Jake lowered his voice inaudibly, no doubt over lighting

one of his vile cigars.

Cane: "Besides supplying you and your clients, what else?"

"Smut, sir...floodin' the town...don't distribute though."

"So that's it."

"...link...." Jake always was a soft-spoken man, especially when he had weighty matters to communicate.

"Not mixed up in any of it, is she?"

"Not...turned up other evidence...protect your innerests."

For a moment, Cane hesitated. "How's that?"

"...been trailin'...not easy workin' out the details...."

"Skip your methods—and watch the ash, Landry, no need to leave a visiting card. Are you sure about her? No blackmail or anything like that afoot, is there?"

Jake's dignity momentarily found a corresponding dynamic level: "Didn't your Pa always trust Jake Landry like his own kin, sir? Fam'lies been associatin' together from way back, ain't they?"

"In a business way, Landry. I'll make it worth your while... depend on her being out of it. Just spare me the particulars."

"...out of your way, sir in a day or two."

"Out of *my* way? What *are* you talking about, Landry?"

Here was the smug Landry I recognized: "Why gettin' rid of that colored granddaughter of Frances Boullet's, sir, that's been such a headache to you and yours."

"Your neighborhood intrigues, Landry, are of even less interest to me than your small-time peddling. I'm only concerned with whatever that roofer chap is up to with my niece."

"I thought you wanted, sir...."

"Don't try to put yourself in my place, something your grandfather understood perfectly, and nothing's changed there. Just be sure that man knows where the line is, call his bluff, if necessary."

"...beggin' your pardon, sir, but I don't b'lieve your friends would like it if—well, you know, the...."

Did he say "cheat"? "The cheat?" Who might that be?

Cane's voice, low with dangerous significance: "I don't care for your insinuations, Landry...what's all this absurd business about old Jeremy Wentworth?"

"Hill a beans, sir, like you say." Landry was getting his second wind. "That trash...moved...."

"Need I remind you that the Wentworths haven't always been what they are today? In any case, the disadvantaged of whatever color or station are properly objects not of our loathing but of our compassion. Let's remember that."

Jake moved so close to the wall I could have whispered in his ear.

"Yessir, like you say, 'disadvannaged.' Well, sir, it seems Tom found 'im lyin' here near dead and mumblin' 'bout his fam'ly bein' all doped up an' such crazy stuff as that. Him havin' such a longtime connection with your Papa—and, beggin' your pardon, sir, that ole colored woman too—I thought I oughtta keep an eye on things. And then Tom took it into his head one day to go down to the station—"

"Who did you say?"

"Plumber, sir. Evans. Makin' mountains outta molehills, thass all it was."

"Awkward."

"Lucky thing my buddy Sergeant Peaden—well, sir, less juss say whatevcr he finds out will be oh-fishal if you get my meanin', sir. The chief—" (Aha! That's what it was, "the chief." One of Dr. Cane's "friends," who wouldn't like it if—if what?)

"What else did Wentworth convey to this—who did you say?" Clinical again, supremely cool about the whole absurd business.

"Plumbcr, sir. Mr. Jeremy Wentworth kep' sayin' there was somebody out to get rid a him, sir, an' he had some ole papers to back 'im up...legal dockymonts, he said."

Low: "...see them?"

"Don't nobody know what happen' to them dockyments, sir—could be...well, sir, the granddaughter, sir...."

"Who?"

"Or if there even was inny," Jake quickly corrected himself. "No point stirring up imaginary problems, hear?"

"Like you said, sir, let all 'em sleepin' dogs lie."

"Mind your ash, Landry."

"Yessir, I'll see to it that this here en-tire case...like you say...."

"Well fine, Jake, fine. We of the 'good ole families,' as the phrase goes, cannot afford to relax our vigilance. Right, Jake, ole man?" Such a burden to have to explain, even tongue-in-cheek, what is so ineffably patent.

"...my philosophy," or words to that effect, I'm sure. In a pinch, I could have made a great understudy for Jake.

Mumbling, as they move away, across the room.

And pausing, at the library door most likely. All quiet, yes; coast clear. Dr. Cane's voice, firmly at the habitual ironic distance of the Southern gentry—just the proper degree of intimacy reserved for valued helpers not of his station—heard projecting back into the room to Jake, no doubt a deferential step or two behind: "Miz Cane wouldn't—doesn't do to let the ugly side of life get too close, know what I mean? If that fellow sees my niece again, call my office, Landry. Right?"

Steps out on the landing, going down, no hurry—never know when you might bump into the new owner. Could be awkward. Front door clicking shut, opening; best to leave everything as it was, now that no one need be the wiser. Let sleeping dogs lie.

An engine sprang to life and sped down Valencia Street. Inviolate at any cost, the family name of Cane. Breeding, training, education, all function in him to censor alien traces the slightest of which, whatever their origin, signify present danger calling for immediate destruction. The only issue: the choice of appropriate questions. For who does not know that strategic questions lead to their own answers?

psycheme

Today I am tempted to turn away.

From a makeshift stand in narcissism I nod in your direction. You there, *mon semblable, mon frère*.

Soeur, if you like.

A moment free of eroticism, free of desire because satisfying in its Resistants. Almost.

I call them Resistants because they resist language, because they cannot be represented, because they have no meaning and possibly no being. Because their very acknowledgement requires, but can never be more than, a simple act of nodding in their direction. There. And there. The gesture toward the Resistant is the only possible affirmation, I have heard Harding say. It loosens the organism, allowing experience to shape in the orifice of language.

A turning of our bodies.

Away from each other to unchain signs from the feeling-of-meaning. We would have signs reveal themselves, we would together know these our creators.

This places us in an unnatural relation. Not supernatural or perverse, *un*natural. One in which we collaborate to escape, not the activity of signing but the domination of signs.

Almost.

XV

Friday evening's slow rain, which lasted through the night and on and off all Saturday morning, washed the mud off the shells. In the grey end of afternoon, they shone up at me with the pallor of old bones, and in the rain's aftermath I longed for a shower, a pot of brewed tea, and rest. Rest more than anything, somewhere far from Tarragona, far from the Randall Canes of this world and all their mignons. Two refurbished chandeliers for the library converted from gas lamps and polished to a soft gold sat upright in the back seat of my car like persons of privilege. Sliding one of them out by its tall center shaft, I glimpsed—who else? He wouldn't dare snoop around like that at Segovia Crescent, what with Miz Cane's delicate sensibilities to worry about!

My chandelier and I advanced. We bore down on him so resolutely his pencil stopped dead as I positioned myself before him with both hands gripped around the gleaming shaft, a one-woman crusade for calling his bluff.

"Seein' you wasn't here, Miz Dumot...fack is, I couldn't get this here angle juss right"—chin and pencil point plotted a line to the roof of the Boullet House—"with all 'at commotion over here ever' day this week."

"You know, Mr. Landry"—it was gratifying to roll off his name in anticipation of getting a few things off my chest—"this house has been here a very long time, and you've had any number of opportunities to draw it from every conceivable angle for just about every imaginable purpose, and even some I wouldn't dream of imagining. True, the carriage gates stand wide open, and anyone can unlatch the other two gates and stroll right on in, front or back, just as they prefer, but the fact that there are ways to enter does not negate the equally incontestable fact that you are standing, at this very moment, on private property. You will please remember that this back yard and everything within the bounds of this iron fence"—I gave him a moment to take in its full circumference—"is *private property*, and you are hereby advised that I intend for it to remain *private* at all times in the foreseeable future." And I lowered my standard with as much dignity as its considerable heft and span would allow.

Jake lit a cigar without his usual folderol and flipped the match into the alley. "That's just it, ma'am, with the house bein' so near ready now—leastways from the outside, don't know nothin' 'bout the inside of course, juss what I hear..." (Bald-faced worm of a liar!) "Fack is, I'm juss drawin' that chimney there in line with your fence here—have to get this one down exackly." An urgent case, he explained, wielding his pencil with overbearing dexterity; couldn't wait.

"Urgent is it? Bet you've turned up some brand new evidence that old Wentworth was poisoned by shooting toxic gases down the flue, right? With all I have to do, I'm behind on the local gossip, not to mention on my ratiocination."

Flick went the cigar ash, in a rare pique. "That wasn't really what you'd call my case, ma'am, juss he'pin out a colleague in the police on that one, y'unnerstand."

I did, of course, more or less—help keep a lid, like they say, on whatever it was that had old Wentworth in such a mortal rage, and divert suspicion, maybe, to an old woman growing poppies in her back yard. Both missions, now, called off from on high.

"This here case," he was saying, engrossed in his sketch, "well, I have a personal innerest in this one, you might say."

"I can see you're a busy man."

"Could be related to the lil accident you had over here, coupla days back."

Harding says she looked provocatively into the pale fish-eyes. "A scratch, nothing to set tongues wagging."

"Good thing you carry liability, ma'am. How 'bout life insurance? A woman with children like yourse'f, ma'am, would be well-advised, like they say. Well-advised." Closing his sketch-book, he took a corrective nip from the end of his cigar. "In case of any more accidents on your proppity here...."

The man was a hidden camera, and for all I knew he'd been nosing through my personal papers and bugging my phone conversations. "Look Mr. Landry, I've had it with you and everybody else around here congregating at my place as if it's the public fairground, and I'd be much obliged if you would take your leave presently—this very second, as you might say. And stay out, unless invited in. By whom, I can't imagine, certainly not me."

"Sure thing Miz Dumot, reckon I forgot myse'f," and with cigar poised a fraction of an inch from his vermiculate lips, "thinkin' a man's life might be that important."

The chandelier and I were right at his heels as he made for the alley gate and slipped out in a huff. "If that clumsy insinua-tion," I said, "is anything more than an idle pretense, let's have it out—the facts." Shades of Randall Cane, I hoped, lending my request authority.

"I b'lieve you already got some of 'em, ma'am, but you ain't seen fit to report 'em." With the fence safely between us, he flipped open his sketchpad to a clean page. In a few skillful strokes, he drew a hand, fingers curved inward to grasp a thin pole—the end of a broomhandle possibly, or a cane—sinewy fin-gers, but so slender and finely proportioned as to appear grace-ful, like the hand of a man, maybe even a woman, of leisure. Only the dark ridges at the tips of the nails, appearing swiftly at the end of Jake's pencil like flyspecks, gave that impression the lie.

"Look familiar?" On the other side of the iron palings, he held up the notebook for me like a placard.

Images blurred through my memory fast as cards fanned down into a closing deck: you glimpse a face as they fall, but too fast for recognition. The hand was as familiar, somehow, as the one-eyed figures in their cascading descent, as elusively sinister as that forever averted two-dimensional gaze.

"This here hand is mixed up in some bidness I wouldn't care to mention in front of a lady. Sure you ain't never seen it?"

I was sure I had, but that was all, and I wasn't about to give him the satisfaction of even qualified assent. Along the bottom of the drawing, in fussy black letters, he printed EXHIBIT A: MURDERING HAND, and let me have another go at it, close up.

Me hoisting my chandelier once again: "I wouldn't know, and I most certainly haven't got time for guessing games." There was no way, in the end, to keep from being stage-managed by the man except by exiting, and even then you had the inescapable sense of doing it on cue.

"Won't be no guessin' to it, 'fore the night's out," he mumbled as he folded up the pad. "Somethin' for you to remember, ma'am—for future reference you might say," he called after me.

He was still posted like an officious sign on a highway when Sergeant Peaden's patrol car drew alongside him in the alley a few minutes later, whereupon our investigator of human arcana tucked away his book with these final words to me, as I stood searching my trunk for electrical tape: "Don't say Jake Landry didn't give you alla facks, ma'am."

xvi

When I came back out for the other light they were both there waiting. "Lemme get this out for you," said Sergeant Peaden, taking hold of my fixture in an unprecedented act of chivalry. In the hall he set it down like a crate of eggs and looked to Jake for further direction.

"The Sergeant here has a lil po-lice problem you might be able to he'p 'im out with, ma'am. It's about that ole colored woman they was lookin' for a while back, you know the one."

"Name of Mary Louise Bernard," Peaden supplied officially.

"We got to thinkin', ma'am, how there wasn't really no solid evidence, like you said, for detainin' her...."

"Do you mean *in jail*?"

"Yes ma'am, thass just it, you see...I put it to Sergeant Peaden here, who, as you may recolleck, was lookin' into that Wentworth bidness—"

"And mighty obligin' you were, too, ma'am," Peaden intercepted somewhat to Jake's annoyance. I could tell, because the cellophane crackled a bit louder than usual as he slid it off the cigar and stuffed the latter summarily into Peaden's mouth.

"I was tellin' the Sergeant 'fore you come out, 'that Miz Dumot,' I said, 'that's one highly edjicated lady right there, an' she cain't see no case to speak of neither,' I said."

"And you was kinda like a witness...."

"Bein' the first to come on the proppity like—"

"And gettin' a good look at the deceased."

"An' the Sergeant here," with a bravura extraction of a match from a nearly empty book, "the Sergeant agreed with us one hunnerd percent that there wasn't no sense goin' on with inny of it no more. No sense atall."

"So what's the hang-up, Sergeant?"

Peaden removed the cigar and lowered his jaw, but no sound issued. His head dropped to one side and rested almost on his shoulder, while he chewed his gum so slowly and deliberately as to suggest that the question called for more than ordinary study and circumspection.

"Well you see," Jake stepped in, "this here rookie officer that's learnin' the ropes, like they say—"

"Young Gorrie, ma'am, you've seen the boy."

"A novice, ain't that the word?"

"Yes?" Jake's lexical retrenchments for compelling my attention got on my nerves worse than his drawings, which had at least the authenticity of craft beyond mere guile.

"The boy got real caught up in the case, ma'am," reluctantly from Peaden, "lookin' for a chance to get ahead, I guess."

"Claims he got some kine a new evidence. Don't 'mount to a hill a beans, a course, but now the Deppity Chief has her down at the jail, like you said ma'am."

"And that's the whole story right there," Peaden concluded, falling snappily back on his gum, case closed.

Landry passed him a light, and Peaden turned his blind glasses toward me over the first puff.

"What Sgt. Peaden means to say," Landry prompted.

"What I mean to say, ma'am, is, if it was me that picked up the accused—"

"Accused of what?"

"You see, the Sergeant here could of kept things strickly under his own control ma'am, no problem."

"None atall," Peaden concurred amidst more quick, shallow puffs, while Landry's eyes transfixed him with their watery pallor. "But now it's outta my hands dontcha see."

"Won't be no indictment a course, but the Sergeant here is real anxious to git her released—"

"Quiet-like," the officer emphasized, "no sense disturbin' the peace."

"Like they say—"

"I mean it would save—"

"It would save the ole nigger woman a big heap of trouble."

"Gettin' upset and all," Peaden amplified guiltily.

"I see." Their little, almost surely self-serving, strategem, aborted at the eleventh hour by the eminent Dr. Cane for the dimmest of reasons, had ended on my doorstep where I could do with it, not exactly as I pleased, but one of two things: take it up as mine, or sweep it, stone-hearted, aside. Either way it looked like I was to be in on it up to my neck.

"Where you come into the picture, Miz Dumot," he explained under tense scrutiny from Peaden—and with the earnestness of one who, having stumbled on a miscarriage of justice, forges on, trusting that decency and humanity will exact cooperation from all, and if they don't it's because not everyone, contrary to first impressions, is decent and humane—"where you come in is kine a like a character witness, you might say."

"For Miss Mary Louise? Is that what you had in mind?"

"In-die-reckly ma'am. You see, all they got is Doc Shibbles' word, an' you an' me both know he's lost his mind, let's face it. Don't know Mond'y from Tewsd'y an' visa-versa. Claims she come over here the day old Wentworth passed away an' did some kine a hoodoo act on them back steps out there, an' there was dogs barkin' and she threw 'em somethin' to quiet 'em down some."

"But," I took up the thread in the softly ironic vein Jake's account had opened for me, "the Wentworths took the dogs along when they moved themselves and most of their possessions out, and that was the day *before* the old man died. He was still alive and kicking next morning and no dogs in sight—am I right so far?" Jake nodded his approval of my deductive powers. "So it couldn't have been *that* day Doc Shibbles saw Miss Mary Louise with the dogs, as you say—not to mention the little matter of the back steps...."

"They was broke off a good while back, like you say ma'am—matter of fack, it's been a good two or three years now. I can see you got a real good unnerstandin' of the case. Now if you was to repeat all 'em facks to the Deppity Chief, an' if you could put in some a them edjicated words...like you might say it was just a vay-ga-rie...why, it would he'p out ever'body concerned—all around, ma'am."

"And you have to do it real quick!" Peaden popped out.

"Yes," I said, "I think I see just what you mean." Possibilities were flashing on and off in my brain like neon lights in Times Square.

"It couldn't hurt either if you was to state that you know for a fack Doc Shibbles makes things up that don't have no basis," was Peaden's bold addition.

"Somethin' else you wanna bring up too," Landry persisted, so absorbed in our collaborative ratiocination he was letting his own cigar go cold.

"And what might that be, Mr. Landry?"

"You see ma'am, your plumber...I b'lieve he's your plumber, am I right?"

"Go on, Mr. Landry."

"Well your plumber, ma'am, Tom Evans, he mighta been the last man to see ole Wentworth alive, ain't that right Sergeant?"

"It's a fact. Tom was fixing to make you a bid, he says."

"Says you wrote 'im a letter, an' he knew you was due here any day. Well like you say, ole Wentworth had plinny a life in 'im that mornin' when he let Tom into the back bedroom, dragged out a bunch of ole legal papers in a box an' carried on somethin' awful, Tom says. He wasn't right no more, a course. Hadn't been in a good long while."

Both men eyed me closely as Jake let this truth sink in over a warm-up of his cigar. "If you was to put your mind to it," he suggested, "you might juss recolleck seein' them dockyments yourse'f, ma'am, although natchully inny upset a findin' a dead body on your proppity you wouldn't of paid 'em no mind."

I'd gone over it in detail after taking in Randall Cane's spe-

cial interest in this aspect of the case. There had been cardboard boxes amid the garbage strewn through the house the
day I came; one, I remembered, was spilling over with mail-
order catalogues, moldy issues of *True Confessions*, and any
number of half filled-out orders, bills and receipts, tear-out
renewal slips, old envelopes bulging with who knows what.

"There may have been papers of some kind," I agreed
vaguely.

"Now that you mention it," Peaden chimed in, "I recollect
seein' some official papers myself, clear as day, when Miz Avery
called us over here to remove the body."

"I don't wanna put no words in yore mouth, ma'am," Jake
encouraged me, "but if you was to say that you saw some dockyments that afternoon, like you said, that was still on the premises
when you come inside—'bout two-thirty wasn't it?—why it
surely would he'p out that ole colored suspect in question."

"Suspected, I gather, not only of doing away with Jeremy
Wentworth that very morning, by some mysterious hex, but also
of breaking into my house afterwards, presumably when he was
safely dead, to steal these old legal documents."

"Yes, ma'am, I do be'lieve that sums it up about correckly,
ridickulous as it sounds now that we all three know it ain't so."

In a spasm of coughing, Peaden stubbed out his half-
smoked cigar, relieved once more to don the hat of police official
asking routine questions. "Just what did happen to those, unh,
boxes and, unh, papers, ma'am?"

"You've thought to make a thorough search of the dump,
I'm sure—not to mention asking the Wentworths."

The Sergeant slid his glasses uncomfortably up and down his
shiny nose; again the glimpse of mild hazel eyes astonished me.

"Yes, ma'am, I mean as a matter of fact I didn't, ma'am,
but Miz...Professor, you might mention at the station—"

"What Sergeant Peaden is saying, Miz Dumot, is that he
looked all up and down this house way back then, top to bottom, you remember?"

"Way back *when*, Sergeant?"

Evasively from Landry: "Hardly a day or two after all that
garbage was hauled off."

"We didn't have no reason to be suspicious before," the

Sergeant blurted out.

"You mean before they hauled off the garbage?"

"No ma'am...before Tom Evans came to us...that is...."

I could see their threads of intrigue withstood examination about as well as cobwebs a good swish of a whisk broom.

"It's a cryin' shame," said Jake, always adept at making the critical shift, "that pore ole colored woman is just another victim of circumstance, you might say. But now if *you* was to...like I said, ma'am, a college P-H an' D like you...."

"If you was to go down there right away," Peaden contributed with the alacrity of a law officer aiding and abetting the social order, "you could still catch the Deputy Chief in, I bet. It's his Saturday on duty."

The Landry eye, I had long known, had its peculiar powers of detection. He might miss the motive, but he had an unfailing instinct for catching its import, even as he caught the salience of a stoop, or a laxness in the midriff, or a droop of the mouth. "Which way is the police station?" I inquired.

"Why it ain't two blocks from here. Allow the Sergeant to drive you down, ma'am."

"Patrol car's right out in front," Peaden affirmed.

With identical flourishes, Jake swung open first my Spanish gate and then the door of the said patrol car, considerately disposing of his cigar in the gutter along the way.

And that was how I came, a few seconds later, to be speeding through a sleepy stretch of the old Quarter with Sergeant Peaden to one side of me and Jake Landry, private investigator and artist of the essential, on the other.

psycheme

It should come as no surprise that, in my view, the language someone uses can tell you more about that person than almost anything else.

It can but it probably doesn't. Today I intend to describe so clearly where I'm coming from that there's no way you can miss placing my voice when I say: cut the vulva. Has a richly suggestive ring, doesn't it? That no-nonsense imperative, clean and

direct, of telling somebody else to cut it out (whatever and wherever *it* is) as in: cut the bull, cut the horseplay. Stop being vul-
gar. Just stop. The command to cut invokes the snap of the
filmic guillotine excising from the camera's gaze everything but
what it seeks. As if to free what the eye takes in from intervention. As if what goes on beyond its range is so vulvaraceous it
undercuts all serious attempts at objectification, a.k.a. *vulvation*
(alternatively: *vulvuration*) as in: to undergo vulvu(ra)tion, very
promising, nowadays, as an outpatient procedure with multiple
applications, or, altering our stem ever so slightly: *evulvution*,
as in the theory of, not to mention the whole problem of evulvuating this or that, other people's characters, for instance, as
when we say that someone is, or is acting like, a real vulva, or
that he/she is the most vulverted person around (cf. the political
act of vulversion). And then there's the physio-therapeutic practice of revulving (can be painful but effective), I'm told, not to be
confused with the earth revulving on and on (or various revulving personal habits), nor with Divine Revulvation, nor with the
French, the American, or the English Bloodless, or, come lately,
the information revulvution by which you and I are instantly
linked with everyone, everywhere—it just keeps coming.

Cut the vulva.

The fact is that one can spew vulvumes without anywhere
near exhausting the morphemic, semantic, and pragmatic
transmutations of cut vulvas (a.k.a. *cunt-outs*), especially when
passing over to the participial form: *cutting the vulva*, the vul-
vacity of which details a wealth of vulvid analytic incisions
describing the *langue* generating all possible vulvarisms. Isn't
that what *langues* are for? (Once awake this morning, I actually
entertained, and left hanging, the possibility of a truly vulvanoid
linguistics—making it my life's work, that is, as one would have
to, with the aim of rendering its previously unrecognized theoretical status avulvable to the interested, however few, along
with at least rudimentary critical and therapeutic applications.)

The very first association I myself had was with cutting the
mustard. You may have an inkling why. But rather than going
on, I'll content myself with situating the phrase in question
within the purview of my life, thereby allowing you at least one
little go at evulvuating its status. It came at the tail end of a

dream I was having when my alarm went off (it's one of those shrill old-fashioned ones that rip you right out of unconsciousness, no frills)—you'll see that the fact that I'd been studying, while drifting off to sleep, examples of language pieces irrupting with delusionary force is not irrelevant. All I can remember of the dream is that I walked into a butcher shop to pick up a cut of fresh ham. The butcher—presumably it was the butcher—a heavy-set, middle-aged, balding man, rather Greek-looking I thought, sat in a chair with a hunk of meat on the table in front of him. He appeared to be dozing, but I distinctly had the impression that his sleep might be feigned, that he might be peeping at me from under his not quite closed eyelids. At any rate, he was waiting, it appeared, for me to come for my meat. It had an elliptical shape, crinkly at the edges and a tiny whorl spiralling to a spot more or less in its center. Partly not to bother him and partly for no apparent reason except that I simply found myself doing it, I grasped a huge meat cleaver that appeared like magic from nowhere, leapt lightly up on the table, almost floating easily and naturally with no firm foothold—it was definitely me there except my sexual identity had gone hazy even though mostly I seemed female—and swung the cleaver down to a line I envisioned on the meat at one end of the ellipsis. As I did this, I considered three possibilities clearly and simultaneously: 1) he really *was* asleep and I could slip away with my meat and no fuss; 2) he was watching me with amusement, enjoying seeing what I did with a piece of meat when he thought I thought he wasn't looking; and 3) he was watching and ready to jump on me the second I did anything out of line (in this version, it was not clear whether my action was or was not out of line and I could only find out by doing it—it wasn't even clear, it occurred to me in the instant of bringing the cleaver down, that the meat on the table was mine, or any portion I might chop off, in which case I was sure to hear from him).

My alarm went off about the time the cleaver reached the table and I leaped out of bed without seeing whether I had successfully completed the slice. Slumped half asleep in an armchair, eyes closed, I strained to revive the dream, see how it ended. It was then that an apostrophaic voice spoke jubilantly: cut the vulva! (I forgot to say that when I was up on the table doing my thing with the meat cleaver, there was a somewhat shadowy figure of a woman standing behind him in the room. I had not seen her before, I think, because she did not appear to be a part of the action although perfectly well aware of what was going on.)

xvii

Saturday at the Tarragona police station on Cadiz Boulevard and Arriola Street when the clock reads 5:00 p.m. more or less, neither footstep nor cough, not even the telephone ringing perturbs the chilled air pumped into the reception area's fluorescent, musak-lulled vacancy. Except for the fact that the revolving door has admitted her, the place might be shut down for vacation or remodelling, or forever. Or stilled, merely, in anticipation of the night's campaigns against wanton acts of destruction, or crime aforethought, or simple ill-doing, or ill luck. The hours to come will yield plenty of each if *The Sentinel* is any authority in these matters.

Not quite empty styrofoam cups, soda pop cans, and match books trash the floor under the metal folding chairs and the sand-filled ashtray stands that signal an area for waiting—one of those places where you wait for service or bad news in surroundings so like its counterparts in sundry clinics, public assistance offices, motor vehicle bureaus, or regional bus stations, that if the hiatus of a yawn or of eyelids drooping could transport you spontaneously from one such vestibular space to another, you would hardly stir in your seat for all the difference your translation has made. Even in the late seventies, says Harding, we didn't yet realize that we were fast nearing the end of an era when such public spaces, no effort having been made to distinguish them from each other, gave the sense of an eternal present. The floors never seem to get a really good scrub between coats of waxy finish smeared on in haste; the walls are dreary with institutional paint, the windows (if any) with the precipitates of modern post-industrial life accumulating year-round. The liquid gurgled out by the hot drinks machine arrives with a foamy chalk on top that makes all of them taste pretty much alike. The candy dispenser is out of the best and freshest pieces, and the musak tapes have gone unchanged from day to day, month to month, always in season.

From the rim of a long counter opposite the entry on the Boulevard side, hang pens fastened to chrome ball chains, and on top is a scatter of official forms torn in half or into little bits. No one seems to be in attendance out here, but at one end of the counter, over a cubicle like a closed ticket seller's window, this hand-written sign has been posted: "Ring Bell for Service."

I did so, says Harding, and waited.

Above the wainscoting in oily institutional drab, the wall behind the counter has been papered over; recently, by the look of its design. The paper startles with its simulation, in a single repeated frame—a blow-up—of Tarragona's historic heart as rendered in picturesque detail on the tri-colored Bicentennial street map issued free of charge to all by the Tarragona Visitors' Bureau, in celebration of our country's two hundred years of doing something right, with compliments of the Chamber of Commerce. A dozen or more stately Hernando Inns march along the length of the wall, each run of paper rolling out its minutely graphic depiction of the tree-filled Plaza, the giant oaks garlanded with moss, the little lanes on three sides, the gaslights, a monster-torn DeLuna Bay at its southern edge, and residential Valencia Street to the north, cut off at a slant. The angle of vision is such that the backs of the Boullet House and its neighbor appear in three quarter view near the top of the cropped blow-up; you seem to be peering through a powerful telescope into a quaint old neighborhood at a great distance.

The shutter rattles up and a woman's face, vacuous, heavy make-up, halo of bouffant hairdo in rigid glittering blonde, appears in the window and looks out at me in disbelief. "Next?" The hum of activity from the room, or rooms, behind her—a dispatch radio, the hunt-and-peck of an old-fashioned typewriter, someone taking a phone call, the low undertone of conversation—confirms that business, after all, is going on here as usual.

My statement that I have information for the Deputy Chief pertaining to a case under criminal investigation is received with a skeptical "unh-hunh," and a curt warning that I'll "have to wait." Behind the window-lady, an invisible double seems to be urging an opinion of sorts as the blind rolls back down leaving me to the musak once more, how long is anybody's guess. Treacherous, the ways of power in old Tarragona, though by now familiar enough to suggest that it might become necessary to enlist outside help.

Gazing inattentively at a bulletin board, I peeled tiny bits of encrusted paint from my cuticles, the musak blandly harassing my consciousness (thinking, by the bye, that only aberrant people, probably all women in mid-life, are distracted by such insidious forms of trashing; only the aberrant actually pay attention to it or expend energy and will to shut it out instead of yielding to its banality, going with it, breathing it in like smog or letting it roll off the surfaces of perception mildly like newspaper headlines, or acid rain). I considered, or reconsidered, my approach.

Facts and figures posted before me, crimes and arrests, police successes, make favorable comparisons with other municipalities, nearly all in crime-ridden South Florida. The "Officer of the Year" award has gone to a good-looking one just promoted to lieutenant, with deep-set eyes, an aquiline nose, close-cropped dark hair, and a wide smile uncovering a set of admirably straight white teeth. He is Leon Zamora, whose people, the article says (getting down to the really relevant facts), have resided in Tarragona since earliest times, the name Zamora having been spotted in sixteenth-century records authenticating the Ponces, the oldest documented family of European descent, it is said, in the New World. Having proven himself in homicide, he has been put in charge of a special task force created in response to widespread citizen concern about police effectiveness. His big opportunity is knocking.

"...help you ma'am?" Long and lean, from his feet to his neck and down to his bony fingers, Zamora is the very incarnation of his photograph. His impeccable uniform signals that what others keep to as regulation he adopts as an ideal of personal fastidiousness. But his speech has a hasty slur to it, the doe-brown eyes are on guard. Fending off the ghost of ancestral color, are they? There is the smoothly stretched olive tone of the man's skin—Tarragonans are still hyper-sensitive to such apparitions, especially among their oldest families.

Over his brand new institutional desk, where disorder runs

energetically rampant, he explains to me that, although not officially on duty this evening, he will gladly be of help if he can—or
something along those lines, said with a curious swell of pride
vaunting diffidence: "…excuse…mess…urgent proposal…late
tonight…reorganizing…recently…bad…." His talk is so fast and
runs so lightly over the tongue, you strain just to catch the general drift. Barely. Two unframed posters occupy one wall of his
small office lately partitioned from a larger room. One poster is
inscribed with the motto "The word ADEQUATE does not exist
in my vocabulary"; its companion is a black and white portrait
of Robert Kennedy in open-necked sports shirt, the nostalgic
mass image of contemporary democratic man. "…always…step
ahead." He's reached a stop.

The man's time is not his own; something is driving him to
the top of his profession. An adjacent wall exhibits his diplomas
next to colored enlargements of the impeccable lieutenant with
his pretty wife and two strapping toddlers. Posed in front of
their ranch-style home, in one of the outlying fringes of Lavallet
or Basington Woods, most likely, where all the rising young
couples want to live, all four beam obligingly into the camera.

The best approach to this one, so zealous about screening
access to the Deputy Chief—and who cannot decide whether he
is a closet elitist or a closet egalitarian—is that no-nonsense
brand of sincerity and candor which shows not only that you
have a heart but that you know how to keep it in the right place.

"I've come here," I said, "because I'm concerned about
Miss Bernard."

No fudging on his part either, no feigned disengagement or
ignorance of the case. "Just…your interest…old lady, Miz
Dumot?"

I jumped right in to make all the points on which my infor-
mants had briefed me—with one or two original turns thrown
in—winding up with: "So you see, Lieutenant, I couldn't just sit
back and not speak up in defense of a wrongly accused elderly
woman, practically a neighbor of mine. And I'm sure the police
don't want to give the impression of being engaged in mere
harassment either."

He, too, takes the candid and sincere route—as dictated to
him by his new burden of official responsibility, however, and at

his characteristic gallop. The drift: he himself has not been convinced that earlier incriminating testimony would hold much water, but new information has come to light thanks to the dedication of a young police trainee who, in his off-hours, has taken it upon himself to observe the suspect's home, where he has witnessed nightly gatherings of black children and adolescents, different ages congregating on different nights—data on this insufficient for him, Zamora, just who they might be or where they come from—but these reports may have a bearing on whatever is behind the original allegations, if anything, and, in light of certain other evidence which he's not at liberty to divulge, constitute grounds for holding the woman in police custody.

The muscles of my face hurt from the effort of trying to catch his express train of an account, uncertain even at that of what I was hearing. "Miss Bernard," I submitted, "is a former schoolteacher. She's probably doing some tutoring in her home—plenty of kids around with learning problems. All ages."

He takes to this explanation. Too readily, perhaps, inasmuch as he seems to harbor a suspicion of some kind about her nightly young visitors. Whatever it is, he chooses to evade it by launching into a full-speed reminiscence of his boyhood in the old Quarter: "...nobody there I didn't know...black kids by name...not a bad place...even...hit bottom...grandmother knew Miss Mary Louise...high regard...changing times...all sectors... said hold her."

"I gather you're not comfortable with the situation, then?"

"...following up...routine...place for feelings...old lady... colorful...memory...," faster and faster, eliding more and more connections, "house...books...requested...jail...," until an agitated shuffling of papers betrays that he feels himself caught and exposed in a snarl. Abruptly, he peaks his lean fingers on the paper-strewn desk in front of him and looks at me with doe-eyed circumspection.

"Excuse me," he says and leaves the room, returning in a matter of seconds. "Deputy Chief...shortly. Meanwhile...how... obtain...knowledge...police records?"

I obliged him with a terse run-down of the visit from Peaden and Landry and a somewhat lengthy sampling of my opinion of the latter.

Lt. Zamora is so deep in thought his speech decelerates almost to the pace of ordinary mortals. "I wonder," he ventures, "if you aren't jumping...allowing personal...enter in, ma'am... information does show concern...." A man aiming at greatness must, before all else, be fair and impartial to all no matter what, give credit where credit is due, or at least appear to. And a man fending off ghosts, more than most.

The owner of the bouffant hairdo sticks it in the door without knocking and snaps, "Depitty Chief says come on in."

Smiling, the same beckons me to a seat across the desk from his own leatherette swivel chair out of which he has just risen, and with an economy of timing that is entirely *comme il faut*, both mannerly and official, he settles back down into it. A pleasure to meet the old Quarter's most notable restorationist, he says, who is to be congratulated on a lovely choice of exterior colors, and the fine brick steps—not original, he assumes, but a credible touch. How does one get that kind of unusual detail past Greeley Connor?

The Deputy Chief is in his prime, if slightly overfed as they sometimes are in their prime, with a razor haircut to match his trendy mustache. More the Yuppie in appearance than a good ole boy like him has reason to be.

"Greeley's flexible enough if what you do is in keeping with the general character of your restoration," I lied as charmingly as I could (having added the steps only over his strenuous objection: "Inauthentic in this part of the country, you know—only wooden steps are appropriate to a home such as this").

Lt. Zamora recapitulates my arguments in defense of Miss Bernard and, surprisingly, the Deputy Chief has no trouble at all deciphering his morse code. Up and down glides the Adams apple on Zamora's elongated throat as he clears it confidently for the summation: "...suggest sir...light of...consider...Shibbles...delayed search...untenable...."

Buckminster opens one of the folders on his nearly empty desk and leafs through it as if for the first time (or perhaps because he wishes to avoid my gaze). He expresses the police department's appreciation for my interest. My points, he grants, are well taken. Very well taken. "But this fellow Gorrie, he's the most promising rookie we've had here in a long time, isn't that so, Leon? Takes his job very seriously, can't dismiss his findings out of hand."

"What findings?"

He glides right over my question. Selective inattention has brought the Deputy Chief this far and no further. Admitting just the start of a grin to his face that makes him look the cheeky boy he may once have been, he comments waggishly that everybody knows about the old lady's unconventional ways, "don't they, Leon? Goes around stickin' pins into dolls and chantin' a lot of mumbo-jumbo." The greenish blue eyes dance merrily in his almost handsome face.

"Surely you can't charge people with that, not even in Tarragona—then again, who knows? A woman can lose her job here for teaching novels that offend the police chief's family."

Lt. Zamora is about to grin but controls himself in the nick of time. It will not do to have a future Chief go on record as having laughed at his predecessor.

Buckminster has turned thoughtful, as though he is considering my point seriously—or as though he has glimpsed the inauthentic detail of the brick steps in a new light. But his voice is perfectly bland when he declares, "As a matter of fact, there *are* grounds for a charge here, and have been for a good long while, except that nobody worried about it until Miss Bernard got mixed up in this Wentworth business."

"Don't you mean 'got mixed up *with*' the Wentworth business, as you call it? Who got her mixed up in it was Landry, as I told you."

"Until she was suspected of being mixed up in it," Zamora offers in an agile, word-perfect compromise.

The Deputy Chief strains his neck from side to side, as though his open collar is getting too snug on him. "Miss Bernard is known to be a practitioner of voodoo—a type of black magic, or whatever you want to call it—may even be holding illegal sessions in her home, at night."

Harding says she laughed, wishing for once she had a cigarette for exhaling a magniloquent cloud of disbelief.

"Is that what your promising officer's 'findings' have turned up?"

He pulls a manila envelope from a desk drawer and delicately shakes out a little blue-eyed figurine with a red-topped
straight pin stuck in its chest: found in the Boullet House, no
less, back in May. Old Wentworth was gripping it so tight under
his blanket it had to be pried loose from his fingers. Now Gorrie
thinks a search of the suspect's home may turn up other imple-
ments of the dark art; a warrant is already in the works.

Lt. Zamora folds his slender arms, palm over crooked
elbow, and stares sideways down at the Deputy Chief's blond
and tanned family captured in a photograph on the Deputy
Chief's desk, maybe to disassociate himself from the more dubious exhibit in the Deputy Chief's outspread hand.

"Frankly, that doll looks to me like an improvised prop for
a kid's horror movie. In a country where cultism is practically
fashionable—not to mention that it's protected by the Constitution—you can hardly prosecute someone for their religious
practices, can you?" This last directed mainly at Zamora's
ascetic profile.

He has yielded to his superior, who explains that Tarragona,
like many an older township across the country, has never
rescinded certain outdated laws on its books which continue in
force technically. The assiduous Gorrie, it seems, has turned up
an old anti-voodoo ordinance dating back to an effort, in the
eighteenth century, to control a notorious cult imported along
with slaves from the West Indies. Absurd and anachronistic, he
well knows—and so, of course, will any judge or jury. No one is
going to be convicted on such a basis in this day and age, and if
voodooism is her only problem the Afro-American woman will
go free in due course—no more than a technicality. On the other
hand, it's probably just as well to discourage any gangs of people,
of whatever age or color, from meeting for no good purpose anyway.

And chances are, Zamora adds in a leap to fortify good
sense with better, that old Wentworth's heart just plain gave
out, finally, in the ordinary run of things.

"All by itself? No voodoo-induced coronary failure?"

"The doll is a problem," Buckminster intervenes sternly,
but a bit uneasily nonetheless, "it's not just a question of intent."

"Jailing people for their thoughts, you mean?"

"I meant we may be dealing with certain dangerous substances here."

"Such as?"

"Toxic preparations, potions that folks in the neighborhood say the Bernard woman dispenses to them...we're having some analyzed." For good measure, he throws in a reference to Doc Shibbles' statement about seeing the suspect perform strange rites at the Boullet House on the day of Wentworth's death.

"Which testimony, as I've demonstrated, is totally worthless."

"Some good will have been accomplished," he says, leaning forward over his desk with the doll still cupped in his hand, "by clearing a dusty old ordinance off the books. Makes the system more efficient."

"Meanwhile" (lowering her voice, Harding says, to its most reassuring contralto range) "meanwhile the Afro-American woman is free to avail herself of the exemplary comforts of the city jail, even to the extent—if I understood you correctly Lieutenant?—of being permitted to read her own books, all in the interest of deleting a quirky old statute. What else would an old woman do with her time anyhow? Why you're practically doing her a favor, gentlemen, giving her a chance to be socially useful in spite of herself!"

Even though the Deputy Chief has been showing signs of flushing at the roots of his ash-blonde hair, his manners are beyond reproach. "I didn't make the rules, Professor," he says quietly, "but it's my duty to uphold them. Otherwise we'd have anarchy."

"Well in that case, let's have it! The more anarchy the better. Down with rules, procedures, duty, orderliness, technicalities, findings, equilibrium, and the common good—and most especially, down with all the pretenders to the lot of them!"

Lt. Zamora speaks up, more slowly than one could have believed possible. "The arresting officer was exercising his prerogative. We'd be setting a very unusual precedent."

"Police Officer of the Year, is it? At least *he*," pointing rudely at Buckminster who sits very still, "can be said to have the excuse of class upbringing for his involuted perspective, but you're a man who has actually *chosen* to delude himself so that he can have the privilege of seeing a little less every day as he rises in the world. You'll go far, Lieutenant."

Into the silence that bristles with this oracular charge, as if someone had turned the volume up for an intermission, rolls the musak's pastiche of great classical themes distended in metronomic majesty.

A darkness, as of hurt or resentment, passes over Leon Zamora's face. But the Deputy Chief, whether from some personal code of courtesy towards a lady, or from professional etiquette, or simply because he does not consider such unseemly displays worthy of a reasonable man's notice, has himself and his vascular system fully in hand. And I—I recognized quickly enough what afforded the luxury of my eruption. Had I not known, after all, that these two are better than most, that with them I could indulge myself and exploit as a weakness what is probably best in them? Still: are they not what they are despite knowing better, and isn't it precisely this that makes them worse than others of their kind?

I said something to the effect that my remarks had expressed more feeling than fact. There is only one recourse, under such circumstances, for a civilized man and a seasoned public servant like Buckminster: he ignores both tirade and half-hearted retraction and becomes excessively formal in dismissing me. Are the pointers of his watch not pressing on past five-thirty? "Professor Dumot," he says, "if you're all that concerned about this woman's freedom, I suggest you make an appointment with Chief Fleming first thing Monday. Lt. Zamora or I'll be glad to assist you in putting the case to him." It is a proper remedy, and a proper sort of route for the old Quarter's most notable restorationist, given though she may be to off-beat behavior of one kind or another.

"I'll do better than that, if you'll kindly allow me a few more minutes and show me to a phone more private than this one."

Caught off balance, he rises as though by the impulsion to save appearances and nods to a small enclosure at the back of his commodious office. But he immediately thinks better of it and warns that the Chief of Police is not a man to be rushed into things.

"I wouldn't dream of calling Chief Fleming on a Saturday evening. This will be a personal call. A quick one—and certain to get immediate results."

His curiosity awakened, he runs a hand through his hair, shrugs, then plunks down a phone directory, and politely shuts the door behind him. The enclosure is hardly more than a phone booth—no window, just the instrument on a desk, beneath an overhead fluorescent strip.

xviii

Randall Cane is having a few friends in for drinks. Would Elizabeth care to join them at Segovia Crescent, where Aimée has just now been singing her praises?

I put the situation to him succinctly, omitting all references to his family's connections with Miss Bernard and appealing solely to his rationality, his sense of communal justice and fellow feeling—Jake's strategy with me.

He asks me a perceptive question or two, offers his surmise that the Chief of Police knows nothing of the affair. "Surely this young Gorrie's energies can be channelled more productively," he says.

"One would think so, yes."

"I know J.W. will find this bungled absurdity as preposterous and as unworthy of the force as you and I do. What did you say this unfortunate lady's name was?"

"Bernard, Maria-Louisa."

"Sounds familiar of course, so many of the names here do. By the way," (it is the sort of afterthought by which friends prolong contact) "I get the idea that you think someone engineered this whole business, put old Shibbles up to telling that nonsense to the police and so on—any idea who?"

"Oh yes. I'd be willing to bet on it."

"Really?" (Is that caution's reserve carried along the wire?)

"A man by the name of Jake Landry, lives here at the Hernando. I think you know him—at least he certainly knows you, has done some quite interesting drawings of you and Mrs. Cane."

"...Landry, oh yes...used to be an errand boy in Daddy's firm when I was a youngster. Fancies himself an artist. I seem to recollect seeing him about a year or two ago at one of the local fairs—'officious,' as they used to say in nineteenth-century novels."

"And a compliment in his case."

He chuckles, says he imagines it's just a case of misplaced self-importance.

"You've been so generous with your time already, Elizabeth, do you mind just staying where you are a moment more and holding the Deputy Chief there while I give J.W. a call?" Chief Fleming, he's sure, can be relied on to do the sensible and humane thing.

"I'll wait."

Help has come every bit as readily as anticipated. The trick in these transactions is to find just the right leverage, applied all around at critical points. Human relations, in this way, may be reduced to a straightforward problem in mechanics.

Will I be at the house tomorrow? He's eager to see my progress—but then he will, he just remembers. Isn't it Monday the Board is slated to come around for an official look?

And then: "Oh, incidentally, I don't think it would be—well, you know, politic, for the men down there to know about my part in this. Might undermine their faith in the efficacy of police routine."

We laugh together. But to me my own laughter lacks conviction.

psycheme

Today, I shall sing one of my little original compositions for you:

> I got a cravin', yes, I got a cravin'
> It's so bad my bones are goin' thin
> I cain't stop it 'cause I cain't he'p it
> An' I don't mean no needles and gin
> The Man, he say I'm talkin' 'bout sin
> Ever' time I holler for my or-i-gin
>
> O, O, O, that O-rigin-al Sin
> It's so satisfyin', so ga-ratifyin'

I got a cravin', yes, I got a cravin'
Ain't no way to keep me from misbehavin'
The Man cain't stop it cause he cain't he'p it
Ain't no way to turn off this ravin'
Till I done settled in my din
And sweetened up on my or-i-gin

O, O, O, that oh-ri-gynal sin
Oh, oh, oh, my oh-ri-gin.

xix

Buckminster checks his watch and plucks warily at individual hairs in his mustache following my announcement of an imminent call that will set all to rights. Zamora, who bears me no grudge, offers paper cups of water from the cooler and resumes flipping through the Wentworth file. European classics give way to the fiftyish pop nostalgia of "Ebb Tide" as he becomes absorbed in watching me finger the rag of pyjama material on the voodoo doll—snipped, it would seem, from an article of clothing belonging to old Wentworth.

At last, he says, it comes to him: the thing reminds him of the old Dollman's junk art.

"There you are, Deputy Chief, one may as well conclude that old man Hurd is a voodoo devotee and that *he's* responsible for Wentworth's death—whites have been known to indulge, you know. Yes, I believe the Lieutenant's right—this one's definitely his style, too clumsy for a really skilled practitioner. But then, maybe the old man made the doll, Miss Bernard said some mumbo-jumbo over it, and a person or persons unknown dropped it at the scene of death, in which case we may be dealing with a whole voodoo gang—"

"A witchcraft conspiracy!" Zamora bursts in with rolling of eyes and pointing of a long accusatory finger at the exhibit.

"Just who did ferret out the origins of this wicked piece of work?"

Although the Deputy Chief seems relieved by the light turn my visit has taken, his reply is uninformative.

"Bet I can—"

The strident ring commands silence, and Buckminster jumps forward to take the receiver.

"Yes, sir, about lunchtime...no, on his own initiative...back in May...Peaden, sir...Landry...not much to it...no, as far as I know, the papers haven't got wind of anything." He puts his hand over the mouthpiece and looks to Zamora who shakes his head "no." "We certainly don't...would strain our resources, all right...couldn't agree more...I'll be sure to convey that to him...Good night, sir...Just as soon as I get off this phone...well, I appreciate that, Chief, same to you."

Buckminster relaxes in his swivel chair and beams good will all around. "Chief asked me to tell you, Leon, be sure to put something in that new manual about those out-dated old statutes. Says he doesn't want any more incidents of this kind. Waste of good manpower."

"So it *was* Jake Landry?"

"Ma'am?"

"My unprofessional guess was right on the mark—Landry turned up his 'evidence' for hanging that little exhibit on Miss Mary Louise and passed it along to his not-so-vigilant pal, Sergeant Peaden, who probably didn't appreciate the full significance at first of what he'd pried out of the old man's hands. And our promising young Mr. Gorrie took it from there, am I getting warm?"

"Well, let's just say it's all water under the bridge now."

"Lucky for Mr. Busybody. I wouldn't put it past him to have planted that incriminating piece of trash on the corpse in the first place."

Buckminster's sense of his position is coming back to him. "Actually professor," he says, "it was Landry who discovered, while sketching the doll for our records, that it had enough morphine in it to put away more than one old man. It's not exactly implausible or far-fetched that a woman known to advocate euthanasia might give a little push to somebody who needed it, maybe—somebody she'd been doctoring with her potions, from what I'm told."

"I too believe in euthanasia, a fact from which it doesn't follow that I'll practice it, or even intend to, at least not on others."

Not letting himself be drawn into further time-consuming and irrelevant speculation, he says firmly and finally, "Chief Fleming, as I'm sure you gathered, ma'am, has authorized me to release the sus—Miss Bernard, and that's just what I intend to do, right this minute."

"Yes, I was sure you would." I collected my beat-up leather handbag, which like everything in my daily life now had smears of paint all over it.

Standing up simultaneously, prompted by the reflex (formed, I suppose, through years of habit) to a lady in proximity arising from her chair, Buckminster says: "I don't know who it is you know, ma'am, but it worked like a charm." Given my penchant for impulsive openness, I may blurt out the powerful name.

"Like a charm," I repeated, with a residue of irony so faint it probably came off as self-satisfaction. I have shown that I am someone to be reckoned with, and he respects me for it. From the reception window, back out in the lobby, the face with the bouffant hairdo gawks with new interest at sight of the handsome blond Deputy Chief and the busy Lieutenant with the kind heart swapping friendly farewells with that straggly-haired one who doesn't know enough to stay out of the sun.

Leon Zamora walks outside with me where the air has begun cleansing itself with breezes from the Bay and promises a fair evening. Would I like to accompany him to the jail, he asks at the last moment. In light of...something indecipherable...he feels like doing the job himself.

I said that I believed I would come along, yes. "I've never actually met the, uhn, suspect."

"...drop that now," he replies with some irritation. On the way, though, relaxing through the thin Saturday traffic, he confesses with youthful ardor, "...really glad you did what you did, ma'am...grow as a police officer...human being too."

If I'd had the heart left for it, she says, I might have tried to explain just how little I relish contributing to anybody's "growth." (There are those who have even suggested that my house plants could use more nutrients—incidentally, not one of my plants has ever died on me.) As it was, the best I could offer the Lieutenant was a neutral silence.

psycheme

No doors to close in my head and the inevitable reaction: pulped to the consistency of nothing but feeling, the bog of undifferentiated affect metastasized through every body part, here, where endurance alone prevails—and even that victory goes flat—here I am, distilled to this obscene drip of mere survival. I speak of pure suffering, that movement of life turning on itself, nerve-sensitized repetitions forming new organs of transmission—suffering so pure, so fully itself, as to be unequivocally meaningless. Purposeless passing of meaning to and fro without end, mindless immortal force forever on the loose. Look at me, gaze upon a clarity more fundamental than Descartes' *cogito*. My certainty: I do not want to suffer. If it helped to have others pulped to my consistency, I'm not above accepting such sacrifice from you, but the ontology of the bog legislates that more pulp only softens the ground farther out, and so I must say no! when you reach out an arm to save me, must insist that the protective glass behind which I stand exposed to your view not be moved, that you do so at a certain risk, that experience, if you have learned from it, shows how dangerous it is to be in the vicinity of the bog—if nothing else, others unwittingly breathe in the rot and the pollution. Such is the minimalist ethics of the bog. How it weakens me, the bog and this fierce desire to escape it. I am not among passion's addicts, having lately survived both romantic and naturalistic devotion to it. I am no underground man. I do not value suffering, I abhor it in any form and under all circumstances, all guises. Suffering precisely articulates the living condition in which there is no value, none, and through its very fineness of articulation, the very rigor of expression, suffering secures the differences against which I measure all value. I have no desire to live life fully. Life, fully lived, brings us here where it is suffered in all its strangulating depths, all its intensity without the usual modifications that idealize death or uglify life. I wish to live life well, to swim freely at life's surface. To live well without the myth that more value is to be wrung out of its extremities. Clearly and distinctly: life in the raw kills. My life is worth living only when I have time free of the bog. I would practice dying on other terrains, from deserts to gardens of value watered in diversions of life's flow from its own victimized necessity. I would speak obscurely from obscurity. Little existential oxymorons get their sharpness from the stupidities of reflexivity, but my certainty is grounded here where we live out the power of powerlessness, soggy with the unrelieved earth-pulp of hopelessness. The deadening of feeling, the apathy of the living dead, may bring some relief, but I have never experienced apathy to speak of and I recoil from the living dead at rest in their premature graves. I always know too much about the bog of myself to settle into the balm of apathy, and too much is any consciousness of the bog whatsoever. Nothing, absolutely nothing do I wish to be free of more than this, forever and ever...ah, a surge of anger as I hear your judgments on me everlastingly rendered from halos of ignorance, not to mention your want of interpretation, much less your reading problem. To jump to the conclusion that I'm seriously depressed, perhaps even a potential suicide struggling with an enervating death wish, shows just how little attention you, given an unqualified opportunity, pay me. "Nothing more than" does not exclude "just as much as," and I emphatically wish to escape death *just as much as* the bog no matter how much, from within the bog, death's promise of ultimate satisfaction, sweet closure, offers itself.

I could hardly finish that sentence before my anger washed away, looking like grumpiness, into the bog. Too bad. Any strong direction of feeling will lead out—I said "strong direction" not "strong feeling"—any will do, some identifiable feeling that individuates itself and thus sets a course compelling allegiance. That's why there's so much rage. Rage by virtue of the kind of feeling it is points an immediate way out. It's the easy way, but without an Achillean steadiness even the bridge of rage sags and slides its pulp back into the bog, merely multiplying bog-power geometrically. My tragic dimensions reach no mean depth but are not of heroic breadth. The full intensity of life narrows and darkens all but itself.

Life turned on itself. "How hard it is to die," she said as she lay dying in the bog, yearning for her own death and too weak with age to welcome it. Here where life unprocessed goes on in its crude state as the raw material of death. Here where the place of unlimited feeling and that of no feeling falsely converge, collapsed into the same psychical space, the one lived and the other projected from your eyes. Already I can see myself dying a perfectly natural death as the exhaust of my last breath rises from the bog even as I'm pronounced dead there and then, my motion in time frozen for all eternity. But what can be identified as the same place in space can never be so identified in time. A difference infinitely unquantifiable remains, the difference between me alive and me dead. The bog of raw life, pure suffering, homogenizes all differences except this last. As for knowledge, it's always limited to what it is of, and knowledge here is never more than knowledge of suffering. Gaze long upon me from your protected place: I offer proof positive of a knowledge not worth having.

Another time I'll tell you what sucked me in. I can't tell you how I got here, I never know—panic, you understand. I can only remember what happens before I'm suddenly gone, bogged down. But not here, not now. From where I speak I cannot bear to tell it. I cannot yet hear words compelling remembrance. Another place, another time. Please. Please.

XX

In the last block of Valencia Street, there where the old houses still ramble and sag and weather the years without the Preservation Board's nod, Lieutenant Zamora let us out at Miss Mary Louise's door. We surprised none other than Martin Kingston (lately in the employ of Tony Krasner who took him for his kind of man and paid him accordingly) making himself at home in the front room of her four-room shotgun cottage. He turned his book face down, beside the peppersauce red of an old Kutani cup, on a little carved table, and wordlessly embraced her.

"No," she said as I looked from one to the other, "I haven't taken leave of my senses in one last fling. My father remarried and had a second daughter shortly before he died, in Haiti. His new family settled in Trinidad afterwards where Martin was born. My nephew."

"Then you," I said to him, "are Frances Boullet's great grandson?"

"The same." His chuckle registered fond amusement at the wondrous irony of circumstance—life in its mindlessness playing out what may resemble the whimsy of an infantile god. "Mother used to tell stories about her that she'd heard from grandfather, and about Maria-Louisa too. She wrote letter after letter to her 'Florida kin,' as she called them."

"I never got a single one. I never even knew of my sister's existence until Marty turned up full-grown."

"Mother finally stopped writing when one of her letters came back stamped DECEASED."

"The Canes," said Miss Mary Louise. "They'd taken possession of the house by then and forgetting became convenient all around—even for me, non-existence has its utility."

"I never forgot," said Marty. "I resolved early on to look for any trace of my Florida kin some day, and once in Tarragona, it didn't take me as much as a day to find her, publically deceased but privately far from it."

"As in 'dead ahead,'" she quipped. "Is everyone safe, Marty?"

He briefed her on his placement of the latest arrivals. Refugees from Haiti.

"That will have to do for now," she said, "this place is off-limits until the authorities forget about me again. In a crunch," studying me thoughtfully, "the old house may have to be put back in service."

"Too much coming and going there," I said quickly—too quickly—"all those inspectors and sightseers, not to mention, at all hours, the insufferable Landry and his cohorts."

Her short, husky laugh passed into a kind of carefulness, the prudence of one for whom deception and self-deception hold no more mysteries. "My kind has long dealt with the Landry method of keeping community records," she said, "and we know how to turn it to good use."

"His drawings," said Marty, "produce the same effect as do overly talkative people: they tell too much and reveal only too plainly what's missing from them."

"Outwitting Jake Landry has become a favorite pastime for some of us natives—it was Jeremy's one delight before he died."

"Wentworth?" Here he was again.

"Like so many others, he had personal reasons for hating Landry," said Miss Mary Louise, her violet eyes cool and steady, though not unkind. "We had an understanding, Jeremy and I, about the upstairs of the house. The rest of that family were easy enough to keep in their cherished ignorance, as you can imagine, especially since they were all convinced that the ghosts flitting up and down the staircase at odd hours would do them no harm as long as they kept out of the way. They wouldn't have dreamed of going up there."

"So the wild, spooky stories about the Boullet House are promoted not a little by your own doings?"

"Just a little fattening of selected fictions on fact," with a more than ordinarily delighted chuckle from Kingston.

"I must have presented quite a problem for you when I set out to restore the house—no more safe hiding place—so you started bringing the refugees here, till the assiduous Gorrie concluded, in line with 'evidence' furnished by our specialist in demonology, that you were demoralizing the young—casting spells. Voodooing them into criminality, or insurrection maybe."

"Something like that," she smiled. "Nobody's imagination has helped more than Maria Zamora's, aided of course by Greg Shibbles. Poor dear, there was a time when he was gone on me, long ago in our teens—and I was not without some regard for him, but he lacked the intelligent will to move beyond his mother's framing of the world in which I, of course, was taboo. And I've certainly travelled in a direction diametrically opposed to the childlike innocence he turns to in Maria. They've served me well, those two."

"I see," I said, "although nobody believes either of them, their tales have done wonders to keep a useful old prejudice against the house alive."

"The young Lieutenant may have other ideas. But for the time being, he'll keep them to himself."

"So what led you at this point," the West Indian drawl interposed, "to my aunt's rescue?"

I ran over the Landry-Peaden "investigation," not without a sense of bearing old tidings until I arrived at the sketch Landry had made for me that afternoon. The swift efficacy of my call to Randall Cane had them both nodding even more, with an understanding I wasn't at all certain I shared. When I finished, Miss Mary Louise set a blank sheet of typing paper in front of me, and a pencil.

"Draw it," she commanded, "exactly."

I started off haltingly, drew the hand more or less like Jake's—making several corrections with little feeling of further success—and on somewhat surer ground, reproduced his caption: EXHIBIT A: MURDERING HAND. She snatched the pencil from my hand, and, with the telling strokes of an accomplished artist, copied my awkward attempt on a piece of drawing paper of the kind Jake used—and so like his original I could not distinguish a difference in my memory.

"Yes," I said, "that's it exactly."

Her eyes met those of Martin Kingston who stood as if on alert. "Get a car," she said, "and be back here by 7:15."

That I should, after those weeks and weeks with their little horrors and absurdities draining the life out of me, possessing my time, find myself there with her in that high, spare, clean, hospitable front room, two people getting to know each other by rambling on without purpose about their ways of sensing and making sense of the world, the late sun obliquely fading around us—it had the uncanny feel things assume when they seem unfamiliar because so very close, close as the life of your own body.

After a while, she excused herself, and in this pleasant condition of drifting about in my own time, as it were, I could only stare, uncomprehending, at the woman who re-entered the room, literally unable to put together what I saw until she spoke.

"You're sure?" she said, studying the two drawings intently.

The turban gone, heavy hair brushed back and gathered in a full bun at the neck, an appealing wisp or two escaping, she wore a soft, sleeveless off-white cotton shift, full and as finely spun as silk, a pale yellow pin-striped shawl of the same material flung over one arm, and a rather large knitted purse. She looked white, just as much as before she had looked definitely colored, of African origin. She could have been an aging Southern white lady, elegantly dusky but hardly as much as, for instance, Lieutenant Zamora, her skin lighter at that moment than mine. She could pass, and I realized this was precisely her intention.

"Absolutely certain," I replied. "But what—what is this about?"

She disposed of my smudged piece of work and tucked her own into the purse, neatly rolled. She was waiting for Marty to drive her to the KKK meeting at the Community College, she informed me.

"Why there of all places?"

"Because," she replied (just the least bit put out over the effort at explanation), "it is there of all places that I expect to get the kind of information we may need now. Don't discredit *everything* Jake Landry says. 'Before the night's out,' remember?"

And that is how it happened that, with a long evening still before her, the old Quarter's most notable restorationist came to be riding home with Maria-Louisa Bernard, Frances Boullet's granddaughter, in a rather old but reliable sedan chauffered by Martin Kingston, the ghostly lady's great-grandson. "At least you can rest assured," said the latter, "that our local Daumier won't be peeping in through your shutters tonight. Still, it might be just as well to lock all the doors and windows." Maria-Louisa gave a nod from the back seat and touched my arm so lightly as I stepped out it might have been nothing more than the edge of her fine-spun shawl brushing against me.

xxi

An eerie cry careened down the alley alongside the Boullet House and away to the old Hotel. Sunday morning, five past six.

Jimmy's scream—for that, unmistakably, was what woke me up, some more than ordinary eeriness in the familiar sound—thrust me out into the morning adrift on the vivid tatters of a dream: a child squatting at the tide's fluid edge, warm water swilling around the ankles and sucking them down into the sand...a white dress...crescent of red at the hem floating on a shallow, translucent tide...in and out...a pale rosiness spreading away in the water and no one to be seen anywhere along the beach. Only birds dipping at the waves with faraway cries, ripples of dread and loss.

Dread—stranded as I felt myself to be at this borderline of

dreaming, she says, I stayed in bed a few moments longer. I'd found that if I gazed at the ceiling long enough, an intense gathering of light drew my eye upward into a rich pallor without barrier, as if through a gateway of opalescent air. *Trompe l'oeiul.* Captain Boullet's library fresh in the early play of light, its creamy whites tinged with the palest of greens, warblings of high summer in the boughs of the old oak tree, sky framed in the sparkling tops of the dormer windows—clear, almost autumnal blue sky—had a way of quelling the urge to be up and about the instant I opened my eyes, and so this lingering for a while, letting the room compose itself in my seeing, was a kind of ritual to forestall the pressure of those final days to get on with the chores, the list, get moving, be done with all that finicky finish work, work my way out, get away. Miss Mary Louise had agreed to visit one day this final week to see what I had done to the "old house" as she always called it.

And that was when it came to me that the boy's scream, eerier than ever, had been a wail of triumph.

Dread propelled me up from my bed at the blare of sirens nearing, on to my feet and into my clothes like a shot. Car doors slammed in rough succession, footsteps crunched fast over my new shell drive and back of the house. Voices, a whirr of them, clustered in the alley as if galvanized out of nowhere, out of dream-cathexis, to rally behind that sleep-shattering cry.

I burst out to the back gallery—white shells blazed up at me through the sun's diagonal glare. Over the gleaming white parking area, against the vista of yard where the shells ended and the sandy ground reached back to the cool penumbra of the old wall, figures pressed past each other like shades with auras of gold suspended in a two-dimensional plane, floating forward two or three steps and stopping, another two or three steps and stopping, toward and over the shell walk curving off in the direction of the alley gate. There, half-blinded by the sun, all of it like a luminous cinematic frame prolonged unnaturally, I saw it, in a haze of stillness, filling the top of the frame: something white billowed over the gate top. It could have been a long down cushion hung out into the alley for an airing, which for some unaccountable reason was drawing a swarm of spectators to itself like ants to an edible dropping, all around, on both sides of the fence, crowding closer, pulling themselves up tall and straight to crane past other necks and heads in that rudely festive, jostling expectancy of onlookers at the scene of a calamity.

Propped against the fender of an ambulance at the back of my driveway, like one improbably posing for a picture in Sunday best, maroon tie a couple of inches above his waist, was Jimmy Hurd at the crest of a frantic victory.

"Tell 'im what you seen boy!" Miss Annie made swipes at prying Jimmy's fingers from his mouth. "Tell 'im!" The Dollman scratched the underside of his chin and grinned over all and sundry at a hump-backed tilt, while old Mrs. Hurd circled the ambulance and waved her hands at the crowd by the gate to ward them off. "Oh Momma," Miss Annie screeched, but oddly enough she kept on looking at me, "cain't you be still Momma, cain't you go home?" And the Dollman cupped his ears for better reception.

I wedged myself between Jimmy Hurd and a bewildered policeman with a snappy "What is all this? I own this property," when an amplified voice from the alley drowned out everything. "Stand back folks. Please! Clear the area. Repeat: Clear the area." None other than Sergeant Peaden and, by the sound of it, firmly in charge for maybe the first time in his life.

Jimmy kept on pointing in the direction of the gate and gibbered wildly, excitedly. I watched his mouth. "...came down the alley," I prompted, "and you saw..." Feet, it sounded like. He saw feet and shiny shoes. To my translations he nodded in hilarious assent, head bobbing, forearm jerking up, down, up, forefinger snapping out pistol-like, here, there. "Shooo, shoooo, shooo"— the word held him mesmerized in a bubbly drool. The policeman turned away, whether in frustration or to answer his Sergeant's call, and Jimmy's "shooo" broke into giggles that doubled him over from the waist like a marionette clutching itself in a theatrical mimesis of the human body gripped by pain.

All in one smooth, swift arc, the old man's hand swung out with an upward blow at the convulsed boy that set off a sputter of further speech. "Ma...ma...wok...aw rooo...." Jimmy's forearm swung a few degrees, the pistol pointing at the Boullet House clean and glittery in the sun, "...aw wa loo...feey... shoooooo," jaw jutting out at me. I got "man on roof," and somebody looking at somebody's feet, or shoes.

The line of policemen was making a wedge through the crowd on our side. "You cain't make no sense outta him today," said Miss Annie as the pistol swerved along its arc and took aim at a heavy-set grandmotherly woman clutching a large black purse in the center of the parting throng. Momentarily, the pistol dropped as if for reloading and snapped back at three or four huddled across the alley, faces turned away and nodding in agreement. Among them, I recorded the green turban.

"Sergeant wants to talk to you, Miss Annie," said the officer with distaste as he butted up against Jimmy's swerving instrument, "stick around." The boy's eyes, I saw, were closed tight, the pistol finding a purely random aim. She'd have her say right then and there, and started to: "Boy come runnin' home like the devil was after 'im, all dressed up for early Sunday mass like he was, couldn't nothin' hold 'im back to wait on me an' Momma, she's always so slow, hard to manage, an' all of a sudden here he come runnin' home fit to be tied, kep' yankin' at me to go outside with 'im till he drug me right up to it—oh that turrible sight up there on them spikes, never will forgit it, no siree, not in all my livin' days, an' him always such a partickler man. I run right home then an' I called the police an' I—"

A fourth police car rolled into the drive, siren blaring, toplights imperiously flashing.

"—an' all the boarders come runnin' out with the boy yellin' an' hollerin' like that, woke 'em all up, an' people off the street, an'—"

"Later," said the officer.

"Shhh...," from the old woman, raising one bony finger gravely to her lips, scanning the scene with the wide open eyes of the sleepless and mad.

Out jumped Lt. Zamora fingering the knot of his tie as he opened the back door for a man with a leather satchel. The wedge of policemen broke a path for them and held it clear, so that I got my first unimpeded look at what hung over the top of my Catalonian fence—a reddish brown stain soaked through the billowy white shroud to blazon its insignia on his chest, neck straining out and down to the side like the twisted gullet of a game bird, thin rills oozing darkly over the bluish lips and through the stubble of the exact mustache, downward along a nostril, the bridge of the nose, over one palely gaping eyeball, across the temple and smudging the scalp under the mousy straggle of hairs limply afloat in the morning breeze. Between rigid teeth, in the corner of his mouth, a panatella tilted groundward still wrapped in cellophane. Right side up, Jake with his fresh cigar angling jauntily up past his nose would have looked as if his scalp had hemorrhaged at the hairline.

Since the eye does not easily pick out the gate to the alley from the run of the fence, the placement of Jake's body there seemed, from the instant I saw it plainly, to have been calculated for effect. And, especially, perhaps, for its effect on me, with my newly laid shell walk like a curved arrow gleaming through the yard to the display of death billowing on the black spears. "...feey...shooo...feey-shoo...feey...shooo...feey-shoo...." Jimmy's refrain gained a syncopated momentum. On the alley side, from under his snowy integument, Jake's shiny patent leather shoes could be seen pointing outward in dainty display. Mrs. Hurd moved in so close that her ruined face brushed mine, dry as a great moth's wing in the night, then drew back in alarm and fixed me with singular clarity. So quietly, that no one else could have heard, she whispered, "Nothin' but justice," and backed off in confusion with a "shhhhh" that lengthened as she withdrew, disowning all possible complicity with the likes of me.

On Jake's upside down midriff fluttered something like a starched dinner napkin stained with the same reddish brown. I had an involuntary full-blown vision of myself in Dr. Cane's office, he leaning back in his excellent chair all the better to observe me read the stain, as if for a Rorschach test. "Obsessional self-reference...sexual displacement...paranoid fantasies concealing schizophrenic fragmentation...," he would later diagnose into his state-of-the-art recording device, being of that generation who rarely saw symptoms of mood disorders.

Out in the alley I looked for the green turban. But as I started toward her, Miss Mary Louise walked past me along the fence with no sign of recognition other than a quick, definitive turning away of her head. A warning.

How did I know? asks Harding, forestalling the skeptic. Under the circumstances, it was the only reading that could have made any sense at all.

xxii

"…take him down, sir."

Buckminster, lately arrived on the scene for a look around, nodded. "Watch that thing pinned to his chest, Leon." Two men came carrying a stretcher.

I'd brought out coffee and we were alone in the shelter of the back gallery drinking it. "Seems to be some kind of a message," volunteered the Deputy Chief, setting his empty cup down with care.

"Can you—am I allowed to know what it says?"

His blue eyes blinked away. "'Dead men tell no tales.'"

"Very original. With a pen, or what?"

"They spelled it t-a-i-l-s."

Leon Zamora on my rented stepladder—the one from Evans had long found its way back to his dogshed—was removing the note with gloved hands. Whoever had impaled Landry, backwards, had jammed him down so hard he had to be prised off by four men, two on either side of the fence under Zamora's direction. The word going around for what had been done to him was "spiked," with graphic speculations about the effect on Jake's anatomy.

Doors banged shut. The patrol cars backed through the gates first, making way for the ambulance. "Can use the packing down," said Buckminster with an abstracted survey of the rutted shells as we walked over.

"Yeah, but more evenly would have been better."

He sighed, tamping down a ridge with the heels of his shoes.

"What now?" I said. "What comes next?"

"Questions. Checking into this 'n that."

"What killed him…and of course who. Opportunity, motive."

He was staring up at the iron palings where Landry had been, smudged as if the side of a paintbrush dipped in reddish ochre had brushed them in passing. "For starters," he said, "the body was left here, on your property."

"Why would somebody go to all that trouble, right?"

Back in the shade he said, "There was more to the message: 'You could be next on the fence.' Any idea who that 'you' might refer to?"

"Could be anybody, or nobody in particular—or somebody very particular...me, I suppose. Is that what you're thinking?" It was right up Jake's alley, that sinister indirection of the second person pronoun. Referential indeterminacy—problem of deixis: what an addition these would have made to his lexicon.

"Any unusual noises last night?"

"Would I be standing here making you quiz me like this if I'd heard any?"

"Would I know what you'd do if you had, Professor?"

Harding's account of herself the night before (the night in question) is as follows: worked straight through till midnight more or less as always; showered and to bed. It had seemed stiller than usual for a Saturday night—no drunken brawling, no screeching of tires around corners to trouble sleep. Nobody using Valencia Street for a racing strip at two a.m. Nothing. As peaceful a night as you could ask for.

Didn't it strike her as a little, well, unbelievable, he wondered, that not a soul saw Landry on that fence, not before the boy found him, when, according to preliminary findings, he'd probably been up there most of the night?

People didn't use the alley after dark, not for any licit purpose. "No lights to see by," she said.

What about somebody looking out their window? From the back of the Hernando, for instance, or....She had, indeed, looked briefly out one of *her* windows before retiring, yes—a dormer window, at the front of the house, though, opening not into the alley but on Valencia Street. Stars were showing, tiny bursts of light behind racing clouds. "No nocturnal assassins anywhere, or would-be-victims wrapped in white—what was that long billowy thing he had on him anyway?"

He passed over my question, she says, and seemed to be having second thoughts. So I added this superfluous bit of explanation: "My dislike of Landry, although quite real, wasn't such that I would actually relish the thought of his corpse hanging up there a minute longer than absolutely necessary. Nor—" just to drive my point home—"despite a summer in training so to speak, has my musculature quite reached the point where I could have hoisted him up with my bare arms."

"Somebody did, that's for sure. And then they smashed him down backwards."

"Already dead, I presume."

"Shot to death."

xxiii

Lt. Zamora was down on his impeccable knees in the shelled walk, assisted by Peaden and two other officers, minutely examining the area where the body had hung: investigator on the trail of a reputation, embroiled in the ever-tantalizing mystery of the datum. Barred from the alley, onlookers straggled around in the Hernando's back yard, that unruly stretch of verdure having found its use at last as a public vantage point for peering over at the latest. It wouldn't have surprised me to see the Dollman getting into the business of charging admission, with Jimmy in on it. I turned my back on the scene.

Doc Shibbles and Maria Zamora in a pale blue frock, fanning herself with the uplifted corner of her pink-checked apron, looked on from the other side. Even in death, Landry's presence couldn't be ignored. Not enough to have suffered his palaver and the reek of his cigars all summer long; now his blood was on my property, one more clean-up job of unknown dimensions—soon, no doubt, to rouse the entire Quarter and environs into a solidarity of ogling. Already a reporter with a cameraman in tow had managed to get through one of the police cordons at either end of the alley and was fraternizing with assorted officers. Buckminster had promised me a twenty-four hour patrol, "to discourage thrill-seekers."

His cup of coffee on my porch rail had gone cold when he passed back by, apparently for a last sip.

"What about the sketchbook," I said, "have you got it?"

"What's that got to do with anything?"

She says his question seemed to be inviting something more than she might intend to be saying. In these situations, the ulterior motive shifts from the margins (where Harding is always in the habit of looking for it, and it is precisely her persistent scrutiny of these marginalia that seems to render her behavior, her very sensibility, so off-center to others)—the ulterior motive, as I say, was shifting from the margin to the center, a magnet to attract the inadvertent remark, the unguarded look that temporizes, incriminates. This we accept as the critical shift to the investigative mode, which is the mode of ulteriority proper. What is aberrant sensibility in one context becomes, in another, methodology, something for which Harding and I both have a healthy regard. One reason why its fulsome display by Landry ticked her off so, she says.

"Well, I'm not really sure," she replied. "At the time, it seemed like another of Landry's odious ploys for attention, but," and she told Buckminster all about how Jake had made his drawing and insisted on showing it off.

He would pass the story on to Zamora, who would be taking down a formal statement in due course, he said. They would want a detailed description of the drawing, possibly an approximation of it.

"How well did you know the victim, ma'am?"

The voice surprised them from behind, and Buckminster instantly took charge. "Whatever you heard, Markit, I don't want to see any names in your paper except what I o.k. personally. Who let you fellows in here?"

"No problem, sir," said with hands forward in pacification.

Not two weeks earlier, he had attempted to interview her for what he strongly hinted could shape up to be an exposé of restoration politics in the Quarter, rumors of kickbacks and favoritism and other corruption in official places that she, as someone who must have had dealings with certain agencies and individuals, might wish to confirm or disconfirm. I, she says, had time for neither—besides which, I envisioned my opinion, say, of Greeley Connor or Randall Cane set tendentiously adrift between quotation marks. Reticent, no doubt to distraction, she had failed to put off Roland B. Markit, who had taken his leave without apparent ill will, journalistic zeal intact.

"Whoever did this thing isn't just fooling around, Markit."

"Understood, sir," voice weighted with the gravity of the

moment as he clicked the mechanism of his ballpoint in and out. "About that robe he was wearing, with that hood, you know—some folks that got a good look say it might be one of the ones exhibited at the Klan rally last night."

"Teach-in," Buckminster corrected. "See what I mean? Slip in a word here and there—tells an entirely different story."

"You got me there, sir, but considering that demonstration outside and the vandalism downtown—"

"What demonstration?"

But Markit's unfailing pursuit of the main story line circumvented her. "You haven't ruled out a racial motive in the killing, have you sir?"

"I'm gonna tell you something, Markit. There's a lot of just plain pure and simple hatred in this town, in case you didn't know. Landry had a way of riling people, all kinds—all colors, right, Professor?"

What is it about these situations, says Harding, that seems to press for demonstration of the obvious?

"Let's suppose for a moment, though," Markit was saying as he snapped pen to shirtpocket in the casualness of things being off the record, "let's suppose that Landry *was* a member of the KKK—after all, who else dresses up in Klan outfits? Now isn't it just possible that the robe and his murder—"

"Sure, sure, we could suppose this and that and the other thing. That's your line of work, Markit. Exploit the angles, keep 'em glued and guessing. Our job is to turn up facts, plain and simple, in the interest of...of getting justice done, you know?" To his credit, the Deputy Chief seemed the slightest bit uncomfortable falling back on his dignity like that.

If my historic property was about to launch a spectator sport, what would that mean for my chances of finishing and disposing of it? Just the previous week, Markit's *Sentinel* had reported on an isolated homestead somewhere in central Florida becoming a tourist attraction after the scattered remains of nameless (and literally countless) females, ranging, on osteological evidence, from ten to twenty-five years old had been dug up there, with prospects of more of the same at deeper levels. Investigation, the paper said, was being hampered by droves of the curious as the earth yielded fact after fact.

"Check with us at the station later on, Markit," said Buckminster on leaving, "and remember: easy on the names. Discretion's the word on this one."

The photographer was attempting to snap pictures of the baleful fence from various perspectives with Roland B. Markit of "Then and Now" fame, resting one foot three steps above the other to support his writing pad, making notes at a purposeful clip. Landry at least had not died without issue; immortality may be as various as it is reported to be long.

"Have you got a garden hose, ma'am?" Sergeant Peaden asked, curtly tipping his cap, no gum in evidence.

Sickened, I pointed him to an outside tap with its coil of dark green hose. Only right, of course, that he should be doing his bit to expunge the mortal traces of his late collaborator and doing so with a new-found discretion that must be warming the stilled cockles of Jake's heart, perhaps even lighting a fire under his panatella across the far reaches of the grave.

psycheme

Pure and simple: have you ever wondered if I exist when you're not looking at me, when I'm not here exposing myself to you? I'm not a tree falling in any forest.

xxiv

"I've come to turn myself over to them." In their mask the eyes were like stones. Doc Shibbles was on the point of making some terrible last stand, half-raising a hand in the air, a straw in the infinite nothingness, and let it fall. Maria Zamora tried, again, to turn him around, lead him back home, but he pushed her roughly away and pointed at the fence, changeless and dark in the sparkling air, then at me, saying, "You above all know what I have done, and why it had to be."

"Who was that on the fence?" I said, hearing in my own voice the echo of officialdom's probes.

"Who?" Doc Shibbles half-bolted toward the alley, where

the last of the policemen were making ready to leave, then turned back to me in confusion. "Who? Who? Can you ask?"

"How did you do it, sir?"

Maria took his arm, and this time he submitted. "He wouldn't drive out to her grave with me yesterday," she explained, "said he couldn't go back there till it was over and done with. Is it done with now, ma'am? Is it over?" I was astonished to see in her eyes a resigned deference to me as administrant of chaos, as if she were asking, "Are *you* finished now?"

"Absolutely," I lied. And he let Maria lead him away to their cottage, mumbling an accusing appeal at me over his shoulder, "I told you...the words...I told them...violence...sex."

"I can't see that old man slinging that corpse up there, can you?" said one of the officers who had taken Landry down.

"And breaking his back," another said. For, it was, in some way, not so much the murder itself as the image of it, the white-robed figure gored upside down on the Spanish fence, that had taken hold of everyone, the consummate details of brutality like an unmistakable yet cryptic logo for all to ponder.

XXV

Zamora seemed lost in an uncharacteristic gloom as we strolled over to the police car backing into the drive to pick him up.

"What kind of paper was it?"

"Hm?"

"Lined, scrap, stationery—could you tell?" I was determined not to get the slip a second time.

"...heavy-textured...thick."

"Artist's paper, maybe? Torn out of a sketchpad?"

He paused thoughtfully before sliding into the front seat. "...keep on looking." A pity, I thought, that Jake's sharp eye couldn't be enlisted in the service of scrutinizing his last hours in Tarragona—or wherever.

Markit was waiting for me on the gallery, perched on the banister slick with three coats of dusky salmon, perusing his notes. "I wonder," he said tapping his pen on his pad, "if the police may not be dismissing Shibbles too lightly. He's not what you'd call a deep thinker, our Officer of the Year. Obviously, you can't depend on the old man's 'confession,' but I have a hunch— just a hunch mind you, sheer intuition—that he's got usable information of some kind."

"Usable for whom and for what?" I was really curious about this.

"The problem," he said with sophomoric gravity, "is how to pull it out of him in usable form, see? How to free it of the old man's powerful sense of being caught up in some terrible fate, some inexorable pattern of violence, some—"

"I, Oedipus, accursed...." (I meant, Harding says, to offer a plausible encapsulation of what he was after.)

And he, not surprisingly: "You're looking at him, Dr. Dumot. Playmakers, Chapel Hill 1972."

"Have a turn for tragedy, do you?"

"Not so much *my* turn," came the modest repartee, "as the turn we humans keep making." He looked frankly into my eyes, no doubt to assess if I was capable of following him, and decided to take the risk. "My work gives me a chance to give pointers, tag the tragic elements adrift in a world without form—or so I like to think of it."

Modesty, sure of itself, disciplining an intelligence that might otherwise grow too lively, too penetrating for everyone's good—it was this, I decided, that lent him that obnoxious air of youthful certitude, and that arrogance of a vigor restrained by ever probing psychical antennae like a dendrite of his sensitivity.

"Why just 'pointers'? Why not delineate the whole turn? Journalistic objectivity? Or is it that a world without form has to be represented by a turn without form?"

psycheme

If you think that all your gaping has resulted in the faintest notion of who I am or what I'm like, you're as full of it as the dead man on the fence. Anything of any interest or value to or in me goes on only when I'm not here.

xxvi

It stumped him only momentarily, a challenge. "Good point. I like to think it's some kind of integrity anyway, but I'll admit I'm not up to any new world-shaking development of tragedic form. My stock-in-trade is strictly pathos and—I won't deny it in present company—fear. Pity and fear grow even stronger detached from any reasons for them, I notice. You have to know how to punch the right message in, as with everything else."

"And the cold facts?"

"Even a journalist, a reputable one, is aware these days that anything is a fact from *some* point of view. I'm in the business of gathering the news, all the news that's fit to print you know, and even some that's unfit if I can get away with it. And 'the news,' of course, is those facts in which there's some reason to think people will be interested."

"So you can always kill 'em with facts arousing pity and fear, especially if you can work a slice of love into the pity, and the odd bits of hate or disgust or revulsion into the fear. A dynamic mix."

"Exactly! You make an appreciative audience. Even the day's obits and the market quotes can work wonders. Presto! rabbit *ex nihilo*—well, practically."

"No need for form when you've got all the formulae. Sounds downright experimental. *Avant garde*."

He looked at me, I can only say "eagerly." "You may be onto something there, ma'am. You see, when I follow through on a story and show day by day how the pieces change and move around, even if just the tiniest little bit, and how they get put together again just a little differently than last time—well, there comes a time when my readers realize there's nothing more there. Nothing new, you see. A good newsman has to know when that happens."

"I recognize the moment all too well."

"So, you see, that's why it's important to keep more than one story going: they all play out on you in a few hours, days at most, even the great ones."

"Somehow, though," I said, hanging on in there for no

good reason (missing breakfast, like lack of sleep, can make Harding grimly tenacious), "somehow I still suspect there's a difference between a performance that lives so briefly—or dies so lengthily, as the case may be—that we expect nothing more of it, and the TV soap with its eternal serialization, always the same bits arranged and rearranged *ad nauseam*, always to be ended on time and continued on time."

psycheme

Coming before you is an act with neither a positive nor a negative effect. A zero grade act.

xxvii

"Do I perceive, ma'am, the scorn of the litterateur for mere media pastiche?" Though the question was put with light good humor, he receded even as his psychic antennae converged about me and ran rapidly over me, touching, feeling, tapping, but finding nothing there to arrest them.

"To the elitism of your 'litterateur' I may plead guilty, but to the contempt? If so, it must be self-contempt, because the daily news, however dead it goes, is almost as important to me as my morning coffee." The brief lift given by each, I didn't bother to explain, is addictive, especially when the two work synergistically as they invariably do for a while.

But the glimpse of his own limits made him more aggressive, even a bit eloquent in his aggressivity. "All right, all right, so I butcher the carcass to feed the public necrophilia. But I do feed a *real* need—maybe even in the best way possible today, meaning the least reprehensible. My public is increasing beyond my wildest expectations, and..." he glanced at his watch here, "they're clamoring for me right now. I've got to be off to concoct their daily feast."

"For the first time, I have a glimmer of what it means to meet a deadline!" Without the forbearance to withhold my witticism, I was not surprised at his lack of response.

But as he was rounding the corner of the gallery and I was thinking he had withdrawn from me entirely, he poked his head through the balustrade with a grin, "Catch the morning edition tomorrow. The late Jake Landry shall live again very shortly. Presto!"

xxviii

A few feet below where Jake's blood-streaked eyes had gazed from their inverted perspective into the bright morning, the upturned oyster shells were miniature vessels holding a palely rose-tinged liquid. My impulse was to scratch them under; instead, I marched over to the garden hose rolled into even coils by Sergeant Peaden, hauled it back to the gate and stood over the spot a good ten minutes, contemplating and ratiocinating— until I'd flushed the shells bone-white again.

psycheme

Me again, but here under duress this time.

Having come to know Paul Dumot fairly well last time around, I feel I should have anticipated something like this happening. Still, even though he took me by surprise, I would never have consented; I would have treated the idea as a joke not worth a moment's consideration, merely suggestive grist for his flirtatious mill, had it not been for Harding herself.

I'd just finished reading my latest installment of Text One (all of which, by the way, he keeps referring to as "Her Long Hot Summer Without Big Daddy," or "The Frustrationist," for short), the murder sequence just concluded. Helen and Vanessa were delighted with it. One of them had dug up the phrase "morning made hideous" from an old Klan pledge in a library book and thought it would make a great chapter title, if I used any. I sat basking in a haze of authorial gratification. Harding was sketching a faintly Hibernian border of upright spikes interlaced with vines, or possibly snakes, along the margins of the newspaper that lay beside her demitasse; she'd been at it for a while and was on the point of turning the last corner.

"Really Jael," he said, "as your heroine once put it to pore ole Jake—or so you say: 'You have a flair.' Why not turn it to something, well, more ambitious...more, shall we say, human and engaging? More accessible, universal. These are so characteristically Harding's stories, we never get another viewpoint. Gets downright claustrophobic." Shudder. "Why not spice it up a pinch and a dash? At the very least, get in a story *about* the lady, if she's your focus, which I take it she is, rather than *by* her?"

"It's Jael's book, Dad." Helen's voice held the gently stern reproval of a parent reminding a child of good manners.

"She's reading it to get our opinion, isn't she? I'm giving my honest-to-God gut reaction, that's all. But wait—" the stopper clinked back into the decanter—"hold it just a minute here, I think I'm on to a creative solution. A little suggestion for you, Jael, a lit-tle proposition." The bowl of his brandy snifter slid deftly between his fingers into the palm of his hand communicating excitement in the quickened tempo of its tiny circular movement. It was his third one on top of numerous apéritifs and steady refills of Chardonnay throughout our excellent meal, and his rituals of pouring and partaking were getting ever more elaborate. The brandy swirled away from the center as he drew the glass to him, stuck his nose down in it, closed his eyes and inhaled as deeply as if anticipating inspiration therefrom. Harding, I noticed, was alertly studying him, pen suspended over the front page of "Arts & Leisure."

"Well, what do you say, Jael?" He flashed me one of his laid-back, sideways half-smiles, soulful, no-sweat-no-pressure-no-problem-no-nothing.

"To what?"

"You're doing a great job," he began expansively, "with what you have. It's a tough thing you're after, really tough—tricky—I understand the problems of authorship better than you think, Jael, though I must admit your psychemic appearances leave something to be desired—or maybe nothing, and either way you're stirring up one great big can of worms. I take my hat off to you. But your real trouble, I'm beginning to see, is with the leading lady. You only know what she *says*—or pretend to—and you're knocking yourself out to be sure you tell it like she does (supposing she's telling it straight). Barely a twitch into fiction, not a *soupçon* of authorial license—Harding in your hands becomes a missing person, my dear. What makes you think anybody wants to listen to her? You've got to make your storyteller less of a stranger, that's the secret, *chérie*, move in on her so we can get a better look at who's doing all that talking. And who, I ask you, knows better than her own husband?"

"Ex," Harding corrected.

"Very important point, that," he conceded, "verrr-ry important. Who knows better than her ex, and incidentally the acknowledged father of her two exquisite daughters?" A bit of cognac savored from his snifter, and: "I can give you the material you need Jael, a story *about* Harding. A close-up, and I humbly offer my services this very night."

I laughed and suggested that he write his own book, let me do mine my own way. Helen piped up with an embarrassed, "Oh Dad," but Vanessa, whose first year in college has reinforced the experimental strain in her, was of two minds, agreeing with Helen and me but still intrigued.

I thought he would drop it, get absorbed in comparing the newly decanted brandy with the previous bottle. He didn't. He came up with a stream of witty arguments to show that "one little story artfully inserted" couldn't hurt a thing; in fact, it was bound to enhance the effect of the whole by opening new depths in the narrative *ethos*. Vanessa shortly gave in to the prospect of all that charm, while Helen slipped into the prim silence of one who has judged another to be a hopeless case. Harding said nothing but seemed to have turned her attention to a study of her daughters, both self-possessed young women, if still easily shaken.

"Ah," he said, "you haven't heard my proposal out, to wit: before we gather here tomorrow evening anon, I shall have ransacked my highly specialized ex-knowledge of Elizabeth Harding, ex-Dumot, processing my computer eye for that one little thread, that finely telling detail of her personality—no, no, an *act*! I think it will have to be an act that captures, if not her essence, her character. Yes! The character of her existence, no less, recorded forthwith on my worthy word-processor to orthographic perfection and printed out for your private perusal and meditation, not to mention delectation, ere we two—three, five, excuse me—meet again. What I offer I give freely. I ask no thanks for my contribution, expect no recompense, pecuniary or intangibly otherwise—and you can edit and clean it up to your heart's content, Madame Author, frame it as you please, though I strongly advise you to ease it in naturally."

Rhetorical deflation, the drop from giddy seriousness to dead seriousness, signals a shift with Paul in the play of his irony, in this instance from self as tragic comedian to self as mouthpiece of the-way-things-are-in-this-modern-world-of-ours. "Truth is, Jael—and I don't know how you managed this—you've got Harding's voice all right, but somehow she herself remains a closed book, as uncomfortably evasive as a paranoid projection. I'm prepared to give you the stuff to change all that, but only on your promise that you'll incorporate it in your text. Say "I do" and Uncle Paul is at your lady's service—no promise, no tell all. How's that for a good deal, no strings tied?"

"Oh Dad, you're bluffing!" blurted out Vanessa, a poker fan, "You're just dying to get into Jael's book any old way you can." Even Helen looked tempted. Still this, after all, *is* my book, and I could have (and no doubt should have) dismissed at once his offer to disclose new and vital material—writers are forever getting such "gifts" presumed by their donors to make up for any perceived literary defects—but I had been observing Harding, quite at her ease though gone very still, and I acknowledge that I misread alliance with me in her sculpted silence.

So, playfully like Paul, but with the conviction of her assumed support I said, "Enough third-person references, let the subject speak for herself. Let whatever she says be final, and I promise faithfully to abide by her decision."

She sighed deeply and spoke in a way so at odds with our levity as to sound profoundly sad, and so quietly we all leaned forward to listen. "Under these terms, then" (directing herself to him alone): "No more than twenty typewritten pages double-spaced, with one and one-half inch margins, no less, to be completed and turned in by tomorrow evening, no later. Let it be finished, then, once and for all." Turning to me, lightly, almost gaily, she added, "As if a murder isn't enough to resolve, you can now prepare for a twenty-page debacle."

And that, precisely, is how I have experienced it. Paul

remained shut up all day, did not appear for dinner but left his gift to me some time before on the table: title page (Bedroom Knowledge Of The Inner H, by an Ex-Husband) plus several more than twenty crowded, unnumbered pages that trail off in mid-sentence. I brought his manuscript to my room after dinner and have just finished with it. So much is clear: it does not and cannot fit anywhere in my text. I've considered trying to make use of it in revised form, ease it in somehow as he said. But however I imagine incorporating the thing, the result is a different book, not mine.

Yet I'll do nothing if not keep my promise, and so I insert it here with no changes and no attempt to work it in. Why exert myself to smoothe the edges of its intrusion? Let it stick out for what it is. Those who prefer more continuity and coherence may simply skip it, as well as those who thrill to erotic experience only under more conventionally romantic moral covers. To the latter, I offer apologies; I share with them at the very least a resistance to contemporary pressure to be always and interminably talking about our sexual escapades, which presupposes not only that we must always be engaging in them but that nothing else matches them in interest or importance, whether in life or in art. I hold to the Foucaultian position that exposing oneself in sexual discourses has become a primary mode of mass pacification, the principal instrument of unreflective political subjection in Western societies. We all now have ample opportunity for abjection in the guise of consent; I can extol my captivation in the irony of naming none other than myself as captor/captive.

PAUL'S THING

There are, in the final analysis, meaning that which must be lived out in the long run, only two ways for a man to exist alongside H. Either he holds her at a legalistic distance, keeps her where she touches nobody, nothing, or he doesn't even try to make it with her, just plain gives up and treats her as gut feelings command, and that's a sure and fast fall into sado-masochistic depths. She makes me suffer for having taken the latter course, the bitch. I pay dearly for having treated her like what she does indeed call for, oh yes. Talk about a victim it's her. She can't accept the benefits of her sex, status, education and, yes, even her nationality. Of course she's had them all, a fine endowment. When I say she doesn't accept them I mean she never takes full advantage of them—these, after all, are opportunities less fortunate women throughout the world would pee all over themselves for, even half of them. And it isn't just that she doesn't take full advantage of them, no, worse than that, she takes advantage of them grudgingly, and as sparingly as possible, as if all the goodies of Western civilization have come into existence not exactly to plague or tempt her but to force themselves on her. So every time she partakes, every little sniff of the goodies she so loves comes off as a violence perpetrated on her.

If H, as some of her women friends seem to believe, harbors a hermetic knowledge it's because of her expertise (read: expert tease) in the field of rape. Rape! Rape! Rape! that's what she's all about. If I say a man can't lift his pinkie without raping her, I'm speaking literally in the sense that his slightest movement invades her, and a little unwanted penetration is as much rape as a long drawn-out go at it unwanted. That's one of the bits of knowledge to be reaped from living with her, note. But her range is broad, from infinitesimal rape to infinite rape, the entire spatio-temporality so to speak of rape. It doesn't in the least surprise me that you want to write a book about her Jael, but deny it as you may, the disguised eroticism can not escape an eye trained like mine.

I'm not saying any of this to dissuade you, but just to emphasize what it is you've got on your hands, *chérie*. Eros (our kind anyway, though I think it's equally true of, for instance, Indian erotica to the very extent that their representations are stylized, not to mention impractical) can't live without the cover of innocence of the very kind this woman feels herself called on to remove. No, that's too mild a word; rip away is more like it. Ignorance, God bless it, in all its forms, be it the informed, the deformed, or the reformed, or in full-blown form the Form of forms, is the bliss without which eroticism dies of exposure. Peeking, you're right, is fine—eroticism can thrive on such apparent dangers—but peeking is erotic exactly to the degree that it doesn't accommodate the eye with a good hard look. Rip away the cover of eroticism and what you have left is mere pornography, but she's so busy killing the one she never sees the birth of the other, the pornographic phoenix.

Oh she's a killer and no man knows it better than I. If she suffers any life around her it's either because she's recouping for the next round, letting the poor innocents gather around for a preview, or she's too damn tired of rape and murder to care one way or the other.

This is not quite true. She has what she thinks of as "manners." "Good

Manners." These exercise some constraint on her by keeping in a tenuous boundary what otherwise becomes savagery beyond all belief. Before I get prejudged as a misogynist (and misjudged like my fellow-worker Nietzsche) let me say that the word had a purely intellectual content for me until I became intimate with H. To put it very simply, she takes the fun out of things. Or maybe the meaning. Actually it's neither, or again it's both, as if she's always saying permissively "Sure, go ahead, have your fun if that's what it is, and your meaning if you've managed to hold on to any." How the hell can you have fun in the presence of a doubt that what you are having is fun, a doubt filling the space and time of a female body? Her body is doubt in concrete form. Can you imagine what it's like holding it in your arms, not to mention the shock to a vulnerable organ of penetrating it?

Here's the perfect opportunity to bring up what I consider to be the great paradox of her character: you can have more fun with H than any-body. I remember times I laughed so hard I couldn't stand it. That's just it: *I couldn't stand it.* Or understand it. Or maybe I couldn't stand not under-standing because that's where it always gets with her. I don't know whether the laughter took us there or that was what we were laughing about, the infinite configurations of nothing that can't be understood, but there are things you don't want to be that funny, almost everything in fact. This is what makes her hateful and I'm walking proof that she is. She inspires hatred in me with great ease and with limitless bounty. Cornucopious hatred. People are as susceptible to laughter as to viruses and far more sen-sitive to when and where it's in the air.

Sometimes people who have met her find her repellent, and I'm using the word in a way she would approve of, precisely. If not, it's usually only a matter of time before they're getting suspicious and skittering off to a more comfortable distance, ready to turn away at the flick of one of those perfectly grown eyebrows—especially the stupefied (those made stupid by ignorance, or elective blindness, or just plain habitual obtuseness). That kind are awak-ened by H to a sharpness of mind far beyond their usual capacities. Seeing in her one who fails to put being attractive, pleasing, engaging, to good use, in short one who in spite of many personal advantages can't seem to come on strong with anything positive, they demonstrate the force and alacrity with which the accumulated fears of a lifetime rise up in nothing less than universal form and speak their self-validating language of cultural verities— incontestable, powerful, barely a hairline's difference from Eternal Verities. All this merely to be rid of her, put her some place where she can be seen winding a path shorn of responsibility because without effect, without consequence to the world as it really is, without promise, without, that is, The Positive. A path strewn with milestones scrawled over with NO. It is as if the Positive delivers its judgment on her: this is what it means to be what you are: nothing going nowhere, cultural outcast silently sidling along streets from door to door, curb to curb, babbling idiocies in your endlessly rocking cradle. H is enough to make me believe in the concrete reality of archetypes like the Scapegoat, the negative forced to function positively.

I better get going because I have something special in mind for you Jael, but: in writing this, a new insight into the psychodynamics of how she manages to bring out the worst in me is shaping up. There's no difference in the final analysis between what she brings out in the stupefied (see above) and what she brings out in me, except in them it's their best and in me it's my worst. The stupefied have at least the dignity of their collective stupidity while I become merely hateful. Being hateful herself she makes me hate her, and by hating her I catch a residue of her reflected back to me in the mirror. What's more I get separated off from the stupefied by being jerked off into a place where I can see how silly and pitiful we all are. Now obviously, H picked up my responsiveness to her early on, and in those depths over which none of us has control it attracted her that I was a man she could thus jerk off, right down into the pits of humiliation with her. And that, as I have intimated before, is what her hermetic knowledge is all about: a knowledge of negs to be had only by being dragged through humiliation. That's her special mystery, ladies. Not a man's *nada*, oh no, her negs are specific negatives given inimitable form. I will admit that with her I arrive at what has at times felt like a moral urge, an experiential imperative to get out of it all and stay out for all time. Who wouldn't? Maybe only a man strong enough to save the sadist in the sado-masochistic routine. If our biological circuits demand sado-masochism and our pleasure lies in variously meeting this demand, H must be seen as a killer of life-forces. She simply unwires the circuits at some point. And this is what people pick up, even the stupefied, something unnatural about her. I want to make clear what it is: as guide extraordinaire in this realm of humiliation, she brings you to a place where shame becomes the coloring of all experience, any experience, no matter how innocent or harmless or beautiful it might previously have seemed to you. It isn't that what was innocent or harmless or beautiful before now seems less so; worse, these things become the very hues of shame and each experience a layering of shame-hues identifying it, a veritable stratification of shame. There's no redeeming value here either. She doesn't save you from what she gets you into and if there's a way out she's certainly no guide, her finger points strictly one way. A knowledge with nothing positive in it is not knowledge, so let's not dignify the experience she leads us into by the name of knowledge.

I'll be frank with you Jael. I want you to see how silly and pitiful *she* is. Silly and pitiful. I don't yet trust you to present her free of the mythical guises others may project on to her in an admirable if misplaced effort to make her more palatable. To humanize the experience of humiliation is to suffer it, be warned, that's her essential trick. Seduce 'em into according dignity and value, even a harsh kind of beauty, to that destitution of heart and imagination you call her "sensibility," so that she can jerk the old rug out from under you all the more briskly, and all the more murderously. You want to make something of her, right? Get at what kind of human being this woman is? Whatever you make of her she won't let it stand, *chérie*. She'll find a way to undercut you. Cut you down, that is.

Let me tell you a little story about her.

In the days before I came to grips with what it was I had married, I spent what little time I had alone looking for the perfect gift. I have a thing about the perfect gift. Have you ever noticed how much H values the eighteenth-century silver teapot she inherited from her grandmother? I'll admit it's a beautiful object, perfect of its kind, but I wanted to find a gift that would surpass that teapot in perfection so absolutely as to relegate it to another order of things. Perfection itself, embodied so as to become her standard of all value to live with day in and day out. I wanted to find it, hold it in my hands, and give it to H, the perfect woman she was for me then. I looked at everything from perfect flowers to perfect houses to perfect art objects, perfect necklaces, clothes, anything and everything perfect. None of it would do because, although each was perfect in its own right, none was the perfect *gift*. I discussed my problem with the perfect man. Yes, I'd found him too and he too fell short but he saw my predicament instantly and suggested that we ourselves fashion the perfect gift. We sat up several nights on and off drinking our way into a perfect friendship shaping up from our collaborative impetus to create the perfect gift. What made our friendship so perfect was how the very fullness and richness of our shared creativity brought us together in a kind of integrity, a wholeness such as exists only as the trace of a great creative energy, and from this integrity of feelings and interests we saw that we must breathe life into our creation. Who, we agreed, would deny that the greatest gift of all is life? No gift can be wholly itself, wholly a gift lacking in nothing, except that which is itself gifted: the consummate gift.

We knew how the perfect gift must be crafted of course, but saw too that one aspect of our craft had a kind of necessity in it on which all else depended. A gift is a false gift to the very extent that it contains any element of debt going in any direction. (I got this from H herself, I'd never thought of it before.) What I mean is the giver cannot give his gift with the notion either that he owes it to the recipient or that the recipient owes or will owe him something, because a true gift is something that comes to its recipient through no act on her part, for no reason, and no strings whatever attached. It had become evident, you see, that we, he and I in our creative collaboration, were engaged in a specie of the gratuitous act. There it was: only by means of a gratuitous act could our gift be freed of extraneous accumulations, achieve its true form. We felt ourselves immersed in a purification ritual without cause and without consequence. A heady experience, the act of giving.

Once we got this far we saw the importance of H not getting wind of what we were doing for her because even the slightest whiff of the role she was to play in creating the perfect gift would transform her otherwise natural, spontaneous responses into knowing cooperation with our creative enterprise. What was a wholly gratuitous act for us would become for her, should she have any knowledge of it, an act fraught not only with the creative goals we had set but also with the whole spectrum of her own self-interest and desire, since the created object was to belong to her alone. Not to mention that enamored of her as I was during this whole period of creativity—it flowed through my whole life you see, and so it was no accident that I produced some of the best work in my field at that time—I suspected even then that H incarnated all the dangers of a little knowledge. In her, a little spreads malignly until it reaches full critical proportions. Better to prevent that altogether for her own as well as everybody else's good than to bank on trying to excise it once it got started. (Even the inevitability of an eventual knowledge explosion though is far and away the lesser of two evils when the alternative is to see the creative charm of any activity whatsoever dispelled, exposed and killed dead in its incipient tracks.)

So we proceeded slowly, cautiously. *Sub rosa*. As you Jael with your quick understanding have surely surmised by now, H was to receive none other than the perfect man's sperm. Her body, we figured, could be depended upon to do the rest & the foetus would very likely reach a substantial growth before she would even be aware of the change in herself. In all its strength and vigor her body would bear the child, proudly, happily, naturally. Birth would consummate our gratuitous act of creation. I would never lay claim to this child because of not having technically fathered it and yet it, the perfect gift, would carry my name and grow from perfection to perfection under my tutelage. Nor would the perfect man ever lay claim to the child he had so fathered because doing so would corrupt his own creative act by tying strings to the created object. In sum: we had perfect faith, he & I, that the perfect gift could only be realized in the form of the perfect child & the perfect child could only come from the gratuitous union of the bodies of the perfect man & perfect woman. Of course, it was this necessity of having it just happen for no reason that both made our project creative and presented us with the whole range of problems, possible solutions, techniques, and so on, that one always encounters in any creative endeavor as you well know. I could in fact write a book recounting the story of our failures, the time expended on traditional approaches & efforts to retool them for our purposes, followed by more and more experimental methods, etc. All threatened to subvert our project with insinuating hints to H. Just you try giving her anything whatsoever, much less something for which you can never want nor expect any return, and you awaken a suspicion which cannot be quieted except by her own steadfast refusal of the gift you wish her to have. She has a thing about freedom as you know, and to accept anything from anybody for any reason seems to infringe upon it (Rape!). To be fair to her, if she accepts anything at all from anybody, she either assumes she'll have to pay back and a hundredfold probably, or she decides the giver is worth bringing into her life in some small way, worth establishing a tie or two with. Usually she does both, but never without a profound sense that her freedom has been contaminated—and this extends even to you Jael, much as she may rejoice in your friendship for the time being.

To shorten a long story (page-count really cramping my style here) we came in the course of the 2nd year of our project to the only viable creative stance. There was to be no approach of any kind. We were however to be prepared at all times, at the ready. Our craft was to lie precisely in a disciplined suspension of all designs, the better to be poised for the opportune moment into unpremeditated creativity, the spontaneity of the unaccountable happening (an aesthetic, Jael, you could do worse than ponder). H knew something was up but had not an inkling what.

She came at this time (I later began to expect such distortions from her) to accuse me, playfully at first, of living in what she called "the solipsism of a narcissistic high." Correction madame: I experienced my condition as hermetic rather than solipsistic and what gave my admitted narcissism its high was the extraordinary phenomenon of seeing myself transformed by, for, & in your reflection. When in love Jael, I'm given to hyperbole. But remember, I could discuss with no one the true state of things, least of all her, the personal anguish of stepping aside for a man no matter how perfect, the spasms—so like jealousy—at the thought of it, the strength of commitment it takes to sustain the fictions creative of the gratuitous gift—this & so much more. In the thick of it H took to asking over a woman she had claimed as her best friend ever since they'd met at a prep school in Vicksburg. Talk about two good-looking women. The perfect man & I agreed that, objectively speaking, you couldn't find better anywhere, approaching thirty, both of them tinged with enough secondness of youth's blush to be interestingly lush as opposed to merely so. It shortly became evident that wife & friend conspired as did we but toward the end you might expect, namely, they were setting friend's cap for the perfect man who was far from offering any objections. She was beautiful, of an old and good New Orleans family, in line for a considerable inheritance & nobody's fool. Imagine it Jael, the atmosphere so heavy with eroticism it was like swimming through a custard packed with the dancing flesh of fat women. A Fellini extravaganza—you get the picture.

The perfect man's courtship of the perfect woman's best friend seemed just the fateful development needed to expedite our gift-giving. It would have seemed positively inhospitable, then, had the four of us not gathered at our house one lovely June night a few hours after all doubt dissolved with the question popped, just the 4 of us, the making of an all-night feast, no disturbances, nothing to interfere with amatory currents and nothing to destroy their civilized forms. My idea, this, Jael, of a well nigh perfectly framed situation for the play of life. Play, it goes without saying, like art must always be framed, and that's a thing H has never really appreciated or denies appreciating for the sheer killing fun of it. Do you know I very much like being in frames with you Jael? And methinks no higher praise and affection expressed than in the obit "A fine playmate was she." But sitting here in the northern cool twixt midnight and morn I get chills...I get chills.../ I shall quaff my bottle & take more pills. Ooo-eee, feel that fire trickle down the old gullet. My ancestral frogs distilled hell's mystery in cognac they did. "OO-eee, oo-eee!" I said that when I was about five years old in a class set up by my parents *et amis* to give us kids an early start learning French. First week and we'd heard all about how expressive the language should sound and practiced screwing up our faces getting the sounds to the front. Came my turn to read: *Oui, oui.* I lifted my very soul to my screwed-up mouth, drew in a deep breath and let go loudly, proudly,

"Oo-eee, ooo-eee." Expressive as hell, a stuck pig's squeal, truly a formative experience. Onward. Some time twixt midnight & morn it was back then too, and even H was brimming with spirits when we left the happily engaged couple sprawled on pillows in the dark of the music room and stumbled upstairs to her boudoir. With her so slowed down by food & drink you'd think she was already *enceinte*, I threw off my clothes (man has to learn how to hold his drink in case he's called on for action), got up in a hurry & did bang about getting downstairs, heard her laughing at me, the bitch, already used to my penchant for a last quick shot before bed & not very delicate about it. Quiet as a little mouse I crawled into music room over to perfect man caressing brow of wife's best friend, pretty knocked out & moaning a little. Lifted his hand off her & replaced it with mine. She never opened an eye & I snuggled down beside her as he crawled off & banged back upstairs. I was listening so hard I held my breath while stroking wife's best friend, by comparison with H easy problem to handle keeping best friend quiet & happy. Two, three minutes passed, all quiet on the upper level, perfect man could handle things, I'd coached him. With his perform-ance capacity & my know-how he couldn't fail. *Don't think*, I told him, the minute you lie with her run your hands over her body hard & fast, don't stop, don't hesitate, he who hesitates is lost, get between her legs & be ready, then mount & penetrate, go at it till she starts to sound like a little girl crying—then come & leave fast, I'll take over from there. Don't worry about foreplay, she likes all that afterwards I counselled him, and what I'm telling you to do will be like foreplay for her anyway. If you leave her like that she goes into shock briefly, time enough I figured for him to make it back to his woman and for my return to make love-amends. Like everything else she has a taste for, sex is not something H pursues hungrily but, if unrestrained, something she binges on once it comes, or she does, so I had every intention of demonstrating my love for her in every way she savored once the perfect man had delivered his genetic message. I actually ached and yearned to express fully what I felt for her.

Meanwhile, down in the music room: unanticipated problem dawning on me. Although not relevant to story about H, it had come to our attention (by way of same) that best friend was in spite of her age, & gorgeous too, a virgin. That's right, pure virgin. Touched to discover perfect man, sexual prowess written all over him, was intimidated by this. As one who may not have perfect man's stamina in any damn bed but who knows a hell of a lot about how to go easy making love when his woman is sensitive, I had offered my services in deflowering her. Seemed a loving and fair exchange all way around, no strings attached there either, my gift to perfect man. I had just begun to relax into the pleasure of giving, slowly, sensuously, important not to hurry this one, when it occurred to me: duration of my gratuitous act had to be lengthy, his short. Real time problem there. If I got too deeply into my act & he burst in any second—I hate this kind of problem, no logical way out, but H removed horns of dilemma crashing downstairs that very instant bellowing "Rape, Paul! He's trying to rape me! Paul! Paul!" Lights snapping on simultaneous with my dash for the door, I stopped just short of her & stood staring into the frantic, appealing eyes of the perfect man in hall behind her, arm half-stretched out as if unsure whether to exercise restraint on himself or on her, half-Adonis, half-Hermes, full mouth stretched into a slit, teeth set in unmistakable grimace of man caught red-handed & in dire need of red herring. The one commodity that never fails me, H & I are a lot alike in this way, is words (in the service of what she calls "fictions" when she uses them and "lies" when I do), and they had begun to tumble out of my mouth when the virgin suddenly sat up, opened her eyes, took in the three of us frozen stark nude in the doorway and asked in the imperative tones of swift, comprehensive assessment: "Is there a fire?" Bless her pure little womb, it was all the cue I needed. I grasped the still-extended hand of the perfect man and pulled him forward. "Look ole Buddy," I said, pointing to the virgin now herself wearing less than strictly called for, "I found her for you," I said, "tole you she in house somewhere," & gazing over my shoulder at H, "ole Buddy los' his bride," whereupon I jerked his half 'n half arm hard enough to buckle his knees & crumpled down beside him. H instantly pulled me to my feet, dragged me back upstairs, me mumbling all the while about how ole Buddy'd been rampaging all over the house looking for his betrothed. "Well shut up," she said, "he can rape the right one now," & wrapped herself around me. Need I say I felt called upon to perform as never before? I knew it would take fire & passion aplenty to erase any spectres of question marks lingering in her mind, but I did it—matter of fact I had not downed over two real drinks that whole night and was sole member of party in full control of situation. Even that early in our marriage she would never have believed me capable of such continence in the presence of so many bottles.

That night not even the perfect man could have surpassed me, and I succeeded. H binged again and again, sexual bulimia—but don't let's get off on that—followed by extreme anorexia. It wasn't two months before she announced she was pregnant, and only two days later when they married in a surprise private ceremony witnessed only by yours truly & wife. After a week in the Caribbean, they returned and promptly bought a home in the Garden District. We invited them to dine the night of their return but a few hors d'oeuvres were enough for me to sense a profound change, no fun being with them anymore. On the face of it they were simply where H & I had been two years or so before when we first married and got heavily into home-making. She continued to see quite a bit of them during the next few months but I more or less dropped out, had work to do. Then she too stopped seeing them, never said why except when I asked her replied people come to see each other differently in time, one of those observations nobody can quarrel with. She makes them when concealing something. Had the new husband spilled more than his sperm to the presumably now-deflowered virgin who would certainly have reported same to H? She's quite capable of biding her time before using such knowledge but will do so with a vengeance when and if. I waited and became more and more convinced that something was amiss, but nothing from H who in fact, once she stopped consulting with the newly married couple about the endless options available to newlyweds, seemed not so much absorbed in the coming of her first child as released from some habitual bodily restraint on her already enormous vitality, so that life flowed as freely from her as if she were its source. "You look," I said to her, "absolutely radiant, like someone experiencing fulfillment, is it so then?" "It's normal," she said, "if nothing intervenes I always look this way two or three days in every month, hadn't you noticed? The only difference is this has been going on ever since the second month. I'm sure I'll pay for it before it's over."

And before her eighth month was out, she did. That look that marks her out, almost humanizes her if you don't think about it, became visible. You know it as well as I do Jael, hard to picture but as if hosting some indescribable pain to which she is resigned, not to be assuaged or even acknowledged, calling neither for struggle nor reconciliation, so rarefied as to be always slipping away but never altogether gone either, as if it lurks inside her eluding capture by swift, clandestine movement among folds of organic tissue. Not that she ever looks pained, oh no, nothing so human as that, but as if she is getting pain rather like she's getting lines on her face. There may be more to the comparison now that I think of it than mere verbal trope. The older she gets the more her aging seems to reduce to a body escaping pain's assault only by providing it sanctuary. I won't deny I still have a certain curiosity as to precisely what experiences of suffering she has been compelled to accommodate, and you can be sure she *has* been compelled, in some way or another. She has neither the fortitude nor the greatness of soul to meet any such experience head-on. Quite the contrary, the one excess that always escapes her control is her loathing for suffering in any shape or guise whatsoever and her contempt for a species in which, she puts it, "a knowledge-jig has evolved to the strains of pleasure and survival preferably so harmonized as to confirm the delusion of rhythmically ordered transcendent movement. Jig, jig. Jug, jug"—and you've heard this one I'm sure: "I need not think, therefore on and on past death, past life, in the wilderness of eternal beginnings...." On & on indeed, she'll be brought to her knees & (not that I'm proud of this but I'm human enough to admit it) I shall treat her like all others on their knees. That's called getting what you deserve both in her case and my own, eh what Jael? Told you you'd learn more about her in two or three (oops, forgetting to count) pages from me than from all her so-called stories. Another case where experience matters. Good ole British empiricism teamed up with American pragmatism can keep a sorely tried man reasonably sane.

Story's not done, takes a turn here. Helen born, incredible baby, perfect. Only thing I couldn't help noticing from the very start, she didn't look remotely like me or any branch of my family. True, she doesn't look like H either but you'd think if she didn't look like her side she'd bear some little family resemblance to mine. Not a trace, not a sign. I watched her closely for nigh unto two years, lovely, lovely, intelligent beyond belief, learned to talk, walk right, everything, quickly, easily, naturally, but not one little mark, not one. A daughter to be proud of & I loved her as only a father can, fiercely I loved her, & I was telling the truth when I prefaced my question to H with assurances that her answer would in no way matter, in no way change my feelings or how I would act in the future. "I want to know," I said, "the name of the father." She genuinely, I think, did not understand at first. I had carefully concealed my suspicions from her but as there was no question as to my feelings for Helen it seemed to me I had a right to know. Had she roared with laughter, suspicion might have been quieted, but she didn't. She treated me to a woman I had never seen before, warm, understanding, concerned, kind and responsive, anything but the derision I had come to expect. Left the impression her sympathy with my delicate position flowed from knowledge of something more than mere irrational fears. Even now when I think back I would swear she had too much real feeling, she understood only too well. (Too well, that's another of the impressions you have of her without any reason you can ever point to if you live with her.) "No," she said, taking one of my hands between hers and holding it next her cheek as she looked earnestly, lovingly it seemed, into my eyes, "you need never doubt it. You are her father, of that you can be sure." I withdrew my hand and she did not move off as is her usual way, conditioned reflex at the slightest rebuff. Had she been any other woman she would at that moment have been all that any man could wish for. But as much as I wanted her to be what she seemed at that moment I knew better. You learn from her—I already knew her too well. "We are not discussing textual transmission, or closure in the short story," I said pushing her away. And then, standing in front of her with a hand on each of her arms and looking down into those darkly emerald eyes with at least an equal depth of loving-kindness, "Come, you were attracted to him, I know it, and I don't blame you. There. It will make no difference between us or in my feelings for Helen either, I promise you." This time she did pull away from me. "That's what I thought you thought," she said. "But I not only know you to be the father, I'm just as sure of the date I conceived." Asperity sounded in her voice for the first time then. "It was the night the proud bridegroom raped the happy bride-to-be and you raped me."

"I *what*?! You drug me upstairs, rammed me down on the bed and literally didn't let go till I was so weak with exhaustion I was crying mercy! And of course we both know what got you off to such a good start. Just how long was *he* in the sacred place before me?" Then spoke the woman we know so well: "Oh you would eat that up, wouldn't you? A special application of the master-slave dialectic here...." I steeled myself for the barrage, but again, none. Instead, the cool calm which can mark despair as well as reasoned resolve. "Let's stop this before it goes any further. If you've had doubts about Helen's paternity I suppose my last pregnancy reactivated them." She'd just given birth to Vanessa about three months before. "But why," she asked, "focus on Helen? Why not this one?" "Because I don't have a doubt in the world about her and don't think I have any reason to," and I'm sure you've noticed like everybody else Jael, that Vanessa is the spitten image of her Daddy. "None in Helen's case either," she said. "Please, please, these two years since her birth have been the happiest in my life. Let's not spoil that I beg you." There were tears in her eyes, actual tears and—mind you, they are the one behavioristic signal you can depend on in her case—if she ever cries, her feelings whatever they are, anger, love, grief, joy, you name it, have overpowered her. (Of course you may never know just which one it was but you damn well know that something in there is getting the better of her for sure.)

Now I've never quite figured out why I feel this way but when H mentions happiness it's like hanging bull's balls on me and waving a red flag.

Somehow I've never felt she's in the right place for shooting off her mouth about it, although God knows she carries on without an iota of empirical support about all kinds of other things and I never pay much attention. It's not just that women set such indisputable value on happiness—I'm probably less sexist than most men Jael, I believe you'll be pleasantly surprised on that score, as well as a few others I could mention but I'm running out of space dammit! Still, when she mentions happiness, & she seldom does, it's like some special kind of speech act, as if she has the attitude that without my intervention happiness flows in her like her own blood. (For those like us Jael, on less cozy terms with it, the sweetest taste does but confound the appetite & turn our tongues to acrid seasonings.) I felt, back then in the moment, not now of course, that if she had been happy for the last 2 years it had been at my expense and some kind of inequality between us needed to be rectified once & for all.

I border on getting defensive about what I did next, what with a pleading tearful woman standing in front of me hands lightly on mine begging for mercy and eyes widened in a desperate appeal for my protection of her happiness. But away with old sexist expectations & give a man audience for a word or two! "We'll not drop it," I said, "until I hear truth from your own mouth, in your own voice. Sorry your need for happiness will have to give way to my need for truth this time." Bowing her head so her hair brushed my chest she slid with hands firmly passing over my hips and half-way down my legs to a kneeling position where her head came to rest in my crotch. Now ask yourself Jael if my reaction was not that of any normal man, any normal *person* in intimate circumstances with an object of desire. (Remember too that it was as unthinking a reaction as a reflex.) My head tilted back, eyes closed, breath caught, body went as erect as if each cell of it had been roused simultaneously with the others from biological slumber to sudden sensing of its own possibilities for a separate living existence, as immediate as electroshock. You recognize the experience, eh Jael? You never know when it can take you like that, always fresh, by surprise, usually at the first touch between lovers, the sudden stiffening that signals surrender, remember? The body's ritual of passage into the sweetest unbearable trembling anticipation. At my age one has something like a premonition of how & with whom this miracle may occur, a minor miracle not because restricted to the current uniting two bodies or because of its rapid quake-like passage but because we so often go on afterwards without change, as if we had not crossed some boundary. I've come to think we deny where we've been so as to cover up a loss of nerve, the magic circle of union articulated like a plosive sounding the difference it makes, sweet meaning twining bodies in the delights of its sensuous depths. Forego this? Deny this? How Jael, how? Shall we stand outside that circle in the cynicism of false maturity ever fearful of possible enchantment, unable to make a sensuous distinction between the Chaos of creativity and the abyss of hell? Not you, I think, Jael. Certainly not I. Readied for the risk we are, both of us, & why not plunge together into the weightlessness of sweet meaning before time and circumstance eat away all possibility, for possibility—lovely, oh lovely Jael—erodes so fast the shock waves never reach us, no warning, no sonic boom, a speed that makes a lightyear a mere drop in a vacuum as if the soul's departure begins with its entry at birth and takes its leave of us possibility by possibility. Let before be now then, and should we be so fortunate as to receive the energy flashing from that bolt of pleasured anticipation I for my part shall welcome and treasure every sign, every sense, every act, every touch, of what can only be experienced as biological grace. Two adults, willing and knowing, joined in the most meaningful and satisfying of all personal explorations—think of it, yes Jael, but whatever your response touch me in the spirit of the same feeling I lay open to you, in the spirit of the same feeling. For it can happen otherwise & with her it did. Judge me a fool if you dare but remember that my absurdity derived not from my reception of grace but from her lack of it, her gracelessness. My arms were already reaching for her head when I opened my eyes. Her torso, as if suspended in mid-air, suddenly lowered and came to rest on arms stiffly outstretched behind her. She sat still, the figure of abjection at my feet looking up at me. Ah Jael, the revulsion, the undisguised revulsion for me in her eyes. The contempt, the absolute contempt, for me who the instant before had surrendered my soul to her. And what I felt as I looked down on her and touched her hatred, the purest hatred I have ever faced, was that life had passed out of me as the Greeks represented its passing, the breath exhaled at death, and that she, she had taken it—my very soul—away from me.

It has never quite left me, that. I am still a man looking for his soul Jael, but one far better prepared to house it. Give the devil her due. "Truth," she said in the husky low voice of passion, but I heard it clearly now as the passion of hatred, "truth, is it? Well, you shall have it unadulterated, meaning without the adultery you are determined to impose on it, the truth of your desire, Master of the Household, the truth of your little obsession: the economics of hubby's eroticism. But no mystery there, merely common household resources like the little wife who fulfills hubby's desire, who desires what hubby desires, and, so, filled with hubby's desire but without hubby's mastery of erotic management indulges herself in his desires with wildest sexual abandon down to receiving what he hungers for most: the fertilizing sperm of his choice! Baby grows & so do hubby's suspicions, baby born & so is hubby's paranoid jealousy, baby develops into beautiful child, clear evidence of desire escaping household management while fulfilling itself right under hubby's nose." She threw her head back and closed her eyes, moaned and drew a deep breath, "Mmmmm, smell it, this classic example of truth! Do I smell a homosexual pimp in the house!" I kicked her in the ribs so hard she collapsed to the floor. It was the first time I'd ever struck her, I don't excuse myself for it & I swear I'm not the kind of man who abuses his wife, but even now when I recall that mock ecstasy on that mock-erotic face I feel like kicking her to the ground & smashing the sole of my shoe down on her face until nothing is left of her. Can't you see Jael, I'm not writing an apologia for my behavior, I'm trying to warn you about what can happen to a person who gets too close to her. I can see you've been taken in by her but it's not too late if only I can make you understand. You've already become a little like her you know, but a little of H is not all bad & it sure goes a helluva long way. Leave off now and you'll even profit by what you've picked up from her. I'll help you, I want to help you Jael, I want to help more than I've wanted anything for a long time, but more than that it makes sense. There's some way we've both been prepared for this, both baptized in intimacy with her, readied thus for the crucible of a relationship formed out of that experience. Together we can save all that she would destroy. That psychoanalytic drivel of insinuation pouring from her lips parted in passion—oh the passion of that hatred!—I only wanted to escape it, to prove for once on her own ground that she was wrong, dead wrong, had misjudged me, misinterpreted whole situation from start to finish. Lying there on the floor holding her side with legs pulled up and head bent almost to her knees like a foetus, I let her have it, the whole truth, how I knew all along what the attraction was between him & me, never denied it, took it for granted in this day & time we all knew, but what she was too stupid to get hold of was her place in it, how she'd been the fountainhead of the whole thing, & we had built an erotic life all right but she had been the source, the medium, the goal of it. I told her how we worked with the eroticism for her own sake, to give her the perfect gift, tried to explain how we wanted to sublimate all sexual feelings for her sake, create perfect baby, thought we had failed but maybe not, maybe successful & she too afraid to tell because she had not known the real goal of our desire, that far from having any real jealousy of him, paranoid or otherwise, I had had the unique pleasure of dreaming a dream with him about her.... Absurd? Only as all existence is, no more, no less, even she would admit that. I was angry, sure, & anger can loosen a man's tongue with a woman as much as alcohol with a man but even then I think I still had some dim (or dim-witted) notion that she was out of the ordinary, different & acute enough, sufficiently daring to walk with me laughing into the absurd. "Pardon," she stood up rubbing her side, exploring for injury, "the truth is slightly more intricate than I supposed but I'll answer your riddle with equal truthfulness Paul. The Father—& the Friend & the Mother & the Child, even the Virgin in your scenario—bear each & all of them one & only one name: your own." She drew herself up very straight then, left arm stretched across waist holding side, a stance like a dignitary about to realize he's been shot, eyes gone full of fear & shame, suddenly large and hollow like a holocaust survivor, a look I'd come to be wary of, but the words came out soft & pleading, hopeless, "Let her be, Paul, whatever the scenario, let *her* grow free of it," and then she laughed, she laughed, oh how she laughed, a full & bitter laugh like other women cry, like it carried her some place she could claim, & did, & would never leave again, "So teddibly sorry, old boy," with her pseudo-British accent, "no time for the chah-ming myth of Narcissus." Jael, Jael, hear me, I won't deny my narcissism but I was working on a new ending for that myth. She was my mythic center, hers to experience the playfulness of meaning made to raise her with me, both of us together, above the traditional pedestal, no lies, no expectations, hers to accept a love that wanted only to make of her a new and more powerful mate in a man's life, not out of the old need but out of our ever-present consciousness of our absurd creativity. Echo with her body restored to her. A matter of play, Jael—oh! if you want to write about her come away with me & let us, you & I, collaborate on a fictional creation we can both enjoy—but no, no, the book is yours Jael, yours to write—& my part? Methinks mine to be your ideal audience vibrating to your every touch, for us a new erotic whole, every part fashioned by us together, every part an erotic microcosm for no reason & no purpose, desire joyful, away from the abyss of that cold hell wherein she reigns—Rape! Murder! Horror! confuse us not the hope, the promise, the challenge, the risk, replacing pen on this my worthy machine processing loving words, yearning, hell's no exit beyond retrieval, no Dante I, tour-guide of that marital inferno, all memory erased, type NEW while stuff endures & ends well, one system command from your hand &

Paul's twentieth page ends here; I am under no obligation to include more. He has already cheated substantially by leaving virtually no margins and running paragraphs together. Presumably I can now return to my work without further interruption.

xxix

Good as his word, Roland B. Markit refrained from identifying me by name in the relevant paragraph buried in the middle of Monday's front page:

> Landry, a private investigator, is said to have boasted he was working on an "important case." According to a neighbor on the scene, the victim exhibited a sketch he had made of an unidentified "murdering hand" late Saturday afternoon, ironically near the spot where his mutilated body was found early Sunday morning.

Giving him the benefit of the doubt, Markit's theatrical training may have preserved a stricter sense of what is ironic than one ordinarily meets with in the mass media nowadays, where practically any concatenation of events can acquire the label. Irony, the all-purpose filler in stories composed for fast, indifferent consumption, as in: "Ironically, the convoy crossed the overpass moments before the supports collapsed." Rhetoric's Big Mac: the ironic twist without the old flavor. What Markit's "ironically" bridged with such a facile resonance of possibilities was precisely the gap between Jake's exhibition of his accusing sketch on Saturday and Sunday's exhibit of Jake's abused corpse, and that, it would appear, was the heart of the mystery. He'd managed also to evade the issue of "the neighbor's" sex, but to anyone in the know about Landry's habits, the neighborly presence by the Boullet fence left less room for guesswork than I might have desired.

I let the phone jangle—about a week of it in the house and already a source of irritation, my brief morning peace shattered. Markit's headline loomed up from the marble kitchen counter:

KKK KILLING

Murder as victimage or as retaliation? Jake martyred for the Klan or by them? Either way, a grainy photograph of the Boullet fence, cropped so that the sinister spikes pointed unequivocally to the headline itself, dragged my property into the thick of ambiguity.

Lt. Zamora on the line: "...sketchpad...saw him without it?"

"Never," I say with delayed comprehension. "You would have thought it was growing out of the man's armpit."

"...not there now," muffled laugh, "...quite a haul...room... not at liberty...worry him to death if...portfolios...no blood-stained hands."

"Who said they were bloodstained?"

"...what do you call it? Figure of speech...right word?"

"Close enough, it's a transferred epithet." The image, suddenly, was as sharp as if Landry himself had inscribed it in my brain for fast recall—not just any generic human hand, but *this* hand and none other: capable, deft, gliding over a leather strap, wound around a glass, at rest on a switch. A hand not so much accurately observed as apprehended at being itself, caught "inny ack," as Jake would say.

"...unusual brutality." Zamora must have been studying, as I was, the photograph's caption: "A section of the eight-foot tall death fence atop which the victim's body was brutally hoisted."

"Landry's car," I suggested, "have you looked in it?"

"Clever...professor...sure?...not supposed to understand... except...you read, I always heard."

He had that much right.

"...College parking lot...cigar ash...dents...no sketch pad... traces...page three."

"Let's see, 'Drug Connection,' that the one?" The perforated stream, however, directs me to the final paragraph of the lead story carried over:

> It is not yet known whether blood smeared on the vinyl back seat of the blue 1967 Plymouth matches that of the victim. Asked whether police were proceeding on the theory that Landry may have been gunned down in his own vehicle before being impaled on his back over the Boullet fence, Lt. Zamora of the homicide squad replied, "We go on fact, not theories. We're not TV cops."

I considered asking Zamora how you would know what to investigate or whom, or even what could count as a "fact" if you purified your methods of "theory." But, then, justice too may require sanctuary for its existence.

"...if convenient...statement...glad to...never know...right now?"

I was on the point of telling him the probable owner of Jake Landry's "Murdering Hand." But responsible for what? Surely not Landry's own death (as Markit's "ironically" might have implied). All I had, as Zamora would view it, was a prime-time TV fantasy stimulated by an alleged drawing that seemed to have vanished without trace.

He evidently was interpreting my silence as antagonism of some kind to the law (had I not flaunted my disdain of it only day before yesterday?), for he reminded me, a bit sharply, that I was a "key witness," and something else that sounded a lot like "public innerest." The tonalities of language were indelibly washed with Landry colors.

"It's just that I won't be able to make it over there till later. I'm being investigated at nine.'

"Ma'am?"

"My house, it's being inspected, people from the Preservation Board. A whole delegation of them is coming here to authenticate my restoration, not that the place is anywhere near finished.

"Afterwards...run into...holler."

"How's that?"

"I said...trouble, just holler." That his tense staccato phrases reached my ear with such trustworthiness adhering to them struck me as an anomaly in the case of one whose behavior was, on the whole, so circumspect as to approach shiftiness.

I lingered a bit longer over the morning paper and its continual piquing of the appetites it catered to. For instance: Officials would not disclose whether the victim was wearing the robe at the time he was shot in the chest with a .38 calibre handgun, or whether the long white garment in which he was found is one of the rare antiques exhibited at the Klan's teach-in Saturday night. Spokesmen for the organization have not been reached for comment. The lure of what has not yet transpired, is not yet determined, though transient in the nature of things, speeds the next deadline.

As for Jake: he seemed on his way to becoming not only a facilitator of history's minute unfolding (a part his life had, in its way, foretold) but an instrument for transmitting its archaic truths as well. Whatever the circumstances of his brutal end—in the robe or out—some Klan member's wife, maybe herself daughter to an original seamstress, might undertake to rehabilitate the precious artifact for future generations, bleach out the stains, mend the bullet holes—if any—and the irregular gashes no doubt made by the iron spikes of the Boullet death fence, all in the spirit of purification and continuity...but then, it might just serve its purpose better unpurified, gore, gashes, bullet holes and all, a communal relic authenticated by its stigmata. Oh but who would have thought the little man could have had so much *bone fide* red blood in him?

xxx

The rehabilitated doorbell rang serenely down the rehabilitated hall, sun brilliant on the sparkling glass above me, just as my razor blade twisted, despite my vigilance, against a hardened splatter of paint on the last window pane. A pinprick of red showed on the fleshy mound of my right thumb. I sucked it clean, let the bell ring, chastened yet again by the miracle of having managed to survive the summer with only exhaustion, only bruises and cuts, abrasions and pricks, ripped nails—no crushed bones, no loss of limb, no major irreparable mutilations deflected to my own body out of that unfocussed incrementation, day after harrowing day, of danger and dread as of an atmospheric immanence readying itself for the starlit hours of Saturday night, for the billowing morning-clear horror. A pin-prick was an innocuous anti-climax, but no assurance that more might not be still to come, no reason, after all, to relax my guard.

I sprang to, surprised that they would manage to arrive close to ten minutes early on a Monday morning, this Monday in particular, when all the Board's members would no doubt feel acutely the delicacy of our venue.

In ambled, not Greeley Connor with half a dozen colleagues in tow, but Tom Evans—as if he were expected—followed by Son nudging the door shut behind him, the polished doorknob gliding heavily from his hand. That was it, of course: in some cranny of my fear, I *had* expected them. The moment the doorbell rang, too early, my sense that they were bound to come started surfacing. Only my timing was off, the door open and shut again on the three of us, inside, before I had hold of what I knew, and only because I feared them too much to trust that what I suspected was so. That kind of doubt-ridden fear will keep putting off the moment of truth (even, sometimes, in the counter-phobic individual, a fact not dreamt of in Jake's philosophy).

"I see you're locking up now like proper folks," said Evans with his fine fat smile. "Can't say I blame you none after what went on down here," slicking back his sandy hair with both palms, beaming approval at ceilings and light fixtures all around. Aubrey twirled a dead match between his fingers, its tip the color of the ridge under his nails. "Watch yourself, boy," Daddy snapped, "you don't wanna mess up these here fine old floors."

I dumped the sheathed razor blades off the saucer I had set on the bottom stair and presented it to Aubrey for an ashtray, who winked as he strolled off, uninvited. Down the hall he went opening doors like someone enacting a plan for reconnoitering the layout.

"Forget something?" Fingers closed lightly over the blade I'd been using for a scraper.

"Little oversight, honey, 'pears Aubrey forgot to install traps in your new faucets—but I don't have to tell you shuga, that boy can't ever do things just right. Not the fine things, honey, we both know that. Home alone?"

A brief volley of barking from the street cancelled out the gentle creak and shuffle of Aubrey's searching footsteps, and Evans' lips widened in a smile displaying the irregular front teeth inherited by his unsatisfactory offspring who was pausing at the kitchen door.

"You and me need to come to a little understanding," eyeballing earnestness at me, "you don't know what you got yourself mixed up in here, honey."

"You're so right," reflecting his earnestness, "I had no idea what this restoration could turn into—too much for me."

"An' your health's a heap more important than holdin' on to this old house." We could hear Aubrey in the kitchen whistle softly to himself, definitely not installing any faucet traps. "Give it all up while you're ahead, shuga," the voice of compassionate authority fully cognizant of realities not to be evaded, "so the bigger things won't fall in your lap. No sense pushin' your luck—like I just been tellin' Leona, you got to step aside now and let the trouble you're in roll right on past you."

"Pore ole Jake," Aubrey sighed over the front page of my *Sentinel* which he'd picked up from the counter (still chomping, if I wasn't mistaken, on one of my juicy little Indian peaches). "It's a wonder one of them niggers didn't get him before this, Daddy." Paper plunked down at Daddy's feet as if from loss of interest and flashing me a big smile.

Evans shook his head ever so sadly. "Just between friends, honey, this can be dangerous territory down here. Hurricanes, floods, tornadoes, vandalism, you name it. If it ain't one thing it's another. Why we've had storms here when the water come right up to your waist in front of this here very house."

"Man ain't that the truth!" said Aubrey in a lusty expulsion of smoke. His tee-shirt was an impeccable black this morning, and freshly lettered in red across the front was the legend "Only your plumber knows for sure...."

"There's always a risk if you own anything, isn't there?" I replied nonchalantly, noting as I brushed away a hair with the back of my wrist, that my watch read six minutes before nine. "From one thing or another?"

"I just hate to see a little lady like you get burned."

"You could lose one heck of a lot, babe, just like Daddy says," Aubrey seconded.

Skin glistened damply behind the paternal glasses; soft drumming on the newel post, "Dum-da-da-da-Dum-da-Dum-da-da-da-Dum."

"Mr. Evans—" fingers pressed against the flat of the razor blade, I took my chance. Keep them idly talking and listening—in a word: pacify. Any moment they would all be at the door—Greeley, Randall Cane, Margaret Avery and the rest, and that would be that for Evans & Son. The Board's very inflexibility now presented itself to me as a tag of more than ordinary reliability. So what if not a one of them aroused the warmth and trust of affection, not mine anyway, were we not allies in a common cause?

"Still '*Mister* Evans'? You make a man feel like he's your ole grampa, shuga."

"Well, then, Tom," I corrected myself, a line of communication opening hazily before me. "I've been wanting to ask you about something, Tom—" fingers ceased their drumming— "never had the chance because we've all been so busy. Something interesting I came across not long ago...in some of my reading."

"Readin'?" The drumming recommenced in a slower measure, at his ease yet alert. *Adagio con moto.*

"Well, you know, it's in my line of work."

"I guess you'd know more about that than me, honey. A family man don't have a lot of extra time on his hands for readin', not like you honey—readin' and what not." Treacherous ground.

"Well," (he'd given me my theme now, which I grabbed hold of for all it was worth) "as a matter of fact, Tom, it was some old *family* records I turned up, old Tarragona families... you know the kind of thing I mean, Tom."

"Family records, you say...guess you know how to study up on these old homes, shuga, do things up right...." More on his mind than he was letting on, the rhythmic drumming modulated without interruption into a mysterious *pensoroso.* "Don't think I don't care about authentic colors and all that—I was pullin' your leg that day, honey. That's all a part of the way things used to be around here, when family life still counted for somethin'."

Aubrey patted his stomach and belched "'scuse me," rendering absurd the notion that he, at least, had either the wit or the energy for something as demanding as a murder whether by malice aforethought or on raging impulse, even on orders. "Yeah," he looked at his father, "we go way back too, don't we Dad?"

"I thought so—I, well...it's all so interesting, this, unh, reading I was doing, you know, all about the Boullets, the family that originally owned this home." Which, thank God, I have as good as sold, I didn't say. Yet it was the one thing I might have said to get me off the hook. If convinced that my goal was to sell and leave within a few days (which it was), they might have ambled out at that point. But I had to be sure of what I already knew, and I kept talking, playing for time—as I had during my whole restoration project, for that matter—counting on the authorities of authenticity to appear as unwitting saviors. It was a kind of error in judgment, you might say.

"The captain," I was going on, "married a Howard, you know—"

"Cap'n Claude Boullet," from Aubrey, evidently to invite a more serious estimate of his character, "had an eye for the ladies, didn't he, Daddy?"

The elder Evans directed the merest grunt at his offspring and switched from drumming to fondling the satiny wood again. *Pianissimo, dolce, dolce.*

"Yeah, and built the Hernando, too, I guess y'all know that. Killed in Cuba during their war for independence, in the 1870's, so I read." Nothing that anyone couldn't get from the plaque beside the Hernando's half-dissolute entry.

"Didn't stay home much," Aubrey snorted furtively. "These here walls seen some hanky-panky in their day, right Daddy?"

The Senior member averted his eyes disdainfully as I pointed out in the lightest possible fashion that these particular walls were too new to have witnessed much of anything other than my own struggle to get through the restoration. "Though that alone," I chuckled, "could fill a book."

Smarting blunted the edge of Aubrey's prurience. "I was talkin' about that crazy daughter that lived here while her daddy roamed all over, her an' her colored pals. An' after he died, too. That's when things really got goin' good, didn't they Daddy?"

Evans' placid silver-rimmed eyes were on me. "I know you're a big reader, honey, and real particular," he said. "Now about them ole records you been readin'—you musta found 'em in here—but what's all 'em records got to do with me, honey?"

It was a critical moment, nearing nine o'clock for sure, and from out beyond the door the silence reached inward like a dead hand come to claim my all.

"What I wanted to get straight, Tom, is this—and you realize I'm no expert on local history—well, Captain Boullet's wife died young, in childbirth it seems...."

"The Howard girl was a little on the spoiled side," he explained graciously, "came from El Inglès, a big plantation east of here."

Aubrey, who'd been sulking over his cigarette, whipped it out of his mouth like a sudden encumbrance and looked at his father, whose gaze shifted carelessly to the newel post.

"Well, these documents, Mr.—I mean, Tom—they mentioned—"

"Great-grampaw Jonas!" Aubrey burst in excitedly, "and great-uncle Bobby, they headed up that ole plantation, didn't they Daddy?"

Tom Evans' hand fished up the *Tarragona Sentinel* from the landing, stacking the sections as if from belated solicitude for the tidiness of the place.

Would Greeley Connor's exacting standards, so influential with his colleagues, permit him to visit premises so lately tainted by death? But if they were not coming as arranged, surely one of them would have called by now?

"Guess you been findin' out blood still counts for somethin' in these parts, shuga." He glanced down the front page at arms' length as he began rolling the paper with both hands, very neat and tight, as though he meant to put it to some special use. "My grampaw and his brother Bob were overseers at El Inglès before the War, honey, like Aubrey said."

"And not a better pair in the whole county, I bet."

"Them documents you been readin', just what kind was they?"

"Well," I considered his question, "they gave me the idea that the Evanses moved over this way, and made a name for themselves."

"Did their part in upholdin' law an' order in this here community, rough as it was back then. Family's been looked up to ever since. I think maybe you oughtta show Aubrey where you keep them documents, honey." He took a deep, patient breath and slapped his fleshy thigh with the rolled *Sentinel*. "Didn't I tell you to watch your ash, boy?"

Aubrey tapped his cigarette over the saucer like a juvenile complying with the school code. "Bet the lady didn't read nothin' about what went on here in Reconstruction days, Daddy."

"Lady knows her history, son." The hand kept smacking the paper, briskly now. *Accelerando.*

"I mean right here in this house, that night they come ridin' up to that foreign nigger like—"

Aubrey's simile remained forever unformed. The lash of *The Sentinel* over his mouth sent the cigarette flying. Fingers clenched around the paper roll in its upward arc showed the Evans hand to full advantage, incongruously slender on the thick tattooed forearm and supple with the economy of a performer whose living is in his hands, a concert musician or a master of illusions. Aubrey's hand, which jerked palm outward to save his Winston, was its double, coarser, less pampered, but kin.

"Ole records, shuga, that ain't all you been lookin' at," murmured Evans as he caught my eyes watching the pages unfurl from his grip and scatter to the floor. "I just had a hunch it was you that talked to that reporter."

Nothing had been said anywhere in that morning's paper about what Landry's "murdering hand" looked like, and I myself had described it only to Miss Mary Louise and Martin Kingston. If Evans read meaning in the unguarded fixity of my look, if he had caught the flare of certainty there and of fear, it could only be because he himself had seen the sketch and had recognized the resemblance to his own hand—or, if he had not seen it, because he had good reason to know whose hand Landry might want to sketch and why. *Why* was still a problem, but if all was as it seemed, I had hold of a fact—all three of us, variously, in the grip of this fact.

Even Aubrey was putting it together, no doubt about it from the nervous way he moved in on me. The blade lay hot in the palm of my hand, its damp, paper-thin edge chafing a groove in my skin, but Evans was like one made invulnerable under the spell of his own knowledge. "What you don't understand," he said, "is what kinda man Jake was, and how he was always usin' them drawings to get his way and slander folks he had a grudge against."

It was awesome how, even now, the quiet voice and the eyes behind their twinkle of steel compelled belief, trust.

"He was a snooper, honey, a busy-body without no sense of common decency."

My opinion exactly.

"Why that s.o.b. was just up to his old tricks, tryin' to throw suspicion off on me an' my boy here to cover up all the slime he was mixed up with."

Highly plausible.

"And I'll tell you somethin' else, shuga. He had somebody workin' with him."

I might know more about that than he suspected. I carried on a bit, then, about Landry's contemptible methods, skipping anything the whole Quarter didn't know inside and out.

The dogs' vicious eruption at a truck roaring past broke into my faltering ploy for time and recalled their master to a proper sense of what he was up against. "I just get the feelin' all the time in this fine home, honey, that somebody's about to drop in on us, don't you?" Aubrey's fingers were kneading the front of his tee-shirt, leaving damp crinkles on the smooth new black cotton.

I'd managed to get my arms behind me without attracting either man's notice and slipped the razor blade from my left hand into my right. If I can claim to be more or less ambidextrous in matters of strength, when it comes to agility, I trust only my right hand.

"Why," I asked, "why would he frame you of all people? A man with your kind of reputation?"

Voice honey-smooth, heartfelt as of old, he gave his son a peremptory nod, "To get back at me, shuga, but it's a long story." And as if the nod had released some spring of action in him, Aubrey gripped my shoulder. "I'll tell you a secret—think you can handle that, boy?—somebody's been keepin' them Wentworths furnished with a powerful lotta fancy dope."

"Yeah, an' even you, Miz Professor, can guess who that somebody might be." Speech and manliness resurgent, Aubrey turned my neck toward the door in a bruising squeeze.

"Easy does it there, boy. I didn't name no names, all I did was repeat some things the ole man tole me hisself before he died, an' that's what got Jake's back up."

"Oh, I see. That's why he acted so fishy all summer about old Wentworth." At my side, Aubrey rubbed the nape of neck half-brutally, half as if he meant to reward me for good behavior while pushing me up the hall toward the front door.

"Now shuga," back of me, Evans' voice levelled out in my ear like a newscaster's, "we're just gonna drive over to the old Bay bridge where we can talk over this problem without interruptions. Forget about that cop down in the alley, honey, he cain't see out front."

"And I'm gonna make sure he cain't hear you neither." Clapping a hand over my mouth by way of demonstration, Aubrey was at his best when he could function as an extension of clear-cut authority. "After we get out, shuga, you just walk down those pretty brick steps between me an' Daddy, nice an' easy like we're just havin' a friendly visit." We were almost at the door. "An' don't let Daddy's dogs scare you half to death again, hear?" He giggled. "Daddy'll—" A ferocious round of barking cancelled out the rest, followed by growling and whining, then another volley of barking, louder and more urgent. Panicked, Aubrey released me from his sweaty grip, eyes turned to his father for instructions.

"That's Greeley Connor and the whole Preservation Board— Randall Cane!" I yelled above the ruckus. "Didn't I tell you I had an appointment?"

The bronze door knocker rapped with all the authority of its weight descending on an oiled hinge, thrice. Aubrey tried jerking me toward the back door.

"Idiot," Evans whispered, "the truck! They can see we're in here." In my ear his breath was huge as the swell of the sea inside a whorled conch. "Go on, honey, and tell Greeley an' them that you're just too upset right now about that murder on your property to keep your appointment. Aubrey'll be right behind you."

Softly, the doorbell rang as Donner and Blitzen whined like crossed children. Evans positioned himself at the newel post again, just paying a little neighborly visit in a time of distress, giving succor where needed.

"And I'm sure you won't have a lick of trouble selling this fine old home, Miz Dumot," he said. "Am I right Aubrey?"

"No trouble atall, Daddy," Aubrey echoed close by.

On the porch stood Greeley Conner, a slim white envelope flapping over folded arms, behind him not the half dozen or so members of the Preservation Board but, unaccountably, Martin Kingston in sunglasses with the opaque sheen of obsidian.

"Where...where is everyone?"

"We thought under the circumstances," Greeley mumbled stiffly, "Margaret, that is, and Dr. Cane and myself, er, that it would be an imposition...we agreed to postpone, unh, the formalities in light of this unspeakable business...fine job you've done here, no hurry."

Kingston elevated his dark glasses about a half inch over the bridge of his nose and, as he seemed to flick something out of one eye, looked keenly at me.

"Good morning, Mrs. Dumot," he said, "nearly finished?"

"Nearer than you think," I replied in a tense whisper.

"Been mighty rough on the lady, Greeley," Evans, ambling up beside me, slipped in with the sort of cadence that must have inspired the salt-of-the-earth designation.

Greeley took an awkward step back, tact written all over him. "I...I....," but Kingston's unmoving presence served as a reminder that, even at a time like this, work and its rewards make their demands on a practical man's attention nonetheless. "I ran into Mr. Kingston outside, Tom, and thought I might take him over to my new place on Arriola and get him started on tearing off my roof—got a minute, er, Tom, to come over with us and give me your opinion on the sewer system?"

"First thing tomorrow be all right for you? You know how it is, Greeley, payin' my respects to Miz Dumot here," fatherly arm closing on my shoulder in an iron lock. And softly, as if he were in church, "after all she's been through lately."

Martin Kingston uncrossed his arms and straightened.

"Of course—" the enigmatic little smile twitched over Greeley's lips—"meanwhile, ah," and he handed me the envelope as if surreptitiously.

"Killers!" I screamed, not so much a charge as a signal to Kingston that it would have to be now or never. The grip shifted down my left arm in a camouflage of protectiveness as Greeley bent to retrieve his fallen statement of account, and the Evans voice, avuncular, intimately warm in my hair, said "Nerves kind of raw here, Greeley." I swung out of his hold, a split-second's movement, slashing my razor blade down the length of his forearm right across the tattoo. With a surprised yelp he let go, and

I was out the door, accidentally driving one knee into Greeley's upturned face as I went.

"Police!" I screamed for all I was worth, Aubrey after me and Evans' babies letting loose with the full fury inscribed in their names.

"Son of a bitch!" I heard their master roar behind me.

At my car I met the patrolman breathless from his run out the alley. "The Evans men," I said, "stop them!"

He raced up the porch steps, gun swinging. With Aubrey underfoot, Kingston pinned Tom to the door jamb, the raised arm streaming with blood. Pale and baffled, Greeley Connor had already withdrawn to the periphery of it all—the last, as it turned out, I saw of him in person.

Donner and Blitzen's harsh shrills of attack pursued my car down Valencia, and even as I rounded the corner towards the police station, they filled my head, the two of them still hurtling against the wooden rails of the truck bed, again and again, in violent, mindless need for the space of unleashed rancor.

In Zamora's office, I saw that the razor blade was still in my bloodied hand. "...just radioed in," he said, "...dispatched...now?"

psycheme

I had so much to say. I have forgotten what it was. I meant to share myself with you, give myself over to you. It has all simply evaporated.

Only this, fulfilling, satisfying: I hate you. All along, all the time, I want to be rid of you. And now, freely, purely, without reason, without motive, I hate you.

Bad Blood.

IV

❧

Finish Work

i

Tuesday morning's headline was sensational, bold and big, smack across the front page:

NEW FACTS IN KKK KILLING

In the upper left, just under the logo-type, was a passport style photo tagged familiarly Miss Mary Louise, in the opposite corner one of Tom Evans, Chief Suspect, blamelessly round-faced as in life, and between them, like an oddly assorted family, a double row of smaller shots: Aubrey Evans (Suspected Accomplice); Jeremy Wentworth (Foul Play), not a year over fifty in bow-tie and blazer; Jake Landry (Victim); and, in a fuzzy newsshot beside the death fence, who else but our Visiting Professor. There was also Tony Krasner, darkly handsome (Missing Link?), and—gasp of disbelief—Randall Cane III (Prominent Psychiatrist). The brazen swath of headline seemed to balance us all aloft like members of a show gone on the road.

It didn't take more than a quick look to discover how overnight developments had already consigned the Evans' attempted kidnapping of me the day before to background detail, integral but definitely recessive. A whole new miasma of narrative possibilities had formed out there, swirling around the inner quiet of the Boullet House, maybe even getting ready for another incursion.

ii

EYEWITNESS LEADS

by Roland B. Markit
Sentinel Staff Writer

A bizarre case of mistaken identity may hold important new clues to the murder of Jake Landry, private investigator and victim in the grisly KKK killing.

In a surprise statement taped early Monday afternoon in her home on Valencia Street, Maria-Louisa Bernard, long-time Creole resident of Tarragona's Historic Quarter known locally as "Miss Mary Louise," related how she became an unwitting participant in a bizarre masquerade involving Landry perhaps minutes before he was murdered late Saturday.

Bernard stated that she attended the KKK's Saturday Teach-in at the College auditorium hoping to view relics and antique robes slated to be displayed there. "As a lifelong student of local history, I naturally had an interest in the Klan's program to educate the public," the former elementary school teacher said.

After three men who identified themselves as Klan members had addressed the audience, a fourth unnamed individual came forward to model an antique robe designed and fabricated in a local workshop at the beginning of this century. KKK organizers denied the press entry to the event, but later released an account for publication.

"This person had been sitting toward the dimly lit rear of the stage," the Creole woman said. "Before he pulled the hood over his face to demonstrate its effect, I recognized Mr. Jake Landry, a familiar figure in the Quarter." Independent witnesses also identified the man demonstrating the garment on stage as Landry.

"He was so much a part of the life around here," said Bernard, "his absence will be felt by one and all."

According to the KKK news release, members of the audience were invited on stage to view various exhibits and to try on selected garments. Security personnel at the College have reported that an unexpectedly large number crowded on stage creating a possible fire hazard. "It's the fascination with a past way of life," Bernard theorized, "especially one surrounded by so much controversial lore."

"I was right up there with everybody else. I picked up a specimen of an old robe which looked like a twin of the one Mr. Landry was wearing and put it on with the hood over my face. I was curious to know what it feels like to be on the inside of a thing such as that," said the Creole woman.

The over-sized garment was too long for Bernard and, as Landry, a slight man, had done, she sashed it at the waist and took several steps to a nearby table covered with Klan memorabilia. Still hooded, she paused to examine cabalistic symbols on the blade of a knife made in Sheffield, England, when, suddenly, someone gripped her arm from behind.

She stated that a man's voice whispered in her ear, "It ain't healthy to spread this kind of phony evidence around, Jake."

Bernard identified the man as Thomas Evans, a local contractor. "He was carrying an oversized artist's sketchbook of the kind I have occasionally used myself," she said. "The young man with him wore a pale blue shirt inscribed with a slogan, the kind of vulgarity one sees posted on cars, you know, and pickup trucks."

John Leonard, a data-processing major at DeLuna Community College who also attended the event, confirmed that he saw a man on stage wearing a tee-shirt with "Are your Pipes Taking A Leak?" stamped across the chest in bright orange. A Sheffield knife of the type described by our informant has been verified by KKK spokesmen as appearing in the organization's on-stage display Saturday night.

According to Bernard, Evans "shoved" a pencil sketch at her with the caption "Exhibit A: Murdering Hand." She said the sketch depicted a human hand holding a tube or pipe of some kind. A former art teacher, Bernard had in her possession a drawing she claimed to be "a reproduction from memory" of the one she was allegedly shown by Evans Saturday. At her request, the drawing was subsequently conveyed to authorities.

Professor Elizabeth Dumot, present owner of the Boullet property where Landry's body was found early Sunday, has stated the murder victim drew a hand in her presence the previous afternoon. It is not known whether the drawings the two women claim to have seen were one and the same or whether the alleged original still exists. Landry is said to have been in the habit of carrying around an oversized sketchbook which he exhibited to others.

"I tried to object that [Evans] must be mistaking me for someone else," Bernard said, "but he whispered back, 'Shut up Jake, keep walking over to the exit. We got to settle this thing about your pal Krasner.'" Our informant hypothesized that Evans may have been referring to Anthony Krasner, a local roofing contractor. Krasner, who has not been located, is reported to have left town.

Police have so far refused to speculate on this and other aspects of the three-day old murder case which has shaken this entire Gulf Coast community. According to Lt. Leon Zamora of homicide, officials are investigating "all productive avenues."

"The crowd was so thick," the Creole woman said, "that I managed to slip away from the two men, removing my hood and robe as I went. I did not want to become involved in their problem." A minute or two later, she saw the Evans men "leading a hooded person out the back entrance between them," she said.

It was about 9:30 at this time, Bernard said, and she herself left the auditorium shortly afterwards to meet a friend who gave her a lift home.

Medical examiners have established that Landry's death, caused by two .38 bullets to the chest, occurred no later than midnight Saturday. The murder weapon has not been found.

At the time, the Creole woman surmised that she had somehow become a party to a quarrel of a personal nature and dismissed the incident. It was not until Monday morning when Martin Kingston, a relative of Bernard's from Trinidad who works for Krasner, told her about the attempted abduction of Dumot by the Evans men (see page A-5) that she decided to make her story public.

"Whatever the links among these events if any," said Bernard, "the violent abuse by these men of a visitor to our city made it incumbent on me to come forward. It may be that others have information which, like me, they considered unimportant. Perhaps they will change their minds and speak out once they read my story."

On Bernard's account, Landry, who was a resident of the Hernando Inn, also had dealings with the late Jeremy Wentworth of 321 Valencia Street, which she believes may have a bearing on the murder. Wentworth, formerly a partner of the now defunct law firm of Cane & Wentworth, died on May 19th of this year of undisclosed causes. (See "Foul Play?" A-2.)

iii

I suspected Miss Mary Louise of having alerted Markit to the journalistic possibilities of both her account and her copy of Jake's "Murdering Hand," for he had been extraordinarily enterprising in his use of them. Before delivering her testimony to the police as charged, he'd managed to pay visits to the

Evans men in their respective prison cells—along with eliciting authoritative opinions from other quarters. There was a little article squeezed in at the bottom of the page, like a corroborative footnote to Miss Mary Louise's bombshell of a story, called Copy Credible, Expert Says. The Creole woman's sketch (purportedly drawn from memory after an original by the late Jake Landry which has not, thus far, been located) was pronounced by Robert J. Hartley, Curator of Art at the Tarragona Historical Museum and Professor of American Studies at the Community College, to bear "the unmistakable stamp of the Landry style."

> "The dead man," said Hartley, "seems to have carried on with little change a naturalistic style of portraiture developed by his artist great-grandfather," Jacob R. Landry (1808–1893), active on the old Howard plantation in Leon County, El Inglès, during the ante-bellum period. The family style of both Landrys," explained the curator, a specialist in 19th century domestic portraiture, " is pared down to brilliantly observed details which compel the viewer to identify the artist's subject beyond any doubt."

In a nice civic touch, Mr. Hartley informed the reading public that the old Landry collection, heretofore accessible only to scholars, would be mounted for general viewing "at the earliest possible date." It would be a timely exhibit, said the curator, adding that the Tarragona Historical Museum is open Tues.–Fri. 10 a.m.–4:30 p.m. and Sundays/Holidays from 2:00–5:00 (closed Mondays).

iv

Tarragona seemed about to come apart all over the pages of the local paper, says Harding, but following developments from day to day, you could never be sure which was happening, disintegration or climax, or whether there's even a difference worth bothering about when things have progressed that far. *The Sentinel*, true to form, made no authoritative statements, no far-reaching generalizations, avoided all speculation, and let its readers decide. She enjoys reading clippings from it aloud, in full or in snatches, her voice modulating into character on a quotation, still unmistakably Harding but Harding possessed by the voice, the tenor, of another—Miss Mary Louise, Tom Evans, Randall Cane. Inscribed voices. Aubrey Evans *et. al.*, with a difference.

V

Shown Miss Mary Louise's sketch, he allowed that it looked like his own hand all right, but charged that it was part of a dirty plot by Landry (at the very least) to ruin an innocent man. He's sure "that woman is involved somehow," which I took—rightly, it turned out—as a reference to me. Tom Evans' boy flatly denied, however, killing Landry and also that he or his Daddy had forced Jake to leave the auditorium with them as related by the Creole woman. In on it up to her teeth, he believes.

All of this comes out in Markit's other story on Tuesday's front page, a long piece headlined Evans vs. Evans, catchy angle leading off with the astonishing sentence: Aubrey Evans, junior partner of Evans & Son, a local plumbing firm active in historic rehabilitation, confessed yesterday that he watched his own father, Thomas Evans, murder Jake Landry. Here's Aubrey:

> Daddy and me waited in Jake's car because he said he had something important to talk to us about after the meeting...still wearing that KKK robe when he come out into the parking lot...about nine p.m. I'd say. He did have that notebook on him, that part's true, and he showed us the picture...said anybody could tell who that hand belonged to, but Daddy said he would see to it nobody got the chance. That's just how he said it. Then he took out the .38 and told me to sit still...told Jake to drive out to the fishing bridge [to DeLuna Island]...when we got there Daddy shot him...made me drive Jake's car to the old Boullet House and pull right up by that gate in the alley...we got up on the car with Jake's body between us and spiked him over the top.

Questioned about his father's possible motives, he clammed up saying only that "Daddy wanted to protect the family name."

> The thirty-four year old plumbing contractor stated he was prepared to sign a formal statement "right then and there" accusing his father of murder in return for immunity from prosecution as an accomplice.

Somebody official (possibly Buckminster, or Zamora slowing down to his chief's tempo) is quoted as accusing Markit of "gross journalistic irresponsibility and interference with the processes of law enforcement." This same official also denies any indiscretion or connivance on the part of police and refuses to speculate on the significance of the Creole woman's testimony or the veracity of the junior partner's confession.

Tom Evans, after initial resistance, read the Creole woman's story (in full, quoth Markit) and withheld comment. But as Hamlet was mad only when the wind blew north by northwest, so Evans practiced stony reticence selectively—where I was concerned, he could still turn a fulsome phrase or two.

> Evans, whose right arm was bandaged due to a razor blade wound inflicted by Dumot during an alleged kidnaping attempt, charged that "the woman professor has a tendency that's well known to everybody in the Quarter to get jumpy and hysterical."
>
> "Anybody with a little bit of horse sense," the suspect said, "would know right off that the drawing Jake made ain't evidence for me being his killer, or Aubrey either. That just don't add up." Whatever Landry's reasons might have been for making such a sketch, Evans said, it could not have been for the purpose of identifying his own murderer. "Poor lady's gone over the edge," he said, referring to Dumot.

Informed that his own son had only moments ago accused him of shooting Landry, Tom grew close-mouthed, venturing only to comment—under pressure from *The Sentinel*'s enterprising staff writer—that "Aubrey always would say whatever anybody wanted to hear, if he got scared enough." Somebody on the police force let it out that Tom was refusing legal counsel: "them lawyers are just after your money...the law don't know a tap about justice." He'd likewise refused to post bond, either for himself or for his weak-kneed son: "An innocent man don't need to buy his way out. My boy's going to learn a few things from this experience...." By way of Jake's passing—if not by his outright murder—Evans seemed to have assimilated a side of the victim which, in the paternal timbre of his voice, resonated with a philosophical gravity that had always somehow eluded Tarragona's living historian.

Aubrey confided to Markit that the old man was a fool; he himself intended to obtain the best legal advice available: "It'll take the best and then some to get me out of this mess you-know-who got me into." One could only applaud Aubrey's sense of linguistic decorum before the public, even if it did leave him at some loss for words in his not uncomfortable jail cell.

vi

One thing you will not find in *The Sentinel* is Miss Mary Louise's reproduction of Landry's "Murdering Hand"—at the center of the whole miasma, yet nowhere visible. Clearly Zamora (or perhaps the matter had been decided even higher up) had put his foot down when it came to that; it wouldn't do to have every Tom, Dick, and Harry in the country getting pet vendettas out of their system with this or that self-serving identification.

On page three or four, amid the spillover from the front page, an unnamed staff writer wonders: Did Victim Identify Own Killer? Even though Tom Evans, detained along with his son on a charge of attempted kidnaping—no more as yet—seems to have driven the nail into that one, an unidentified police spokesman speculates that "Landry may have become a marked man when he claimed knowledge of a killer on the prowl." The theorizing tendency was everywhere escaping management, Jake's melodramatic death releasing bursts of cerebration (and ratiocination) that might have unsettled even him, and *The Sentinel* democratically quoted all.

vii

Poor scheming Jake. I threw out the last of my coffee, which had gone cold and sour, added two or three more items to my list of finish work as they occurred to me, and turned my attention briskly to page two—the remainder of Miss Mary Louise's statement to the press which Markit, the indefatigable, had worked up into a separate story with the collaboration of Ellen Rappaport, staff-writer. The reason this part of the Creole woman's testimony did not appear on the front page could only be because it threw off more than a whiff of old news—though anything but quietly dead news.

Foul Play at Historic House?

When Dr. Elizabeth Dumot of Athena, New York, took possession of her newly purchased property at 321 Valencia Street, known as the Boullet House, on May 19th of this year, she found a corpse in one of the empty rooms on the first floor.

The dead man, Jeremy Wentworth, formerly a junior partner in the prestigious law firm of Cane & Wentworth founded towards the end of the last century by Judge Randall Cane, was a long time tenant of the historic house. No foul play was suspected at the time, according to police.

Surprise allegations by a Creole resident of the Historic Quarter implicating Thomas and Aubrey Evans, owners of a local plumbing business, in the Landry killing have raised the possibility of a connection between the KKK case and Wentworth's death last May.

"I want to be very clear about this," the Creole woman, Maria-Louisa Bernard of 403 Valencia Street, said. "I want to go on record here and now as taking sole responsibility for what I am about to say." Bernard stated that she had decided to make certain information about Wentworth public "in order that more competent individuals might be able to judge" its relevance, if any, to Landry's murder.

The Creole woman, rumored to be a practitioner of voodoo, first met Wentworth many years ago when her grandmother, Frances Boullet, who was skilled in the herbal treatment of disease, aided his recovery from a severe bout of fever to which he had become recurrently subject. "After her death, Mr. Wentworth, whose problems were complicated by alcoholism and later by addiction to heroin, turned to me for treatment," said Bernard.

According to Bernard, Wentworth "became obsessed" in the last years of his life with the idea that his family had been the target of deliberate efforts by Judge Randall Cane and his son Randall Cane, Jr. [father of Dr. Randall Cane III, noted psychiatrist] to bring about their ruin. "He never tired of telling me how Randall, Jr. had tricked his father, Jordan Wentworth, into signing over the family's share of several businesses to a Cane trust while inebriated and not responsible for his actions," said the Creole woman. After his father's death, Wentworth took his place in the law firm in return, allegedly, for a promise from the Canes to forgive a large portion of the family debt.

"Although it was never legally cancelled during his twenty years in the Cane & Wentworth firm, Mr. Wentworth said he assumed the Canes would make no attempt to collect on their so-called losses," Bernard stated, adding that Wentworth told her he had not suspected until 1935 that his father had been swindled. At that time, shortly before her death, Frances Boullet, then owner of the property at 321 Valencia Street, sent him a packet of documents pertaining to the Cane family's real estate and business interests.

Frances Boullet was the only child of Captain Claude Boullet, the local shipping magnate who built and owned two landmark properties in the city, the Hernando Inn and the Boullet home on Valencia Street. The Committee for the Preservation of Historic Tarragona, until recently trustee of both properties, sold the Boullet House to Dumot in May. The Hernando Inn, continuously in operation since 1838, was for over thirty years home to Jake Landry, the recent murder victim.

The Creole woman said Wentworth confronted the firm's senior partner, Randall Cane, Jr., with evidence he had spent years amassing, but Cane denied any wrongdoing on his part or that of his deceased father, Judge Cane. "Mr. Wentworth confessed to me that in the course of this discussion he himself may have had a drop too much to drink and was escorted home by Mr. Landry who was at that time employed as a messenger by the law firm," said Bernard.

According to Wentworth, Cane claimed that the Wentworths' debt had substantially increased over the years and suggested that the family would be well-advised to place the modest remainder of their investments under Cane trusteeship. "He would go into a rage about that," said the Creole woman, "especially when he had a worse bout of fever than usual, insisting that he gave in after many months only because his sanity was called into question by young Dr. Cane." In 1945, Dr. Randall Cane pioneered the practice of psychoanalysis in Tarragona after extensive training abroad.

Our informant said that Wentworth considered Landry an agent of the Cane family hired to bring about the destruction of the Wentworths and, specifically, his own death. She was of the opinion, however, that "no one would take seriously his story impugning the honor of one of Tarragona's first families," but speculated that the unlimited supply of alcohol and drugs which Wentworth claimed had been furnished to him by the late Jake Landry was "a pay-off of some kind." Landry may have been buying Wentworth's silence, according to Bernard, in regard to illicit activities at the Hernando Inn involving narcotics and prostitution. "Those activities surely were and are no secret," she said.

Two days before Wentworth's death, he sent for Bernard to receive treatments. "He was barely coherent," she recalled, "and kept muttering fiercely that Mr. Landry's days were as numbered as his own."

Wentworth told Bernard that he had no intention of vacating his property, by which he apparently meant the Boullet House. He referred to its new owner as "an out of town speculator and nothing more than the latest front for the Cane conspiracy."

"I suppose he meant poor Mrs. Dumot, who is certainly from out of town but as innocent in all of this as you or I," said the Creole woman, referring to Professor Elizabeth Dumot of Athena, New York, currently restoring the Boullet property sold to her earlier this year by the Committee for the Preservation of Historic Tarragona.

Police spokesman Sgt. Tommy Peaden disclosed that a thorough search made soon after Wentworth's death brought to light no evidence of foul play. Chief of Police J. Winston Fleming has ordered an immediate investigation of alleged mischief at the Hernando. [See "Probe," B-3.]

All of this placed me and my restoration in an illuminating context, and if not exactly new, at least sharpening the contours of things, like a sudden overhead light in a room known to you only in the obscure glimmer of dusk: everything turns out to be pretty much what you thought, only more so. Little wonder that I was always coming up against Wentworth traces all over the house, since it was, now, clearly Wentworth property I'd been restoring in the sense that houses—all material objects, for that matter, like purely ideational ones—belong ultimately to those whom they possess. Only the Wentworth kind of possession confers that feeling of natural ownership which is unshakable, however tenuous in law. A natural owner is always an innocent. And if the restoration amounted to this—a wresting of the house from the old man's dead grip—the sense I'd had, all summer long, of a purgation in progress came from none other than our entwinement, his and mine, in the innocence of our joint possession. Purging the house of Wentworth traces, was I not ridding it of myself and myself of it?

Poor Mrs. Dumot, with her deed from The Committee for the Preservation of Historic Tarragona, alias Randall Cane III, as sole proof of ownership, so hard at work, so slavishly wresting her own property from its natural place in her life to a moment of sublimity, a moment free of possession, before its return to the natural order of things. Poor, innocent, possessed Mrs. Dumot. As for Miss Mary Louise, (no innocent, I concluded) she played the situation for all it was worth in the next few days and emerged, in short order, as a thoroughly fascinating and marketable public character.

viii

Except that his was by no stretch of the imagination a self-sacrificial nature, one would almost have suspected Jake of having set it all up, engineering the ultimate communal record by absentee management. News lines daily spun out the widening web of his murder. I followed them avidly—snapped them up, hastily sandwiched between myriad details of finish work.

Front page: Tom Evans bound over to grand jury to await action for indictment.

Special feature: unsullied Anglo-Saxon pedigree of Wentworth clan dug up in Rappaport interview bolstered by unspecified "archives." Recollections of former affluence, erstwhile ties to prominent people. Existence of legal documents said to be possessed by the late Jeremy Wentworth, proving deforcement of rightful belongings, not established.

Pro-Evans voices (KKK visitors, self-proclaimed): "Jake knew too much. The higher-ups figured they'd shut Tom and Aubrey up along with Jake by pinning his murder on them, but Tom has special friends to protect his interests. Tom's always been well-liked in this here community." Between the lines: new power base in formation, with directing voice embodied in Tom Evans and "special friends"; higher-ups well-advised to fill subordinate role or none at all. Apparent disintegration here of old-style benevolent paternalism, Judge Cane's bloodline thinning out in the socially mobile world of his psychiatric heir.

Harding browses through these clippings, pulling out this one and that to show how the news unraveled from day to day that final week. She proffers, like a choice dish, a statement from Randall Cane's attorney:

Although Dr. Cane's sympathy with the Wentworth family's plight and regard for their former association with his own family preclude detailed comment, he finds himself regrettably constrained to respond to their recent allegations, paranoid projections founded, he fears, in a congenital instability aggravated by substance abuse and, in the case of the late Jeremy Wentworth, senile dementia, Dr. Cane's prognosis being that, with supportive care during a monitored period of withdrawal in a rehabilitative context, members of the Wentworth family may be expected to attain a reasonable emotional equilibrium.

Page two: Missing Link Discovered in Captiva Island. Krasner lounging on a yacht, beachrobe slung over shoulder, sporting *arriviste* recently appointed caretaker of Palm Beach estate of Julia Howard Stein, widow of David J. Stein of Long Island and, along with Tarragona's Randall Cane III, heir to El Inglès, one of the Panhandle's oldest and most important remaining ante-bellum plantations.

ix

And here, says Harding, a personal favorite, because it is such a fine example of how a medium can outdo itself even against its own best interests: THEN AND NOW, supposed to be linking past and present in significant resonances, featuring Life on Southern Plantation in 1830's: Typical or A-Typical? A full-page spread on El Inglès reproduces a sketch by the late Jake Landry's artist great-grandfather (the plantation's head overseer, it turns out) shortly to be on exhibit at the Tarragona Historical Museum: two males of African descent attired in early nineteenth-century morning dress examining hand-crafted jewelry displayed on a table. One of them casually lifts, with end of riding crop, a gold chain studded with gems, while the other watches, speculatively, over an open Bible in hand. Artist's caption (so like Jake's) in upper right: PARSON WILLIAM AND PARSON JAMES. Authorities consulted by news hound Roland B. Markit offer diverse hypotheses in historical context, e.g., Professor Alain Coulert (stimulating theorist and visitor at Tallahassee, formerly a structuralist):

...Landry drawings show traces of unprecedented socio-economic situation requiring a new language for plausible description...early nineteenth-century experiment in radical socialist capitalism, it would appear…utopian attempt to sustain, within a self-sufficient socio-economic structure, a kind of egalitarian polity whereby primitive satisfaction, equal but separate for each individual, was maximized….

So goes the new descriptive language, but the former structuralist notes that the artist's renderings of managerial figures on the plantation "betray certain behavioral signs of dissatisfaction not exhibited by slaves," e.g.: the tall, slim, fashionably clad young Caucasian male captioned HEIR TO EL INGLES (not reproduced in Markit's column, but subject to scholarly inspection at Museum by arrangement with Curator) has in all situations a kind of enervated sag in lower body parts, especially the knees. Coulert:

…foundering of experiment in failure to maximize primitive dimensions of satisfaction for owners and managers? Thereby permitting emergence of alienated group within community…master-slave dialectic bringing master class to consciousness of self-deceiving ideology…not to be taken as interpretation, but merely as direction for further analysis.

Here our staff writer sticks his neck out and speculates (boldly, one feels): Did radical socialist capitalism at El Inglès evolve into individualistic capitalism?

X

More voices—the essence of a newspaper is that it commits to print the dialogue of the community, or, depending on your hearing, its babble.

Greeley Connor: dwelling, safely after the fact, on the happy coincidence by which his "concern for authenticity in details" led him, as consultant, to drop in at the Boullet House at precisely the moment Dr. Dumot "felt herself in need of a protecting hand."

The Creole woman: local amateur authority on antique Klan protocol and fashions invited by College to present lecture series on "Klan-destine Iconography: From the Outside In." Elsewhere, hers is now the voice of a regional aesthetic warning all concerned of "dangers of aestheticism" in the work of historic restoration. "The surest way to miss the experience of beauty, like the closely allied one of happiness, is to make it the object of a pursuit." (She who bends to herself a joy, doth the wingèd life destroy—Miss Mary Louise recycling old poetic verities into new shibboleths.)

And here again, the Wentworths: male head of family, William Royal, turns away all further approaches from media after stating that no one meant to hold the Canes responsible for the misfortunes of his own family, or words to that effect. A step towards "reasonable emotional equilibrium?" A first, faltering, independent step, or....?" How old Jeremy Wentworth must be raging in the courtrooms of the Great Beyond!

xi

Somewhat to Markit's surprise, the piece on early plantation life at El Inglès touched off a burst of interest in the community to rival news of the murder itself, partly, I imagined, because of a suspicion among many that something amiss in the life style depicted in the great-grandfather's portfolio might have been set straight by the great-grandson's killing. In response to a barrage of phone calls immediately after the morning paper went out, Markit, true newsman that he was, arranged to follow up his article with a talk show, that very evening, on the College TV network. A full hour of it, with himself as moderator. His panelists: Curator Hartley, Professor Coulert, and none other than Tarragona's own Creole Woman.

Thursday's paper—the first I heard of the program—nailed it as a historic breakthrough and captured it at some length.. Markit, who must have been working round the clock by this time, appeared in some danger of losing a proper sense of his audience, caught up as he was in the heady drama of experts facing off.

CURATOR, once more attempting to draw fellow panelists' attention to overlooked evidence of four drawings of a woman identified in one exemplar as BRIDE OF FREEDOM: obviously neither master nor slave...distinguished by queenly self-assurance and an American Indian costume magnificently simple in contrast to the fashions of the day.

MODERATOR: Possibility that ante-bellum plantation life

depended in some way on this Indian woman...primitive but complex bartering patterns?

PROFESSOR, eyebrows raised over half-glasses and eyes lowered in *Sentinel* still: socio-economic system in question was almost certainly grounded in Native American myths and rituals dramatizing religious or transcendent rationale for its historical existence.

CURATOR: Fascinating....

PROFESSOR:...thus we may assume a period of success on the part of the Seminoles in radicalizing the plantation systems within their cultural purview.

CURATOR: reminds colleagues that the name "Seminole" is very likely derived from Spanish *cimarron*, meaning "wild."

PROFESSOR: Just the kind of false etymology the ritual of a profane marriage might have celebrated. Earlier speculation that radical socialistic capitalism was destroyed from within by emergence of alienated master class may have to give way to likelihood that system met its end through victory of colonial man in Florida Indian Wars.

CREOLE WOMAN: Holding up several sketches of black slaves, one by one, before camera. Points to bodily mutilations: scars, missing fingers, eyes, ears, other body parts. Evidently, Seminole institutionalization of freedom involved structuring daily life in patterns of ritualized violence?

PROFESSOR: Demonstrating intellectual flexibility, gracefully waives earlier hypothesis that traces of violence might date from pre-radical period.

CREOLE WOMAN: Exhibits, sequentially, four drawings of Indian Woman's black consort and invites response from colleagues.

PROFESSOR: One sketch labelled MATADOR, FINE STUD, suggests Native American woman mated in a type of "ritual polyandry" with males of various social factions selected for sexual prowess.

CURATOR: Fertility figures, no doubt.

CREOLE WOMAN: Points to last drawing labelled KILLED...(remainder of caption unreadable, some word or words having been smudged out). Black fertility figure lies in pool of blood, face blown off, recognizable only by his elegant attire.

CURATOR: Most expressive.

PROFESSOR: modifying initial hypothesis,...difficult to avoid suspicion of ritualized violence in this social structure...obligatory death of Seminole's consorts and her periodic remarriage...not an unusual rite among primitives...no derogation intended, only that such social structures allowed for expression of primitive inclinations psychologically shared by all human beings.

Markit, summing up: After further lively discussion, views were found to converge. Whether it was the effect of this controversial talk show or of Markit's exhaustive report of it in the paper, interest in nineteenth-century life on one of Florida's oldest plantations instantly dried up. Two brief letters to the editor testified to the general dearth the morning after.

Dear Editor,

While it is probably futile to oppose the rising tide of journalistic myopia (viz. Markit's biased report on the ante-bellum Landry drawings), I respectfully commit to the public record my view of the French anthropologist's speculations as unqualified nonsense. The work of the artist in question, in which I have a longstanding interest, shows an aversion to all fanciful touches and is to be viewed therefore as the objective representation of daily slave existence it purports to be. Nothing more or less. One notes In Professor Coulert's labored comments the sorry spectacle of "theory" lost in its own tergiversations.

Wm. Albright
Professor of American History
DeLuna Community College

Dear Editor,

I teach a night course down at the high school on how to manage your own portfolio, and all I can say is that it really takes a mind divorced from reality to think that socialism in any form, however modified, could ever have existed in this great state.

R.J. Pickering, Jr.

xii

If she did not answer the signals of others calling for response, the telephone and doorbell, along with numerous notes and letters in her mailbox (some commending her civic-minded restoration of a historic home; a few intimating that she had overstayed her welcome in Tarragona either because she belonged up North, or was "overly intellectual," or because she was a woman doing man's work, or a woman living alone in a questionable district—not a residential area really—or some combination of all; two from up and coming young businessmen, very polite and to the point, seeking to acquire restored properties suitable for "professional uses"; the rest from people like Greeley Connor who offered both his good wishes and his "services" should she still require them, Aimée Hulin expressing concern for her emotional welfare amid "all this sleaze and violence" and hinting that some mysterious, gripping new influence had entered her life about which she could not yet speak, Margaret Avery assuring her on blue butterfly notepaper, informally dashed off, that the Boullet House was still "highly marketable," and Randall Cane, ironic and witty, praising her "impeccable taste" all around and sending his condolences for the lack of it shown by the local paper in mounting her among "the roster of native villains," since, he writes, "I would imagine that yours, too, is a family adhering to the old code under which one's name appears in the public news twice only, once at birth and once at death, all other events presumably being private and under one's own control")—if, then, our restorationist did not respond to any of these signals, however intended, the thud of *The Tarragona Sentinel & Sun*, pitched every morning from a passing car so as to strike her front door with unvarying accuracy, resounded enough like a token of the world to impress on the solitary pace of her finish work the urgency of a race-against-the-clock in its final stretch.

xiii

Meanwhile, just as you thought that the community, deafened by its own noise, was about to be restored to its senses: Aubrey

Evans pipes up to repudiate his earlier accusation against Daddy as "just one of those dumb stories I concoct when I get good and mad...didn't mean to get the old man into trouble." And from Klan spokesman Jimbo Townsend: "They got that confession out of Aubrey illegally, everybody knows that. Not one officer around to read him his Miranda warnings before he told all them lies. Ain't no case against Tom, and the boy either."

Momentum gathering in another quarter: the Hernando's habitués surface as newsworthy material in diverse interviews and testimonials of their transgressions. However degraded, all are "born again" (or praying to be) irrespective of denomination or political persuasion. Themes etched by repetition of typological (if not naturalistic) pattern: pure Old-Family-Blood running through veins of one and all; Fall-into-Corruption through Unfortunate-Surroundings; Expiation-of-Guilt to be suffered in Fallen-Environment, etc. The inference seems unavoidable that the degenerate of the Quarter (despite some flatness of character) constitute a community more real and less hypocritical than most. Something else: two familiar names getting linked at last like the heading of an established firm, "Krasner & Landry, Agents of Corruption, Inc."

Reading between the lines: due to dwindling inventories, hoarding in face of future scarcity, loss of income from sales and so on, anarchy seems imminent. *Ergo*: growing demand of mass market (in the main, roughly two thousand African-Americans and Southeast Asian refugees jammed pell-mell into Segovia Villas) about to impact on community, and whenever things get to "impacting," somebody had better sit up and listen! Spokesman for Segovia Villas, one Flanagan J. Prideaux, gives voice to submerged but perceptibly rising clamor for Krasner's return. No regrets, though, for his partner's passing.

xiv

On the point of discarding the paper at about half past eight on one of those mornings towards the end, I hear the doorbell ring, not for the first time that day, in synchrony with an importunate banging of the knocker. Through shutter slats I spy three policemen, Roland B. Markit and a fifth man behind him, a photographer, grouped around the entry.

I open the door far enough to push my head out a few inches from Sgt. Peaden's one-way mirror glasses (same old Boschian grotesque—*plus ça change*...).

"Yes?"

"Sorry ma'am, been trying to contact you don't know how long, need your permission to check over the house. Lieutenant Zamora's orders, ma'am, and strictly for your own protection, unh. We'll just walk on through, won't touch a thing."

Since Jake Landry's demise, Sgt. Peaden has become positively masterful in the execution of his duty. Getting cozy with the press too, I see. He peels a wrapper off a fresh stick of gum which he pops neatly into his mouth, rolling the paper into a tiny silver ball between puffy palms.

Reasoning that the fastest way to get rid of this bunch is to let them do their business, whatever it might be, I throw the front door wide open and step back as the photographer, following right behind the three officers, starts snapping pictures of me and the long, wide hallway. "Very nice," he says.

"You don't mind, do you ma'am?" It's Markit.

"How could I? I'm just on the staff here, haven't you heard?"

His mildly chastened look does not deter him from inquiring where I have been for the last seventy-two hours and what my plans are for the Boullet House "now."

"No comment on either subject." I do this surprisingly well.

Producing a xerox of Miss Mary Louise's sketch, he asks me if I can confirm with any certainty that it is a replica of the one shown me by Landry the afternoon before his death, to which I reply that I have no doubt whatever the sketch is a remarkably exact facsimile of the one I watched Landry draw. (Omitting that I also watched the manufacture of the facsimile.)

"That would seem to clinch that part of it," Roland B. says with frank enthusiasm.

"It certainly would," I agree.

Sergeant Peaden assuring me—more staidly than I had thought possible—that everything seems "in order," I usher all five of them out the door and down the steps.

Markit lingers beside the hydrangea as if it were a horticul-
tural anomaly, angling for an interview. "It would certainly be
interesting," he coaxes, "for our readers to get your viewpoint
on what's going on."

"Afraid I have none newsworthy."

He waits. I decline to elaborate.

He tries a new tack: "Just a couple of questions—"

"No. Not ever. About anything."

But his parting query to my back manages to inspire a
retort. "What's your reaction," he asks, "to the charge of the
Evans men that not a word of what you claim happened here
can be trusted?"

"Slanderous," I say firmly, "I'm entirely reliable." And
then, before closing the door on further news in the making:
"The problem is that they are not reliable judges of who I am
and what I am doing here."

It was all the same to me that all of them would now agree
in secret with Evans that I was jumpy and hysterical, unquote. I
kind of enjoyed the idea, actually, as I went about calmly locking
and bolting the front door and set to measuring, sawing, and
tacking into place the already painted toe molding. There were
roughly a thousand running feet of it to go.

XV

And after that, there was always more—and still more finicky
work to get through, time foreshortened, and foreshortening.
The glandular secretion of fear, without pity or compassion,
worked its rhetorical finish to my project as emerging perspectives and events crowded together for dénouement. After
Markit's aborted attempt to interview me (when, unlike the Creole woman, I sought to remove myself from the purview of the
news media) the journalistic sequence daily unfolding into
minute novelties collapsed into a restive texture of relations with
an ever-shifting focus, and my snatched readings of those last
pressured days came to exist in memory as a montage of fact and
fancy, lacunae and excess, exposition and innuendo, unaccountable reversal, inadvertent and deliberate mystification, alternate

solutions, complications, whole new perspectives, inconsistencies, and just plain bunk. Stock situations peopled by stock characters calling for stock responses.

Among the gathering clouds of archetypal formations in the falling action, my own image hovered over me like the fatal woman. Could I, would I work my way out of it all, be done with it before time closed on any ending other than that imposed by its own necessity?

xvi

Face to Face With Ellen Rappaport

Is he a brash man of the world scattering obscenities like inflated coins? A romantic individualist? A devil-may-care loner?

Dark-eyed, with salt and pepper curls and beard, he is Anthony Krasner, roofing contractor, the suspected "missing link" in the nearly week-old KKK case, who appeared seemingly out of nowhere early yesterday, reportedly to cut a deal for immunity from prosecution. Highly placed officials would not disclose what information has been obtained from Krasner or what charges, if any, may be pending against him.

We talked to him at Sandpiper Marina on his thirty-foot cabin cruiser "Night Owl," just as the sun was slipping into Tarragona Bay. Full of twists and turns, true or false, this is his story to the public. Deletions of offensive language are so marked.

Q:　I'll go straight for the big one, Mr. Krasner. Who killed Jake Landry?

A:　What do I get if I tell you baby? (Lighting the first of many unfiltered Lucky Strikes washed down by nearly as many cans of Michelob from a well-stocked ice-chest on board.) No kidding—I wouldn't know. Cross my heart and hope to [unprintable] die.

Q:　What about the Creole woman's story?

A:　Smells a little fishy, I agree. But look at it this way: how in hell would she make up a connection like that?

Q:　A connection between you and...?

A:　Whoa! Easy now baby. Want a beer?

Q:　Did you work for Landry?

A: Would a member of the *fair* sex ask me a [unprintable] lowdown question like that?

Q: Who *do* you work for?

A: Tony Krasner works *for* Tony Krasner, *capisci*?

Q: What exactly *was* your association with the dead man?

A: Sure you can handle this scoop dear? (Draining his can nearly empty.) About a year ago I was making a regular delivery when Landry came up with—

Q: What kind of delivery?

A: I don't mean postcards or babies. I'm a roofing man, remember? High wire. You ladies are all gab (smiling wickedly through rings of smoke).

Q: Drugs?

A: You said it dear, not me. Where was I? Landry had a line on some hard porn, but he couldn't distribute it here himself because he was "too vulnerable," he said.

Q: How so?

A: (Wink) Careful as he was—and Jake was one careful guy—he still ended up on that fence, dear, which just goes to prove you can be *too* [unprintable] careful, get me?

Q: So you became Landry's distributor locally—drop off the dope, pick up the porn?

A: You're rushing me dear.

Q: How *did* it work then?

A: Jake needed a couple of local hicks to peddle his dirt, some guys that would be so [unprintable] into it themselves they could be counted on to keep the inventory moving.

Q: Tom and Aubrey Evans.

A: Bull's eye! Bought one of everything—cassettes, pictures, gadgets, you name it. Real churchy folks in the daytime, but come sundown, man! We offered them a wholesale discount on buying in quantity so they could see the money in it.

Q: Did they bite?

A: Crying for it babe. Dirt started moving up and down this coast like it was a sewer. Piece of cake, and then the [expletive] hit the fan when that chick at the College used some sexy little book in her class.

Q: Did you read it?

A: A man can't waste his time on artsy-fartsy porn any more than the other kind.

Q: So the thing at the College hurt your business?

A: Let's just say that all those [unprintable] letters in the paper, and all that [expletive] about cleaning up the smut trade cooled off Uncle Tom real bad.

Q: And what about Landry?

A: Squeezing me from the other side dear, to keep Daddy and Sonny-boy in. I figured he was setting them up to take the rap, just in case, so I told them I might have to let the [unprintable] cat out of the bag if they didn't cooperate.

Q: Did they?

A: Sonny-boy caved right in, he was hooked on the stuff. But Dad went nuts, and I do mean nuts—haywire, loony, turned as red as a baboon's behind and kept screaming about the [unprintable] "family name."

Q: Were you surprised?

A: In this trade dear, you figure your goons pretty close. I saw right from the start that flushing out old historic [expletive] was Uncle Tom's idea of a really fine business. He'd do anything to protect his "position-in-this-here-town," and I do mean anything.

Q: Is that an innuendo?

A: Wouldn't know one from a [unprintable] dear.

Q: Did he give in to you?

A: Are you ready for this? I picked up a great big load of canned stuff from Landry and delivered it at Evans' place in the usual way.

Q: Which was?

A: Disguise, baby. I dressed up in a uniform like a delivery guy and drove a van with "Top Star Chow" across both sides of it, right over to that doggie-barn behind his place. He's got a couple of Dobermans, meanest [unprintable] devils you ever saw, but I made him install remote control so they'd keep away from yours truly while I slipped the goodies in through the back.

Q: Is the story you're telling me the truth?

A: You're hooked on this stuff, aren't you?

Q: What are *you* hooked on, Mr. Krasner?

A: Wanna hear the rest or what? Gets more exciting. Like I was saying, I dropped off the doggiechow as usual, all boxed up and juicy, and I called Evans from a payphone to let him know. Seemed just like old times, not a [unprintable] peep out of him, so before I hung up I just happened to mention how glad I was he'd decided to stay in the corporation. He said he'd thought it over and now he was seeing things in a different light. A different light, [expletive]!

Q: You must have put the fear of God in him.

A: That's what I thought, and I was [unprintable] wrong! I'm not an easy man to fool, but I had a lot of [expletive] on my mind just then, overloaded the old circuits I guess. Want another beer?

Q: What happened?

A: Sitting on the edge of your round little seat, aintcha? Dig this: that little [unprintable] tried to rig a fatal slip-up for me on the roof of that woman's historic residence we've all been reading so much about lately.

Q: The Boullet House?

A: Lucky my [unprintable] number wasn't up yet.

Q: Are you saying that Tom Evans...?

A: Sonny-boy, darling, that snot-nosed [unprintable] tried to pull the plug on yours truly, and it didn't take a lot to figure out who put him up to it either.

Q: Is that an accusation?

A: Am I under oath sweetie?

Q: Did you report the incident at the time?

A: I'm no dummy lady.

Q: So the Evanses scared you off—or was it Landry?

A: When your job is to be middleman, that don't mean you have to take it right on the old [unprintable], get it?

Q: Bet you thought up a smart comeback!

A: Flattery will get you everywhere sweetie, but you should learn to be a little more subtle.... I got in touch with Uncle Tom pronto and told him his secret was safe, he could count on me, but I just had the feeling Landry wouldn't be satisfied with trying to make a patsy out of Sonny-boy. I could see that fat old [unprintable] didn't trust me an inch.

Q: When exactly was this?

A: A few days before ole Jakey passed on to the wild blue yonder. (He hums a snatch of the famous Marine song in a scratchy voice.)

Q: But you lied to Evans, didn't you? His secret is *not* safe with you after all?

A: A man has to protect himself, but you wouldn't understand that—it's the only thing I've ever had against your sex.

Q: Lack of understanding?

A: You see? That's what I mean. Gab.

Q: Mr. Krasner, are you a member of the KKK?

A: A what?! You've got to be kidding! That [unprintable] bunch of closet pansies? (Wrenching cough) Where was I? Oh yeah, I got tied up with a hot little number and took her for a ride in my boat, same night I set old Tom straight on his porno connection.

Q: Are the police in contact with her?

A: (Charming smile, more coughing.) Never squeal on a lady dear. Here's the rest of the story, interested? Monday morning, bright and early, I dock at this little marina down the coast to pick up some beer, and there he is, front page—hit the news all over the place, big picture of ole Jakey in KKK dress on top of that woman's fence. Cigar and all.

Q: Any idea who killed him?

A: [Expletive] honey, folks were practically standing in line to do that [unprintable] bastard in, and frankly I don't give a flying [expletive] which one of those sickos got to him first. But you can take it from me, I'm not playing sitting duck for anybody.

Q: When you left town, you headed South, is that right?

A: Boat and all sweetheart.

Q: How come?

A: Pursuing opportunities.

Q: What kind of "opportunities"?

A: Jake kept blabbing about an opening for some kind of hot-shot caretaker on a big place over on the East coast. Good money, easy hours. "Plenny of everything you'd want," he said. He said they'd appreciate my talents down there—he always talked that way, called himself "a student of psychology," poor bastard.

Q: One with rich contacts, though, down South?

A: I never dig too deep.

Q: Dangerous? Too much trouble?

A: Not my style. Anyhow—I kept putting him off, figured he was just try-ing to set up on his own, maybe work out a better deal. But once I saw how the wind was blowing, I thought what the [expletive], and I took off. Docked on Captiva and drove over to glorious Palm Beach so I could cash in on my caretaking talents. Ain't that something?

Q: And you told all this to—who exactly *did* you discuss your case with?

A: You're a better listener baby.

Q: Why did you wait all this time?

A: You mean to get to know you babe?

Q: To go to the authorities.

A: (Drains a whole can of beer, slowly.) I know how to take care of *numero uno*, and that's the bottom line, see? I'm a man that knows what he wants, and I know how to get it, every [unprintable] time, got that? Maybe you need to turn your gadget up a little louder.

Q: Are you saying you just didn't *want* to cooperate with the police ear-lier? Didn't feel like it?

A: Damn right! I don't have to go running off my mouth to anybody, and especially not to some publicity-starved [unprintable] on a little local rag that thinks she's got a right to snoop into my private business— follow me?

Q: Your *new* business, Mr. Krasner? In Palm Beach?

A: Listen, and listen good. I'm my own man, always have been. You got that on your [unprintable] tape recorder, Miss Susan B. Anthony?

Q: Just one final question, Mr. Krasner. Do you use drugs yourself?

A: Never touch the stuff baby. Never had any need for it. Let's make a truce— want another?

xvii

From one of the inside pages, a caption: Adele Evans, daughter of Aubrey Evans, alleged Porno Prince, listens to her grandmother, Leona Evans, explain that women and children have no business in the doghouse. The photograph itself—portly woman in heels too high for comfort or grace, straight skirt confining her too tightly, white blouse with a ruffle at the neck around which hangs a piece of costume jewelry—I found unaccountably moving. Her hair is freshly done up for the weekend in the style of Tarragona's neighborhood beauty salons (perhaps this is why I feel I have seen her somewhere before?). Framed by the side door to the Evans home, redwood picnic table on patio, she extends one hand to a slim girl who looks up trustingly at her; the other holds a bulky purse (possibly, it comes to me, the one that, according to Evans, safeguards the snub-nosed .38). Donner and Blitzen, hanging on the chain link fence, rage at uniformed officers of the law hauling away boxes marked "Top Star Chow."

xviii

In the making: the longest, biggest religious revival in the collective memory of Tarragona. Various denominations, however bent on splitting hairs in the past, express their unanimous desire to restore the community to one version or another of moral purity. "Atonement" is on everyone's lips; "at-one-ment with ourselves, at-one-ment with each other," goes the rallying cry. Church of the Moabites, young but enthusiastic, spearheads effort. Minister and founder Jonas B. Dabney explains: "Conceived and born in sin, we live in sin, and we attain salvation only through routing Sodom and Gomorrah from within our midst." The revival's text, "Moab is my washpot," signifies that "we must all become as God's spiritual washpots whereby the whole community may be cleansed of God's Enemy Number One." The soul as divine laundering facility, soaking, churning, rinsing, spinning away the inimical pollutions of the flesh in suds of Cheer. Already, it is reported, hundreds have come forward to become "washpots for Jesus" and to "increase and multiply their commitment to Christian renewal." The aroused spirit turning back to its ancient commerce.

Puzzle: how does a community authenticate its own renewal? Who will be found competent to inspect the blueprints, materials, workmanship in so massive an enterprise of rehabilitation, not to mention the façade that this community of cleansed souls will turn to the world, its hues and mien? What Greeley Connor can rise to such a task? (And what will it all cost?)

On behalf of Tom Evans, who continues to refuse both legal counsel and bail (no longer news, really), this voice from the Klan: "It's a set-up if there ever was one. Everybody knows Tom and his boy are hard-working, God-fearing Christians, never been in an ounce of trouble."

Meanwhile, Aubrey's latest confession becomes the subject of a probing feature by Roland B. Markit, still dishing it up tirelessly after nearly a week, though no longer on page one.

We honestly did try to get out of the porno biz, Daddy and me...somebody might want to write a book about my experience with porno as a warning to others.... It's kind of like everybody up there got together and planned out how to put the blame on two little guys, first that professor lady with her cock'n bull story, man! Like Daddy says, she's got a mighty high opinion of herself. And then that other one, not a single true fact in what that old colored school teacher said, and everybody is acting like it's gospel.... I got a theory, more than a suspicion, that somebody's paying them two off, but good.

Plain, ordinary working man as technocratic society's unacknowledged victim. His alleged attempt on Krasner's life? "Just wanted to scare him into treating Daddy and me right, teach him a lesson on his own turf. Old pro like Krasner always hangs on some way."

xix

Text for the upcoming sermon at First Baptist Church on Laurel Walk (where, it will be remembered, no mocking bird sings): "The Lord Taketh Pleasure in Them that Fear Him." The deacons there were said to be appealing to authorities for permission to release Evans & Son for the duration of the service, at the congregation's recognizance.

XX

By seven at the latest each morning, I fold the paper, throw all but the occasional snipping from it in the trash and put away my few breakfast things, allowing no trace in the kitchen of present habitation. As the house nears completion, I take increasing satisfaction in its cleanliness and in the gradual removal from it of all personal signs of my life there. Clothes, shoes, superfluous tools and toilet articles, the odd pencil, stray pins and clips, all find their way piecemeal into the trunk of my car in a steady evacuation, ready to go, so that with nothing at all left lying about but the barest essentials for concluding my project, every inch is exposed to my ceaseless scrutiny as I continue to ignore the doorbell, the thumps of the brass knocker, the taps (exploratory, persistent, or furious) on the window panes, the quick footsteps crunching inquisitively over the drive like the specter of Landry collecting material for his still living history.

psycheme

I have not forgotten my promise to tell you about what happened the time I found myself in the bog.

It was a rainy, dreary day but I was so wrapped up in my work I noticed nothing around me until the sun suddenly burst out and laid its warmth over my shoulders tensed in concentration on the writing before me. I was reminded to take care of my ordinary needs and called a friend to meet me for lunch in the little park across the street. I darted to the vegetarian deli on the corner, where I picked up three or four cartons of tastily prepared salads, a slender cut of brie, and a round of sourdough French. Ordinarily, I would have spread our picnic cloth on the grass, but this day there were puddles shining all over, so I laid it over a portion of the one empty bench left and put out my assortment, leaving room for my friend to sit on one side and myself on the other. I no sooner settled in my place than a young blue-eyed woman plopped down beside me with just enough room for her picnic basket between us. The line-up: her at one end of the bench, then her basket, next me and my picnic cloth spread out, then the empty place at the other end for my friend. I was mildly surprised that anybody else would choose this bench because space was tight and I so obviously had taken it. Still, she might be tired, I thought, resting a bit, maybe planning to eat out of her basket. There are ethnic groups that comfortably space themselves so close to strangers you can feel their body heat, even the texture of their skin—I had seen her around before and she didn't look like one of those but you can never tell. There she was, anyway, definitely looking as if I and my arrangements did not exist. Well, my friend and I would have to make the best of it, and if she could stand it we should be able to, since we at least had the space necessary for our lunch. I saw my friend approaching at the end of the block and went to meet her. We decided to split a bottle of cider and had almost passed the bench on our way to buy it when I noticed that the cloth with my assortment of cartons, bread, and wrapped wedge of brie on it had been pushed way to the end of the bench, apparently by the black-haired young woman who had joined the other one and was laying out a picnic cloth. Both then began emptying the contents of their large basket on the cloth between them. I was incredulous but, politely, if somewhat coldly, controlling a hostility that any analyst would abstract from its setting in a patient and identify as psychotic for a fee of one hundred plus, I reminded the blue-eyed one of the history of our relations on the bench, how originally I had had the whole thing, having used about two-thirds of it to establish myself and my friend for our lunch, how that had already been accomplished when she came along and sat down with her basket thereby taking over the remainder of the bench, how I had not objected—after all, it was public space and we could share—but how my friend (who was nodding vehemently) and I must ask them (and we were sure *her* friend had not understood the situation) to please remove their picnic things from our space on the bench. She stared at me with a kind of bland amazement as if struck that speech should issue from one whom she had not even known to exist. "Oh," she said, "did my friend do that? I didn't realize." "Yes, she did," I replied, "please move your things, we'll be back in a minute." "Sure," she said. Back with our apple cider, the scene as we approached was as follows: two elegantly casual young women, a gay cloth with cheeses, fruits, bread, and wine in confiture glasses spread between them, having a leisurely lunch, sparkling in their conversation, heads tilted back in laughter, eyes almost closed to catch the delight of the sun, apparently unaware of both the quickening interest of passing young men and the benign smiles of older ones; and at the other end of the bench, my cloth, with cartons, bread, and cheeses piled up and teetering on the edge like leftovers forgotten by previous picnickers not as fastidious as these two. They paid us not the slightest heed until we stood within a few inches of each other and I spoke: "I must ask you again to move your picnic things from our part of this bench." The blue-eyed one looked into my eyes and said, "Oh, I forgot, but we're eating our lunch now," and turned to her friend. "You're a manipulative, exploitative little bitch," I said. "You either remove your things immediately or I'll throw them *and you* into the street." "Jeannie," she said, appealing to her friend, "get this witch away from me." Jeannie promptly responded with angry contempt: "Are you afraid we'll mess up your precious bench?" "Move," I said and reached down to jerk their cloth and all its contents up. Black-haired Jeannie instantly jumped to her feet and backed down, voice quivering with rage, "All right, all right, for Christ's sake, we weren't even going to be here very long! You'd think you owned the place." She dumped the remains of their lunch into their basket, threw the cloth over it, and reached her hand toward the other one. For a second, that one didn't budge, blue eyes floating forth from her head, pustules of pure hatred erupting and penetrating the pores of my body like sperm whipping their tails to the female gamete in the complicity of biological reproduction. Then, she rose, hooked one arm under her basket and the other through Jeannie's arm, and off they went like models, tall, erect, flashing glances at an admiring public, too professional at being women to admit of or experience dislocation. As if blue eyes might return to claim her place, my friend and I carefully avoided a space the size of a small ass at her end of the bench as we took over the rest with our cloth and food between us. It is not that we failed to experience pleasure sitting there with each other in the sunlight eating our tasty concoctions and drinking cold, sparkling, full-bodied

cider. But it was not a wholesome pleasure. More as if a threatening cut had taken place, and ours was now that place where the
mind still knows and consciousness still appreciates and feeling
still hurts although there is no body. Where my body, cut off, sur-
rounds me, takes possession of me and beats me in sado-
masochistic frenzy, berserk, back into shape. I understand it
well. If I come out of it, I come out weakened but whole again,
back in shape but different. I suppose I may once have believed
in the mind-body dualism like others, I don't remember; that's
an issue tangential to living in it. And so we sat, my friend and I,
almost in silence, taking our pleasure without having it. Only
time quiets such a convulsion of the body, shrinks it to its normal
cuddly size and brings it to snuggle once more in itself, whole
and half-asleep, buoyant and time-rapt.

   It took months for me to tell you this. Weeks and weeks
passed before I could bring myself to so much as recall it. I have
fulfilled my part of the bargain here, I have told it. I wish only to
call your attention to the fact that what brought me to this pass
was not the threat of thermonuclear war or ecological destruction or criminal transgression or terrorist attack, nor the spectacle of starving hordes, dying children, disease-ridden communi-
ties, nor perceptions of economic and political injustice, nor a
personal loss either of a loved one or of deeply held convictions—
nothing, in short, of momentous stature. Nothing, indeed, of any
stature at all.

xxi

Tom Evans denies, absolutely, any association with pornography ("the boy's just saying whatever that pusher wants to hear"), and
Klan voices transmit his bitterness escalating now into out and
out rancor directed at the community in general, washed and
unwashed. A supporter citing him: this town ain't worth a lick of the
work I've put into it."
   A different view:
   Me and Daddy don't exactly see eye to eye on the porno biz, never
   have...ain't nothing wrong with it if you run it right...don't nobody
   want their wives or their mothers to have nothing to do with it, or

their kids neither...Daddy said he'd kill me if I ever let on we had anything to do with it...my idea is to make a legitimate business out of it,
do it out front like...build it up gradually...times are changing, don't
nobody think nothing about it no more...don't matter to me personally, but it's easy to see there's big bucks out there....

Slithering shamelessly out of his natural father's grip right into
the clutches of Big Daddy Capitalism.

xxii

I've always distrusted the motivating fantasies of future accom-
plishments with their tendency to lure one to a disregard for the
signal presence of obstacles. In those final days, I would push
myself till one or two in the morning, later and later, before
falling into the uneasy sanctuary of a few hours' sleep. As I
checked off items on my list, I would restrain impulses to speed
up the finish work, knowing that every chore, to be well done,
with a minimal risk of deforming botches, requires its own
tempo for living time. The discipline under which I had placed
myself allowed no indulgences in the tension of deferred pleasure, the vision of all being finished and perfected. The future as
a realm of unpredictable promise is suspect—it too easily
tempts one into forgetting that all promise, if not made good,
amounts to less than nothing.

psycheme

As Paul says, who wants to listen to her? Who cares what she
says? Obviously, I do, and as in all caring "why" does not matter
precisely to the extent that you do care. Obviously, too, Paul's
version of Harding has ruptured my text, refracted her image.
Less obviously—indirectly, like reflection returning to its source—
it has left its mark on me. Since his unwanted manuscript
appeared (he, to no one's surprise, disappeared quite amicably
soon thereafter), little has been said about the whole affair, and
that by me—one morning at breakfast I asked Harding to write a
piece about herself for me, not that I want or expect her to make

any reply to him as such, but it seems only fair that she have a chance to give her side of the story. She looked impassively out into the garden and changed the subject. I see her now about the house—the sun room, the kitchen, early in the morning before anyone else has thought to stir—with a legal pad and pencil, writing in longhand. She is oddly taciturn even with the girls, looks preoccupied during our daily long walks; the evenings she spends shut away in her study and forgets to say goodnight.

And so it stands between us, undetermined, unsettled as to what or when, while I forge on with what is left of Text One, toward the end. If you want to be really finished, she would say, you have to do it all exactly right, meaning that details as such disappear into and, thus, little by little, imperceptibly articulate the whole. Everything has to function with decorum, nothing calling attention to itself, as if it had grown there naturally, like a vital member of a healthy organism. Say you are touching up fresh paint around electrical switchplates, outlets, heating vents, wherever workmen have left their handprints: better not let the attention lapse for a split second, no accidental spots or streaks allowed on your polished old brass, no dribbles on your fine floors glistening all over the restored house. Any tiny break in concentration, any wishful or rebellious drifting away from what is immediately and materially before you, and you condemn yourself to doing it all over again. Careless finish work engenders more finish work and there's no end to it.

No end to it, yes. The question for me is not *why* I am so fascinated by her stories about that summer in Tarragona but where they have brought me—to what end. Where is this? And where are the others?

As any worker in a tradition knows, such work means you need not calculate anew the effect of the whole once enough of it has been materially collected; taking it all as if given, you merely select and arrange details under its legislative presence until exhaustion cages you in your ghostly lawgiver's arms of sleep. Not that the work turns automatic, says Harding, anything but. It requires that you absent yourself as a relevant factor in it even as it exacts your undivided attention, utter subjection from moment to moment—indistinguishable, she says, from abjection. Who performs these final tasks matters only to the extent that the worker see clearly what is needed and can act accordingly: someone prepared, in every sense, to function as an irrelevant necessity. This becomes increasingly evident as all room for play, for variation, closes itself off. In Harding's case, the very completeness of her involvement demanded her release from it; that release in turn came about only by way of the discipline that refuses to countenance any arbitrariness in bringing work to an end. And, so, as the restoration edged toward completion, each minute task moved her to a more definite circumscription of the critical activity required for her freedom, toward an ever finer judgment of what was necessary to please and ease her.

How very, very different it is for me, here in this curiously unpopulated place where neither I nor Harding nor you have any reality. I would linger here or, if speaking from another place, malinger, in this absence of opposition between knowledge and ignorance. My love of this emptiness knows no waning and my passion for this silence no pathos. I wish for no power other than this spinning of values webby with you and Harding, tatters in the wilds to wrap around my body.

xxiii

Over a tiny staff photo of *The Sentinel*'s Afro-American columnist in Section B, a headline: Gallery of West Indian Art to Open Locally. Pictured are Miss Mary Louise and a respectfully smiling Aimée Hulin at ease in graceful wicker chairs beside a draped table in a little sun room with tropical plants sitting and hanging in jungly masses, in the background a large Haitian primitive (one of several masterpieces purchased by Dr. and Mrs. James R. Hulin III on a recent trip to the Islands). Amanda Howard Hulin, wife of the noted cancer specialist, to cooperate with Miss Bernard of Creole woman fame on ongoing projects in the West Indies and Haiti in particular; Boullet House, late scene of KKK killing, still unsolved, soon to change hands, giving permanent home to new Gallery of Caribbean Art (second floor, above new law offices of Stavros, Stavros & Ribaut) which is to sponsor apprenticeship programs, financed by local contributors, "whereby promising young people from the area will have an opportunity to work in the Islands with native masters in the developing Haitian tradition." Aimée's voice, too, freighted with a new authority.

There is more: something called the Haitian Reintegration Organization (HRO) has been formed. Its main thrust: food production and work opportunities for Haitians in their own land, a projected network of diversified crafts, services, and small village industries, some producing specialized parts for national and multi-national corporations on a contractual basis. Stabilization of these networks by association with local agricultural cooperatives is to be organized by HRO, which hopes to enlist the aid of such progressive organizations as the Institute for Food and Development Policy, also support from concerned private individuals in negotiating with landowners to buy and/or rent portions of their land for food production by local cooperatives. Ms. Hulin said to be involved in the latter aspect of HRO's work. Says Miss Bernard, former elementary school teacher now retired:

> Our aim will be to reintegrate Haitians into their own rural culture where food produced for local use and work generating wages are critical necessities. The future of Haitians lies in Haiti, not on boats to Miami, and the successful creation of such a future has become a test for the very soul of the Western Hemisphere.*

Martin Kingston, a relative of Miss Bernard now employed in historic restoration, will, among his other duties as director of HRO, spearhead the group's family planning efforts in Haiti.

xxiv

Elsewhere, digging really deep, a human interest story with photos has another retired school teacher recalling Tony Krasner in her third grade homeroom as "a beautiful, dark-eyed boy, smart as a

---

*After circulating this clipping from the late 70's, Harding dryly updates the condition of our hemisphere's soul by citing several more recent headlines: HAITI IGNORED BY THE WEST; HAITIAN TALENT LEAVES COUNTRY; HAITIAN BOATLOAD DROWNS; and, most succinctly, from section 4, page 6, of a major national newspaper: HAITI IN CHAOS.

whip, and too full of life not to stir up trouble, but never really a bad boy."
But this is stalking ghosts: since his interview, Krasner (whose
talent for appearing and disappearing at his whim I know only
too well) has once more faded from the scene, perhaps down the
coast again, and over to the other side.

psycheme

Dear Reader, no matter how many showings of myself you get,
you can never be sure you're looking at one and the same one.
Every appearance under my name could be merely another
understudy. Not merely another identity but literally another
body. Body after body running in claiming to be Jael B. Juba. A
kind of performance art.

Unsettling as they may be, multiple identities are no real
problem because we all know we have the minds to constitute
ourselves interminably. What you need to get at is the body
problem, remembering—for this is what you forget—that identities are what bodies have.

Nor are mirrors any good here. For all I know, you see me
as nothing *more* than a name (although I never experience
myself that way). I had hoped, actually, that we might be proceeding under a sort of agreement: when you see me you see into
a body changing its mind by the hour, bits of identity showing,
the name giving it all a stable reference point of sorts. Unfortu-
nately, though, it occurs to me there's no real way to avoid reversals as in Juba B. Jael. Nor displacements, as in Baal J. Aub or
Charlotte C. Bell.

It would appear—what do you think?—that our only recourse
is a proper pronoun. The letter rather than the spirit of the word
bespeaks me; not who, what, or where I am, but *that* I am the capital *I*. Try it: look at me, read me, and say *I*, to be continued however you please. While I continue,

yours truly.

PS: And Harding too. I hear her typing away, ever so faintly.
Transposing from her legal pad likely.

XXV

A more than curious tale, appearing at week's end like an after-image stubbornly persisting on the communal retina:

Child Encounters KKK Victim on Eve of Death

Once again the trail in the week-old murder of Jake Landry leads to last Saturday's teach-in at DeLuna Community College.

On the school grounds of the First Baptist Church on Laurel Walk where she was playing with friends, Adele Evans, daughter of Aubrey Evans, confessed Porno Prince, told of encountering the Klan-robed victim on stage some time before he was shot twice through the heart that same night.

The eight-year old said that she and her grandmother, Leona Evans, wife of alleged Porno King Tom Evans, joined other members of the audience on stage to view Klan exhibits. In the crowd, she was briefly separated from her grandmother, Adele said. During those few minutes, a man wearing a KKK robe whom she identified from photographs as Jake Landry, approached her.

"He showed me a big picture book," the blonde, blue-eyed girl said. "He told me I was real pretty and did I want to be in a picture show so I could be a child star."

When her grandmother found her, the child told her of the incident. "Grandmomma said I shouldn't talk to strangers," Adele said.

The same man later followed them out to their car, according to the pert eight-year old, and said, "You two ladies can help me get Tom and Aubrey out of the trouble they're in." Her grandmother "yelled at the nasty man and told him to keep away from our family," the girl said.

"He got real mad and showed us a picture of Daddy's hand," she said. "He told us him and Grandpa killed somebody." At that point her grandmother made her get inside their car, before locking the doors and telling the girl to stay there and wait. The child said she fell asleep and did not wake up until her grandmother started the car some time later.

The Evans woman confirmed the man's identity as Jake Landry whom she described as "an evil influence." "I wanted to get him away from the child," she said.

She said Landry tried to frighten her by accusing her husband and son of attempted murder and claiming that powerful people stood behind him.

When she pressed Landry for more information, he refused and she returned to her car and drove home.

Her husband, Tom Evans, and the girl's father, Aubrey Evans, were out walking the family's dogs when she and the child arrived at the Evans home on Park Lane about 9:30 p.m., the soft-spoken housewife said. Returning a few minutes later, the two men assured her that Landry was "a big liar" and that she should not have given him "the time of day." About 10 p.m., her son drove home with his little girl and she and her husband went to bed, Evans said.

Asked whether she believed her husband would be charged with murdering Landry, she said, "I know for a fact Tom didn't do it, but whatever he decides it'll be the right thing. That's just the way Tom is. He always puts his family first, me and Aubrey and the little girl, all of us."

"These two females may have been the last people to talk to Landry before his death," police officer Pat Gorrie speculated, but would not comment on the apparent conflict between their story and earlier testimony by Miss Mary Louise Bernard describing an incident she says took place the same night involving Landry and the Evans men. The Creole woman claims to have seen a hooded figure she identified as Landry leave the College auditorium with the Evans men about 9:30 p.m. last Saturday.

Lt. Zamora who heads the investigation into Landry's murder stated that he had no knowledge of any past attempt by police to collect evidence against the Evans men for murder or attempted murder. Neither of the two men, owners of a local contracting firm, has any previous criminal record. They are being held on charges stemming from an alleged attempt earlier this week to abduct the Dumot woman from her house in the Historic Quarter.

xxvi

Sunday's editorial, One "Murdering Hand" or More, or None? reminds everyone that the original of Landry's sketch, known to authorities only through the Creole Woman's reproduction, is still missing despite all-out police efforts.

Individuals claiming to have seen it: Dr. Elizabeth Dumot, on the afternoon of the murder; the Creole Woman, at KKK teach-in, evening of same day; Mrs. Leona Evans and grandchild Adele, ditto; Aubrey Evans, ditto (but has recently repudiated his entire original statement). Questioned about the credibility, from a psychiatric standpoint, of these reports, Dr. Randall Cane III gives as his opinion that the drawing "may be non-existent in the ordinary sense," citing accounts by the Evans men of how an overwrought Dr. Dumot turned on them, slashing the arm of the elder Evans (the wound required fifteen stitches and will leave a permanent scar). Dr. Cane:

> She reacted to them as murderers because of having watched the late Jake Landry, a self-appointed and, I believe, vivid chronicler of life and mores in the old Quarter, draw (or so she has claimed) something suggestive...unusual stress...traumatic experiences...the image of the hand may have been a hysterical projection...not impossible therefore that her description stimulated a phenomenon of group projection in which suggestible individuals, each of them having perhaps seen a Landry sketch of some kind, succumbed to the belief that what they had indeed looked at was the very drawing Mrs. Dumot described.

The first time, says Harding, I can recall being credited with instigating a *group* projection.

Then again, assuming that a Landry original *does* exist (in the ordinary sense), and if it can be demonstrated that anyone saw it or anything like it *before* the Dumot woman did, it must follow from her testimony that Landry himself (in the ordinary sense?) produced more than one "Murdering Hand." If, however, the Evans women—or anyone else—saw the drawing only *afterwards*, the likelihood is that, given the time factor, all who saw it saw the same hand, if indeed there was such a drawing. Right.

Summing it all up:

> These and other points of uncertainty in this baffling case must be frankly acknowledged before the application of cool, tough-minded logic can dispel mere speculation and spell out anything like a probable sequence of what took place that fateful day. This is the challenge for those charged with conducting the investigation, which we believe to be in very capable hands.

Protesting too much already?

xxvii

As it happens, police report a record number of arrests in and near Segovia Villas over the weekend, but the narrative stream in Sunday's paper is slowing to a trickle. Even in the ordinary sense, August was turning drier than usual; bright, sunny days ahead, no sign anywhere of a change in the weather.

psycheme

A person's language may tell you something, but, unless you know how to register it, nothing much about the one speaking. The trick here is how easily and how fast you can psychically turn, dip into her utterance, down whatever the draught tonguing every drop for all its flavor, sweet or bitter, and be on your way, not with thirst allayed, necessarily, but having sampled yet another specimen from the lonely limitless well of words. The place, the source, the origin of what's being said—where it comes from, where it's coming from now—makes all the difference in the human world (not that anybody knows much about it, or cares, you must admit). Others can be slightly motivated to tag along where it's obvious they don't know their way around as long as they're reasonably sure they can get out when they want. We learn that way, but such knowledge never reveals more than the conditions under which the person we're with makes her own signs—under which her psychical moves take place. Note well: whoever would make any sign do for her own ends must first produce it, must have, so to speak, her own movement.

Some years ago, I wrote what I regarded as a story. Once during hard times, it begins, a newborn infant was abandoned in the labyrinth of psychical movement. I describe how well-fed she was on the organic nutrients produced there, how healthy and strong of limb, and yet—here's the story's problem—yet she never budged at all, not even to crawl or cry out. The idea is that any efforts at movement on her part are unmotivated for the simple reason that she is always on the move anyway, effortlessly and without pause as on a feeder belt, conveyed through maze after maze by the ubiquitous flow of signs. And so, during her formative years in the labyrinth, the child acquires a knowledge of sign-elimination she does not know she has but takes for granted as a domestic animal does its daily food supply. At five years old she is found. By her looks, she gives every indication of being a healthy member of our species with an unusually stable emotional balance except for the curious fact that she never moves, never makes any sound, never lifts a finger to make any sign of any kind. Taken to be deaf-mute, she is diagnosed as irreversibly catatonic, a victim of post-traumatic labyrinthine stress.

Here, I myself enter the story. I am new in the American land of opportunity, an immigrant child having that first great triumph mastering the English language, while the foundling (about my own age now, placed in a home for the disabled on the very block I inhabit) is to be seen bundled in a wheelchair on the sidewalk, often unattended, silent and still. I befriend her and more or less keep up with her as we grow up (this part of the story, sketched in broad strokes, suggests my efforts to make contact by vocalizing freely around her on whatever happens to be in my head). As we approach puberty, the sense of an enormous potential vibrating in her body lends it an unmoving grace that impels me to work up a gestural communication for her use, to which she never responds with so much as a nod or a blink. I persist nonetheless. In my college years, I resolve to devise a language that will reach her and lead her out to the rest of us. I realize it is not simply a matter of finding the right communicative channel (i.e. tactile, auditory, visual, etc.) but of constructing a language so much a part of her life in the labyrinth that she cannot fail to recognize its sphere of reference and experience its usefulness.

Whenever I return to the neighborhood during vacations, I discourse to her about psychical movements every chance I get. I compare and contrast her experience in the labyrinth with everyday life. "As surely as the air you breathe," I explain to her, "the food you eat, the sights you see, the sounds you hear, the things you touch, imprint the inside of your body, as surely does what's in your body press out of it, and just that surely does that inside out action shape into psychical guts spilling into the world without your choice as to whether it will happen, but possibly with a bit of a say as to how and when." Never a twitch of response. "What you have," I tell her, "is a block—a signing block to be precise," and I forge right on under the conviction that the glow of intelligence settled so beautifully over her face unlined with meaning, and into her eyes undimmed by experience, comes from her perfect attunement to me. It is bound to be, I tell myself, purely a matter of time. Patience. Skill of exposition. Exactitude. "Signs," I say with the deliberation of one incising precious metal, "perform the marvelous function of depositing spaces that vanish in the very act of signing, leaving, at most, quark trails of material and memory traces." I broach the socio-linguistic dimension: "Our exchange of psychical guts makes for an intricate global commerce: the human economy—largely unconscious—of space deposits." And I stress the implicit psychological dimension: "What is always and forever escaping us is the whole process of the body's inside out movement by way of its signing." It's easy to get confused, so I pull apart the tropes of my own talk as I labor to turn it, ever more precisely, to her experience: "The intestinal tract normally stays inside," I explain, "in place, while its contents move out through it, whereas the psychical gut, with little or no defined content, is just that which always turns inside out and thus can only feed back to us outside in. What feeds back to us is what we feed *on*." Luminous with what I believe to be the knowing reception of my sign-surge, she sits in her wheelchair, absolutely stock-still. "We do all of this unwittingly," I emphasize, "situated as we are in the normal alienation of inner/outer from our psychical guts—we do it unwittingly, with the consequence that all the good and all the evil we partake of in this human economy of ours comes from eating our own body products." What does she think of my excursus into morality, I wonder, searching her eyes time and again for some signal of corroboration or dissent. I pass at least one entire vacation soliloquizing on this horror whereby we can-nibalize ourselves, the horror beyond which there is no good or evil—"both the haloed and the hornèd head are all too human" becomes my *leitmotif*. And, always, to no effect; only the radiance of her still life as I speculate peripatetically on the sunny sidewalk, pushing her wheelchair to and fro, that we humans both fear and adore the spatial excretions of psychical movement, our psychical guts, with good reason, and that we do so because it is from them that both gods and demons speak. I am forced to admit, hearing my own solitary voice return to me on the street, that our inside out movements thread no way out of the labyrinth.

The above is a highly condensed account of my attempts, during successive breaks and homecomings all through my college years, to create a language both describing and reflecting psychical movement, by which I might draw my friend out. In my last meeting with her, before going abroad to graduate school, I talk about the failure of psychosis as a solution to the labyrinth because, I say, psychosis misses the signals of directionality and merely forces you to box yourself into emergency latrines. For the first time (I never understood exactly why) I clutch her hand in mine while considering just why it is I'm always avoiding certain expressions that I feel sure would be meaningful to her if uttered. And then it strikes me: you don't come right out and say what's on your mind when it degrades the very place where a person has spent her entire life—her home. I couldn't simply say: "Look, we're always in the shit." Not to her. What I do say, finally, with an awkward sense of its inadequacy is: "Since the body's fundamental trope turns its own insides out, all the more reason to watch your language there."

Still holding her hand while deliberating further about this aspect of our signing problem, I am startled to hear her speak with the hoarseness of an untried voice, but without any hesitation whatever. It's as if the mechanism of her body, long wound up, has been set off by the pressure of my hand. After a sentence or two, she stops, obviously having said her piece and, just as obviously, signing off. "Wait," I implore, "come back." Her hand lies peacefully in mine. "Please," I plead, "we can talk, you and I." But I cannot pull her back, I cannot find her, I cannot see into those rainbow-colored eyes. I was never able to remember thereafter what she said, word for word—something about my species being always already domesticated by space and time, and the ignorance necessary for a body like mine to talk. Something like that, so my story ends.

I sent it off (it's still my idea of what a story is all about) to a number of magazines, both conventional and rather more forward-looking. All returned it with remarkably similar comments, the most succinct being: "This simply falls between too many cracks." But I never go back to my old neighborhood without running into her still, trundled along in a wheelchair, moved more and more, it seems, through ecstasies of silence I can never know.

xxviii

That final Sunday became, as it were, my métier, a time wherein every moment promised and fulfilled itself and my future spread out before me like the uncluttered harmony of the restored Boullet House.

At a few minutes past two a.m., Monday officially, I checked off the last item on my list, permitting myself no exultation, and fell immediately asleep, happy in the assurance that the house would provide me its sanctuary for a final night, however brief.

psycheme

A few days ago some of Harding's old friends called from New Orleans to discuss a project they wanted her to take on. Even though the city belongs to her and her past, she referred them to me—"this is much more up Jael's alley," she told them. They're organizing a new women's krewe for a debut in next year's Mardi Gras. Their stated goal is to capture the spirit of the occasion with a new twist—"to somehow make the mystery," as one of them put it, "crystal clear to the uninitiated." As you can imagine I was quite intrigued. Carnival, saturnalia, masquerade of every kind from sacred to soldierly is, if not exactly up my alley, certainly on my mind—and that for some time. A rare photograph from childhood shows me costumed, at about age ten, in the resplendent black and gold garb of a khalif from *Arabian Nights*, complete with gilded cardboard scimitar and a deeply quizzical look on my face.

It does not follow (as I think has been amply demonstrated in these pages) that you know what your signs mean, all those personal properties—words, images, gestures, clothes on your back, in drawer and closet. And that, in my first conference call made from Harding's study to the organizers of the krewe, is what I in essence said when they brought up again the business of trying to render the carnival mystery "crystal clear." I'd agreed to act as their consultant and thought it only fair to say a word or two about where I was coming from, i.e. that when I talk about signs and our feeling that they mean something, I'm not talking about affect or emotion, I'm coming from a more primordial place; I'm talking about how the body's creative feelers, like novice potters, give the first vague shape to meaning. It's that surge of psychical movement—but you already know about the feeling-of-meaning that makes it self-propelling and hard to stop. I didn't say that it moves itself rather like a cycling technology from waste to energy to waste. (Unlike most people, I've never found the idea that humans are machines offensive, or even unsettling—it merely entails seeing matter as having the capacity to live by means of language: from ace to face or quarks to Mr. Marks or, pre-positioning the barred space between psychoanalytic and information theory, from bit to tit.) Well, you can't say everything at once, so I got off on a tack about how sexual metaphors of penetration don't really apply to the sign-generating movement since there's neither any outside from which to penetrate nor any inside to penetrate.

This sparked their interest. One of them enthusiastically declared that what I was talking about was the female body doing its signs, as against the male body that stays inscribed in its inside/outside oppositions. And that remark clued me in to what this job was to make clear, what it's all about: the tradition of celebration. The ritual in which we're all celebrants.

OK, I've got it, I said, I'll try to sketch out what is involved if you really want to make this scene—the specifics will come as we go along. First off, the theme, to be elaborated so as to reveal directly the mystery under carnival masks, right?

Well, not exactly...more the idea of getting behind the mystery of the carnival spirit.

Just so, I said, but of course you have to approach these things pictorially.

By way of tableaux, they all agreed.

I paused and let myself regress intellectually to pubic parts and public parks. Immediately, I had my cue (yes, I thought, Harding's right, this is my forte).

Let the stage be dark, I began, except for one spot directed on an ordinary man in ordinary dress (your King of Carnival) who stands beside a white backdrop on which up-to-the-minute bits of world news, silent and pallid, are projected non-stop. Fly gaping, and oblivious to all else, he inspects his pubic area with alternating expressions of wonder, fear, joy, pain, astonishment, exultation, despair, abjection, anguish—occasional movements there appear to emit arcs of colored light that propel the eye forward across the stage space to *tableaux vivants* lighting up here and there until only stage center remains in darkness. The audience will understand that these tableaux, materializing one after the other, project what the ordinary man sees in his concentrated self-inspection: dozens of you, all costumed as penises, but penises masked again as animal or plant or insect, larva, half-this, half-that. Periodically, each turns her other side to the audience to show the penis in the mask of a gorgeously costumed woman. But, I advised, go beyond the frozen tableau; add dance accompanied by music and words, a total script—for instance, a choreographed set of transformations, with each mask rapidly taking the place of another, the woman-side showing at intervals like punctuation, and stage effects (false snow, etc.) suggesting the passage of seasons. While this is going on, let a female chorus in stark whiteface down to off-the-shoulder floorlength sequined sheaths of various dark hues chant in unison from the margins of the stage—we can compose and set it later, but something like this (I hammered it out over the phone in jaggedly improvised phrases):

> The law/the law of the penis/is occultation/occultation/ Thou shalt not/know the difference/the difference it makes/ The one supposed to know/can only jack it/up and down/up and down/Satisfaction comes/by way of ultimate/occultation/ The law/makes speech veil/ penis preening/preening under the power/of the divine mystery/and the dream/the dream of a common language/is only a dream/a dream/for penis prevails/prevails in ordinary speech/transforms ambiguities/into the clear mask/of obscurities/for the law/the law of the penis/is occultation/ occultation/But we are come/to

reveal the mystery/we students of the occult/we come to tell/how penis signs/itself in the act/the act of occultation/ Beware the knowledge/ the knowledge we bring/the knowledge of penis/engendered in a female body/We are come to tell/of penis gendered/by its place of origin/in the female body/We are come to reveal/ penis bearing always/always bearing/the seal of Woman...

The ordinary man's absorption in his penis has begun to take on a disturbed, distracted quality. His elbows lift convulsively as if to ward off attack. He glances anxiously around and back down. His body twists from side to side, his mouth moves, and his head shakes vehemently as if he is arguing with himself. He obviously suffers great anguish which he is trying to deny, and the chorus of dark-sheathed, sequined women chant on:

Receive thee/the secret of the Mysteries/Here and for all time/penis becomes Woman.

The ordinary man in ordinary dress stiffens and throws his head back in fear and horror, his eyes gazing blindly up, toward the darkness of center stage. On the floor of center stage a train of fine mesh material is glowing from the stalk of a giant fleshy facsimile of *Phallus impudicus* with a great satin sash at mid-height tied in a huge bow. As the light slowly moves up this towering dummy vaguely suggestive of a svelte, sybaritic female model, the masked dancers strip off all costume parts down to a flesh-like sheath replicating the giant fungus. The light finally reveals the head of the huge stinkhorn crowned with a wig of serpents, whereupon the ordinary man in ordinary dress creeps forward and falls to the floor in a swoon before this central figure, as the chorus announces, speaking plainly now, like a single voice amplified over a bullhorn:

Dionysos Phallos! The name of penis-become-Woman is Dionysos Phallos! Listen, and ye shall learn the formula of this wondrous transformation: Wheresoever you see *Woman*, read *penis*. Repeat: for *Woman/she*, read *penis/it*.

(Acting under the inspired guidance of the moment, I reached behind me and pulled a volume at random from Harding's bookshelf—Kierkegaard.) Behind the chorus, I continued, there is a row of old oak book cases suggesting a large library. Let one of them pull a book from the shelf and begin to read aloud in an ordinary, rather businesslike voice (I started to read, more or less at random from the open book in front of me, transforming as per formula):

> [Its] head is a perfect oval, and [it] bends it
> a little forward which makes [its] forehead seem
> higher, as [it] rises pure and proud, with no external
> evidence of intellectual faculties.

In synchrony with the reader's words, Dionysos Phallos inclines His head a little forward while the masked women begin a slow graceful dance wherein one body part moves first—an arm, a neck, a belly—and, the rest of the body, part by part, joins into the movement like a rippling effect spreading among all the dancers (I should have been a choreographer, I can just see this dance). It is the Dance of the Phalloi, performed around the base of the giant Phallus. The ordinary man in ordinary dress has revived but is obviously demented.

(I glanced back over Harding's shelves, cheating a little, like a scientist, to save time and pulled out a text I knew I could depend on.) A second reader, I said, pulls another book from the shelf and proceeds:

> ...whatever [penises] write about ['penis'], we may in the end reserve a good suspicion as to whether ['penis'] really wants or can want enlightenment about [itself]....

She passes Nietzsche smoothly to the next reader, who continues:

> Unless a [penis] is looking for a new adornment for [itself]—perhaps [it] is seeking domination.

And the next:

But [it] does not *want* truth; what is truth to a [penis]!

And so on, sentence by sentence, Nietzsche passing from reader to reader without pause or vocal modulation:

> From the very first nothing has been more alien, repug-
> nant, inimical to [penis] than truth—[its] great art is the lie,

[its] supreme concern is appearance and beauty. Let us confess it, we men: it is precisely *this* art and *this* instinct in [penis] which we love and honour; we who have a hard time and for our refreshment like to associate with creatures under whose hands, glances and tender follies our seriousness, our gravity and profundity appear to us almost as folly.... We men want [penis] to cease compromising [itself] through enlightenment.

The last reader delays briefly, turns to the others as she flips back the page and they all nod:

[Penis] wants to be independent; and to that end [it] is beginning to enlighten men about ["penis as such"]—this is one of the worst developments in the general *uglification* of Europe.

The dancers straighten and go into a mechanical warlike dance. This is the Dance of the Penes performed as the ordinary man in ordinary dress, who has been babbling to himself, suddenly joins the chorus of readers along the edges of the stage, assumes a visionary pose, and declaims like a prophet:

Beyond good and evil
Behold a world where penes move in full strength,
Now gloriously nude, now fashionably dressed,
Sporting the latest head-covering.
Behold their achievement of full independence
Like Gogol's Nose,
Subject to no law
Other than the push of their own desires,
Their innate will to power.
Behold how they enlighten all in their purview
About themselves,
Without intervention or cessation.
Pleasing themselves as they please,
Coming and going and coming in absolute freedom,
Untroubled by the needs of any other,
Denying themselves nothing,
O happy and healthy—
Full of feeling,

No neurotic idealization of castration,
No male member cut off from its male body
And held aloft in glorification of Woman
Denuded, no effeminate symbol,
No dismembered penis born again as Phallus,
No ritual here to celebrate the mystery
Of Woman, transvestite,
No myth to tell the name of....

Gagging, the prophet grasps his throat while the head of the giant Phallus which has begun a gyrating motion in the middle of this vision becomes violently agitated and fades from view back into darkness. Flinging off their penis costumes the dancers, now nude and indisputably female, attack the ordinary man in ordinary dress, clawing off bits and pieces of him to play with.

In the final tableau, center stage still dark, the nude dancers and the chorus of chanters-readers are seated formally at a banquet table. There are flasks of wine and a huge tray with an ordinary penis on it. The ordinary man in ordinary dress reappears, battered and walking gingerly, and proceeds to slice up the penis with great care, serving it in thin wafers to the women. The dancers taste it hesitantly at first but then bite into it with increasing zest and finally wolf it down with great abandon. The chanters-readers neither eat, speak, nor make any other movement as if frozen in a watch over the penis-feast of the other women. The penis-eaters, still chewing the meat, begin a series of grasping movements that seem to pull them away from the table into the unity of a final dance: the Dance of the Carnivores. They whirl about longingly in search of their cast-off penis costumes, don them lovingly, and move, uncertainly at first, back into the slow, sensuous movement of the Dance of the Phalloi while the giant Phallus at center stage gradually lights up once more. The women of the chorus rise one by one, each alone, and take their place again at the margins of the stage where the sparkle of their sequined dresses can be dimly seen as they chant:

The law/the law of the penis/is occultation/occultation... Fadeout.

That's a sample of what I'll work up for the tableaux at

your ball, I told them, their theme to be carried out, of course, in your parade. Since, I said, I understand you only have funds for one float your first year, let all the masked krewe revolve around it on foot—classical masking opportunities abound, and anything goes, but the goat, the bull, the snake are indispensable. Your float should be a boat-wagon bearing the giant *Phallus Impudicus* with your king and queen seated in front—I suggest you make your king the goat and your queen the bull or vice versa if you prefer, or half one, half the other. Instead of krewe members throwing trinkets, the head of the giant Phallus can be constructed to whirl about, scattering penis-shaped lumps of dried fruit into the crowd. The uninitiated, I assured the prospective Captain of the Krewe and her lieutenants, will not easily lose sight of the mystery being rendered so palpably.

They had all been listening most politely to me the whole time. Now one or two objected that my "approach" seemed unnecessarily psychotic. I tried to argue that the continual eruptions of history's holocausts can only be explained in terms of a psychotic reality. The horrors of human cultures, I said, socially enact biological processes for relieving the body of its signs. The sexed violence of war—that psychotic theatre of action—marks communal failures to satisfy this biological necessity of expression, and all sexual violence prefigures a final biological solution in ultimate mutilation. Dismemberment. This line didn't wash with them, even though I expressed it fervently, so I shifted gears and said it was not a question of *being* psychotic but of *entertaining* the Dionysian reality. After all, I pointed out, something psychotic always passes in any little movement through non-pathological openings (here I had to control a strong urge to expound on psychical movement) but, I assured them, your job is not to *become* psychotic but to *represent* the psychotic dimension. What's crazy, I added, is to confuse your carnival costumes with your real bodies.

"Oh," said one, "it's not that I mind playing like I'm psychotic—I just wonder why it has to be *that* psychotic."

"Because you sommoned the spirit of carnival," I said.

"As a women's krewe," a soft Southern voice explained, "what we have in mind is something having more to do with women, a fertility myth, maybe, like maybe Demeter going down for Persephone—I love your idea of dances alternating with the *tableaux vivants*, but we could concentrate on the mother-daughter theme with the dancers dressed like fresh-picked corn, green with different pastels of silk for the tassels. And no choral chants—"

"Or readings, for sure," another joined in, "just music would be all we need really."

"Yes," a third collaborated, "beautiful and light—then, to get across a sense of the mystery dominating all, we could have a very large corn dummy on center stage clothed to represent the goddess of the harvest."

"Remember the corn cob in *Sanctuary*?" I began, but no one did, and, anyway, they were too enthralled with visions of mother-daughter vegetation rites to take a good look at their corn cob goddess center stage. They thanked me effusively for my suggestions and said they had enough to work with for the moment. Today, Harding got a call from the krewe's captain expressing their appreciation for having been introduced to "the woman with such clear ideas" and reporting that they had voted to go ahead under their own steam with the mother-daughter theme. They'd decided to name themselves "The Mystic Krewe of Agave" and promised to send both of us invitations to the ball. This call sent me the double message that I need not expect a juicy consulting fee in the mail and that they have stolen my ideas, put them in mask, and will stage a watered-down version. A more authentic restoration of the carnival spirit than my own, I'll admit—Harding's only comment between bursts of laughter, mostly at my expense: "It just goes to show you can't take people at their word when they say they want to see clearly."

xxix

At six-fifteen, on my day of departure, Valencia Street twittered in the unobtrusive quiet of early morning—the same innocence of birdsong and soft breezes returning again and again despite and after all else.

Upon awakening that last morning in Tarragona, Harding, we may imagine, makes a final tour of inspection through the house with hammer, screwdriver, pliers, machine oil in hand. Does she twiddle her tools (those tokens of work accomplished) as she goes, stopping to test, or tighten, or tap at this or that with the unconscious dexterity of a master craftsman? It would be only natural if an element of bravura were to enter her actions now that nothing remains to be done, now that this solitary, high-spirited wielding of her instruments may function purely as a ritual of proprietary endorsement, a leave-taking. Fun, she says, but the very kind of narcissistic play that risks a senseless nick or scratch.

Controlling impulses to premature jubilation, she slams down the lid of the Chevy's filled trunk with a clean snap of her arm. No fevered last minute packing; no rushing around or cutting corners to make it to the closing on time. All is ready. Inside the house remain only her typewriter (never once used that summer), her briefcase (never once opened), the dress she will change into in about two hours for the act of sale at the offices of Stavros, Stavros & Ribaut, and for the journey afterwards. Her workclothes, uniform and insignia of her stint as a restorationist, will end up in the green plastic trashbag slumped open on the floor of Captain Boullet's library. (The trashbag will, in the orderly course of things, land somewhere in the city dump more or less on top of the discarded mattress and fourteen bags stuffed with pampers, beer cans and other Wentworth castoffs.) May she be allowed to take the brick steps up to the porch of the Boullet House lightly, two at a time? They are wide and shallow, the only ones of their kind the length of Valencia Street or anywhere hereabout, easy steps that will age well because she has built them to last—over Greeley Connor's say—out of rosy hand-formed Spanish bricks (declared by Doc Shibbles to be Mother's and put into service by Jake Landry as the foundation for his spy perch on the back of the Boullet House).

Unaccountably, now, after a summer forever cramped with too much to do in far too short a time, this quiet stretch of morning is hers, and the house, finished in every smallest detail, is nearly rid of her habitation in it.

Monday's *Sentinel* lies neatly rolled on the threshhold where the paperboy pitched it not long before she must have stepped over it, without looking down, on her way out with the handtools. She slides off the green rubber band, drops it with only a second's hesitation in the trashbag, and flattens the top section, not over the kitchen counter whose marble top lies perfectly clean in the soft Southern light, but over her crossed legs on the floor of the library upstairs, next to her few belongings.

"I'm the only one that knows what really happened, because it's true I'm the man that killed Jake Landry," she reads, looking for what she hopes is the last time into the wide fleshy face, the tiny smiling eyes behind their steel-rimmed spectacles.

EVANS CONFESSES.   A startling twist of events, but inevitable once it has been broached. Once the stream of words begins, once the voice gets going, the story tells itself. A question not so much of who killed Landry as of how it came to pass that it had to be done—and there remains only the issue of whether the right voice speaks even as the self-authenticating persona of Evans has its confessional say. Charged, finally, with the murder of Jake Landry, first degree, he has made a deal with Roland B. Markit: a scoop that will "set the public straight," in return for editorial assurance that his bombshell of a story will be printed in its entirety, "like you did them other two" (referring, apparently, to what he has taken as unexpurgated utterances by the Creole woman and, more recently, Tony Krasner).

I'm sick and tired of every John, Dick and Jane in this town taking advantage of me and my family. It's time to tell the whole story, from start to finish, and I want it all printed in the paper just exactly like I'm gonna tell it. It's either that or nothing. Don't want anybody putting words in my mouth or leaving any out, no two-bit lawyer and no reporter either.

The man, says Markit, has an equal right to be heard and he as a journalist has the obligation to keep the public fully informed, refraining from comments of any kind, with the result that Evans' verbatim account makes its appeal in an earnest, manly, Hemingway style of tightlipped refusal to whine or offer excuses. He, Tom Evans, has let the close leash of community taboos slip from his hand, and this, not murder, has been his real crime. Himself possessed of inalienable rights to pornographic knowledge, he has failed in the obligation which such rights impose on their possessors: he has exposed those in his charge to contamination, has allowed filth to become publicly

associated with the family name. There's more than a suggestion here that his fall has come about through the unprincipled
machinations of others. And now, understanding that through
Landry's death the law has created a demand for a scapegoat,
he would compel admission from the community of his true
mission as a minister of its justice: "It ain't no accident the way it all
got started," he says, "Landry was a snake if there ever was one."

So it goes.

One night Krasner asked my boy Aubrey over to his boat, for some
fun with girls, he said. They spent a few hours looking at stag pictures, and he told Aubrey he owned the stuff and there was more
where that came from. Then he gave the boy a few samples, to show
his buddies, he said. Jake put Krasner up to it, and that's why I say it
was no accident the way this thing got going.

Now Aubrey ain't a bad boy, but he's got his weak side, which is
why I always look out for him the best I can. I noticed the boy was getting mighty popular around town, going out nearly every night and
dropping off his little girl at the house with my wife Leona. I got to
thinking that he wasn't spending enough time with the child like a
good father should, and I told him so.

That same night, he asked me over to his place so I could see for
myself he wasn't doing nothing but having a little fun that paid off.
That's how he put it to me, and like he said, there didn't seem to be no
harm in it. Folks would call up and ask if they could drop in on such
and such a night, and he would line up a party for them. Wasn't any
time before he had him a bunch of regulars. Why some of them fellows would drive down from Georgia and over from Alabama and all
the way across the state, but it wasn't like he had a business going or
nothing like that.

I said why didn't we split up the regulars by age with me hosting
the parties for the older men at his place on the nights he wasn't giving a party himself. You got to realize that all ages wanted to come.
We didn't allow no minors, of course. One fellow from a little place in
Alabama, about my age, he never missed a single one of my parties,
drove that car away full of samples every time. He started his own
parties back home, and that's how this thing spread and grew.

You got to understand that nothing went on at these here parties
that don't ordinarily happen at old-time stag get-togethers, bunch of
fellows horsing around, drinking a little maybe and having their fun

without bothering nobody. Just men being men, you get the idea. The magazines and pictures and movies and the other items just gave us something to use for recreational purposes.

It got so we had to set up special events for the tourists out on the Island. They come down from the Dakotas, Minnesota, Ohio, New York, Maine, you name it, even a few foreigners like them West Germans and Dutch. The tourist demand got so heavy we finally turned the Island crowd over to a Canadian that's retired out there, nice fellow, family man. He'd drive across the bridge in his camper every week for a regular pickup.

Now I have these two big guard dogs, Donner and Blitzen I call them, pure-bred, and about this time the young one, Blitzen, was getting full-grown. Nothing I wouldn't do for those animals. I got the idea of building them their own doghouse in my backyard and fixing it up for extra storage, you know, so the supplies wouldn't fall into the hands of the wrong people.

Everything was going along real good, wasn't bothering the community in any way, like I said, when that rat Krasner up and come to see me with a colored dude called himself Flanagan. Flanagan Jones Prideaux, from that housing project [Segovia Villas] over by the old Quarter. This dude started bragging how he headed up all the business at the Villas, and he was out to see his people got their fair share.

That was when it started to come out, the position Krasner was trying to force on us. I told Aubrey right then, "Son," I said, "this man is trying to make pushers out of you and me, boy," I said. "You see that, don't you?"

This Prideaux character had some nerve, though, telling me I better "cooperate," or else. "Or else *what*?" I said, and he said he didn't like to make no predictions but there was my fine pair of attack dogs for one, and he could not say what else me and Aubrey might stand to lose, but he would be glad to give it some further thought. "I be *glad* to give it some further thought," that's how he talked to me.

I told him certain friends of mine would be mighty upset if I lost anything at all. If he wanted something, I said, he would have to get it from Krasner. Those two deserve each other.

Afterwards, I had it out with that skunk [Krasner]. I told him he was betraying his own kind and he had to realize how some things wasn't right for them studs in the Villas. He got sassy with me and said he didn't see no point "discriminating on the basis of color." Any white girl, he said, that gets her kicks from showing her stuff in dirty pictures was just right for them black studs and wasn't worth protecting anyway. Then he let it out: "Landry's right about one thing," he said, "color don't count in the smut trade."

"Landry?" I said, and that's when it hit me who I had to deal with. I let Krasner know loud and clear I was not in the business and didn't intend to be forced into it by him or anybody else, period. And I took the opportunity to let him know I didn't think my friends would appreciate his racial attitudes either. Krasner said he didn't like to get rough with me, but he figured I knew there were higher-ups looking after his deals. Considering who they might be, he said, my friends would lose interest in him real fast once he slipped them a name or two. "They'll [evacuate] in their sheets," he said. Got a mouth like a sewer, that man does.

So I asked him, "Seeing you got so much protection, why can't you deal with the colored trade direct?" He said that wasn't his style. Things would get out of hand if there was more than one distributor in the area. "It's cleaner this way," he said, "keeping the dope and the porn peddlers separate. A doghouse for smut makes about as good a cover as the old idiot's basket for dope. Take a day or two to think it over, Tom, and watch the papers."

I didn't know what he meant until about a week later when the story broke about the lady professor dragging indecent books into her classroom at the College. Krasner asked me if I'd read the morning paper. I said I didn't see the connection. This was a woman, and a professor, and she was abusing her position by exposing young girls that would be wives and mothers some day. I said they ought to kick her clean out of the state. There was no similarity to our case at all that I could see.

The rat [Krasner] jumped on me and said he didn't call up to argue "the finer points," that's in quotes. He just wanted to remind me that the finger could be pointed at me and Aubrey just as good as the woman professor, and the public was in no mood right then to listen to my side of it. One thing I hate about that weasel is it's always "*my* side of things," or "*your* side." Man's got no sense of right and wrong. That's something I always tried to teach my boy.

What Krasner didn't know was the kind of a hand I was holding. You see, old Wentworth had just passed away a couple of weeks before, and I had good reason to believe it was an overdose. There's no telling who might have been monkeying with him, what with all them old papers he had stashed in that Boullet House. He bragged to me about how he had a claim to it and a lot of other property around here. Talked plenty before he died, but a poker player don't let on about his aces. I just let Krasner know I'd been down to see the police to pass along a few facts about the shape the old man was in the day he died. I said his partner Landry might appreciate hearing about it, and I had a lot more of the same up my sleeve—that's all I said to him.

Well, he hung up, and I swear I didn't have time to feed Donner and Blitzen before he called me back, all buddy-buddy. He said I was absolutely right not to fool with that colored dude [Prideaux]. He could make his pick-up from my doghouse once a week and leave his money out there. That way me and my boy would have nothing to do with the dude, wouldn't even have to lay eyes on him. No problem, Krasner said.

And that's the God's honest truth. That's how me and Aubrey was forced into distributing for a while. But let the record show I never did take it sitting down. I've got connections, and I kept turning the screws on those rats [Landry and Krasner] so me and my boy could get out of something we never wanted any part of in the first place. We've always been honest, and God-fearing too, me and my boy. I had them two skunks so nervous the whole summer they might have let me and Aubrey out if the police hadn't hushed up old Wentworth's death just like they always do.

The question I'd like to see somebody answer is, just what did happen to all them legal papers Wentworth had? Somebody must have snatched them away mighty quick after he died, and whoever it was used that [Dumot] woman against me. The way I figure it, it had to be Landry, and he must have showed her enough to let her know she ain't got clear title to that old place she's been doing up so fine, all authentic and historical. I happen to know for a fact she spent a lot of time looking into old documents, told me so herself last Monday. Seems like a mighty suspicious stroke of luck for her the old man died when he did. Don't it seem that way to you?

But Landry made his biggest mistake when he tried to trick Aubrey into that monkey business with the shingles on the Boullet House. When I found out about that, I knew right away he was trying to kill two birds with one stone, get rid of Krasner and blackmail us into doing his dirty work all at the same time. That's how Landry operates. The police swept that under the carpet, too, so it was up to me personally to see to it that justice was done in this here community. I wasn't going to allow the weakness of the law to interfere with what's right.

And that's what was going through my mind when me and Aubrey waited in Landry's car for him to come out of the KKK meeting that Saturday night. Let's just get one thing straight, though. Every word of that old colored woman's [Mary Louise Bernard's] story is an outright lie, from start to finish, like my boy said, and that's one of the main reasons why I want to get this off my chest and down in black and white, so the public can know what really happened that night and not be stuck with some cockamamie story. Let me tell you, that's all it amounts to, that woman's so-called "eyewitness testimony."

What really happened was we waited for Jake out in his car—that's what happened, no matter what they told her to say, or anybody else. When he got to us, that snake was still wearing my grandpa's KKK robe. That was the last straw. It made me so mad I held a .38 special on him and told him to drive out to the old fishing bridge [to DeLuna Island]. Jake didn't know what I might do in the state I was in. He was sweating it out.

He admitted right away he was just using Aubrey to get at Krasner, but he wouldn't try to trick us or nothing like that. "I just wanted to get a little message across to you gentlemen," he said. "What message?" I said. He said the point he was trying to make was our problem would be taken care of if we got rid of Krasner. The higher-ups would see to it we was protected, and, afterwards, the three of us could split the profits from the porn business right down the middle, fifty-fifty. I got the idea somebody up there thought Krasner was getting too big for his britches.

I said nothing doing. He said that was all right by him and no hard feelings, because he could always find another dealer for such a "profitable enterprise." That's a direct quote of the way Jake talked. What that snake never could get through his head is that money ain't everything.

I was thinking about letting him go, but Aubrey kept saying, "Jake's right, Daddy, he's making a lot of sense," and other foolishness like that. I told him to shut his mouth, but he said he was sick and tired of me butting into his business and he would make his own deals from now on.

I tell you that wasn't my boy talking. It was those skunks getting to him. When I told him to think about his little girl, he said that was just the thing, "I *am* thinking about her, Daddy, and she'll be riding in a Mercedes same as the others when you're still mopping up other people's you-know-what." Now I don't mind telling you, my boy ain't never talked to me like that, not before all this happened. He hurt me real bad when he used that language.

I could see it was high time to put a stop to this thing. We had to get rid of Jake, and it was up to me to do it. I didn't have no thought at that time of killing him. I just meant to see to it he got out of Tarragona for good.

I asked him if he knew protection was off of him. He thought I was lying at first, but he got scared when I mentioned who stood behind me. And then he made the same mistake as that other one: he tried to scare me. I don't scare easy, not like that boy of mine.

Jake must have been pretty scared himself to make a mistake like that. He pulled out that notebook he always carried around and showed me that picture with the label on it ["Murdering Hand"]. It was supposed to be kind of like a hint that a certain party at the Boullet House knew about Krasner's slip on her roof. "You ain't the only one that's seen this picture," he said, in that whiny voice he always had. Some smart individual, he said, was bound to figure out sooner or later which hand might be up to killing folks in the old Quarter. That investigation I set off into Wentworth's death might just boomerang on me, he said, because I was the last one to see him alive with those old papers. That's how the police look at things, he said.

"Tell you what," he said, "you put away that gun, Tom, and we'll drive on back to town, this very minute. I'll see to it these idle suspicions against you are laid to rest, once and for all. No point opening up a big can of worms, Tom, unless you got no other choice," he said, "that's my philosophy."

Now the whole town knows Tom Evans ain't no killer. I was mad, sure, but I'm not the kind that guns down a man in anger. That would be just plain dumb, and a sin before Almighty God, too. Even then I might have let Jake go, but he thought he had me over a barrel, you see, and tried to strike a dirty deal with me and my boy. That's the kind he was—squeeze you for every drop of blood he could get out of you. Well, he thought wrong. Dead wrong.

We could dump Krasner, he said, because dope runners are a dime a dozen, and he'd split *all* his profits with us, down the line. He'd cut his down to a third, me and Aubrey would get the rest. He was "studying the market," he said, and he had a plan to push profits way up so we could all be millionaires and retire in another year or two. Prostitution, he said, fell off real bad since women started to get their liberation and stopped charging for their services, but he had some ideas for pumping new life into it. Plus, he said, "I've got a whole new type of business in mind, where you increase your profits through what they call 'diversification.'"

The dope and the pornography and the sex was all right, he said, but they wasn't "properly coordinated." That's him talking. "Me and Krasner don't see eye to eye when it comes to the organizing of a business," he said. "It's my belief that every part of a business ought to be used to promote every other part. Why we could produce our own video cassettes because I done a survey and I know for a fact them black studs would shell out big money to see theirselves performing on white girls." Just to show how diversification works, Jake had them blacks paying for their stag items by pushing dope, and consequently the dope business was going so good the supply that Krasner brought in wasn't nowhere near satisfying the demand.

Jake was some talker. "Seeing how those little movies stimulate the black trade," he said, "I did what they call a market analysis on the white trade and my figures show what sells best to white men is movies of their group activities. They like a certain mix of the female species," he said. One of their all-time favorites, he said, was two or three colored good-lookers mixed in with an older white woman or a fat one or both, and one young, real fresh-looking white girl. Jake was a talker, all right, and he was talking hisself right into one of my .38 slugs.

He got hisself real worked up. Told about running "a little experiment" where he hand-picked about a dozen of his white clients and fixed up a situation to their liking in the old ballroom of the Hernando. He taped their relations they were having, all without them knowing it, and afterwards, he invited them to an all-male screening. There I had to give it to him: I could see right away this idea of recording your own activities was more interesting than anything else Jake had to offer.

"Ain't a family in Tarragona," he said, "that won't have somebody involved sooner or later, and if everybody takes up associating with it, won't nobody have to worry about having their name connected with it because everybody'll be more or less in the same boat and nobody set too high up above nobody else." He said we might even get a little real democracy going right down here in our own community, like this country is supposed to have, with good opportunities for everybody irregardless of race, religion, age or sex, like it says in the Constitution. But even if there was some higher-ups left, he said, them aristocrats wouldn't have no objections because their profits would be getting bigger all the time, so we could be sure of keeping protection on the three of us on and on.

You had to hand it to Jake as far as being a business man. Like he said, he had thought up a real creative solution. In the first place, you could double-charge a client, one fee for a girl and another for getting his performance on video. Then you could turn around and charge another fee for a private show, and a big whopper of a fee for a personal copy. Not bad. He said every man-soul of them in that little movie he made to try out on the white trade bought a copy for his own personal collection. He named some names, and I could see Jake had what they call "access." I wouldn't want to mention none publicly, of course. They can depend on me not to drag fine old names down through the mud like some.

What got to me, though, was what he said next. He thought he had me hooked on coming in on his business, Aubrey and me both, and he got real talky about what we could do to develop it. "The biggest challenge," he said, "is finding young, fresh-looking white girls for the trade, but I got me another creative solution for stocking up on them." I'm giving you the words right out of his mouth so you can judge for yourself what Jake Landry was.

He had this idea to give free dope and women to the males of any white family that had a girl we could use. First thing, he'd get her in a kind of a soft, cute movie, not much to it, just take her clothes off is all, maybe just down to her panties or something like that. Pretty soon all the men in the family would be hooked on drugs so their protection would be off the girl we needed.

"Once you get them this far," Jake said, "you got something on them, and if they don't have no menfolk protecting them, it's easy to move the girls on to doing some real service for men." Then, he said, when they lost their freshness and started to get a wore-out look, they could still turn a good profit in the video business for the colored trade. That way you wouldn't see no more old women scraping along on Social Security, he said. They'd all have their choice of retiring in style before they hit forty. "Would any woman or child be on welfare if they had a choice like that?" he said. I didn't say nothing, I just let him talk.

There'd be a place in it for everybody. That was his point, and that's when he really stepped over the line. It was the last straw as far as I was concerned. He said he forgot to mention one of the biggest turn-ons, and that was cute little kids. Now just to show the kind Jake was, he had this idea for a video where a man would be laying down after a shower and this pretty little girl comes in and says she wants to be like Daddy and takes off her clothes and snuggles between his legs. Then there'd be this other scene where a little boy comes in and does the exact same thing. Then maybe both of them. Then a woman might come into it. Smut like that.

I heard him out, all of it. Then I told him to get in the back seat. Like I said, I never actually meant to use the little Cobra. We keep it at home, for protection you know, and I figured I might need it to scare some sense into Jake. I didn't see the light till that indecent filth come spilling out of that snake's mouth. That's when I saw I didn't have no choice. I had to use that gun right then and there. Is there any man alive that wouldn't?

I shot him clean through the heart. Ain't no point dragging out a thing like that. He didn't suffer none at all.

Afterwards, I told Aubrey to tie the gun to Jake's picture book and throw the whole thing in the Bay. Let it rot till Kingdom Come. Then we drove to the Boullet House like the boy said, and jammed him down on those spikes, backwards. It was like we were hanging justice up there, upside down, on that same fence where he tried to trick me and my boy into becoming murderers.

Aubrey wrote the note but I told him what to say. "Dead men tell no tales," is an old saying we have in the Klan. It means when you start a job, you should have the guts to see it through right to the end. Aubrey pinned it on his chest. I had the note figured out on the bridge already, when I ripped a piece of that paper out of Jake's book for Aubrey. I did it so Krasner and anybody else that stood behind them two-bit dope pushers would get the message loud and clear and lay off us for good.

The cigar was the boy's idea, didn't mean nothing. Jake loved his cigars, you know. Aubrey said Jake always did run off at the mouth too much to suit him, needed a pacifier to shut him up at the Last Judgment. So you see that part was just my boy horsing around.

Then me and Aubrey parked Jake's car back at the College. We got in our pick-up and drove right on home. It was just about ten o'clock, maybe ten-thirty.

And that's the way it happened. I'm telling it to the public and I'm telling it straight. My boy Aubrey ain't done nothing wrong at all, and nobody else in my family has either. I repeat: nobody. I'm the only one that's personally responsible for Landry's death. I don't believe any man that truly understands what this community stands for would do any different. I believe every Christian man and woman amongst us that hears how Jake Landry was conspiring and scheming to make white slaves out of our children, our most precious possessions on this earth, will hang out both their flags for me, the Confederate and the American. I done what I had to do, and that's no more than any of us ought to do if he's a man and a father. The law says I committed a homicide. So be it. But the people have the last say about whether I killed a man or a snake.

Homicide, overnight, has faded into the tale of Tom Evans, Agent of Justice, who, elsewhere in Monday's *Sentinel*, consents at last to let "sympathizers" post bail for him, set at the modest sum of $10,000, and accepts numerous invitations to make public appearances, including one on a local TV talk show. A familiar voice:

I guess I just horse around and lose my head sometimes, but gosh, I've learned a lot! When I get out of this mess, I'm going to be more like Daddy and become a real productive member of this here community that's been so good to us.

And another:

...frankly, facts revealed about the murder victim make it impossible to view his death as anything but a blessing, perhaps even—in the widest sense of the phrase—an Act of God.

His professional opinion:

The elder Evans, a respected craftsman, has, in his encounter with pornographic materials, evidently so cathected them as to revive the original Oedipal triangle where the murder victim became for him the Oedipal father....Evans killed in the role of the son who both depends on and desires his mother...so understood, the murder is an acting out of his paternalistic protection of the Oedipal mother undergoing betrayal by the Oedipal father....Evans sought to restore the primal scene to its original inviolability by taking the Oedipal father's place...in confessing to murder, he established and authenticated his own identity.

psycheme

You there behind the lattice: if I now reveal the weakness of my belief, will you turn your adamantine eyes away once and for all? I confess that belief in anything whatsoever has never been one of my strong points, but I do more or less believe in this business of psychical movement taken as the signing work of the human body, this marking off of psychical turns in a more problematic body activity than that of dogs but generally with about the same level of consciousness of what we're doing when we're doing it. I have said as much, or in so many words, and I have thought it again and again, even when you were not with me. Will I receive ablution?

I acknowledge hearing a biological voice in all this spatializing and temporalizing to place and orient ourselves, these perpetual trips of human existence from nowhere to nowhere for nothing on which you and I and other such non-entities (not modesty, this, nor bitterness, but plain semantic accuracy) depend;

I avow that the much vaunted Journey or Quest or Pilgrimage, or exploration or tour or wandering, rambling, roaming and roving, escaping, pursuing, flying, creeping, going for it, hanging out—call it what you will—is none other than the endlessly repeated cosmogonic act by which each of us lives her double existence as collaborative creator and collaboratively created;

I grant the power of signs to lay out my place, subject me to them, and I admit that it is my slave position which readies them for use: as tools are said to be ready at hand, signs are ready at body;

I own that space and time are dimensional formations of our sign-generation (not of our sensibility) and that our bodies are construction sites, and I submit that your psyche and world, like mine, are but temporary structures made of signs subject to wear and tear (and demolition), yet strangely, arduously, resistant to restoration;

And I pray that the feeling-of-meaning rooted always in fields of power relations be cultivated without delusions of value in it, and that its intimate power might turn our species—this specific human body—to the restoration and care of our home planet. I have swapped the letch of salvation for war on pain, suffering, distress, and all the rest. But softly, softly—*Vorsicht*! Wherever severed parts come together, collect...you know the rest. A gang is born. The Nature we join up to serve is a killer from way back, bent on holocaust. *Vorsicht*.

Who among you will favor me with indulgence for these articles of my faithlessness?

A plaint: before my creator, the body that signs me into being, manufactures the software laying out my features, I mourn, struck dumb, an infant being born. Long silences, too, from the regions where Harding has been at work on her piece tell me she's winding down along with me, nearing the end now.

xxx

Upstairs in Captain Boullet's restored library, Harding snips out Dr. Cane's analysis—she and I have long had an interest in the status of such discourse—along with Evans' confession. She unzips her old leather briefcase, removes a clean manila envelope from one of its pockets, folds into it the week's accumulated news items (labelling it, in a spurt of tail-end dementia, "Vestigial Growth"), slips the envelope back into her briefcase, and, as the sun plays like a grave child all around her over the wide-planked floor, thumbs idly through the second pocket, which turns out to hold, among other writings, her one-page résumé.

On the point of stuffing the dismembered *Sentinel* into the trash, she glances at the page that lies uppermost. A lone letter to the editor catches her eye—from Naples, Florida, signed "Jon, Last of the Alligator Indians."

Dear Editor:

I address myself to Mr. Markit. The Indian Woman in the drawing was my great-grandmother. Her power did not come from any socio-political system, it came from a necklace she wore. The White Man's gift was removed from her neck at death and given to my grandfather. After that, the Alligator Indians were no longer protected from the White Man's plans and died one by one. I alone remain because I carry the protection of white blood. I alone have the power to continue the breed of Alligator Indians. This lore I received from them as a child before my grandfather took me away for my schooling. I hope this delivers my ancestors from academic speculators and any others who would cast aspersions on our way of life.

No reply from Markit, but editor's note quotes consultant, Dr. Albright: "There is, to my knowledge, no historical basis for the existence of any American aboriginals called Alligator Indians. I suspect the letter to be a hoax, possibly by a college student capitalizing on the unjustified ramifications of this over-sensationalized case."

She salvages both these items and takes up the problem of her résumé. Outside the dormer windows the street lies morning-still; the leaves of the old live oak shudder ever so slightly along its branches.

xxxi

Even there with the end approaching, she is not without gentle tugs of dread, little ripples of it breathed in with the salt-fresh tang of the Bay lapping, she says, so softly, teasingly, at the toes of my sandals. She turns up from the water's edge, cuts back under the moss-fringed shade of Hernando Plaza, taking her time. Dawdling. The hand has just passed 8:30. On the other side of the narrow street bordering the western end, a neat oblong shingle, "Stavros, Stavros & Ribaut, Attorneys-at-Law," signals decorously in the hues and calligraphy of rehabilitation. Her step quickens as she crosses over with the purposeful bearing of one arrived at her destination: fully prepared, as it were, on time.

Down the path of cypress blocks she walks to the Victorian entrance, draws the weathered pine and glass-etched door in behind her and moves slowly, and more slowly still, over yellow tints of fig leaves, pea-greens and off-whites of onion and apple skins, burnished brown of nutshells, indigo blues, over the medallions and stylized parrots and flowers of a long Caucasian runner, pauses briefly at a small mural of Dike instructing her father Zeus framed in an oval of letters that spell out THE WAY TO JUSTICE, and, following the playful arrow drawn as a mere flourish off the final E, takes the first step—not too eagerly, not too haughtily—up the formal, slightly turned staircase.

EPILOGUE

❧

Harding's Piece

Something More*

From the beginning the belvedere harbored a mystery for me supported by years of meaning accumulating as Grandmother, the two of us circling to and fro over paths spoking even to the lake a quarter of a mile down a low hill, instructed me about "what happened" to this and that friend or relative. Except for the addition of the belvedere when she inherited the house, she would remind me, the garden had scarcely changed since her childhood. Every summer since I could remember I had spent a week or more visiting her, and each visit had increased my anticipation of our daily afternoon walks followed by tea in the belvedere set more or less squarely in the middle of the garden. From here, three descending, sprawling levels of lawn and croquet course, herbs, flowers, and vegetables bordered on one side by a patch of muscadine vines and on the other by a fruit orchard, came into immediate view. I was getting the real lowdown on people, I would feel as I sipped my tea, gazed out over the garden, and bit into fresh lemon cookies and tiny, light, hot buttered biscuits with fig preserves.

Back in the early fifties, a few weeks before leaving for my freshman year in college and she an alert if fragile eighty-six year old, Grandmother gave me her last lesson. Before Christmas that year her heart gave out on her.

My mood that day, familiar enough now but new then, placed everything around me in that peculiar relation that combines distance with nearness—what I have come to think of as the place of seduction, where any and every thing may suddenly exhibit a captivating appeal even as all is lost, left behind forever to be whatever it is while the touch of its love abides and moves us forward in time like fingers of the future. What had brought me to this sweet, if somewhat hazardous, condition was my approaching departure from home. In my family, going away to college was a matter of taking the right direction, which was a one-way street from home into the world.

---

*Dedicated, at Harding's request, to Marj Haydon of Itta Bena, Mississippi.

Entering my grandmother's kitchen that day, where she had as usual laid out a tea service on a worn old butler's tray, would have wrung drippings of pleasure-pain from me under any circumstances, but the presence on the tray of a magnificent silver teapot—early eighteenth-century—made me gasp. Various striking objects had made their appearance over the years in this fashion, all referred to by my grandmother as "the family silver," as if, in the aggregate, they were as demonstrably a part of our genetic heritage as the family nose. Both, I'd been given to understand, had made their way somehow down the intricate pathways of lineage through the Manley line.

The Georgian teapot, however, carried the family silver to new heights. Grandmother picked it up and held it raised on the palm of her hand. "From Mama's brother," she said, turning it for me to admire, "Uncle Patrick Smith Manley. Most of the silver belonged to him, what was left of it after the old factory closed down and the debts were settled. It all arrived the same week the twins were born, crates and crates packed full of it with the old Manley factory mark still on them, along with a big packet of drawings, like an inventory, showing details of design and crafting for every piece, and many more we never saw."

The "twins" were my great-uncles, Jimbo and Lee Walker Woolley, now retired from their successful business, both with legendary reputations, Uncle Jimbo for his knowledge of numismatics and period silver and Uncle Lee Walker for his artistry as a smith. I'd heard of the Manley ancestor back in England from whom Uncle Lee Walker was said to have picked up his genius for smithery, but that his factory had been the source of the family silver was news to me.

"Imagine, Lizzie," she set the pot back over its spirit lamp, "imagine the arrival of all that interesting and valuable stuff, the prodigious quantity of it, and such artistry even a two-year old couldn't miss it—that's how old I was, born a year almost to the day from Lee's surrender, when the silver and the twins came.

"Oh, the momentous change it wrought in my life! Almost overnight, we lived in a densely populated world of mysterious objects issuing, it seemed, out of Uncle Pat Smith's death. Some, like the teapot there, were part of his personal collection, but there were also the exquisite models of his own designs, the endlessly fascinating forays into creativity of his apprentices, odd pieces and whole sets commissioned and unclaimed by his customers, and several cartons of silver babies, which is what we called the pieces far enough along to show what they were supposed to be, but not far enough to function as intended. How vividly I still remember all of it, and the boys playing with the silver babies, their first toys."

"Do you still have them, the babies?" I asked.

"No." She was sifting the flour into her dough bowl, concentrating, I thought, a bit harder than necessary, harder than usual. "When I was seven years old, Papa buried all of it. Every last crate. For the boys and me it was unquestionable evidence of his wisdom, and though I'm not sure any of us quite understood, the act meant for us that the world was manageable but must be watched so as to judge what to do and when, as Papa had done in burying the family silver. We liked to be on the lookout all the time, because anything out there might have a bearing on the family secret, our hidden treasure. Any little piece of news that came our way, we'd discuss it, and," she hollowed the tip of the flour pyramid with her knuckles and poured fresh buttermilk into it, "as a consequence, my brothers and I came to consider ourselves secretly denizened in adult society by the knowledge we were gleaning of how things work.

"Especially money. We'd follow railroad-building with as much curiosity as other kids have about how babies get made. We drew maps of railroads constructed, railroads projected, railroads barely hinted at by financiers and politicians in the paper. We knew the mileage of each stretch, how much trade it would likely bring to any area, how much money was paid and owed and expected. We kept up with the balance of trade and how it was going strongly against the U.S., and how too much paper money was deceiving people into thinking they had real worth."

"So that's what got you started on world events." Once I had asked Grandmother how she had come to have such an uncommon interest in public policies and happenings around the world. She had replied vaguely, "Do I really? Yes, well I guess that started so long ago it became a habit."

Deftly, she kneaded the flour into the buttermilk—I would never quite master the lightness of the rhythm—as she talked on about paper money ruining the country back then. "But not us. Never for a moment did we believe paper was anything but paper, useful mainly for outhouse purposes. At best, a convenient way to carry in hand the hard metal behind it. We had very little paper in our household, we couldn't be flashy. We might even look like we were scraping along. Just. When you think about it, Lizzie, isn't it a shame what money can buy? Looking back now it's funny, because the life we lived from day to day was so plain and simple, so pared down that people today, and many even then, would consider us to have been living in poverty. Genteel poverty maybe, but poverty nonetheless, the poverty of land-poor farmers. Yet we went about our daily tasks as if—"

"As if they were the operations of a central bank!" I broke in.

The image seemed to catch her fancy, but she responded only with a dry correction of my anachronism. "Given the times, I would have said the Bank of England."

She looked keenly, if furtively, at me over her spectacles. "The truth was, our wealth was solid, real, indisputable, resting in the earth as serenely indifferent to changes in political tides and economic fortunes as an Anglo-Saxon hoard. When Jay Cooke & Co. suspended in '73 and there was yet another Black Friday at the Exchange, we followed developments the way people do when they've foreseen it all along and acted accordingly. And of course Papa had. By burying the silver for us—the boys and me—to insure our future, he had disposed of our major tangible asset, and so it was as if what we had to lose simply vanished into absolute safety, as invisible as the emperor in his new clothes but still a protective presence walking somewhere among us. A power. Growing day by day, a standard growing in value imperceptibly and dependably, just as the boys and I grew.

"Each of us"—she lumped the dough on her dough board and I handed her the rolling pin—"reacted in our own way. For me, the undefined but ever-increasing responsibility of it meant keeping things straight and dependable, not letting everything get all twisted up. For Jimbo, it meant fulfilling obligations, and he cultivated so many obliging ways that, where the rest of us may have seemed to border on being cocksure or haughty or simply of too private a turn, Jimbo became the lovable one pampered by all. And Lee Walker—well, now, Lee Walker had mixed feelings about the standard all along. He halfway wanted all of it himself, and halfway wanted to get rid of the whole thing. After a while he got really witty at putting the standard down all the time in veiled, biting remarks—and even more so after he spent those months in England with Uncle Pat Smith's old business partners. The rest of us, I have to admit, got so we enjoyed the way he made us feel free of it, like a reminder we could take it or leave it any time.

"The point is, Lizzie, we definitely grew up feeling we had a choice others didn't have, and having that choice made us, including Lee Walker on his good days, feel loved. To outsiders—even to Bone—we Woolleys just seemed an unusually self-sufficient, self-contained family without need for much of anything beyond ourselves. Yes, even your grandfather never did see it any other way, in spite of everything. Yes, I think that must have been it."

Something was starting to worry me here, something hinting at limitations on my dead and revered Grandfather Harding's insight, and I blurted out as much when she paused with the rolling pin over the doughboard, in a kind of reverie. Instantly, I regretted my outbreak which was sure to cause her, I thought, to lose the trail of her own thoughts. Old thoughts.

But she knew exactly where she wanted to be, even if I didn't know where that was. "This profound conviction," she resumed, "that we had nothing to fear from the world, once Papa buried our silver standard, saw us through, without anybody batting an eyelash. Reconstruction was getting a lot worse, Ames was governor and everybody else was in a tizzy, the country in a depression, commercial houses failing a mile a minute. Not us. We sailed along achieving more and more success in living the highest quality of life under the condition of having nothing in public view to lose."

She held out her hand to me and wiggled her fingers. I was not paying attention: it was time for the biscuit cutter. I opened the drawer where it lay among a dozen cookie cutters and passed it across the board to her.

"In fact, I'd say we got so used to our way of life and so good at it that a little superstition crept into it. We could have dug that silver up after the trouble died down around us and sold it, or had the pleasure of its daily use rather than the worn plate we ate with. But, a way of life so satisfying in its absence—and knowing too we could dig it out any time—well, it was as if we already had it, and as if actually bringing it back into the open might somehow divert us from what we already had. You know, Lizzie, when you make a change, you can never be sure where it will begin and where it will end."

"I've thought about that," I said, and I had. "It worries me that you can never know when a change will be big or little, or how much..."

"Papa had his own reason for keeping the silver underground. There was a big hue and cry back in those days for more paper money, nothing but paper and no bonds payable in gold."

"The Greenback Party, right?"

"That's what decided Papa, the Greenbackers and their paper money, and this time he discussed it with all of us, starting with the 'crime of '73,' when Congress completely stopped the minting of silver coins. Four or five years later, they reversed themselves in the Bland-Allison Act forcing the Treasury to mint huge amounts of silver, and then there was all that talk again about printing more and more paper. Back and forth like that.

"We were in our *forte* in this kind of discussion, the twins and I. 'Up to you kids,' I remember Papa saying, 'but we've done all right without it, and if you just hold back a while longer, the pot at the end of the rainbow can only get bigger and fuller.' Papa was a bimetallist." She inspected the pan of almost bite-sized rounds of biscuit dough and marched into the pantry, me tagging behind. "He believed there would always be two standards because those who can't afford gold but can afford silver will force acceptance of a silver standard alongside gold. Although actually independent of each other, each one needs the other one to substantiate its own value, however far one may fall in relation to the other. It might be a little like men and women, he thought.

"To my mind, all this boiled down to a big pot of silver carrying more weight than a little pot of gold. Silver, as I had seen with my own eyes, has many uses," she appeared in the door of the pantry with a quart jar of unopened fig preserves, "whereas gold merely glitters."

"A characteristic you've taught me should never be underrated."

"What I'm trying to get across to you is how the advantages and satisfactions of holding back led us through childhood into a most pleasant and confident adolescence. Here, Lizzie, open this." She rammed the quart jar of figs at me.

"It was just as Papa predicted. And our silver standard, ever brighter and more valuable, had its interest for us compounded by what Lee Walker was doing with it. By the time he was nine, you see, he was fast turning into a master draftsman—kept a crate open all the time to draw its contents, getting down to even the minutest differences between, say, individual teaspoons of the same set, differences in craftsmanship or wear so tiny that the rest of us would not have noticed, and we certainly would not have heeded them had our silver been in use. We all loved to compare Lee Walker's drawings with the designs from the old Manley factory—their purpose had been purely practical, of course, technical."

"So you all had access to the buried silver?"

"Certainly not. Papa had made it clear all along that only he and the boys were ever to know where it was buried. The better to keep Mama and me from worrying, he said."

"Hm," I said, summoning up great-grandfather Wesley Wooley's stern-faced portrait in the front hall.

"But between Lee Walker's drawings and Uncle Pat Smith's inventory packets," she went on, "we became intimately acquainted with an absent silver population of some five thousand objects, from the tiniest spoon to the largest serving piece and the heavy 49-cup candlestick."

I had wrenched the top off and set the jar of preserves before her so she could spoon some into a glass compote on the tray—a sufficiently generous amount, but never in excess.

"The twins and I named our entire silver population. Everybody had a kind of family name, and there were a good two dozen families reposing in those buried crates. Tritons, Wellingtons, Turners, Stuarts, Stouts, Chargers, Hulls, Thackerays, Hobbses. One little set of solid but otherwise undistinguished teaspoons made up the Jones family. As others refer to the teeth of a fork, we distinguished the parts of each silver object by analogy to the human body and so discussed with complete understanding among ourselves the tiny scar on one of the Cromwells' noses or the slight curve of Tutu's neck—Tutu was a pie server. Only good manners kept us from openly criticizing the silver of other people. As you can imagine, Lee Walker never missed the slightest defect. Our closest neighbors down the road had a whole brood of knives with scoliosis of the spine, and the church's entire population, though good .925, had numerous bone diseases crippling arms and legs, not to mention the prevalence of skin cancer in most other silver populations we knew anything about. Our own, we came to realize, was inferior to none, and even some apparent ugliness or aberration in this or that member merely conveyed the family's patrician cast." Pointing to a silver butter knife on our tea tray, she made out the shape of the handle's head with her finger. I saw immediately the elongated receding foreheads of the Mayan ruling class.

"What happened then was Lee Walker got smart-alecky." My great-uncle had begun his apprenticeship as a silversmith in England when he was barely eleven, she explained, "but even before he went over there his drawings were getting different. More and more so all the time. We egged him on, Jimbo and I, until he was giving our population twists and turns they never had, getting more and more fanciful and far-fetched. Papa claimed Lee Walker was the type who learned the most of what he could in a very short time, and any extra would not sharpen his skills but merely give him room for mischief. That's why Papa made him come back home he never got to finish his apprenticeship, you see. Lee Walker was mad as a hornet about that." She shook out the cloth and covered our tea tray with it. "His drawings got so wild after he spent that time in England it was getting hard to tell who was who in them. But it didn't matter, we still got the same pleasure out of them, the same confidence that they somehow preserved our absent silver standard—more, if anything."

Grandmother took a deep breath. "And that's how things were until the silver was dug up. The twins decided. The twins and Bone, the year we got married. I was just sixteen then. Between them, they decided to take the family silver out and put it to use."

She had opened the screen door to the back veranda—it was time for our walk. I followed her out, my mind in a whirl. When I had thought to have heard everything of any interest about everybody Grandmother knew, here was something of possibly far-reaching consequence she'd never so much as alluded to before. I took her arm and we stood a moment on the top step looking out over the garden. "Nothing has changed here in my whole life," I observed in that clutch of feeling so often mistaken for nostalgia, and repeating the words I had heard from her, "nothing has changed here in *your* whole life, except for the belvedere."

She colored ever so slightly, I think. As we took a path curving around by the muscadines, she said, "There was one other change. Between the smokehouse and the outhouse there was once a giant Cherokee rose, monstrously overgrown in every direction. It made a circle over forty feet in diameter, and almost half as tall. One night it was cut down and hauled away, all of it, leaving a brown patch as cleanly cut as that pasture over yonder. I had the belvedere built later on, the better to see everything clearly. The better never to forget what actually happened." A kind of memorial, I concluded, and was immediately filled with the usual delight.

Nothing, as I grew up, brought me any fuller experience of happiness than Grandmother's lessons climaxing in the safety of the belvedere. Before pouring our tea, she would make a complete turn from side to side, fast like an animal, in scrutiny of all around us—wary but not frightened, observing all but somehow skeptical as if looking out for a trick, powerful in judgment, confident but recoiling from it as if from a wound; yet unrelenting and determined, as resolute as a dying person getting on with it, eyes sorrowing but sharp, mouth intimating a smile, and, like a hue over all, a pride as if declaring: whatever and wherever, this was who she was. Because I never saw this expression on her face any other time, it was for me like a secret we shared. I interpreted it as the burden of knowledge she carried and imitated it in practice for carrying the burden myself as I received it from her. Perhaps I took it on so early I got the look without the burden, because that look settles over my face when I'm most happy. One must, of course, discover the pull and play of evil in oneself before mere knowledge of it can function as much more than fascination.

But whatever my gratification, Grandmother was never after entertaining me with her stories. Her purpose was to get the moral across and mine to learn how to get the moral held out to me. A mere story for her either had no moral or had a suspicious one and so was not, at any rate, to be trusted as material for getting the moral across.

And the only material for getting the moral across was what actually happens, although occasional references to Bible stories, historical personages, and biographies were ok because these, after all, are about real people and events. Even a reference to Shakespeare or *Jane Eyre* or Hawthorne was not amiss as long as you tied it in with an account of what actually happened to somebody you know, as if what actually happens can and must place great fictions in their appropriate moral dimensions. Trashy literature (almost everything published, according to Grandmother) is stuff not even the moral value of actual happenings can rub off on. You can tell when literature is trashy precisely to the extent that it wastes your time. The major problem of people all over the world, she would add, is that they don't know until too late, if ever at all, when they're wasting their time.

I realized very early on that part of the job I had in living was to get clear on all the traps for wasting time, and the greatest help Grandmother gave me on that score was her parenthetical reflection that wasted time, like any other waste, is a kind of unused surplus: undigested time excreted as particles of this and that spun off together by chance and dissolving by chance, passingly lingering like a malodorous whiff of the grave. It is by way of the nose that time informs of its sewerage.

We threaded our way among criss-crossing stone, brick, pine needle, and dirt paths with me even more excited than usual that day. What she was telling me about was something entirely new, and, she said, it involved someone we had never really examined before.

My old apprehension returned, exhilarating as always: the fun, the suspense of getting to the moral, whether or not I would be able to grasp it first time around, especially this time, in new material form. Before, we had always gone back to this or that previous lesson in readiness for the moral to come, like a review and a preview all rolled into one. I would be more or less prepared for the new moral, poised to see how it fit with former ones, and indeed how it was a necessary extension of all I had learned before. I no longer had any anxiety at all about synthesizing new moral dicta with old ones; I had been good at that for years. It was getting the moral in the first place where I tended to go astray, thinking I'd got *the* moral when I only had *a* moral, one that a little quick deduction showed might not even fit in where I'd put it.

This time there had been no review, and there was none now. I comprehended the instant the first words came out of her mouth that her kitchen recollection about the silver standard had been no idle passing of the time, and that everything that had gone before—all our years together—had been a preliminary to this: a moral of quite a different order.

"What actually happened in your own family, Lizzie, that's what it's time for you to hear," she opened. "I have to tell you about the family lie."

"'Everybody has a secret reason for self-loathing,'" I quoted from a former lesson, and, generalizing in anticipation, "so does every family."

"No, no, no, child," she interrupted impatiently. Although I may not have known how to label it at the time, I was well aware that I had just committed the fallacy of composition. From previous lessons I had learned that morals were not always bound by ordinary logic—when they were and when they weren't fell largely into a gray area for me. But Grandmother was looking nonplussed, so it couldn't have been merely a matter of a logical slide. Instead of going on, she stopped to think my problem through. "You jump to the wrong conclusions. You've got to realize that a conclusion isn't right just because it's true. To get the moral out of what's going on around you—I'm not talking child talk, Lizzie, this is not an animal fable, this is *me* telling you what happened to *me*. Now, hear me out and pay attention: the moral has to come out from *what* happened and *who* it happened to."

In the years since, when I recall Grandmother's last probe of my moral fiber, I go over not what she meant to say but what she said without meaning to. Sometimes I go over it without remembering it was she who said it without meaning to, but as if she meant this to happen, too. It's then she's no more than an eye-blink away.

"Yes, Lizzie, this one's about me," she said, a first and clear warning that my grandmother has not, mind you, committed a sin but has done what is far, far worse: she has subverted a moral principle. I smiled, wondering how she got caught in the cookie jar. But the anguish in her eyes so palpably digested humble pie that I could not downgrade the moral status of her indiscretion whatever it might be.

"It all came out the year I married Bone, no accident as you'll see. I was almost your age then. What I first noticed was Papa's—your great grandfather's—unusual and strange behavior. Upon looking into it, I found he had taken to hiding with his gun in the rose thicket, one of those varieties brought over from China that grows out of control in two or three years if you don't stop it. For several years it had been piling into a steadily growing mountain, that took up a whole section of the garden and tumbled within a few feet of the muscadines. It covered half the distance between the smoke-house and outhouse by then."

She pointed to the outhouse. All my life it had provided storage for Grandmother's gardening tools and pots, but I remembered her saying it had retained its original function until after her father's death although he was the only one who used it any more. "After Mama had the baths put in the house against his wishes, he never missed an opportunity to express indignation about outhouses being put inside where you eat and sleep," she had once told me. Off about twenty feet to the side of the back veranda, lost among the maze of little garden paths it stood, its iron-latched door facing away from the house in a straight line from the old smokehouse with its well-trod path. Smokehouses in the early fifties had outlived, outfunctioned outhouses, and still furnished a sizeable portion of the meat in our diets.

We were now on a path leading from the outhouse to a large patch of lawn and bellying suddenly around to the smokehouse door. Grandmother stepped off the path and guided me to a thoughtfully determined point at the back of the smokehouse.

"There," she said, "the rose thicket covered that entire side of the smokehouse facing the outhouse and had grown all the way around to where we're standing. Right here"—she pointed to a spot in the air about knee level and about a foot from the smokehouse wall—"was the hole. I'll tell you how I discovered it in a minute, a hole in the thicket big enough to crawl into, and once you crawled a few feet, it began to get big enough to stand up comfortably—nobody else in the family, of course, is as short as me. Openings, every yard or so, through the top of the thicket worked like skylights. Clearings had been sculpted out every few feet on each side where, dim as it was, I could make out stacks and stacks of little boxes under tarpaulins, the kind I'd seen all my life that the shells come in Papa and the boys used for hunting. I knew they liked to save those boxes year after year, as if the shot they once contained gave them a special value.

"My first thought was that I'd stumbled into their secret hunting den. A few more feet and I stood in the heart of the rose thicket's sculpted innards: an egg-shaped alcove tall enough even for Papa to stand up in, with three Cherokee rose teeth cut out about four inches apart, just the suggestion of a battlement.

"That little piece of handiwork might have told me something right away if I hadn't gotten so taken up with the fact that there stood Papa's gun, muzzle poked through an arrow loop in the middle battlement and stock wedged securely in a V notched out of the trunk of a corkwood tree stuck in the ground. What threw me off from the very beginning was that. Wha'cha have to know about the corkwood is that nobody else had 'em. Papa had hauled some in years before from Arkansas and kept a stand of them going in the swamp down back of the barn. He used them for making all kinds of things from floats for fishing lines and bottle stoppers to pole vaults for the twins.

And nobody, I mean nobody, was allowed to mess with his corkwoods except him. So I figured all this business had to be his—besides, Papa was 6'2" and the gun was obviously set at his kneeling eye level. The twins would never have dared touch either his gun or his corkwoods, of that much I was sure."

"Aren't those the trees Uncle Jimbo made my doll out of?" I interrupted. "Remember the summer after second grade when I spent a whole month with you?" The only doll I had ever thought well of, it was not one you dressed up and fussed over, not a real doll at all but one you could play in Delta ditches and bayous with, tease crawfish, even catch them when they latched on to a cork arm or leg.

"Jimbo and Lee Walker kept them up after Papa died," she answered, "but pay attention, Lizzie. Before I discovered the hole in the rose thicket, something else had been going on that showed Papa was not himself. I was already suspicious, I just didn't know what of and, at first, I didn't even try to figure it out.

"But standing there looking at his mounted gun, I couldn't keep my head from filling up with ridiculous ideas like singlehandedly digging up and burning the whole stand of corkwoods because anything connected with corkwoods would be immediately connected with Papa. Lots of men had guns and shells, I figured, but nobody else had corkwoods. Destroy the corkwoods and Papa could no longer be clearly implicated—in whatever it was he could be implicated in. As I've gone over and over with you, Lizzie, it's just this kind of thinking that's nothing but imagination: using what's in front of you for the purpose of looking like a problem is being solved when it's not even clear whether there's any problem or what it is. The reason I bring all that nonsense about the corkwoods up is to show you the twist in my thinking even before I had a good look through the gun sight and realized the gun was trained squarely on the door of the outhouse.

"Well, the goings-on in my head could have warned me if I had been in any condition to see them that way, but right then and there my life was breaking into an impacted fracture: PAPA WAS PLANNING TO KILL ONE OF US. But which one? And why?

"If he had gone this far already, he was not to be reasoned with and I did not have much time to get this business stopped. But I saw it was up to me to stop it. I felt I had been CALLED. Called, at last, to prove my reputation for goodness. Everybody, even when I was a child, has always said I'm a saint, not that I believe it—there's not a Papist bone in my body—but I believed and still believe it's possible to be good if you can keep your mind on it hard enough. And if being good can't stop evil, what's it worth anyway? Well, something like this came to me, and if you can get your confidence back and be in a panic all at the same time, that's how I was feeling when I peered again through Papa's gun sight before I lit out of the rose thicket, rounded it on the muscadine side, and latched myself into the outhouse. I was in no shape to go back in to help Mama finish breakfast until I could go over and get straight what was going on.

"As I said before, Papa had been acting strange for several days, and it was Papa's behavior, especially where Mama was concerned, the way he was keeping tabs on her, that put me on to him and led me to the discovery of the rose thicket's innards.

"I couldn't seem to keep my mind on how Papa had been acting, though, for thinking about why he, of all people, would kill any of us. It would have to be something he couldn't handle any other way. He had always taught us English manners and was religious. His Methodist forbears had come over before the Revolution to practice their religion freely, not to get rich or escape a criminal sentence or anything like that. Stern as he was, Papa couldn't hurt a fly, I thought, well not unless maybe it was something like God ordering Abraham to kill his only son. I had had trouble with the moral there until I realized you had to consider the ending. You know what I mean: how things turned out in the end between God, Abraham, and Isaac. If Papa was hearing directly from God and God wanted him to murder one of us, it must also be part of the plan for me to be called on to put a stop to it. Why else would I be pulled into it? And God and Papa couldn't both be crazy, not anybody as dry-humored as Papa, though the ways of God Himself may be beyond understanding. Given that Papa always had a reason for what he was doing, I could sympathize with the problem of having a reason beyond his own understanding.

"I finally got myself to stop thinking about what Papa's gun was doing in the rose thicket, and made myself concentrate with all my might on what had actually been happening. You see, Papa usually got up about 4:30 every morning. Mama would be up a half-hour before him, go to the outhouse, splash her face, perk the coffee and make the biscuits so breakfast was always under way when I came down to do ham and sausage and eggs. Lizzie, have you noticed how every generation is sleeping a little later into the day? With your Papa, it's 5:30 and with you 6:30. Pretty soon, we'll have a generation sleeping till noon like all the drunks and dope addicts. Well, my mind immediately jumped back to one morning almost a week before when I'd noticed—my eyesight may not amount to much any more, never did, but I can still hear fleas jump in a dog's fur—I noticed Papa tipping out on to the side balcony early and slipping down the tree hanging over it. About time Mama would come in from outside to the kitchen, he was climbing back up the tree to the balcony, dashing into their bedroom and jumping back into bed, quiet as a mouse, until time for the usual sounds he made upon arising. And those sounds were now distinctly louder as if he were saying: 'See, I've been sound asleep all night and just woke up, as you can hear.' The volume of his getting-up noises definitely protested too much.

"I tried two or three mornings to track the direction of his movements once he hit ground—and he always hit ground while Mama was making her way along the path to the outhouse—but it was still too dark and he moved too fast, so after this had gone on a few mornings without any sense to it, I made it to the balcony as soon as he started down the tree and started down it myself the instant he touched ground, taking a chance anybody in that big a hurry wouldn't look at anything but what was in his own head. I might have been like a small version of you when I was growing up, Lizzie, maybe even quicker than you, and at sixteen I could still shinny up and down a tree faster than Jimbo or Lee Walker. I stayed right in behind him but darting between and behind trees just as he was doing because, even if his hearing had started to go bad, he had hawk eyes.

"He made a wide berth around the outhouse where Mama was and, once into the muscadine vines, worked his way through them until he broke across the few feet of open ground to the back of the smokehouse. He stood there panting, pressed up against its back wall like an escaped convict, then edged along the wall to the rose thicket, reached his left hand toward it and made a quick little outward flicking motion with his fingers. It looked like a signal except that he then promptly dropped into the ground and disappeared. Flat disappeared, you hear, with me standing not fifteen feet away looking straight at him. And I swear it wasn't dark enough for any mistake about it, but I blinked and looked good. Gone, dead gone. I ran for the house, forgetting about keeping quiet and out of sight, shinnied up to the balcony and back to my bed.

"I hadn't really been worried until then, lying there with the sheet over my head. Not that I ever believed in magic, black or white, but something scary was happening out there, scary as the devil if Papa hadn't been in on it, or maybe just because he was. I still had complete trust in him, but it was already beginning to look as if some power I didn't understand had hold of him. In about ten minutes or so, I heard him easing into his bed and in another minute more, he bounced out, coughing, dropping his knife on the floor as he put on his pants.

"Too much noise. Our natural quietness, mine and the twins', yours too, goes back to him, not Mama for sure.

"I hardly took my eyes off him all through breakfast. He ate too slow, chewed too hard, and made smacking sounds drinking his coffee, none of it quite natural. Nobody else noticed. Getting to what was going on would all be, I was just beginning to realize, up to me. More signs: Come lunchtime and he hardly took his eyes off Mama, showed intense interest in how she had spent the morning, even down to asking if anybody had stopped by the house to visit, and he paid careful attention, I now observed, to every word she uttered morning, noon, and night. Mama responded in that way people do when they don't know they're doing it. For her, that meant talking and laughing more than ever. As a result, her usual extraordinary vitality seemed to overflow her usual bounds of self-containment. And the more she responded, the more I could see he was definitely not himself.

"Next morning, I took out after him again. And again, he suddenly vanished, same time, same place, same signal, same everything. But by the third morning I had formed a plan. I went down the tree a good half-hour before him, still pitch dark, and picked a hiding spot as close to the place of his disappearing act as possible. This time I was squatting and ready, so intent on him I didn't even bother to hide my head. And this time, once he gave what I had begun to think of as the signal, the stretching of his left arm, held stiffly, to the rose thicket and a little forward flip of his fingers from his wrist, I could see his head was going in first, exactly like a dive into the ground with his feet kicking after him like a swimmer.

"Papa's disappearing act over, I waited, half expecting him to sail straight up out of the earth into the air after wherever he'd been. I waited it out, squatting and squeezed in a clump of Sassafras until, sure enough, his head appeared at about my eye level out of the blackness of the rose thicket—and oh, my lord, I thought it was just his head floating loose. It turned one way and the other and then went up to its proper place followed by the rest of him. At least he'd come out whole one more time so there must be hope, I thought. He stooped, picked something up from the ground, and fiddled, stealthy as a thief, with the rose thicket a few seconds. Covering over nature's evidence of his descent, it looked like.

"The second Papa raced off to climb the tree back up to their bedroom, I popped over to the corner of the smokehouse, pressed my back against it as I edged toward the rose thicket, took a deep breath, reached out my left arm and gave the signal. I'm here to tell you the squeal out of me as I shook my hand free of the thing came straight out of a trapped rabbit's throat. At my feet lay a mess of twigs and vines thickly woven over a piece of fine wire mesh to simulate one of the browning, dying areas of Cherokee rose periodically appearing here and there. I had pulled off this piece of camouflage and there by my side was the hole in the thicket Papa had dived into. I fell to my knees and scrambled in head first like Papa, and—I already told you this part—found its secret heart in no time.

"On my way out, I hastily hooked the woven vegetation back over the two nails mounted on a kind of frame with the Cherokee growing all around it. Only in the privacy of the outhouse—the one place where I was unlikely to be interrupted—did I manage to get some control over myself and this problem of Papa's strange behavior. I couldn't think of it apart from the business of what actually happened between Abraham, Isaac, and God. That brought me to my senses, though: if something similar was going on between Papa and God, I needed to know who the third party was.

"Feeling a momentary relief not because I had any plan of action but because I was prepared both to observe and to answer the call for action, I walked straight from the outhouse in through the back door to the kitchen. The twins on the back veranda didn't even glance up. As they all came in one by one and sat down for breakfast, I noticed just how much I needn't worry about the others noticing me. Papa was watching Mama, Jimbo was watching Papa, Lee Walker was watching Jimbo, and I was watching everybody. We often spent a little time studying each other's ways so none of this would have been out of the ordinary except that I could see all the other watchers were acting just like me. None of us wanted anybody else to know we were watching. I believed what Papa had taught us, and I never stopped believing, Lizzie, that the only good reason under ordinary conditions for hiding anything is to keep from bothering others with it unnecessarily. You know how we are, you're a real Woolley yourself. We Woolleys are so careful not to intrude on others that they call us down for taking privacy to a fault. When Bone was still alive, he used to say, 'I never feel uneasy living in your Papa's house because the one thing Wesley Woolley would never do is look down from heaven into anybody's business.'

"But this time what I was hiding was that *I* was intruding, and I didn't know what into. It seemed like—I'm just saying this is the way it seemed at the time, Lizzie—I never would be able to get out of intruding until I found out what was going on. In a way, that's true: if you push into somebody's place, you have to find a way out even if it's just going right back through the same door you came in, so you at least have to know enough to get out. And all the others, except maybe Mama—I'm coming to her next—were in the same fix. I was sure of this because if any of them, even Lee Walker, could bring it to an end, I figured they would already have done it.

"I wasn't sure about Mama so I set to watching her as closely as Papa was. She seemed to be herself, or anyway she wasn't watching any of the rest of us, that's for sure. Mama at the best of times never paid much attention to any of us. In fact, the better the times, the less attention she paid. That was one of the things I loved about Mama, the way she left you alone. She was the kind of person who loves living so much she never seemed to need more than freedom from pain and the pleasure of breathing without interference. Mama was the very model of what it means not to intrude on others: breathe and let breathe was her motto expressed in a million little different ways every day, letting me know she was all there and knew I was too, and that was that. Well, all I just said about her seemed more true then than it ever had. But it came into my head: too good to be true.

"Looking back I would say, too true to be good. It's not just that she wasn't paying attention to any of us, she was sublimely unconscious of us! I could see this was what Papa was noticing too. Even as she spooned out sausages and fried fish and eggs and buttered biscuit with energy radiating from every pore like warm air from a central heating system, her expansiveness somehow expanded right past us.

"I couldn't make heads or tails out of any of it, but watching Mama was not leading anywhere. She hadn't an inkling of the four horsemen riding through our household right in front of her eyes. Tension had never been allowed to gather in our home. Papa wouldn't put up with it, he couldn't stand tension. If anybody was doing anything that might become a cause of tension, that person, usually one of the twins, just had to stop whatever he was doing. Then and there, too. It had always worked before, but here now tension had spread as uniformly through our home as poison gas in a sealed container. Only Mama was breathing without difficulty and she was inhaling to the point where her voice had gone breathy as it did when she was looking forward to something, or having a really good time.

"And breakfast definitely was going on longer than usual again. Papa as a rule made a point of being out of the house by five in the morning at the latest. Now he sat there eating more than usual, acting more like a town man with leisure to sip coffee, not even telling the twins to get on with it, munching a small bite now and then with his coffee and hiding that he was watching Mama all the while. I turned my attention to Jimbo and Lee Walker, definitely the best candidates for giving away whatever was to be known, I figured. I kept trying to signal to them that I wanted to talk to them before they followed Papa out of the house, but the signals folks use for sub-terfuge were so unfamiliar between us that they simply stared at me as if I had developed a tic.

"As the morning wore on, I got even better control of myself and came up with a plan of action that made me feel good—maybe I should say a plan of no action. Clearly, I had no business following Papa, no business in the rose thicket at all. The awful feeling in my body came from me hiding what I had seen Papa do, and had done myself, pretending to be something I wasn't. For my part I determined to simply drop the whole matter. So what if Papa and the twins seemed to be pretending they too were who they usu-ally were? They'd drop it shortly, just like me. We were that kind of family. By lunch things would be back to normal, but even if not *I* would be. I vowed to be. In proof, I was already doing my part: I would go into it no further. And Mama was already looking less overblown like a Titian painting and just well-filled-out in a normal way, a little tired maybe. But, then, experi-ence had already taught me that an excess of feeling good is bound to lead to a letdown sooner or later.

"By late morning I didn't have the slightest urge to do anything but pick and wash the greens for lunch. Most people who could afford it had at least a cook or a maid, often one or both who did everything, but Mama and Papa never believed in having servants although in an occasional crisis we would take a message to one of our black neighbors two or three miles in the hills and they always gave us a hand when in trouble. In return, we took them meat when they ran out and other help when they called for it, so there was never any real need for servants. I still think they just get in your way, but Lee Walker is probably right: he says none of us ever learned how to use a servant. He picked that idea up over there in England.

"Anyway, I was crouched behind the pole beans picking greens when I saw the two-wheeled cart Papa built for the twins to use for hauling. It moved a few inches, stopped, then a few more inches. Looks like it's rolling, I thought, rolling up-hill, and I stopped picking a second to peep out. Jimbo was bent double trying to hide himself, the blackish-brown slick of his head bobbing up and down so fast it looked like a moving knob on the weathered cart. No doubt about it, he was working the cart toward the opening in the rose thicket.

"I resolutely continued my green-picking," Grandmother pointed to a double row of turnips and collards a few feet from the path we had taken, "but when I glanced through the pole beans again, I had a clear view from down here in the vegetable garden of him sitting up there on his haunches holding on to his cart and watching so hard he seemed frozen stiff. I looked where he was looking but it was only Mama coming down the back steps and turning on to the outhouse path.

"The rose thicket then blocked her from my view, but he kept on watching her. I supposed she had gone inside the outhouse and latched the door because he jumped up and pulled the cart back of the thicket up against the smokehouse and disappeared head first you know where to.

"I paid no attention—I'm not defending myself, Lizzie, but honestly I didn't—I finished my picking, cool as the cucumbers I was snapping off their vines, and thought we should have a few fresh tomatoes, too, and stopped to check on the melons.

"But Mama was certainly taking a long time in the outhouse. Was it possible she was sick in there? That almost supernatural glow she'd been getting every now and then lately, was there a sickness that could make a person look both lax and strong and alive at the same time? And maybe—maybe—I'm ashamed to admit what came into my head—it had even seemed natural, I remembered, when Papa not a month before had had to shoot his fine favorite heifer to save the rest of them from abortion disease, and us too. US TOO: you can get undulant fever from an infected cow. So, although I'd never heard of any such thing, it now occurred to me that there might be dread circumstances everybody was busy hiding. Really dread circumstances, circumstances under which a loved one might have to be killed to save the rest of us.

"It all began to make perfect sense. Mama didn't know her own condition and Papa couldn't bring himself to do what had to be done, so he had turned to the boys for help. I saw Mama's appearance of heightened well-being in a new light. And hadn't I been noticing it off and on for at least a good week without making anything of it? Ever since, in fact, your grandfather, who encouraged us all, even the boys, to stop addressing him as 'Mr. Harding' and call him just plain 'Bone,' had pointed it out when he'd come over for supper the very evening he got in from his last trip to Central America. You remember how he loved to travel, Lizzie. Back then, his trips usually related to business prospects he was investigating for his friend, Minor Cooper Keith, in Costa Rica.

"Bone, a good twenty years older than I, but I'd had more than just a school girl crush on him for the entire four years he'd lived in Starkville after taking the job of Treasurer at Mississippi State. Back then it was the Ag and Mechanical College. Since our land borders the college's, it was almost a straight walk from our house across the back of the campus to his office, not over a mile and a half through fields and woods past the lake. He 'found' us, he said, the very first time he sneaked out to clear his head in the open air. Papa, a little standoffish with most people—'reserved' they used to say—took to him as if put so off his guard he couldn't help but respond to Bone with Bone's own open-hearted warmth. And Bone liked nothing better than to slip out of his office and take the short walk to our farm where he would find Papa and work along with him whatever the job, talking all the while about crops and the need for a new state constitution. He fished and hunted with the boys and was influencing them at Mama's behest to matriculate at the college— back then, a young man could easily get in when he was fourteen or fifteen, and Mama thought it was time. She just loved Bone. He not only talked scripture and literature and music with her but brought over things he valued, like that collection of old prints he bought while at Oxford, and those portfolios of paintings copied from the old masters that you used to pore over as a child for hours on end when you came for your summer visits, Lizzie.

"Of course, I never talked about my feelings for Bone then. What pleased me more was any talk *about* him, and it was agreed, to my great satisfaction, no less than two or three times a week in our household that he was just the nicest man imaginable and, as Mama kept saying, 'so highly cultured.' One of my biggest thrills was to hear Papa in his infrequent exchanges with neighbors refer to 'my friend, Mr. Bone Gentry Harding.' Bone of my bone, I would always think.

"Whatever Bone said, there was probably something to it, although I think Papa saw, like me, that you had to put what he said in the right perspective to get the something out of it. And it was Bone who had carried on with admiration and a touch of astonishment only a few days before when Mama half-collapsed after supper in her Queen Anne wingchair and snugly lolled in the light of the coal oil lamp. 'Why, look at her,' he said, 'She's a Titian in English dress.' Mama's coloring already higher than usual—unnaturally so, it now seemed to me upon recall—went noticeably higher. 'Sacred and profane Love,' Bone murmured like a gentleman in a Chekhov play.

"We all laughed except Papa, I remembered, who gave the smile you automatically put on when others are laughing freely but you aren't quite sure it's appropriate. In the next hour or so during Bone's visit—yes, it was definitely, I realized, *then*—Papa had started watching Mama. And it was the following night Papa had put the Titian portfolio down with some agitation and gone off to bed leaving it open on "The Rape of Europa." More evidence, it seemed: a woman being carried off on a bull's back. A bull, mind you! What that picture would bring to Papa's mind was cattle diseases, Papa who hadn't had much of a classical education and wouldn't recognize Zeus in a bull. But he was good at diagnosing sickness in both animals and people. If Mama had been infected, he would know it.

"And all the symptoms were there: the flush of pink body color, eyes overly bright, a touch of languor combined with a charged-up feeling, and, most rare for Mama, that occasional subdued quietness, not despondency but moving a tad in that direction. That was it, that must be it! MAMA HAD THE FEVER. But surely you didn't shoot *people* with the fever. Still I hadn't known until a month before that you shoot heifers, even the best of them, because such a fever spreads fast. No wonder they were all acting so funny if they had to shoot Mama *now*. What struck me like Zeus' thunderbolt was that MAMA WAS IN DANGER. I knew about this kind of shooting, it had to be fast and efficient. And Jimbo was in the rose thicket hiding, waiting, with the gun pointed straight at the door of the outhouse. Between the eyes—she would never know what hit her.

"I dropped my basket of vegetables and screamed with all my considerable lung power, 'MAMA, NO! NO! NO!' It was a refusal echoing through every hill and hollow around. Mama burst out of the outhouse and stood staring uncertainly around her, the perfect target. He couldn't miss. Everybody in the family, including Mama and me if necessary, could handle a shotgun like Pat Garrett who was Lee Walker's big hero that year.

"I cut through the peach orchard hollering, 'RUN, MAMA! RUN!' She lowered her head and charged toward me with such enormous leaps that we collided on the croquet course. Being the only one in the family of such slight build you could knock me over with a feather, I was sent stumbling and sprawling down the brick step into the next garden level, landing in the hollyhocks with her right behind pulling me up and forward and peering into my face like into a full bucket drawn out of the well.

"On my feet, I broke away from her and confronted the danger. Taking a stand like the twins taunting each other, I flapped my palms against my thighs to emphasize the rhythm of the chant I was shouting into the heart of the thicket: 'Thou shalt not kill, thou shalt not kill....' Poor Mama caught me up around the waist and led me back to the house. I was about to pass out but figured I had made my point for the time being and had staved off any immediate threat from the rose thicket. Mama wrapped one of her shawls around me, the woven dark turquoise Bone had brought back from Mexico the year before, and put me on the little Hepplewhite settee with a stool under my feet while she fixed lunch, running back and forth to check on me every few minutes. When the others came in for lunch, they all stared at me while she explained that I had had a vision or thought I had. Papa glowered at her as if my condition was the last straw. He never had any patience with what he called 'nervous attacks' although everybody on his side of the family gave the impression their nerves had to be kept coated with iron for the good of all.

"Jimbo, who, of course, had firsthand knowledge of what had happened, announced that he was sure I'd had a spell and was out of my head and should be put to bed for the afternoon. I had to exercise all my will power to keep from jumping off the settee and slapping his face. I HATED HIM—and Papa, and Lee Walker too, looking so self-righteous. Never before had I felt like that. See, Lizzie, what was happening to me. I was so agitated I broke out in a sweat, not for the first time in the last two days. I felt hot-and-cold and faint as if I had a fever. A FEVER! I gave up then and there. I—*I* had the fever. Mama didn't seem to be feeling a bit sick but I definitely was. I could feel it roiling through me and heating my brain beyond endurance, and Mama didn't know what was wrong. They were keeping it from her. All that machination in the rose thicket was but to make a horrible necessity less dreadful, a poor but manly attempt to bring mercy, to camouflage the inevitable: they had to shoot me, so much was clear.

"Then, Lizzie, relief rolled through me as light as an Extra Middling sample of long-staple from a Delta cotton gin. I understood early death in a flash, and mine the Achillean choice though for a different reason, not eternal fame but deliverance from evil. No more of the feverish corruptions of hate, suspicion, doubt and deceit I was falling into. No more. I poised myself for my deliverance, there on the settee while they ate, under the cloud, I thought, of my fever. And I closed my eyes as each one silently bent over me before they all went upstairs for their short noon naps. It's no excuse, but playing possum was purely for their sake—I had never felt their love and concern for me so powerfully. They needed any little bit of help I could give them for what they had to do.

"Shortly, Jimbo, just as I expected, crept back downstairs and out the back door. I gave him time to reach the rose thicket and walked, steady as Jane Eyre, to the outhouse where Nature had in fact been calling me the whole time I reclined on the settee.

"It seemed appropriate to empty my body of its waste. I had heard what happens to the body when hung but was not sure what it might do on its own when shot. Now, it's not that my resolution weakened as I answered the call of Nature; rather, it seemed my timing was off. I had not said tiddlysqueak to the one person I cared about in every tiniest little scrap of myself: Bone, your grandfather Bone Gentry Harding. I couldn't do it, I couldn't take my leave of this world without my fill of him first was how I felt. I had to see him.

"But I had a more immediate problem on my hands. It's always been true of me, Lizzie, that no matter how far from the straight and narrow I may drift under some conditions, I have a good mind for what's right in front of me under all conditions, and what was right in front of me was that I had to find a way out of the outhouse without Jimbo seeing me. I felt sorry for Jimbo. I figured he had worked up all his courage to do what had to be done and now I was going to cheat him of it once again.

"It was a symptom of the state I was in that I actually thought one more little cheating episode, even cheating something far bigger than Jimbo, even cheating death itself, wouldn't make any real difference since it was only a matter of time. Just a couple of hours or so. Before sundown I'll be back and it will be over, I told myself. I set about pushing, pulling, and kicking at the plank walls—solid as everything else Papa took care of. There was a spade for shovelling in the lime from the barrel in the corner. I grabbed it and set to work on the side away from the rose thicket where I found a peculiarly soft area.

"It was easy. At the rate I was shovelling, I realized I would have a hole big enough to squeeze underneath the sill to the outside quick enough. But then there was a click. I poked the shovel. A clang. I dropped to my knees and brushed away dirt. A bottle, not one bottle but several, a wooden crate of them set into the ground half in the outhouse and half under the sill where, I judged, it could be dug up and reached from both inside and out. I brushed the label clean on one bottle, and held it to the small shuttered window: 'Mirabelle de Nancy,' it read.

"Start burying things and there's no end to it, I thought, and this buried treasure had to be Bone's! I remembered the whole scene, by then a good six months in the past, when Bone, his visits to our home long a customary event, came striding in late one afternoon with a covered basket from which he lifted just such a bottle and two Baccarat glasses he greatly prized. After completing a financial arrangement in Paris for his friend, Minor Cooper Keith, he had, he said, taken the opportunity to dash over to Alsace for the express purpose of selecting the finest sample of this eau-de-vie for Mama and me. With a great flourish and a pretty speech about the virtues of a liquid "as translucent as the skin of the mother and daughter" before him, he poured what he called 'a spot with Spirit,' into each glass and declared it to be as 'Sublimely mild' as Shelley's 'Spirit without spot' when he held out the glasses to Mama and me.

"O, the smell of it! It held an allure like the fruits of Paradise. I touched the glass to my lips, ran my tongue over them and was astonished to discover my favorite preserve—Mama and I made a batch every year—but in liquid form: the small yellow plum distilled to its purity.

"As I sniffed and marvelled, Mama drained her glass and was laughing with him while he poured another 'spot.' Neither of us had a chance to indulge further, for Papa walked in at that instant, took one look around, sniffed the bottle and stated flatly that no alcohol of any denomination would ever be allowed under his roof. Bone took the glasses back immediately and pointed out how there was just a drop in each, although he proceeded carefully to pour every precious one back into the bottle. Papa replied in his most stern tone that one bite of the apple had been enough to do Adam and Eve in. None of us ever mentioned this incident again.

"Given my situation in the outhouse, the Mirabelle flaunted itself as simply another obstacle to freedom of movement—and one more reason why I had to find Bone faster than ever. In fact, my sense of urgency about reaching him took on proportions lending me more than my ordinary strength. I flipped the loose dirt to the side, heaved the crate up out of the ground, and peered through the hole.

"Shortly, I was outside forming a new plan. I decided to sneak up on Jimbo and tell him straight out I understood everything but I had to see Bone first, so he would have to wait for me. I felt I owed him that much. Moving through the rose thicket, I perceived that it had undergone some change, but I was so dead set on getting to Jimbo I didn't realize what it was until I reached the gun still mounted and pointing toward the door of the outhouse. No Jimbo to be seen anywhere but to one side of the gun were some shell boxes, and it was these that jogged my memory. Only that morning, the clearings on the way to the alcove had been stacked to the hilt with shell boxes and now they were all gone except for this lone stack, admittedly more than enough to shoot one or two women but, earlier, there had been enough for all the feverish women south of the Mason-Dixon line.

"I picked one up, definitely not empty but definitely heavier than any box of hunting shells, and opened it. In disbelief, I picked up another, and another, and opened them. The same in all: the most beautiful silver dollars you can imagine, a lovely frosted Liberty sitting on a bale of cotton and wheat stalks holding her olive branch. Freshly minted, not a mark on them. I turned one over. Under the eagle were the words: 'Trade Dollar.' No bullets, no bullets at all.

"And Jimbo's cart. That was what he'd been doing all day, carting off boxes full of coins. If it had been just Jimbo snaking in and out of the thicket, I would have concluded he had robbed a bank—he'd never bothered to conceal that Billy the Kid was the real object of his admiration behind all his talk with Lee Walker about Pat Garrett—but here was Papa's gun on its corkwood prop and that meant Papa was involved somehow, and Papa could not be led into robbing and stealing. He was beyond all that. More likely he was protecting somebody's money and had enlisted Jimbo's help to guard the stash, in which case the gun was not meant for me or Mama. But that brought the original problem back into focus: why was it trained on the door of our outhouse, making it abundantly evident that danger at its source was to be anticipated from there?

"Everything fell out of place. It was like picking up a basket where pieces of thousands of old puzzles, already half gone, have been dumped. The more pieces you pull out the less they fit together.

"At that point Bone became my only answer, my only goal to reach him. I was having a brainstorm. Since the gun still seemed to be set up to do away with some member of the family if necessary—or, OR MAYBE IT WAS MEANT FOR BONE. Bone, the only visitor who came several times a week, sometimes twice a day, and hadn't I noticed just recently his increasingly regular visits to the outhouse? The Mirabelle! There was a piece here that did seem to fit somehow.

"I carefully took Papa's Enfield from its prop, removed the cartridge, and put the gun back in its former position. With their shot gone, any immediate danger from the men of the family seemed more controllable whatever might be going on. On an inspired second impulse and for added protection, I took the gun down again and jammed the broochblock with dirt, twigs, leaves, anything my hand got hold of and my fingers could cram in, before returning it to its threatening aim.

"Since the passage through the thicket dropped to less than four feet as you got close to the entry, you had to bend over or, if tall like Papa, get down on all fours. I was bolting through it bent slightly from the waist when I collided with Jimbo crawling at a fast clip. Otherwise, we might surely have given each other a good concussion. As it was, his head crashed into my stomach and sent me reeling backwards for the second time that day.

"'Bess!' Jimbo was hissing my name in that loud-low, back-of-the-throat voice you get when conditions don't allow for adequate response to a thoroughly unwelcome surprise. 'You've got to clear out of here. Keep out of this, Bess, forget you've ever been here. This is not what you might think it is.'

"'You mean,' I said, 'Mama doesn't have cow fever, and neither do I.'

"'Oh, Bess,' he said, 'you can't lose your mind just now. There's too much at stake.'

"'I haven't got a single screw loose, Jimbo,' I hissed back at him. And then with an urgency as strong as his, 'I know I've got to get out of here. I've got to find Bone this minute.'

"'Bone? Bone? Bone's waiting for me to bring him the last load. Go hide by my cart in the muscadines, Bess, and I promise I'll take you to him. I swear I will, you just keep quiet.' Jimbo was looking as relieved by the idea of turning me over to Bone as I was. 'Hurry,' he started pushing me aside and edging past me, 'I've got to get the rest of this out before Papa comes in.'

"Shortly, with a look of wild desperation, he popped out of the rose thicket with a sack swung over his shoulder, half stumbling under the weight. He transferred the two or three dozen boxes out of the long sack to the cart already loaded down with them, strapped the canvas tightly back on, and hitched himself up to pull. It would have been light work for his Shetland pony, but for him it was heaving and straining and the cart didn't budge an inch.

"'Push, Bess, push, it's my only chance.' His voice rang so convincingly of man condemned that it now seemed a foregone conclusion the aim of Papa's gun was meant for him. Purely men's business. I wanted to tell him the gun was temporarily out of commission but, not to be deterred from my own objective of getting to Bone without more ado, I threw myself against the cart and labored with all my strength. It squeaked, started slowly, squealed and gained speed until Jimbo was trotting. I kept up a running push, not taking any risk the cart might bed down in a rut somewhere, and this way we proceeded at a lively pace through the outlying orchard, down and up the slope skirting the lake, through the pasture and that stand of pines to the one narrow dirt road from our place continuing on into college property.

"Just the other side of the pines was a wagon full of shell boxes with Bone lounging beside it. He rushed forward to unstrap the canvas covering Jimbo's last load but fell back when he saw my head pop up from behind the cart. Jimbo was unhitching himself and, having surmised that the boxes were to be moved from cart to wagon with all due speed, I set to this job with the same resolve I felt in Bone, and between the three of us, the wagon was rapidly loaded without a word having passed.

"But when I climbed up into the seat beside Bone, Jimbo's tongue started. 'Bone,' he said, 'Bess's mind has left her. She won't stay put. I caught her in the Cherokee and had to bring her along. You've got to make her keep her mouth shut and come back with me. Papa—.' As desperate as Jimbo was for time, it is to his credit that he refused to budge without me. Those were still the days when a young woman, a budding young gentleman's sister in this case, did not climb into another gentleman's vehicle unasked and without the consent of her parents.

"'Papa's gun,' I interrupted, 'is not working, Jimbo, I jammed it. And,' I added in a voice not to be argued with, 'I'm staying with Bone.' Nothing, absolutely nothing was going to keep me from him, I vowed then and there.

"'Rest easy, Jimbo, your job's done. Get along home and I'll take over from here. As for Bess, I'm going to marry her,' Bone said, and eased the reins on his Standardbred. I can still see Jimbo's mouth hang open. We sailed along until Bone cut across the college pasture and up to the back of a building where he sheltered the wagon in a cluster of oaks. It took us quite a while to unload the boxes even with two little push carts he brought out. We stacked them in a basement room to which he informed me that only he had the key. I told him about finding the rose thicket and Papa's gun mounted there, and then the silver dollars, and the crate I dug up in the outhouse. He smiled lovingly and reassuringly until I got to the Mirabelle, at which point he took my arm and hastened back outside. Seating me in his wagon he said, 'I'll explain everything on the way home, Bess.'

"And he did. At least some of it. It had to do with his friend Minor Cooper Keith, who, as the whole town knew because they had so much of their money in it, had gone to Costa Rica about ten years before to build a railroad. The boys and I had heard all about Minor's problems, how it took three years to build the first twenty miles, how Bone would round up laborers in New Orleans to go to Limón, several hundred at a time. Most all of them had died of fevers as well as three of Minor's own brothers—life sacrificed for the founding of a great Central American civilization, said Bone. Minor had never given up even when he had to compete with builders of the Panama Canal for good Jamaican labor, and now his railroad ran all the way from the Caribbean to the Rio Sucio in the Honduran valley.

"Of course, Bone now explained as we trotted along in his wagon, a great project that would benefit all of Central America called for money—a lot of money, more and more of it—so the Costa Rican government had put up *billetes privilegiados* paying 12% for Minor to borrow on. Three years ago, Bone said, he as a newly elected director of our bank had tolled for civilization and arranged funds for Minor backed by Costa Rican paper twice the amount of his loans—the 24% interest to be paid in dollars only. Bone was sure the loans would all be paid back any day now, no doubt about that, but meanwhile at the very time when his friend had to have more money to pull this thing off, the bank might be calling for something more reassuring than the Costa Rican paper it held.

"That's where the bananas came in. Just the year before, Mr. Keith had sent his first full shipload to New Orleans. I certainly remembered that because Bone had been there to meet the ship and had brought back a full stalk for the whole town to sample. Hardly anybody had ever seen banana before and these were small, sweet, and yellow, just ripening. Minor was determined to pay off the interest on his loans, Bone said, out of his own pocket if he had to. And right now, anybody who could invest in a few shipments of banana would not only help Minor earn the money to repay the bank and his other loans—there were a lot more of those, too, in London, and all over—but stood to make a fine profit while contributing to a good cause.

"I should try to get the whole picture, Bone said. He clucked to his horse and gave him full head. The prospects in Central America for the building of an unequalled civilization connected by rail to the U.S. presented the opportunity of a lifetime. After we got married, and once good sewerage and water were assured in Limón, we would move down there. We'd be in on the ground floor of a new world—it was like a dream. Already, Minor had stores along the coast all the way to Belize in British Honduras. He bought and sold everything, and Bone—the two of them had been discussing this for years—Bone could take over this vast network of trade. The important point was, this was a network for world trade. Trade. When he said the word softly, yearningly, you realized how all the fruits of Nature fell and rotted where they lay and how all the products of Industry decayed and rusted, lay useless, until Trade gathered and transported and distributed them in her network. And I—I would be—yes, Queen of World Trade. It was not just a romance that all would move to the top in such a world, but a natural consequence of good education and removing obstacles to individual progress, he said.

"Meanwhile, much had to be done, and my brother Jimbo, upon hearing about Minor Cooper Keith's pressing need for money, and about banana profits, and World Trade, had come up with a solution. We had pulled into the drive in front of the house and were sitting in Bone's wagon as he wound up his explanation, somewhat hurriedly.

"It seemed that the men who reopened Uncle Pat Smith's old silver factory had been pupils of Wyon in the Royal Mint. Partly as a kind of stunt when they apprenticed Lee Walker, they'd set him the task of preparing, under their tutelage, a pair of dies for the US Trade Dollar, and Jimbo, with his business sense, only needed to take one look at those dies again to see the prospects. Bone was proud to say he'd been able to arrange a space for melting and minting in a large disused furnace room of his office building. As the twins dug up one crate after another of the family silver, starting with the babies, they melted it down and minted dollars, then packed them in the shell boxes and stored them in the rose thicket.

"Everything had gone smoothly until Papa, not a week before, had set up his gun there—because, the twins could only conclude, he'd resolved to keep the coins from being carted away. Certainly, Bone said, if Wes Woolley ever had any objection to turning the family silver into coins, he'd have voiced them immediately and unreservedly. He'd had ample opportunity to intervene for close to a year and didn't; in fact, he seemed to wish his knowledge of the whole affair to go unrecognized in any way. The appearance of the gun, however, announced an unmistakable intention to defend the coins against the only two people he thought knew about them, his own two sons.

"Lee Walker was utterly terrified, Bone said, and it was all Jimbo could do to keep him from caving in to Papa's whim and wrecking their opportunity to strike while the iron was hot. It was now or never—those banana shipments had to be kept moving. He was again proud to say, as much as he hated sneaking off the dollars right under Wes's nose, he'd been able to lend a hand there. Since Papa refused even to acknowledge their existence, there seemed to be no other way. The boys were preparing themselves for a ruckus when he found out they were gone, as he would the minute he came out of the fields this afternoon and checked the thicket.

"Here Bone pulled out his gold watch, snapped it open and shut rapidly, but kept it cradled in his hand. He, Bone, knew how Wesley had come to take the silver for granted but, knowing his views on money and the silver standard inside out, was confident of his approval once he understood the situation. The *whole* situation. Jimbo felt that if anybody was going to catch it from Wes, it would be him, because the whole idea of melting down the family silver had been his in the first place.

"Now I'm not defending Jimbo, Lizzie, but his was one of those cases of ignorance which was half a lack of knowledge and half not wanting to read the fine print. As we've gone over before, the family has a knack for this particular kind of self-deception. The way Jimbo later defended himself to me, the government had freed up silver for coinage, and in the case of the Trade Dollar, a coin to be used abroad and not even struck at any of the regular mints, the question of who was doing the minting was really immaterial.

What I'm trying to say is Jimbo would never, never have considered making counterfeit paper money, because all paper money is counterfeit no matter by whom or where issued. We all grew up on that idea. Paper being the real counterfeit, Jimbo was merely correcting the situation at the bank where the entire community had been fooled, lending out and getting back nothing but pieces of paper of one kind or another. As for Bone, the thrust of his explanation to me was crystal clear: judgment day was past due at the bank. Only the Harding Trade Dollars, as he always called them, could bring a period of grace sufficient to turn a profit from bananas. And, he emphasized, only those banana profits could save us at this point.

"I was appalled by the explanation, Lizzie, but never a doubt crossed my mind about the scheme working. As much as Bone might outline his designs on a grand scale, they were never without a hard realistic base, and his business judgment was seldom askew."

By this time, Grandmother and I were approaching the back steps. Instead of going on up, she sat down on the bottom one and motioned me past her, "Go put the biscuits in the oven and turn the kettle on, Lizzie." She was thinking hard when I returned but reached her hand out to be pulled up, and as we took the path through the herbs, she continued. "I'm not defending Bone either. It wasn't ignorance on his part but grandiosity. As he talked, his face lit up with an inner glow like the power of Jesus Christ burning in a human body. It scared me—for me, it was *ecce homo*. Young as I was, I saw he had to be protected from himself.

"Jimbo and Lee Walker, Bone was proclaiming, would do more good than they knew because silver not only has intrinsic value but, in money form, brings prosperity wherever it circulates. Once established in Costa Rica, we could send for them and set up a mint. We could coin both gold and silver—we needn't favor one over the other—in any denomination used by any country anywhere. We could circulate money wherever we found a need, and so share our own progress and prosperity with the entire world without anybody knowing its source. In fact, discretion would be of the essence at first, because money won't work if people don't believe in it. After a few years, given the twins' remarkable skills and the undeniable benefits of having their coinage in circulation, the world was bound to recognize that we were servicing a need never before satisfied in history. 'Think of it!' he said, 'A mint that preserves the integrity of all currencies and provides the little tonic that could prevent ailing parts of the world from really falling sick.' Meanwhile, using the Harding Trade Dollar, prototype of the coming world currencies, he would in his position as a bank director straighten things out at home. That done—and when our own profits came in from the banana shipments—he would be in a position to marry me.

"This last point he glossed over kind of fast after snapping his watch open and shut again and stuffing it back in his pocket. He said he would be right back and rushed off to the outhouse from where he returned shortly running as best he could with the diminished case of Mirabelle. He was tying the canvas over it, explaining its presence in our outhouse as a form of tribute to Mama who had divulged to him an even deeper appreciation of the joys of fine plum brandy than his own and had recently consented to his little strategem for sharing these joys—in brief, Mama, he said, loved to take a little nip now and then and although he himself might have preferred to partake elsewhere—well, here he got no further. Papa came charging at him out of nowhere with his gun.

"That's when I was sure. The target of the bullets in Papa's gun was Bone. Now, however wrong he'd been in bringing spirits on the premises against Papa's wishes, I still couldn't believe Papa would kill for that reason. It would take something a lot bigger and more powerful than either spirits or the silver standard for Papa to break one of the ten commandments.

"All through Bone's explanation I kept noticing that the one issue not cleared up a tap was the very one, the only one, really important to me: Papa's gun and its intended victim. But without a doubt, he was certainly after Bone now and would have attacked him had not the sheriff, gun in hand, come pounding straight up to us on his horse. Papa looked at Bone and Bone at Papa, obviously neither knowing why the sheriff had appeared, and gun ready at that. In fact, both of them seemed suddenly to wilt, as if waiting for the sheriff to take them into custody.

"'Where are they?' demanded the sheriff.

"'Who?' Bone and Papa said at the same time.

"'The bandits! Lee Walker said they had little Bess hostage. Where's the wagon load of money?' The sheriff was looking as if he might round up a posse.

"Bone and Papa were speechless. But I had the picture now. Lee Walker has a mean streak, especially where Jimbo is concerned. It comes from thinking Jimbo is getting ahead of him and doesn't deserve to—pure-dee envy. Lee Walker, I surmised, had gotten cold feet about minting the money and, imagining as he always does, that he's doing the lion's share of the work but is slated to come out on the short end, he'd decided to divert any possible suspicion from himself and to render the whole scheme nugatory. Luckily, nobody ever believed much of what Lee Walker said.

"But everybody always believed everything I said. Papa claimed that if a person has something to hide and can't tell the truth about it, he's not living right. Hiding the silver, we all understood, didn't fit in here because we could tell the truth about it any time but we had chosen not to say anything about it at all. I had tried so hard to live right, never to have anything hidden I couldn't freely and without guilt speak out about if I chose, that I already had a reputation for it. So I up and said, 'Have you ever seen anything like that Lee Walker's imagination! I've been with Mr. Harding here, Sheriff. He took me to meet his friend, Mr. Minor Cooper Keith'—everybody in town knew that name—'Mr. Keith had to hurry on down to New Orleans but he left just tons of silver dollars with Mr. Harding to take to the bank. I guess Mr. Harding is Lee Walker's bandit and Mr. Harding is surely holding me hostage because—Sheriff, you can be the first to know along with Papa. Bone—Mr. Harding and I have discussed it—and oh, do say yes, Papa. We want to get married tomorrow. *Tomorrow*, Papa.'

"Bone and Papa looked equally stunned. Bone said nothing but Papa finally murmured in disbelief, 'You—you, little Bess?'

"The sheriff congratulated us heartily and galloped off to broadcast our forthcoming marriage to the town. Papa seemed oddly confused and broken. Mama did not tell me until after his death what he finally confessed to her, how he'd come to believe she and Bone might be taking a fancy to each other and had caught them exchanging smiles after their outhouse visits. Also the number and length of these visits had increased beyond the necessities of digestion, as if some other necessity had lodged in the outhouse. He suspected it must be their trysting place or a place for arranging trysts. He agonized over it until he'd convinced himself, and upon seeing Bone run into the outhouse and a second later burst back out with something as big as a baby in his arms, something Papa felt to be connected with Mama and coming out of a place so private, too, he would, with the sure aim of his gunsight in the rose thicket, have blown Bone's brains out, Mama said, if his gun had not been jammed. It was the only crazy thinking she had ever known Papa to indulge in, she said. He had never wanted to talk about that time of his life again. He just wanted to put it behind him forever. 'And what is there to say about it?' Mama said to me. 'Crazy is crazy like lightning is lightning, and wherever either one strikes, your only hope is to get out of the way!'

"Well, Lizzie, your grandfather and I were married next day. I slept like a log the night before, but when I got up next morning and started down the back stairs to the outhouse, I thought I was still asleep. But no, what I was seeing was reality: it was gone, the giant monster of a rose thicket. The mountainous accumulation of it growing throughout so many years of my life was clean gone, and the nakedness of the space where it had been stood out like a circle of no growth marked off within our garden. Papa had called the boys from their beds and they'd all worked like fiends the night long cutting and hauling it off to the swamp. Breakfast that morning felt normal for the first time in many days. Nobody watched anybody else and Papa was at peace.

"When the boys and I were still children and Papa buried the silver knowing the crates would be entirely overgrown within a few seasons, he had staggered them, barely covered with soil, along an imaginary path beside the already overgrown Cherokee rose. The boys had carried this imaginary path in their own heads and—so they told me after my marriage—had taken a vow, along with Papa, on the family Bible never to reveal it, not even to Mama and me. Papa lived and died under the conviction that secrecy is contrary to woman's better nature.

"As the rose mounted and turned in on itself, massing to spread its density in a spectacular but uninviting mound, the boys devised what was at first merely a crawling space through it along the silver path. Mama and I both knew they were fascinated with games of medieval knights under all manner of unexpected attacks, but only Papa knew that they were played out within the rose thicket where the boys were slowly hollowing out its innards into the semblance of a rampart with battlements. The camouflage over the entry was Papa's work. Jimbo said they finally got so they never talked about the secret place any more—it was understood that he and Lee Walker would take care of it inside, and Papa would see to the entry. As the thicket spread, he would move the camouflage accordingly. In time, the thicket became a storage place for more and more empty shell boxes saved from their hunts—not, Jimbo rushed to assure me, because he and Lee Walker planned any particular use for the boxes initially, but because he was dead sure they would have a particular and important use sooner or later. 'Little stacked boxes are like little drawers,' he said, 'the more of them you collect the more chance of having a place for all the little parts and pieces that accumulate around you.'

"So, for Papa, there had been nothing unusual about the canvas-covered stacks of shell boxes, especially in his condition, so caught up in his craziness he didn't even see any two and two to be put together. We shortly realized he had not been hiding knowledge of the dollars; he simply had never looked into any of the boxes. Indeed, on his own account to Mama, he had never gone all the way to the heart of the thicket until the week he used it for surveillance of the outhouse.

"Neither Papa nor Mama ever knew but what the family silver was still in the ground and they assumed as a matter of course, when pieces of it began to reappear, that the twins had decided to dig them up. For, Lizzie, about one demand I remained as firm as a judge: Jimbo and Lee Walker were to regain possession of at least half of those coins as soon as possible—I knew Bone could arrange it—and begin the work, using the old Manley drawings and their own proven skills, of duplicating pieces of the family silver. I would tell them which ones. So you see, Lee Walker's reputation as a smith is no accident and neither is Jimbo's authority as an appraiser. The work of restoring choice pieces of the family silver to their original form and use, for our children and grandchildren, has been a lifetime project for us.

"And today, Lizzie, you and I are going to have our tea from the latest and the last of the restorations, the Georgian teapot you earlier admired. It'll be yours in time. I sent it recently to an 18th century expert in London for an independent opinion—you may have his report. He pronounced it to be genuine beyond doubt. A perfect counterfeit, you see.

"My position in the family and in town was, of course, cemented by my marriage to Bone. It was not hard to convince him that his visionary capacities could as well be put to use here as in Costa Rica and that they might benefit from some little restrictions on them. Actually, Bone was almost as chastened as Papa by all that had come to pass.

"The banana boats funded by loans Bone arranged using the coins as collateral did turn a profit. Mr. Keith did faithfully repay all his debts, and our family as well as the local bank, did begin to thrive. All of which your grandfather till the day he died ascribed to the Harding Dollar, incontrovertible evidence, he felt, of his insight into world trade. But neither of us ever had any regrets about giving up the fabulous future that had indeed awaited us in Central America. For, Bone, as usual, was right in his assessment of the possibilities there: had he followed his own vision, he would have headed the Tropical Trading & Transport Co., a kind of early forerunner of the United Fruit Company, and his fortune would have risen with that of his friend, Mr. Minor Cooper Keith.

"But here we stayed, Lizzie, all of us, and we have all had fortune enough. And here, Lizzie, here where we've spent our lives, nobody—nobody, you hear—has ever once doubted my word."

She stopped, leaned forward and searched my face with an intensity that startled me.

"But Grandmother," I said, with as much incredulity as if she had turned into the wolf—for me, it was as if I had just witnessed the inverse of a miracle. "Grandmother, you, you told a—a story—and it was a whopper!"

She nodded, impatient and searching again. "Of course, a great big lie is what I told, and nobody ever seemed to know the difference because they believed in me."

She was stock-still now, up slightly on her toes with her body tilted toward mine, her eyes reaching into mine like rays of my own soul searching its boundaries, and then I remembered, for I had forgotten as usual. It always happened: I got lost in the story rather than listening for the lesson to be learned.

I bent instantly and easily to the task for which she had trained me. Years of practice had left me with a feel for relevant regions confiding their moral intimacies and an equally sure craft in weaving a continuity among them. She was waiting, waiting with that silent concentrated certainty, as confident of my movement in moral realms as her own heartbeat.

But something else was happening between us: as if there were no test, nothing to be proved, not even anything to be learned, merely something more to be told. We had long ago been over the simple lessons about not lying, about not letting greed, lust, pride, and so on overwhelm you, so it was nothing as simple as that. I abandoned all sincerity and put my whole being into saying it right. I felt myself gathering the warp and woof of our mutual confidences over the years; the work was finished and I was knotting, knotting, making the selvedge.

"Love," I said, following the coloring at the border, "is an innocent fall into the depths of whatever we love, and loving an ignorant swim through a cesspit of depths. In the innocence and ignorance of loving, we can't see what is actually happening: debased by what we love, we always demean what loves us—and, so, we come to know where we have been in love only through the surfacing of our moral choices."

She followed the words coming out of my mouth as if taking directions so critical as to necessitate duplication accurate in every detail. Understanding slowly lined the paper-fine skin of her face. Relief and satisfaction too.

But she was very tired, I could see, and trembling a bit. I walked her to the belvedere and left her there while I prepared our tea. She stood up when I returned with the tray. I set it on the iron table and, holding her hand, made the turn that day along with her, this side, now that side, surveying the garden space with a new awareness of all its parts and levels. She smiled up at me with pride and tears in her eyes.

I saw her anguish recede to what seemed a touch of grief abiding in peace as we had tea in the belvedere from the Georgian teapot that became mine only a few months later. And I mulled over how Grandmother had become a storyteller without knowing what the moral was. I had to locate myself in what had happened between us, her not understanding all those years what lesson she was teaching me in the end. Grandmother, tautly stretched in dread toward me, had not known the answer. But she never doubted what I said.

And I continue to mull over what I did not, could not, say then. No, I shall not forget what actually happened out there between outhouse and smokehouse, but the greater mystery, to which I always return, lies in the belvedere.

psycheme

And you? Can you deny that the presence everywhere invisible yet ever felt is none other than your own? My psychemes have succeeded marvellously well, it seems to me, in dispelling the authorial mystery that might otherwise have veiled the triangularity of our interactions, yours, Harding's, and mine. Whatever moves she and I make, pleasing or irritating, frustrating or satisfying, attacking, pacifying, manipulative and hateful, manipulative and seductive, negotiations full of flattery, intimidation, rewards, punishments, reduced to whines and pleas, shamed and shaming, inflamed with loving hate, slyly moral and whetting a contemptuous edge, tales told behind your back, waters tested for how much you'll take, each of us on her own course to you—you the goal here when all is said and done—whatever happens (Does Harding's sale of the Boullet House go smoothly, without a hitch? Without regrets? Does she salvage the letter of Jon, last of the Alligator Indians, from *The Sentinel* solely because it appeals to her sense of fictional absurdity? Does she know more than she tells of Miss Mary Louise's grandmother Frances Boullet and her father the Captain, and the young man on the white horse said to haunt the grounds? And so on, and on) it is you, dear Reader, who stands revealed as the power and the mystery behind it all. None other.

So much, then, for Text One. Harding's account of the restoration ends with her return to Athena late one faintly autumnal August evening, when, safe and sound, hugging her daughters, she stares between their shoulders—unbelieving—into the eyes of Tom Evans earnestly putting his case before the American public on a national news channel, Tarragona's man of the hour.

I lay Text One aside and snap on my own box for an update of down-to-the-minute obscenities the world over: shots, people running, falling, some with guns, houses smoking, explosions, bodies crumpling under rapid fire, a close-up of a woman's dark eyes, fixed, already dead, and down the street behind her more fall, a steady barrage of shots. Is it for real? A preview? An ad? An early movie closing with a high-noon shootout? It has the gritty starkness of films shot before the triumph of special effects, *Viva Zapata!* or some old Western along and south of the border where the tall, taciturn cowboy will appear any minute to show how things stand and set them right. I check my watch, listen to the voice-over: a news-cast voice. Probably real, after all. Strong sun, sand, stucco and palms—the Middle East. But no, the voice locates me deep in my own hemisphere: a small village skirmish. My watch confirms the hour—it's news time, it's real, and I'm moved again over the bodies, some still stirring, and look once more, a brief decisive summation, into the unseeing eyes of the woman, unnamed like all of them, silenced. The voice reviews the new strategy of surprise as more bodies downed in the routines of daily life document it. The facts lie there before you, and we cut to a group of young men tending their guns like vital functions. They congregate under a tree by a church-like building as one explains to the camera in broken English (and all nod) that their mission is to instill fear because this is the only way to win. Fear, he says, fear wears them down. Nobody likes it (his large brown eyes fill with sorrow) but it's the only way. The image, once more, of the woman laid out in equatorial heat to the passing world's gaze, staring, breaks from its media frame, floats free of the ghostly media narrative, and clamps its cellular fastenings over mine, this woman without a name, about whom nothing is to be said, no stories told. And I remember Paul, who casually brings his nightmares to the breakfast table, relating a dream the morning of his departure that appeared so transparent as to make inter- pretation superfluous. "I dreamed," he said, "I was a healthy baby in a crib, well taken care of, two or three months old but with an adult consciousness; for the life of me, I could find no way to reveal my condition even though I never stopped talking in long involved sentences about theoretical physics. Nobody seemed to think this was in the least unusual. The more desper- ate I got, the more I kept on jabbering and the more I was loved and admired for my creativity and scientific probity. Out of the mouths of babes, you know—Paul's eyes went soft and dreamy—if I could only recall what I was saying...." From the mist, Harding reaches out, places something firmly in my hand, and fades from view. (Call it desert or wasteland, call it wilderness, here without you and Harding, without life-giving illusions. Understand, I like it, this pleasurable seethe of energy, strength, feeling to no purpose—as *bona fide* citizen of no nation, sole inhabitant of this intellectual landscape free to accommodate all manner of anarchy down to shiftiness of boundaries, I need a right of passage, an indisputable passport, a *passe partout* enabling me to come and go beyond my intellectual limits whenever I please.) The familiar thrill of a book in hand astonishes me like the sudden appearance of an unknown form of life. It is a fat little book, gaping open, bound in an old smoky leather with the numeral "XL" and the name "FRANCES BOULLET" neatly lettered on the spine in gold. The soft binding flops apart and drapes over my hand like a well-worn glove. On the face page the letters have the enlarged carefulness of script formed by the very old:

> *My Last Writing, wherein the years from December 24, 1860 to December 5, 1935 are recollected in decoupage.*

I finger the texture of Text Two even as the boxed voice connecting once more with the unreliable face of the newscaster drones its sound bites of history in the making.